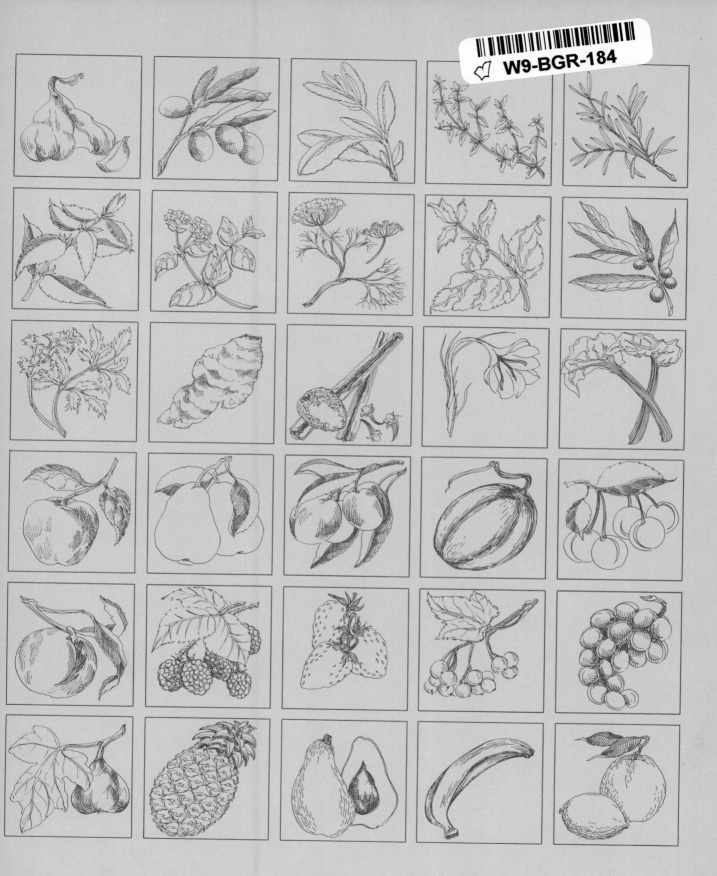

1986 Family Circle COOKBOOK

Other Books by Family Circle:

The Best of Family Circle Cookbook
ABZ's of Cooking
Recipes America Loves Best
Family Circle Hints Book
Delicious Desserts
Great Meals on a Tight Budget
Perfect Poultry
Great Meals in One Dish

To order **FamilyCircle** books, write to Special Projects Dept., Family Circle, 488 Madison Avenue, New York, NY 10022.

To subscribe to **FamilyCircle** magazine, write to Family Circle Subscriptions, 488 Madison Avenue, New York, NY 10022.

Special Project Staff

Project Editor—JoAnn Brett-Billowitz
Family Circle Food Editor—Jean Hewitt
Family Circle Senior Associate Food Editor—David Ricketts
Technical/Copy Editors—Ceri E. Hadda, Wallace A. Kunukau, Jr.
Type Supervisor—Wendy Hylfelt
Typesetting—Vickie Almquist, Helen Russell
Illustrations—Lauren Jarrett
Text Design—Bessen & Tully
Cover Photograph—Gordon E. Smith
Cover Design—Marcon Dynamics

Project Manager—Annabelle Groh
Book Development Manager—Margie Chan-Yip
Special Assistants—Joanne Hajdu, Marty Heebner

Photographers—Mary Bloom, Laszlo, Bill McGinn, Rudy Muller, Ron Schwerin,
Gordon E. Smith, John Uher, René Velez, Ken Whitmore, Susan Wood

Published by The Family Circle, Inc.
488 Madison Avenue, New York, NY 10022

Copyright ©1986 by The Family Circle, Inc.

Manufactured in the United States of America

10 9 8 7 6 5 4 3 2 1

Library of Congress Cataloging in Publication Data
Main entry under title:

1986 Family circle cookbook.
Includes index.
1. Cookery.   I. Family circle (Mount Morris, Ill.)
TX715.B485555   1985   641.5   86-4465
ISBN 0-933585-01-2

1986 FamilyCircle® COOKBOOK

Contents

Cover Recipe, page 272.

INTRODUCTION

Quick, make-ahead, entertaining
low-cost or low-calorie—fabulous
recipes to please every palate.

Family Circle would like to start your 1986 off on the right gourmet track with an all-new collection of the year's "best." With handy menu suggestions and tempting recipes that range from soup to nuts, this fabulous cookbook will help you prepare delicious meals every day of the week.

As you flip through the pages, you'll be pleasantly surprised by the wide range of menus, as well as the diversity of recipes that appeal to all palates and all levels of culinary expertise. So whether your family is strictly "meat and potatoes" or has the urge to go "exotic" with international cooking—it's all here for you.

In addition to creative new recipes, we offer adaptations of recipe classics that use readily available products as well as modern cooking techniques, such as microwaving. And, if you long for some "loving from the oven," why not bake one of our scrumptious yeast breads from scratch!

Because time is such a precious commodity for all of us today, we've added some special features to this book to help you even further. The menus—all laid out in Chapter 1—are coded according to type: Quick, Make-ahead, Entertaining, Low-cost and Low-calorie. We've done the same for recipes in each chapter. We've also provided nutritional breakdowns for each recipe, along with calorie counts per serving. There's no guesswork involved as you plan and prepare a well-balanced meal for your family.

So get cooking—and enjoy it like you never have before!

In This Book

All recipes and menus are coded by type, indicated by the following symbols:

⚡ Quick

《《 Make-Ahead

🍸 Entertaining

🏠 Low-Cost/Family

📏 Low-Calorie

Keep in mind that:
1. *Baking powder* is double action.
2. *Brown sugar* is firmly packed.
3. *Corn syrup*, unless specified, can be either light or dark.
4. Doubling recipes is not wise unless otherwise instructed. It is best to make the recipe a second time.
5. *Eggs* are large.
6. *Egg, slightly beaten* means just break the yolks.
7. *Eggs, lightly beaten* means to create a smooth mixture.
8. *Flour*, cake or all-purpose: most commercial brands of flour come presifted from the manufacturer. Some of our recipes indicate additional sifting to produce a lighter product.
9. *Heavy cream* for whipping is 40 percent butterfat.
10. Herbs and spices are dried unless noted otherwise.
11. Measurements are level.
12. *Milk* is whole homogenized.
13. *Vegetable shortening* is used for greasing pans.
14. *Vinegar* is cider.

Good Meals — Good Health

We all want to be physically and mentally alert and have a happy outlook on life. Good nutrition is one of the keys. A well-developed body of ideal weight, smooth skin, glossy hair and clear eyes are the signs of a well-nourished person.

Eat a variety of foods in moderation to provide a complete range of vitamins and minerals. Eat foods that provide plenty of complex carbohydrates, such as whole grains, fruits and vegetables, for energy and high-fiber content. Avoid eating foods containing a lot of fat, cholesterol, sodium and sugar.

The Nutrient Value Per Serving is included with each recipe in this book to help you plan daily menus that are well balanced and healthful. Refer to the Daily Nutrition Countdown Chart below for the daily requirements of average adult men and women.

Daily Nutrition Countdown Chart

	AVERAGE HEALTHY ADULT	
	Women	Men
Calories[1]	2,000	2,700
Protein[2]	46 gms (184 cal.)	56 gms (224 cal.)
Fat[3]	66 gms (594 cal.)	90 gms (810 cal.)
Sodium[4]	1,100 - 3,300 mg	1,100 - 3,300 mg
Cholesterol[5]	300 mg	300 mg

Calories (cal.) that do not come from protein or fat should be derived from complex carbohydrates found in whole grains, fresh fruits, vegetables, pasta, etc.

[1]RDA [2](12% of calories) RDA [3](30% of calories) Amer. Heart Assoc. and Nat'l Acad. of Science [4](USDA) [5]Amer. Heart Assoc.

Children's nutritional needs vary more than adults', due to rapid growth rate and body changes during the developmental years. To establish a well-rounded diet and healthy eating habits, it is recommended that children's daily dietary intake be closely supervised by an adult in order to insure that sufficient amounts of food from the Basic 4 food groups are consumed. If the supervising adult is not certain as to specific dietary needs for his or her child, consulting with a registered dietitian or qualified doctor is recommended.

Important Measures

Dash	under ⅛ teaspoon
½ tablespoon	1½ teaspoons
1 tablespoon	3 teaspoons
1 ounce liquid	2 tablespoons
1 jigger	1½ ounces
¼ cup	4 tablespoons
⅓ cup	5 tablespoons plus 1 teaspoon
½ cup	8 tablespoons
⅔ cup	10 tablespoons plus 2 teaspoons
¾ cup	12 tablespoons
1 cup	16 tablespoons
1 pint	2 cups
1 quart	2 pints
1 gallon	4 quarts
1 pound	16 ounces

Measuring Equipment

MEASURING FLOUR

Measure the all-purpose flour called for in most of the recipes in this book by spooning flour from the bag or canister into a dry measuring cup, heaping slightly. (Note: The top of the cup is flat; there is no spout in a dry measure, as there is in a liquid measuring cup.)

Place the heaping cup of flour over the bag of flour or canister and run the flat side of a long knife across the top to level off the cup. (Note: Use this technique for granulated sugar too.)

PACKING BROWN SUGAR

Measure light or dark brown sugar by packing it into a dry measuring cup, using the back of a tablespoon.

MEASURING SHORTENING

Measure vegetable shortening by scooping it with a rubber scraper into a dry measuring cup; run the flat blade of a long knife over the top, then scoop it out of the cup with the rubber scraper into a mixing bowl.

● Shortening can be measured before or after it is melted.

● One stick of butter or margarine equals 4 ounces; 4 sticks equal 1 pound or 2 cups.

MEASURING LIQUID

Place a liquid measuring cup on a flat surface and stoop to be at eye level with the measuring cup; pour the liquid to the desired measure printed on the side of the cup. (Note: When measuring a syrup, such as molasses or honey, grease the cup with butter or margarine. Then the syrup will pour out easily.)

Oven Temperatures

Ovens need not be preheated for meats, vegetables and most casserole dishes. Recipes that *need* preheated ovens have the direction inserted in the recipe to allow the 15-minute margin for preheating either gas or electric ovens.

Very Slow	**250°-275°**
Slow	**300°-325°**
Moderate	**350°-375°**
Hot	**400°-425°**
Very Hot	**450°-475°**
Extremely Hot	**500°+**

Casserole Measurement Chart

Casseroles are international dishes. They are imported from all over the world, and each country has its own system for measuring. The chart below will help you to convert your casserole's measurements from one system to another so that you can be assured your recipe will bake to perfection.

Cups	=	Pints	=	Quarts	=	Liters
1		½		¼		0.237
2		1*		½*		0.473
4		2*		1*		0.946
6		3		1½		1.419
8		4		2		1.892
10		5		2½		2.365
12		6		3		2.838

* *In Canada, 1 pint = 2½ cups; 1 quart = 5 cups.*

Emergency Ingredient Substitutes

WHEN THE RECIPE CALLS FOR:	YOU MAY SUBSTITUTE:
1 square unsweetened chocolate	3 tablespoons unsweetened cocoa powder plus 1 tablespoon butter, margarine or vegetable shortening
1 cup sifted cake flour	⅞ cup sifted all-purpose flour (1 cup less 2 tablespoons)
2 tablespoons flour (for thickening)	1 tablespoon cornstarch
1 teaspoon baking powder	¼ teaspoon baking powder plus ⅝ teaspoon cream of tartar
1 cup corn syrup	1 cup sugar and ¼ cup liquid used in recipe
1 cup honey	1¼ cups sugar and ¼ cup liquid used in recipe
1 cup sweet milk	½ cup evaporated milk plus ½ cup water
1 cup buttermilk	1 tablespoon vinegar plus enough sweet milk to make 1 cup
1 cup sour cream (in baking)	⅞ cup buttermilk or sour milk plus 3 tablespoons butter
1 egg (for custards)	2 egg yolks
1 cup brown sugar (packed)	1 cup sugar or 1 cup sugar plus 2 tablespoons molasses
1 teaspoon lemon juice	½ teaspoon vinegar
¼ cup chopped onion	1 tablespoon instant minced onion
1 clove garlic	⅛ teaspoon garlic powder
1 cup zucchini	1 cup summer squash
1 cup tomato juice	½ cup tomato sauce plus ½ cup water
2 cups tomato sauce	¾ cup tomato paste plus 1 cup water
1 tablespoon fresh snipped herbs	1 teaspoon dried herbs
1 tablespoon prepared mustard	1 teaspoon dry mustard

Emergency Baking Dish and Pan Substitutes

WHEN THE RECIPE CALLS FOR:	YOU MAY SUBSTITUTE:
4-cup baking pan or dish	9-inch pie plate, or 1-quart soufflé dish
6-cup baking pan or dish	9-inch-round layer-cake pan, or 8 x 4 x 3-inch loaf pan, or 10-inch pie plate
8-cup baking pan or dish	8 x 8 x 2-inch dish or cake pan, or 11 x 7 x 1½-inch pan, or 9 x 5 x 3-inch loaf pan
three 8-inch-round pans	two 9 x 9 x 2-inch cake pans
two 9-inch-round layer-cake pans	two 8 x 8 x 2-inch cake pans, or 13 x 9 x 2-inch pan
9 x 5 x 3-inch loaf pan	9 x 9 x 2-inch cake pan
9-inch angel-cake tube pan	10 x 3¾-inch Bundt® pan, or 9 x 3½-inch fancy tube pan

Food Equivalents

Berries, 1 pint	1¾ cups
Bread	
Crumbs, soft, 1 cup	2 slices
Cubes, 1 cup	2 slices
1 pound, sliced	22 slices
Broth	
Beef or Chicken, 1 cup	1 teaspoon instant bouillon or 1 envelope bouillon or 1 cube bouillon, dissolved in 1 cup boiling water
Butter or Margarine	
½ stick	¼ cup or 4 tablespoons
1 pound	4 sticks or 2 cups
Cream and Milk	
Cream, heavy, 1 cup	2 cups, whipped
Milk, evaporated, small can	⅔ cup
Milk, sweetened condensed, 14-ounce can	1⅔ cups
Milk, instant, nonfat dry, 1 pound	5 quarts, liquid skim milk
Cheese	
Cream, 8-ounce package	1 cup
Cottage, 8 ounces	1 cup
Cheddar or Swiss, 1 pound, shredded	4 cups
Blue, crumbled, 4 ounces	1 cup
Parmesan or Romano, ¼ pound, grated	1¼ cups
Chocolate	
Unsweetened, 1 ounce	1 square
Semisweet pieces, 6-ounce package	1 cup
Coconut	
Flaked, 3½-ounce can	1⅓ cups
Shredded, 4-ounce can	1⅓ cups
Cookies	
Chocolate wafers, 1 cup crumbs	19 wafers
Vanilla wafers, 1 cup fine crumbs	22 wafers
Graham crackers, 1 cup fine crumbs	14 square crackers
Dried Beans and Peas	
1 cup	2¼ cups, cooked
Eggs (large)	
Whole, 1 cup	5 to 6
Yolks, 1 cup	13 to 14
Whites, 1 cup	7 to 8
Flour	
all-purpose, sifted, 1 pound	4 cups
cake, sifted, 1 pound	4¾ to 5 cups
Gelatin, unflavored, 1 envelope	1 tablespoon

Nuts	
Almonds, 1 pound, shelled	3½ cups
Peanuts, 1 pound, shelled	3 cups
Walnuts, 1 pound, shelled	4 cups
Pecans, 1 pound, shelled	4 cups
Pasta	
Macaroni, elbow, uncooked, 8 ounces	4 cups, cooked
Spaghetti, 8 ounces, uncooked	4 cups, cooked
Noodles, medium width, 8 ounces, uncooked	3¾ cups, cooked
Rice	
Long-grain white rice, uncooked, 1 cup	3 cups, cooked
Enriched precooked rice, uncooked, 1 cup	2 cups, cooked
Sugar	
Granulated, 1 pound	2 cups
Brown, firmly packed, 1 pound	2¼ cups
10X (confectioners' powdered), sifted, 1 pound	3⅓ to 4 cups
Vegetables and Fruits	
Apples, 1 pound	3 medium size
Bananas, 1 pound	3 medium size
Carrots, 1 pound, sliced	2½ cups
Cabbage, 1 pound, shredded	4 cups
Herbs, chopped fresh, 1 tablespoon	1 teaspoon dried
Lemon, 1 medium size, grated	2 teaspoons lemon rind
Lemon, 1 medium size, squeezed	2 tablespoons lemon juice
Orange, 1 medium size, grated	2 tablespoons orange rind
Orange, 1 medium size, squeezed	⅓ to ½ cup orange juice
Onions, yellow cooking, 1 pound	5 to 6 medium size
Onions, small white silverskins, 1 pound	12 to 14
Potatoes, all-purpose, 1 pound	3 medium size
Peaches, 1 pound	4 medium size
Mushrooms, 1 pound, sliced	3 cups
Tomatoes, 1 pound:	
Large	2
Medium size	3
Small	4

1 MENU PLANS

Tulsa Ribs (page 126), Classy Baked Beans (page 144), Chili Corn Bread (page 52), Pineapple Slaw (page 170).

Champagne brunch, backyard
cookout or quick family dinner —
menus for 2 to 12.

I n this chapter, we bring you food for thought: 76 different menus for 2, 4, 6, 8, 10 and 12 people, seasonal menus, menus for special celebrations, menus for the calorie-conscious, even menus for kids. Whatever the occasion or day of the week, there's a breakfast, brunch, lunch or dinner that's perfect for you. Most of the recipes in the book are featured in our menus. To round out meals, we offer suggestions for other dishes as well (for which you probably have your own favorite recipe).

As we mentioned earlier, our menus are classified according to the coding system: Quick, Make-ahead, Entertaining, Low-cost or Low-calorie. You'll find many instances in which a group of recipes will fall into more than one category.

Quick meals usually take less than an hour to prepare from start to serving time. To complete the menu, we select other foods that are easy to prepare, such as sliced tomatoes, ready-to-cook convenience items, such as frozen vegetables, or ready-to-eat products, such as packaged puddings.

Make-ahead meals may be made several hours, days or, in some cases, weeks in advance and require minimal last-minute fuss. These menus also feature foods that are quickly and easily prepared, as well as purchased convenience items.

Entertaining meals are perfect for special occasions when something a bit more elaborate is desired.

Low-cost meals are the wholesome day-to-day breakfast, lunch and dinner recipes that may include meat substitutes or bargain cuts of meat to help you keep within your family's budget.

Low-calorie meals are for the waist-watchers—delicious but nutritious foods you can enjoy while slimming down.

Let your imagination go—mix and match recipes in the menus we suggest. Using the ideas and options we've given you as a starting point, you should have no trouble creating fabulous menus of your own!

MEALS FOR TWO

Breakfast

ON THE RUN
FOR 2
Orange Juice
Dilled Pita Omelet, page 147
(make the recipe twice)

LET'S HAVE PANCAKES
FOR 2
Fresh Strawberries Laced
with Orange Juice
Whole-Wheat Pancakes, page 54
Canadian Bacon Slices

Whipped Butter	*Maple Syrup*
Coffee	*Tea*

NO TIME FOR BREAKFAST
FOR 2
Orange Juice
French-Toasted Cheese, page 150
(make the recipe twice)

Brunch

BRUNCH—
WEST COAST-STYLE
FOR 2
Tropical Refresher, page 253
Steak and Broccoli Salad, page 153
(halve the recipe)
Whole-Grain Rolls
Strawberries in Champagne
Light Red Wine

Lunch

AFTER JOGGING
FOR 2
Chilled Gazpacho Soup
Pasta Salad with Tuna, page 140
Whole-Wheat Crackers
Oatmeal-Prune Cookies, page 210
Milk

COMMUTERS' PICNIC
FOR 2
Broccoli Flowerets and Zucchini Slices
with Onion Dip
Chilled Chicken Rolls Marengo-Style,
page 108
Wild Rice Salad, page 175
Crispy Breadsticks
Cherry-Nut Tarts, page 232
Sparkling Cider (nonalcoholic)

DIETER'S DELIGHT
FOR 2
Creamy Topped Potato, page 171
(bake potatoes and refrigerate,
use 4 tablespoons dressing)
Melba Toast
Fresh Pineapple, Papaya and Raspberry
Compote with Lime
Mineral Water   Iced Tea

GOURMET LUNCH—
DAD'S TREAT
FOR 2
Herbed Meatloaf, page 80   Croissants
Catsup   Mustard   Mayonnaise
Cherry Tomatoes
Honeydew Melon and Cantaloupe with
Grated Coconut
Black Coffee   Skim Milk

AT-THE-DESK PICNIC
FOR 2
Tarragon Chicken Salad, page 152
Savory Cream Puffs, page 53
(prepare only cream-puff portion of recipe)
Orange Wedges on Leaf Lettuce
Fresh Strawberries Brown Sugar Yogurt
Tea

YANKEE-STYLE LUNCH
FOR 2
Onion Burgers, page 78
(freeze remaining 2 uncooked burgers)
Mustard-Onion Hamburger Buns, page 35
(freeze leftover buns)
Tomato Slices and Lettuce
Mediterranean Onion Relish, page 184
Catsup   Mustard   Mayonnaise
Ice-Cream Cones
Cold Beer

Dinner

TO US
FOR 2

Baked Parsley-Stuffed Lobster, page 122
(halve the recipe)
Brown Rice Pilaf   Asparagus Spears
Artichoke Hearts with
Vinaigrette Dressing
Fresh Peas with Roquefort Cheese
White Wine

WAIST-WATCHERS' MEAL
FOR 2

Flounder Florentine, page 119
Steamed Baby Carrots
Cucumbers with Yogurt Dressing
Lemon Sorbet with Fresh Mint
Seltzer with Fresh Lime

WINE AND ROSES
FOR 2

Onion Soup
Salmon en Papillote, page 118
(halve the recipe)
Green Peas and Pearl Onions
Sweet Yellow Pepper Rings
Diced Oranges in Avocado Halves
on Leaf Lettuce
Chocolate Mousse   Whipped Cream
Coffee   White Wine   Tea

HURRAY FOR FRIDAY
FOR 2

Sausage Skillet Supper, page 116
(halve the recipe)
Italian Bread   Butter
Frozen Vanilla Yogurt with
Raspberries in Syrup
Tea   Coffee

VALENTINE'S DAY
FOR 2

Chicken Cutlets Tampa, page 101
(halve the recipe)
Snow Peas
Valentine Cookies, page 214
Strawberry Ice Cream
Rosé Wine Spritzers

MEALS FOR FOUR

Breakfast

EGGS WITH PIZAZZ
FOR 4
Fresh Fruit Cup Laced with Orange Juice
Scrambled Eggs with
Chive Cottage Cheese
Best-Ever Biscuits, page 54

Butter   Jam

Coffee   Tea   Milk

SOMETHING DIFFERENT
FOR 4
Tomato Juice
Honeydew Melon
Bacon and Cheese Strata, page 151

Coffee   Milk   Tea

BACK-TO-SCHOOL
FOR 4
Grapefruit Juice
Sliced Bananas
Hard- or Soft-Cooked Eggs
Morning Spice Muffins, page 46

Butter   Jelly

Coffee   Milk   Tea

SATURDAY BREAKFAST
FOR 4
Grapefruit Halves
Potato-Beef Omelet, page 147
(halve the recipe)
Blueberry-Bran Muffins, page 48   Butter

Coffee   Hot Chocolate   Tea

Brunch

BRUNCH AND BRIDGE
FOR 4
Fresh Fruit Compote
Deviled Eggs Florentine, page 147
Almond-Lemon Muffins, page 48   Butter
Coffee   Tea

SLUMBER PARTY BRUNCH
FOR 4
Orange Sections
Teddy Bear Pancakes, page 55
(halve the recipe)
Sausage Patties
Butter   Maple-Flavored Syrup
Banana-Cinnamon Shake, page 252
(make the recipe twice)

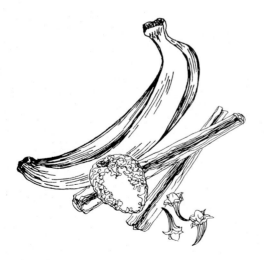

Lunch

MY FAMILY'S FAVORITE LUNCH
FOR 4
Mexican Pizzettes, page 158
Sliced Tomato with Tomato-Garlic
Vinaigrette, page 173
Frosted Brownies
Milk   Seltzer with Lime

WINTER CHILL-CHASER
FOR 4
Hearty Beef Stew, page 84 (halve the recipe)
Wilted Spinach Salad
Parmesan Breadsticks
Warm Blueberry Scone Shortcakes,
page 236
Coffee   Milk   Tea

SUNDAY IN THE COUNTRY
FOR 4
Seafood Salad, page 156
Boston Lettuce Leaves
French Bread Baguettes
Jarlsberg Cheese
Apples   Pears   Assorted Grapes
White Wine

I'LL HAVE SECONDS, PLEASE
FOR 4

Sausage Pilaf with Lemon, page 87
Marinated Cauliflower Flowerets
Crusty Hard Rolls   *Butter*
Nutty Baked Apples, page 242
Iced Tampa Tea, page 253

BICYCLE TRIP PICNIC
FOR 4

Hard-Cooked or Deviled Eggs
Sausage-Cheese Tortanos, page 87
Assorted Vegetable Sticks and Rings
Lemonade with Limeade Ice Cubes
Granola-Fruit Squares, page 209
GORP Snack
(a mixture of raisins, peanuts and
candy-coated mini-chocolate candies)

AFTER-TENNIS TREAT
FOR 4

Fresh Fruit Kabobs
Cold Broiled Marinated Chicken with
Lemon Glaze, page 99
Parmesan Buttered Fettuccine
Curried Corn and Red Pepper Relish,
page 184
Oatmeal Cookies
Sunshine Delight, page 251
(make the recipe 4 times)

TAILGATE PICNIC
FOR 4

Cheese-Stuffed Vegetables, page 150
Cold Confetti Meatloaf, page 80
Tomato Slices and Lettuce for
Salad and/or Sandwiches
Italian Dressing   *Hard Rolls*
Catsup   *Mustard*   *Chili Sauce*
Assorted Fruit
Golden Punch, page 250

BUSINESS LUNCHEON
FOR 4

Vichyssoise
Rainbow Spaghetti with Basil
and Pine Nuts, page 142
Radicchio and Romaine Salad with
Walnut Vinaigrette Dressing
Lemon Sorbet with Kiwi Slices
White Wine   *Coffee*   *Tea*

Dinner

A TWIST WITH CHICKEN
FOR 4
Lemon Chicken, page 102

Rice Noodles   Steamed Julienne Zucchini

Spinach and Bean Sprouts Salad

Cheesecake

Tea

PASTA IS FASTA
FOR 4
Pasta Pronto, page 138

Crusty Italian Bread

Mixed Green Salad with

Vinaigrette Dressing

Ice-Cream Sandwich Sundaes with

Chocolate Sauce and Whipped Cream

Light Red Wine

ONLY 30 MINUTES
FOR 4
Chicken Broth with Green Onion

Stir-Fried Beef and Vegetables, page 82

Vermicelli

Yogurt-Blueberry Parfaits

Shortbread Cookies

Tea

MAKE IT AHEAD
FOR 4
Stuffed Cabbage Rolls, page 79

Onion Rolls   Butter

Cucumbers Vinaigrette

Chocolate-Vanilla Ripple Ice Cream

with Gingered Pear and Lemon Sauce,

page 245

Coffee   Tea

FATHER'S DAY
FOR 4
Braised Stuffed Pork Chops, page 89

Carrot-Yam Tzimmes, page 174

Sliced Cranberry Sauce and Pineapple

on Boston Lettuce

Dad's Golden Car Cake, page 207

Coffee   Apple Cider

VEGETARIAN DELIGHT
FOR 4
Tomato Juice with Lime Slices

Green Gnocchi with

Sweet Red Pepper Sauce, page 183

Dark Pumpernickel Rolls

Sliced Cantaloupe Wedges

Seltzer with Lemon

COMPANY'S COMING AT 7
FOR 4

Curried Apple-Tomato Soup, page 66
Chicken with
Wild Rice Dressing, page 98
Dilled Green Beans, page 166
(halve the recipe)
Orange and Thin-Sliced Red Onion
on Leaf Lettuce
Mixed Berry and Whipped Cream
Parfaits
White Wine   Coffee   Tea

QUICK AND EASY
FOR 4

Alaskan Newburg, page 121
Baby Carrots   Cole Slaw
Fresh Fruit and Tapioca Parfaits
Coffee   Milk   Tea

CHINESE FOOD TONIGHT
FOR 4

Chicken with Broccoli and Fried
Walnuts, page 103
Fried Rice
Chopped Oranges and Bananas Topped
with Granola
Tea

OLD RELIABLE
FOR 4

Creole-Style Chicken Stew, page 105
Mixed Green Salad
Spoonbread   Butter
Chocolate-Filled Croissants
Coffee   Milk   Tea

STIR-FRY SPECIAL
FOR 4

Won Ton Soup
Slivered Pork and Egg with
Fried Noodles, page 88
Pineapple Cubes with Toasted Coconut
Tea

NOT FOR WOMEN ONLY
FOR 4

Rotelle with Shrimp and Lemon, page 140
Mixed Green Salad
Vinaigrette Dressing
Garlic Bread
Pound Cake with Fresh Fruit
White Wine   Coffee

MEALS FOR SIX

Breakfast

LAZY-DAY BREAKFAST
FOR 6
Chilled Grapefruit Sections

Waffles, page 55	Sausage Links
Butter Maple-Flavored Syrup	Honey
Milk Coffee	Tea

Brunch

HOLIDAY BRUNCH
FOR 6
Hot Herbed Tomato Juice, page 253
(with or without spirits)
Winter Fruit Salad with Honey-Lemon
Dressing, page 69
Savory Cream Puffs, page 53
Overnight Seed Bread, page 38
Nutty Maple-Honey Buns, page 38
Frozen Irish Coffee, page 241

Coffee Tea

WELCOME THE NEW NEIGHBORS
FOR 6
Summer Pizza with Sweet Peppers,
page 149
Cherry Tomatoes with
Oil and Vinegar Dressing
Classic Strawberry Shortcake, page 237
White Wine Spritzers

BRIDESMAIDS' BRUNCH
FOR 6
Chilled Fruit Soup, page 67
Curried Chicken and Rice Salad, page 154
Brioches

Lemon Sherbet Sugar Cookies
Wine Cooler, made with Lemonade
Syrup, page 252
(triple the recipe twice)

TEEN BIRTHDAY BRUNCH
FOR 6

Salad Pizza, page 155
Family Circle's Big Burger Cake,
page 204
Lemonade

NEW YEAR'S DAY
BRUNCH BUFFET
FOR 6

Bloody Marys
Hearty Beef Chili with Beans and
Cheddar Cheese, page 78
Assorted Fresh Vegetables
Cornbread   Butter
Individual Caramel Flans
Beer   Milk

BEACH PARTY COOKOUT
FOR 6

Silo Chicken, page 131
Oh My! Potato Salad, page 171
Herbed Tomatoes and Onions on leaf
lettuce, page 173
"The Monster Chip" Cookies, page 209
Watermelon Wedges
Beer   Soda

GRADUATION BARBECUE
FOR 6

Polynesian Spareribs, page 125
Corn on the Cob
Sweet and Sour Cabbage, page 170
Sourdough Bread Round   Butter
Fruit Bowl
Fruit Punch   Soft Drinks

Lunch

FRIENDS FOR LUNCH
FOR 6

Lobster Bisque
Savory Stuffed Tomatoes, page 157
Citrus Muffins, page 46   Butter
Coconut Custard Pie, page 226
Coffee   Tea

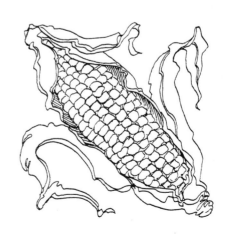

Dinner

MOTHER'S DAY
FOR 6

Chicken Broth with Green Onion Slices
Herb-Baked Scallops, page 119
Baked Potatoes
Spinach and Red Cabbage Salad, page 68
(halve the recipe)
Chocolate Layer Cake

Coffee   White Wine   Milk

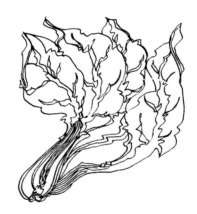

ORIENTAL TREAT
FOR 6

Chicken Broth with Tofu and Spinach
Beef with Bean Curd and
Vegetables, page 81
Cellophane or Vermicelli Noodles
Vanilla Ice Cream
Tea

HERE COMES SUMMER
BARBECUE
FOR 6

Honeydew Melon Balls with Fresh Mint
Buttermilk-Soused Rosemary-Scented
Lamb, page 127
Grilled Mushrooms   Green Peas Amandine
Lemon-Buttered New Potatoes
Pear-Walnut Torte, page 233
Red Wine   Coffee

POOLSIDE PICNIC
FOR 6

Assorted Cold Cuts
Honey-Graham Bread, page 43
Coleslaw   Cold Bean Salad
Boston Lettuce Leaves
Green and Yellow Squash Pickle Chips,
page 183
Mayonnaise   Catsup   Mustard
Whole-Wheat Apple Cookies, page 212
Tea and Lemon Punch, made with
Lemonade Syrup, page 252
(triple the recipe twice)

EASY CLEANUP DINNER
FOR 6

Corn and Cheese Soufflé, page 176
Mandarin Orange and Spinach Salad
Brioches   Butter
Red Fruits, page 232
Coffee   Milk   Tea

MEXICAN FIESTA
FOR 6

Chicken Picante, page 101
Chick-Peas
*Tomato and Iceberg Lettuce Salad with
Croutons*
Warm Flour Tortillas   Butter
Apple-Plum Clafouti, page 235
Limeade   Coffee

THANKSGIVING AT HOME
FOR 6

Autumn Bisque Soup, page 66
Holiday Turkey, page 111
Savory Thanksgiving Stuffing, page 183
Giblet Gravy, page 111
Marinated Vegetables, page 166
Candied Yams, page 172
Creamed Onions
*Mixed Green Salad with Russian Dressing,
page 71*
Cranberry-Orange Relish, page 185
Cranberry Bread, page 49
Pumpkin-Nut Muffins, page 48
Currant-Walnut-Apple Pie, page 229
Indian Pudding, page 247
Coffee   Tea

ISLAND DELIGHT
FOR 6

Sweet and Sour Pork, page 89
Hot Cooked Rice
Celery and Carrot Sticks   Radish Rounds
Ambrosia
Tea

MEALS FOR EIGHT

Brunch

FOURTH OF JULY BARBECUE
FOR 8
Tulsa Ribs, page 126
Classy Baked Beans, page 144
Pineapple Slaw, page 170
Chili Cornbread, page 52   *Butter*
Citrus Chiffon Pie, page 227
Beer   *Milk*   *Iced Coffee*

SALAD BAR BRUNCH
FOR 8
Assorted Raw Vegetable Platter
Creamy Dip
Pork Teriyaki Salad, page 154
New Moon Chicken Salad, page 152
Mixed Fresh Fruit Compote
Assorted Breads   *Assorted Beverages*

Lunch

HUNGRY TEENS' CHOW
FOR 8
Tacos, made with Chili Beef, page 79
Sweet Red and Green Pepper Rings
Hot Fudge Sundaes
Apple Juice

Dinner

FIT FOR A KING
FOR 8
Consommé Madrilene with Chopped Chives
Crown Roast of Pork with Wild Rice
Stuffing, page 94
Poached Pears Filled with Carrot and Pea
Purées, page 174
Green Beans
Herbed Walnut, Mushroom and Orange
Salad, page 68
Dinner Rolls   *Butter*
Orange Chiffon Cake, page 193
Demitasse   *Cordials*

MEAT-EATERS' MEAL
FOR 8

Pork Balls en Brochette, page 61
Baked Brisket with Horseradish-Walnut
Sauce, page 85
Mixed Green Salad with
Russian Dressing, page 71
Hard Rolls   Butter
Almond-Stuffed Apples with Two Sauces,
page 233 (make the recipe twice)

HEALTHY SPRINGTIME
DINNER
FOR 8

Endive and Caper Salad with
Buttermilk Dressing, page 277
Turkey Roll Florentine, page 114
Baked Stuffed Mushrooms, page 176
Steamed Asparagus Amandine, page 166
Dinner Rolls   Butter
Baked Apples with Honey,
Cinnamon and Walnuts
White Wine   Coffee

WELCOME HOME
CELEBRATION
FOR 8

Beef Broth with Mushroom Slices
Leg of Lamb Piquant, page 97
Spinach Soufflé
Mixed Vegetable Salad, page 70
Sour Cream Yeast Rolls, page 39
(halve the recipe)
Butter
Poached Pears
Coffee   Red Wine   Tea

AUTUMN HARVEST
FOR 8

Tomato Juice Cocktails
Mustard-Glazed Pork with Apples and
Cabbage, page 90
Sour Cream Sunrise Rolls, page 39   Butter
(halve the recipe)
Carrot and Raisin Salad
Country Blueberry Pie, page 229, with
Vanilla Ice Cream
Hot Apple Cider   Coffee

MEALS FOR TEN

EUROPEAN CANDLELIT DINNER
FOR 8

Herring, Salami and Head Cheese

Dilled Cucumber and Onion Salad

Magyar Beef Paprikash, page 83

Thinly Sliced Dark Bread   Butter

Dried Fruit Compote Laced with Brandy

Bakery Strudel

Coffee   Tea

PASTA BUFFET
FOR 8

Pasta Rustica, page 138

Macaroni Salad, page 141

*Cheese Lasagne Rolls with Spinach,
page 148*

*Romaine and Chicory Salad with
Italian Dressing*

Danish Apple Dessert, page 232

White and Rosé Wines   Coffee   Tea

APRÈS-SKI
FOR 8

Onion Soup au Gratin

Hearty Beef Stew, page 84

*Romaine, Radish and Cucumber Salad
with Blue Cheese Dressing*

French Bread   Butter

Fresh Apple Brûlées, page 235

Red Wine   Coffee   Tea

SUNDAY BRUNCH BUFFET
FOR 10

Champagne and Orange Juice

*"Eggspandable" Eggs with
Apricot-Glazed Sausages, page 145*

Oatmeal Batter Bread, page 33

Carrot-Raisin Bread, page 50

Whipped Butter

Coffee   Tea   Milk

PRE-GAME BUFFET
FOR 10

Bread Pot Fondue, page 58

Lentil Chili, page 144

Unsalted Crackers

Lemon Mousse, page 247

Coffee   Beer   Tea

MARDI GRAS PARTY
FOR 10

Shrimp Creole, page 122

Hot Cooked Rice   Panfried Okra

Mixed Green Salad

Harlequin Pumpkin Mousse, page 245

Coffee   White Wine Spritzers   Tea

MEALS FOR TWELVE

FAMILY REUNION
FOR 12

Cheese Rolls, page 286
Hot Chicken Salad with Rice, page 104
Marinated Vegetables, page 166
Dilled Carrots, page 167
Watermelon Basket, page 231
Hot Biscuits   Butter
Sugared and Salted Pecans, page 60
Strawberry-Limon Punch, page 250

SOUTH-OF-THE-BORDER
FOR 12

Guacamole   Corn Chips
Chilled Gazpacho
Chicken Enchiladas in Cheese Cream,
page 104
Spanish Rice   Three-Bean Salad
Shredded Lettuce with Chopped Tomato
Summer-Light Cheesecake, page 243
Sangria

CHRISTMAS AND CANDLELIGHT
FOR 12

Creamy Watercress and Leek Soup,
page 65 (double the recipe)
Marinated Fillet of Beef, page 86
Scalloped Potatoes   Steamed Broccoli
Belgian Endive on Watercress with
Red Wine Vinegar Dressing, page 68
Parkerhouse Rolls   Whipped Butter
Apricot Ice Cream and Chablis Ice Bombe,
page 240
Red Wine   Tea   Demitasse

SUMMER DESSERT BUFFET
FOR 12

Almond Cornets à la Crème, page 216
Peach Melba Shortcake for a Crowd,
page 236
Lemon Meringue Pie, page 228
Strawberry Ice-Cream
Brownie Bombe, page 239
Cassis Punch Royale, page 250
Coffee   Tea

2

HOMEMADE BREADS

Fresh from the oven—warm and delicious yeast and quick breads from scratch.

Freshly baked bread is one of life's simple pleasures, almost always awakening pleasant and nostalgic memories. Whether you're the "knead, punch and wait" type or the kind that likes a "quick" quick bread, there's a real sense of satisfaction you get from making bread from scratch.

Thanks to the introduction of rapid-rise yeast, which generally reduces rising time, you can make your favorite yeast bread in about one-third to one-half the time it used to take but with the same tasty results. Our scrumptious Orange Brunch Rolls with Orange-Sour Cream Glaze (page 40) are a prime example.

Quick breads, such as biscuits, muffins, popovers, pancakes and waffles, are—as the name implies—quick to make. Quick-rising leavenings, such as baking powder and baking soda, account for their fast rising time. Some must-try's in this category are our snappy Ginger-Apricot Muffins (page 47) and Best-Ever Biscuits (page 54).

Want to give your family and guests, an unforgettable treat at your next meal? Bake some bread!

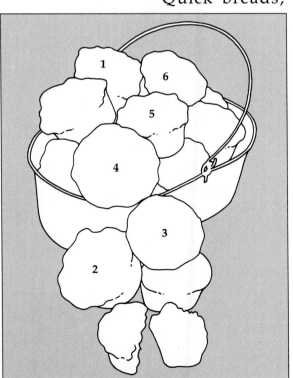

Old-Fashioned Fruit Muffins
1. **Almond-Lemon (page 48)**
2. **Morning Spice (page 46)**
3. **Citrus Muffin (page 46)**
4. **Ginger-Apricot (page 47)**
5. **Applesauce (page 47)**
6. **Blueberry-Bran (page 48)**

Yeast

> **Use Fresh Yeast**
>
> All packages of yeast are dated. For the best results, be sure to use the yeast before that date.

White Bread

Bake at 400° for 40 minutes.
Makes 2 loaves (24 slices).

Nutrient Value Per Slice: 170 calories, 5 gm. protein, 2 gm. fat, 296 mg. sodium, 5 mg. cholesterol.

    2 cups milk
    3 tablespoons sugar
    2 tablespoons butter or margarine
    3 teaspoons salt
    1 envelope active dry yeast
    ½ teaspoon sugar
    ½ cup very warm water
    7 to 8 cups **unsifted all-purpose flour**

1. Stir together the milk, the 3 tablespoons of sugar, the butter and salt in a small saucepan over very low heat, just until the butter is melted. Pour into a large bowl; cool to lukewarm.
2. Sprinkle the yeast and the ½ teaspoon of sugar over the very warm water in a 1-cup glass measure. ("Very warm water" should feel comfortably warm when dropped on the wrist.) Stir to dissolve the yeast. Let stand until bubbly, for about 10 minutes.
3. Stir the yeast mixture and 3 cups of the flour into the cooled milk mixture. Beat with an electric mixer until the batter is smooth. Gradually stir in enough of the remaining flour to form a soft dough.
4. Turn the dough out onto a lightly floured surface; knead until smooth and elastic, for about 10 minutes, using only enough additional flour to prevent the dough from sticking.
5. Press the dough into a buttered large bowl; turn to bring the buttered-side up. Cover with buttered wax paper and a towel. Let rise in a warm place, away from drafts, until doubled in volume, for about 1 hour.

6. Punch the dough down; turn out onto a lightly floured surface; knead a few times; invert a bowl over the dough; let rest for 10 minutes.
7. Divide the dough in half and knead each half a few times. Shape into 2 loaves. Place in two buttered 9x5x3-inch loaf pans. Cover with buttered wax paper and a towel.
8. Let rise again in a warm place, away from drafts, until doubled in volume, for about 1 hour. Meanwhile, preheat the oven to hot (400°).
9. Bake in the preheated hot (400°) oven for 40 minutes or until the loaves are golden brown or sound hollow when tapped with the fingers. If the loaves are browning too quickly, cover the tops loosely with aluminum foil. Remove from the pans to wire racks to cool completely.

> **Soft Bread Crusts**
>
> For a soft crust on a freshly baked white or whole-wheat bread, brush the warm crust with softened butter.

> **Testing Yeast**
>
> To be sure your envelope is alive and well, mix the yeast with a bit of sugar while it is dissolving in the very warm water. A fresh envelope of yeast will bubble nicely within 10 minutes. If not, start with another envelope, and you will not have wasted any of the other ingredients—or your time.

Old-Fashioned Whole-Wheat Bread

Whole-Wheat Bread

Just what whole-grain lovers are looking for—a loaf made with 100% whole-wheat flour.

Bake at 375° for 1 hour for loaves, 25 minutes for rolls.
Makes 3 large loaves or 3 dozen rolls.

Nutrient Value Per Slice or Roll: 146 calories, 5 gm. protein, 3 gm. fat, 253 mg. sodium, 2 mg. cholesterol.

> 2 **cups milk**
> ⅓ **cup honey or molasses**
> 4 **teaspoons salt**
> 2 **envelopes active dry yeast**
> 2 **cups very warm water**
> 10 **cups whole-wheat flour**
> ⅓ **cup vegetable shortening, melted**

1. Stir together the milk, honey or molasses and salt in a small saucepan over very low heat, just until the milk is very hot. Pour into a large bowl; cool to lukewarm.
2. Sprinkle the yeast over ½ cup of the very warm water in a 2-cup glass measure. ("Very warm water" feels comfortably warm when dropped on the wrist.) Stir to dissolve the yeast. Let stand until bubbly, for about 10 minutes.
3. Stir in the remaining 1½ cups of lukewarm water, the yeast mixture and 5 cups of the flour into the cooled milk mixture. Beat with an electric mixer until the batter is smooth. Add the melted shortening and enough of the remaining 5 cups of flour to form a stiff dough.
4. Cover the bowl with buttered wax paper and a towel. Let rise in a warm place, away from drafts, until doubled in volume, for about an hour.
5. Turn the dough out onto a lightly floured surface and knead until smooth, adding as little additional flour as possible.
6. Press the dough into a buttered large bowl; turn to bring the buttered-side up. Cover with buttered wax paper and a towel. Let rise in a warm place, away from drafts, until doubled in volume, for about 40 minutes. Punch the dough down; divide into thirds.
7. Shape one-third of the dough into a 12 x 9-inch rectangle; roll up, jelly-roll fashion, and place, seam-side down, in a greased 9 x 5 x 3-inch loaf pan.
8. Shape the remaining dough into two

loaves, or divide each third of the dough into 12 pieces.
9. To make Rounds: Shape each piece into a ball and place, 1 inch apart, on a lightly greased large cookie sheet. To make Muffin-Tin Rolls: Place the balls of dough in greased muffin-tin cups. To make Bowknots: Roll each piece of dough into an 8-inch rope; make a loop in the center of the rope and pull one end through; place, 1 inch apart, on a lightly greased large cookie sheet.
10. Cover the loaves or rolls with buttered wax paper and a towel. Let rise in a warm place, away from drafts, until doubled in volume, for about 30 minutes. Meanwhile, preheat the oven to moderate (375°).
11. Bake in the preheated moderate oven (375°) for 25 minutes for rolls or for 1 hour for loaves, or until the bread sounds hollow when tapped with the fingers.
12. Invert the loaves onto wire racks and cool completely. Remove the rolls with a spatula from the cookie sheet and cool completely on wire racks. Wrap in a plastic bag to store.

Whole-Wheat Flour

Whole-wheat flour is generally too heavy for delicate baked goods. It contains the entire wheat grain, including the bran, so use it only in recipes calling for it.

To Knead Yeast Breads

Place the dough on a lightly floured surface. Grasp the back edge of the dough and fold it in half toward you; then push down and back with the heel of your hand. Give the dough a quarter turn and repeat the process until the dough is smooth and elastic.

Almond-Raisin Buns

Old-fashioned sugar buns with a new twist—a buttery almond filling.

Bake at 350° for 35 minutes.
Makes 1 coffee cake (9 buns).

Nutrient Value Per Bun: 432 calories, 8 gm. protein, 15 gm. fat, 78 mg. sodium, 91 mg. cholesterol.

½ recipe Golden Egg Coffee Cake Dough
    (recipe follows)
½ cup almond paste (not marzipan)
¼ cup (½ stick) unsalted butter or margarine,
    softened
⅓ cup granulated sugar
⅓ cup shortbread cookie crumbs
¾ cup raisins
1 cup sifted 10X (confectioners') sugar
2 tablespoons milk

1. Prepare the Golden Egg Coffee Cake Dough through its first rising.
2. Beat together the almond paste, butter and granulated sugar in a small bowl until smooth. Stir in the shortbread crumbs. Reserve.
3. Butter a 9x9x2-inch baking pan.
4. Punch the dough down; turn out onto a floured surface. Press or roll the dough into a 16x8-inch rectangle. Spread with the almond paste filling to within ½ inch of the edges; sprinkle evenly with the raisins. Starting with a long side, roll up, jelly-roll fashion; pinch along the seam to seal. Cut the roll into 9 equal slices. Arrange the slices, cut-side down, in the prepared pan. Cover with buttered wax paper and a towel. Let rise in a warm place, away from drafts, until doubled in volume, for about 45 minutes.
5. Meanwhile, preheat the oven to moderate (350°).
6. Bake in the preheated moderate oven (350°) for 35 minutes or until the coffee cake is golden brown and sounds hollow when tapped with the fingers. Remove the pan to a wire rack; cool the coffee cake in the pan completely.
7. Stir together the 10X sugar and milk in a small bowl until smooth. Drizzle over the coffee cake.

Golden Egg Coffee Cake Dough

A rich dough you can use as the basis for many different coffee cakes. This recipe makes two coffee cakes—one to enjoy immediately and one to freeze, if you wish.

⅓ cup milk
½ cup (1 stick) unsalted butter or margarine
½ teaspoon salt
1 envelope active dry yeast
1 teaspoon sugar
¼ cup very warm water
2 eggs
2 egg yolks (reserve whites for coffee-cake
    toppings)
2 tablespoons grated orange rind (optional)
4 to 4½ cups unsifted all-purpose flour

1. Stir together the milk, butter, the ½ cup of sugar and salt in a small saucepan over very low heat, just until the butter is melted. Pour into a large bowl; cool to lukewarm.
2. Sprinkle the yeast and the 1 teaspoon of sugar over the very warm water in a 1-cup glass measure. ("Very warm water" should feel comfortably warm when dropped on the wrist.) Stir to dissolve the yeast. Let stand until bubbly, for about 10 minutes.
3. Stir the eggs, egg yolks, orange rind, if using, the yeast mixture and 2 cups of the flour into the cooled milk mixture. Beat with an electric mixer until the batter is smooth; beat for 2 minutes longer. Stir in enough of the remaining flour to form a soft dough.
4. Turn the dough out onto a floured surface. Knead until smooth and elastic, for about 5 minutes, using only enough additional flour to prevent sticking.
5. Press the dough into a buttered large bowl; turn to bring the buttered-side up. Cover with buttered wax paper and a towel. Let rise in a warm place, away from drafts, until doubled in volume, for about 1 hour.
6. Punch the dough down. Turn out onto a floured surface. Shape and bake, following the individual coffee-cake directions.

◀◀ ▼
Apricot Swirl Coffee Cake

Pinwheels of rich dough glisten with apricots in this attractive ring.

Bake at 350° for 25 minutes.
Makes 1 large coffee cake (12 slices).

Nutrient Value Per Slice: 249 calories, 4 gm. protein, 7 gm. fat, 61 mg. sodium, 62 mg. cholesterol.

½ recipe Golden Egg Coffee Cake Dough
   (see recipe, page 32)
1 package (6 ounces) dried apricots
¼ cup candied cherries
¼ cup raisins
½ cup water
3 tablespoons granulated sugar
2 tablespoons unsalted butter or margarine,
   softened
1 egg white
½ cup **sifted** 10X (confectioners') sugar
2 teaspoons milk or water
¼ teaspoon almond extract

1. Prepare the Golden Egg Coffee Cake Dough through its first rising. Grease a large cookie sheet.
2. Cut the apricots in half. Coarsely chop the cherries. Combine the apricots, cherries and raisins in a small bowl. Combine the water and sugar in a small saucepan. Bring to boiling. Stir in the fruit mixture. Lower the heat; simmer, stirring often, until the syrup is almost all absorbed. Cool completely.
3. Punch the dough down; turn out onto a floured surface. Roll or press the dough into an 18 x 8-inch rectangle. Spread with the softened butter; then spread the apricot filling to within ½ inch of the edges. Starting with a long side, roll up, jelly-roll fashion; pinch firmly along the seam to seal. Place, seam-side down, on the greased cookie sheet. Shape into a circle; seal the ends well to make an unbroken circle. With kitchen shears, make 8 evenly spaced cuts around the outer edge, cutting about three-quarters through, toward the center. Twist each slice, turning the cut-side up to show the pinwheel.
4. Beat the egg white lightly in a small bowl. Brush over the dough only, not the filling. Cover with buttered wax paper and a towel. Let rise in a warm place, away from drafts, until doubled in volume, for about 45 minutes.

5. Meanwhile, preheat the oven to moderate (350°).
6. Bake in the preheated moderate oven (350°) for 25 minutes or until the coffee cake is golden brown and sounds hollow when tapped with the fingers. Remove to a wire rack; cool completely.
7. Blend the 10X sugar, milk and almond extract in a cup until smooth. Drizzle over the top of the coffee cake.

Sifted vs. Unsifted

Most commercial brands of flour come presifted from the manufacturer, making additional sifting unnecessary in many cases. Some of our recipes indicate additional sifting in order to produce a lighter product. Do not sift unless the recipe indicates to do so.

◀◀
Oatmeal Batter Bread

This easy, no-kneading, one-rising-in-the-pan homemade loaf gives you lots of extra time to prepare the rest of your meal.

Bake at 375° for 60 minutes.
Makes 1 loaf (12 slices).

Nutrient Value Per Slice: 168 calories, 4 gm. protein, 4 gm. fat, 190 mg. sodium, 23 mg. cholesterol.

¾ cup boiling water
½ cup old-fashioned rolled oats
3 tablespoons vegetable shortening
¼ cup honey
1 teaspoon salt
¼ teaspoon apple pie spice
1 envelope active dry yeast
½ teaspoon sugar
¼ cup very warm water
1 egg, slightly beaten
2¾ cups **sifted** all-purpose flour

1. Grease a 9 x 5 x 3-inch loaf pan.
2. Stir together the boiling water, oats, shortening, honey, salt and apple pie spice in a large bowl until well mixed. Cool to lukewarm.
3. Sprinkle the yeast and sugar over very warm water in a 1-cup glass measure. ("Very warm water" should feel comfortably warm when dropped on the wrist.) Stir to dissolve the yeast. Let stand until bubbly, for about 10 minutes.

☞

4. Add the yeast mixture, egg and 1¼ cups of the flour to the oatmeal mixture. Beat with an electric mixer at low speed for 2 minutes, scraping down the sides of the bowl occasionally. Gradually beat in the remaining 1½ cups of flour, beating until the batter is smooth. Spread the batter in the prepared pan. Cover with buttered wax paper, away from drafts, until doubled in volume, for about 45 minutes.
5. Meanwhile, preheat the oven to moderate (375°).
6. Bake in the preheated moderate oven (375°) for about 60 minutes or until the loaf sounds hollow when tapped with the fingers. Remove the bread from the pan; cool on a wire rack.

Fast-Rising Yeast Breads

The old-fashioned flavor of yeast breads hasn't changed—but the time you spend making them has! Use the new, quick-acting dry yeast that mixes directly with the dry ingredients and causes the dough to rise up to 50 percent faster.

Tips for Using Fast-Rising Dry Yeast

Follow these pointers for using the new yeast in our delicious breads, as well as in your own favorite recipes.
● Always include water in the ingredients. If your recipe calls for milk or liquid other than water, decrease the amount of liquid by ¼ cup per envelope of fast-rising yeast used and substitute an equal amount of water.
● Combine the yeast with about two-thirds of the flour and the other dry ingredients in a large bowl. No need to dissolve the yeast in liquids first.
● Heat the liquids and solid or liquid fats, but not the eggs, in a saucepan until *hot* to the touch, 130°. This is hotter than the 110°-115° usually required if the yeast is being dissolved directly in a liquid.
● Stir the hot liquids into the dry ingredients; add the eggs, if using. Blend at low speed with an electric mixer; then beat at medium speed for 3 minutes. Stir in enough remaining flour to make a soft dough.

● Follow the recipe directions for kneading and rising (the rising time is reduced by one-half to one-third). Start checking the dough halfway through the suggested rising time in a recipe calling for regular yeast.

Substituting Regular Active Dry Yeast for Fast Rising

When combining the yeast with a portion of the flour and other dry ingredients, combine with about one-third of the flour (instead of two-thirds as with the fast-rising) and other dry ingredients. Also increase the rising times by one-third to one-half.

Sour Cream Yeast Rolls

Bake at 375° for 12 to 15 minutes.
Makes about 3 dozen rolls.

Nutrient Value Per Roll: 103 calories, 2 gm. protein, 4 gm. fat, 95 mg. sodium, 25 mg. cholesterol.

4 cups unsifted all-purpose flour
½ cups sugar
1 teaspoon salt
2 envelopes fast-rising dry yeast
1 cup dairy sour cream
½ cup water
½ cup (1 stick) butter or margarine
2 eggs

1. Combine 3 cups of the flour, the sugar, salt and yeast in a large bowl; stir to mix.
2. Combine the sour cream, water and butter in a small saucepan. Heat to 130° (the mixture should feel comfortably hot to the touch). Add to the flour mixture. Add the eggs. Blend with an electric mixer at low speed; then beat at medium speed for 3 minutes. Mix in the remaining flour, ½ cup at a time, to make a soft dough. Scrape the dough down from the sides of the bowl with a rubber spatula. Cover and refrigerate overnight.
3. Punch the dough down. Divide in half. Roll out half on a lightly floured surface to a ½-inch thickness. Cut into 2-inch rounds. Place the rolls, 1 inch apart, on lightly greased baking sheets. Repeat with the other half of the dough. Cover and let rise in a warm place, away from drafts, until almost doubled in volume, for about 30 minutes.

4. Meanwhile, preheat the oven to moderate (375°).
5. Bake the rolls in the preheated moderate oven (375°) for 12 to 15 minutes or until the rolls are browned on top. Cool on wire racks.

Unruly Dough

When dough has been kneaded to develop elasticity, it is inclined to fight the rolling pin as you roll it out. Just let it rest for 10 to 15 minutes, and it will be soft and stretchy again.

Keep Your Flour Fresh

Regular all-purpose flour can be stored in an airtight container at room temperature. Whole-wheat flour and rye flour should be stored in the freezer in an airtight freezer bag or container if you will not be using them right away.

Mustard-Onion Hamburger Buns

Bake at 350° for 20 to 25 minutes.
Makes 12 buns.

Nutrient Value Per Bun: 345 calories, 9 gm. protein, 8 gm. fat, 831 mg. sodium, 16 mg. cholesterol.

- 4 cups **unsifted unbleached flour**
- 2½ cups whole-wheat flour
- ⅓ cup instant, nonfat dry milk powder
- ⅓ cup instant chopped onion
- 2 teaspoons salt
- 2 envelopes fast-rising dry yeast
- 1¼ cups water
- ⅔ cup Dijon-style or whole-grain mustard
- ⅓ cup butter or margarine
- ¼ cup honey
- 1 tablespoon butter or margarine, melted
  Instant chopped onion, sesame seeds and poppy seeds for topping

1. Set aside 1 cup of the unbleached flour. Mix together the remaining 3 cups of unbleached flour, the whole-wheat flour, milk powder, instant onion, salt and yeast in a large bowl.
2. Combine the water, mustard, the ⅓ cup of butter and the honey in a medium-size saucepan. Heat to 130° (the mixture should feel comfortably hot to the touch). Mix into the dry ingredients. Stir in enough of the

reserved 1 cup of flour to make a fairly stiff dough.
3. Turn the dough out onto a lightly floured surface. Knead until smooth and elastic, for 8 to 10 minutes. Cover; let rest for 10 minutes.
4. Divide the dough into 12 equal pieces. Form each into a smooth ball. Place about 2 inches apart on greased cookie sheets; press to flatten slightly. Cover; let rise in a warm place, away from drafts, until doubled in volume, for 35 to 45 minutes.
5. Meanwhile, preheat the oven to moderate (350°).
6. Brush the tops of the rolls with the melted butter. Sprinkle with the instant chopped onion. Sprinkle half the buns with the sesame seeds and half with the poppy seeds.
7. Bake in the preheated moderate oven (350°) for 20 to 25 minutes or until the buns are browned and sound hollow when tapped with the fingers. Remove to wire racks to cool.

Cornmeal Mush Rolls

Bake at 375° for 20 minutes.
Makes 5 dozen rolls.

Nutrient Value Per Roll: 74 calories, 2 gm. protein, 2 gm. fat, 90 mg. sodium, 8 mg. cholesterol.

- 2¾ cups water
- 2 teaspoons salt
- ⅔ cup yellow cornmeal
- 6 cups **unsifted all-purpose flour**
- ½ cup firmly packed dark brown sugar
- ½ cup dry milk
- 2 envelopes fast-rising dry yeast
- ⅓ cup butter or margarine
- 1 egg

1. Bring 2 cups of the water and the salt to boiling in a medium-size saucepan. Gradually pour in the cornmeal while stirring constantly. Lower the heat and cook for 1 minute, stirring constantly. Remove from the heat. Cool to room temperature, stirring occasionally.
2. Combine 3 cups of the flour, the sugar, dry milk and yeast in a large bowl; stir to mix.
3. Combine the remaining ¾ cup of the water and the butter in a small saucepan. Heat to 130° (mixture should feel comfortably hot to the touch). Add to the flour mixture. Add ☞

CLOCKWISE, FROM LEFT: Winter Fruit Salad with Honey-Lemon Dressing (page 69), Savory Cream Puffs with a chicken-ham mixture (page 53), Nutty Maple-Honey Buns (page 38), Spicy Hot Herbed Tomato Juice (page 253), Overnight Seed Bread (page 38), Frozen Irish Coffee (page 241).

the egg and cornmeal mixture. Blend with an electric mixer at low speed; then beat at medium speed for 3 minutes. Mix in the 2 cups of the remaining flour, 1 cup at a time.

4. Turn the dough out onto a floured surface. Knead for about 5 minutes, adding up to 1 cup of the remaining flour, until smooth and elastic. Place the dough in an oiled large bowl; turn to coat. Cover and let rise in a warm place, away from drafts, until doubled in volume, for about 30 minutes.

5. Grease a 15 x 10 x 1-inch baking pan.

6. Punch the dough down. Shape the dough into 1½-inch balls. Place, side by side, in the prepared pan. Cover and let rise in a warm place, away from drafts, until doubled in volume, for about 25 minutes.

7. Meanwhile, preheat the oven to moderate (375°).

8. Bake the rolls in the preheated moderate oven (375°) for 20 minutes, until golden brown. Serve warm.

Softening Brown Sugar

Brown sugar may be softened by adding a piece of bread to the sugar in a plastic bag or an airtight container.

Overnight Seed Bread and Nutty Maple-Honey Buns

Bake at 350° for 20 to 25 minutes.
Makes 1 loaf bread (12 servings) and 36 miniature sticky buns (12 servings).

Nutrient Value Per Slice of Bread: 167 calories, 5 gm. protein, 3 gm. fat, 108 mg. sodium, 3 mg. cholesterol.

Nutrient Value Per Serving of Buns: 277 calories, 5 gm. protein, 7 gm. fat, 106 mg. sodium, 3 mg. cholesterol.

7 cups **sifted** all-purpose flour
2 tablespoons sugar
1 teaspoon salt
2 packages fast-rising dry yeast
2 cups hot water (125° to 130°)
2 tablespoons butter, softened
½ cup honey
¼ cup maple syrup
3 tablespoons chopped candied ginger
½ cup currants
¾ cup chopped pecans
2 tablespoons poppy seeds
2 tablespoons sesame seeds
2 tablespoons wheat germ
1 egg white
1 teaspoon water
¾ teaspoon ground ginger
2 tablespoons light brown sugar

1. Set aside ½ cup of flour. Combine the remaining flour, sugar, salt and yeast in a bowl. Stir in the water and butter. Beat until smooth. Gradually stir in enough reserved flour to make a soft dough.

2. Knead on a floured surface until smooth and elastic, for 3 to 5 minutes. Invert a bowl over the dough; let rise for 15 minutes.

3. Grease and flour a 9-inch-round layer-cake pan. Combine the honey and maple syrup. Pour into thirty-six 1-inch cupcake cups or a 13 x 9 x 2-inch baking pan. Combine the candied ginger, ¼ cup of the currants and ½ cup of the pecans. Sprinkle equally over the cupcake cups or over the pan.

4. Divide the dough in half. Set half aside, under the inverted bowl. Divide the remaining dough into 3 equal pieces. Roll each piece into a 16-inch-long rope.

5. Cut 3 lengths of wax paper, each 18 inches long. Spread the poppy seeds on one, the sesame seeds on another, the wheat germ on the third. Beat the egg white with the 1 teaspoon of water in a bowl.

6. Brush one rope with the egg wash; roll in the poppy seeds. Brush another rope with the wash; roll in the sesame seeds. Brush the third with the wash; roll in the wheat germ. Reserve the remaining seeds and wheat germ.

7. Lay the ropes, side by side, on a flat surface. Braid together gently, trying not to shake off the seeds. Coil the braid into the prepared layer-cake pan. Carefully spoon any excess seeds and wheat germ into the seedless areas on the braid. Cover loosely; refrigerate overnight.

8. Roll out the remaining dough into a 20 x 10-inch rectangle. Combine the remaining currants and pecans, the ground ginger and brown sugar. Sprinkle over the dough; gently press into the dough.

9. Roll the dough up from a long side. Slice into 36 pieces. Place 1 piece, cut-side up, in each cupcake cup or arrange in rows in the pan. Cover loosely; refrigerate overnight.

10. Preheat the oven to moderate (350°).
11. Bake the bread and buns in the preheated moderate oven (350°) for 20 to 25 minutes or until firm to the touch and golden brown. Turn the buns out onto wax paper immediately, sticky-side up. Cool the bread in the pan on a rack for 10 minutes. Turn out onto the rack to cool.

Sour Cream Sunrise Rolls

Sour Cream Sunrise Rolls

Bake at 350° for 25 minutes.
Makes 1½ dozen rolls.

Nutrient Value Per Roll: 364 calories, 7 gm. protein, 11 gm. fat, 342 mg. sodium, 55 mg. cholesterol.

7 cups **un**sifted all-purpose flour
½ cup sugar
½ cup instant, nonfat dry milk powder
2 teaspoons salt
2 envelopes fast-rising dry yeast
1 cup water
1 cup dairy sour cream
½ cup (1 stick) butter or margarine
½ cup thawed, frozen pineapple-orange juice concentrate
1 tablespoon grated orange rind
2 eggs
Cinnamon Filling (recipe follows)
Sunrise Icing (recipe follows)

1. Combine 4 cups of the flour, the sugar, milk powder, salt and yeast in a large bowl; stir to mix.
2. Combine the water, sour cream, butter, juice concentrate and orange rind in a small saucepan. Heat to 130° (the mixture should feel comfortably hot to the touch). Add to the flour mixture. Add the eggs. Blend with an electric mixer at low speed; then beat at medium speed for 3 minutes. Gradually stir in 2 cups of the remaining flour to make a soft dough.
3. Turn the dough out onto a well-floured surface. Knead for about 5 minutes, adding up to 1 cup of the remaining flour, until smooth and elastic. Place the dough in an oiled large bowl; turn to coat. Cover and let rise in a warm place, away from drafts, until doubled in volume, for about 30 minutes.
4. Grease a 15 x 10-inch jelly-roll pan.
5. Punch the dough down; knead briefly. Divide the dough into 2 equal parts. Roll out each part on a lightly floured surface into a 13 x 9-inch rectangle. Spread one rectangle with half of the Cinnamon Filling. Beginning with a short side, roll up, jelly-roll fashion. Cut crosswise into 1-inch-thick slices. Place the slices, cut-side down, in the prepared pan. Repeat with the remaining dough and filling. Cover and let rise until doubled in volume, for about 30 minutes.
6. Meanwhile, preheat the oven to moderate (350°).
7. Bake the rolls in the preheated moderate oven (350°) for 25 minutes or until golden on top. Remove from the oven. Drizzle the Sunrise Icing over the warm rolls. Serve warm or at room temperature.

Cinnamon Filling: Combine ⅓ cup of sugar, ½ teaspoon of ground cinnamon and 2 tablespoons of melted butter in a small bowl.

Sunrise Icing: Combine 1 cup of *un*sifted 10X (confectioners') sugar, 3 tablespoons of thawed, frozen pineapple-orange juice concentrate, ½ teaspoon of vanilla and 1 tablespoon of softened butter in a small bowl. Mix together until well blended.

Orange Brunch Rolls

Bake at 400° for 20 minutes.
Makes 15 rolls.

Nutrient Value Per Roll: 208 calories, 4 gm. protein, 6 gm. fat, 149 mg. sodium, 28 mg. cholesterol.

3½ *cups* **unsifted** *all-purpose flour*
 5 *tablespoons sugar*
¾ *teaspoons salt*
 2 *envelopes fast-rising dry yeast*
 1 *cup water*
 2 *tablespoons vegetable shortening*
 1 *egg*
¼ *cup (½ stick) butter or margarine, softened*
 2 *tablespoons grated orange rind*
    Orange-Sour Cream Glaze (recipe follows)

1. Combine 2 cups of the flour, 3 tablespoons of the sugar, the salt and yeast in a large bowl; stir to mix.
2. Combine the water and shortening in a small saucepan. Heat to 130° (the mixture should feel comfortably hot to the touch). Add to the flour mixture. Add the egg. Blend with an electric mixer at low speed; then beat at medium speed for 3 minutes. Mix in 1 cup of the remaining flour, ½ cup at a time.
3. Turn the dough out onto a lightly floured surface. Knead for about 5 minutes, adding up to ½ cup of the remaining flour, until smooth and elastic. Place the dough in an oiled large bowl; turn the dough to coat. Cover and let rise in a warm place, away from drafts, until doubled in volume, for about 30 minutes.
4. Combine the butter, orange rind and the remaining 2 tablespoons of sugar in a small bowl; mix well. Grease a 13 x 9-inch baking pan.
5. Punch the dough down; knead briefly. Roll out on a lightly floured surface into a 15 x 12-inch rectangle. Spread the orange-butter mixture over the dough. Roll up, jelly-roll fashion, starting with a long end; pinch to close the seam. Cut into 1-inch-thick slices with a sharp knife. Space the rolls evenly, cut-side down, in the prepared pan. Cover and let rise in a warm place, away from drafts, until doubled in volume, for about 25 minutes.
6. Meanwhile, preheat the oven to hot (400°).
7. Bake the rolls in the preheated hot oven

(400°) for 20 minutes, until golden brown. Pour the Orange-Sour Cream Glaze over the warm rolls in the pan. Cool in the pan on a wire rack.

Orange-Sour Cream Glaze: Combine ½ cup of sugar, ¼ cup of dairy sour cream, 2 tablespoons of grated orange rind and 1 tablespoon of orange juice in a small saucepan. Cook over medium-low heat, stirring constantly, until the sugar is dissolved.

Caramelized Carrot Swirls

Bake at 400° for 20 to 25 minutes.
Makes 4 loaves (6 servings each).

Nutrient Value Per Slice: 282 calories, 7 gm. protein, 5 gm. fat, 349 mg. sodium, 54 mg. cholesterol.

Carrot Filling:
 6 *cups shredded carrots (about 2 pounds)*
½ *cup firmly packed brown sugar*
½ *cup granulated sugar*
½ *cup cognac*
½ *teaspoon ground cinnamon*
¼ *teaspoon ground ginger*
Dough:
 8 *cups* **unsifted** *all-purpose flour*
½ *cup granulated sugar*
 1 *tablespoon salt*
½ *teaspoon ground ginger*
 2 *envelopes fast-rising dry yeast*
1½ *cups buttermilk*
 6 *tablespoons butter or margarine*
¼ *cup plain yogurt*
 4 *eggs, slightly beaten*
 1 *egg white*
 1 *tablespoon water*

1. Prepare Carrot Filling: Combine the carrots, brown and granulated sugars, cognac, cinnamon and ginger in a large skillet. Bring to boiling, stirring constantly. Lower the heat; cook, stirring constantly, until the liquid has evaporated and the carrots are caramelized (slightly darkened), for about 20 minutes. Reserve.
2. Prepare Dough: Set aside 1 cup of the flour. Mix the remaining 7 cups of the flour, the sugar, salt, ginger and yeast in a large bowl.
3. Combine the buttermilk, butter and yogurt

in a medium-size saucepan. Heat to 130°
(the mixture should feel comfortably hot to
the touch). Mix into the dry ingredients.
Mix in the eggs. Stir in enough of the
reserved 1 cup of flour to make a soft
dough.

4. Turn the dough out onto a lightly floured
surface. Knead until smooth and elastic, for
8 to 10 minutes. Cover; let rest for 10
minutes.

5. Divide the dough into 4 equal pieces. Roll
out each piece into a 12 x 9-inch rectangle.
Spread each with one quarter of the filling
to within ½ inch of the edges. Starting at a
long end, roll up each jelly-roll fashion.
Pinch along the seams to seal. Shape each
roll into a ring; pinch the ends together to
make an unbroken circle. Place the rings,
seam-side down, on greased cookie sheets.
With kitchen scissors, make 12 evenly
spaced cuts around the outer edge, cutting
about three-quarters toward the center.
Twist each slice, turning, cut-side up, to
show the pinwheel. Cover; let rise in a
warm place, away from drafts, until
doubled in volume, for 35 to 45 minutes.

6. Meanwhile, preheat the oven to hot (400°).

7. Beat the egg white with the water in a small
cup. Brush on the loaves.

8. Bake in the preheated hot oven (400°) for 20
to 25 minutes or until loaves are browned
and sound hollow when tapped with the
fingers. Remove the cookies sheets to wire
racks to cool. Serve warm or at room
temperature. Store in the refrigerator.

Fruit Kugelhopf

Bake at 375° for 35 to 40 minutes.
Makes 16 servings.

*Nutrient Value Per Serving: 258 calories, 5 gm. protein,
9 gm. fat, 138 mg. sodium, 34 mg. cholesterol.*

　8　large or 16 small dried apricots
　8　dried pitted prunes
　3　teaspoons lemon juice
　¼　teaspoon ground nutmeg
　¾　cup water
3½　cups unsifted all-purpose flour
　1　cup sugar
　½　teaspoon salt
　1　envelope fast-rising dry yeast
　¾　cup plain yogurt
　½　cup (1 stick) butter or margarine
　1　egg
　1　teaspoon grated lemon rind
　½　cup chopped toasted almonds
　1　teaspoon ground cinnamon

1. Combine the apricots, prunes, 1 teaspoon
of the lemon juice, the nutmeg and ½ cup
of the water in a small saucepan. Bring to
boiling. Lower the heat and simmer for
5 minutes. Let cool to room temperature.

2. Combine 2 cups of the flour, ⅓ cup of the
sugar, the salt and yeast in a large bowl;
stir to mix.

3. Combine the yogurt, the remaining ¼ cup
of water and ¼ cup of the butter in a small
saucepan. Heat to 130° (the mixture
should feel comfortably hot to the touch).
Add to the flour mixture. Add the egg,
the remaining 2 teaspoons of lemon juice
and the grated lemon rind. Blend with an
electric mixer at low speed; then beat at
medium speed for 3 minutes. Gradually
stir in 1 cup of the remaining flour to
make a soft dough.

4. Turn the dough out onto a lightly floured
surface. Knead for about 5 minutes,
adding up to ½ cup of the remaining
flour, until smooth and elastic. Place the
dough in an oiled large bowl; turn to coat.
Cover and let rise in a warm place, away
from drafts, until doubled in volume, for
about 30 minutes.

5. Punch the dough down. Let rest for 10
minutes.

6. Combine the remaining ⅔ cup of sugar,
the almonds and cinnamon in a small bowl. ☞

CLOCKWISE, FROM TOP RIGHT: apricot and prune-filled Fruit Kugelhopf (page 41), European-Style Beer Bread (page 44), Orange Brunch Rolls (page 40), Sour Cream Sunrise Rolls (page 39), Cornmeal Mush Rolls (page 35) and Pride O' California Fruit Bread (page 43).

7. Grease a 12-cup Bundt® pan. Melt the remaining ¼ cup of butter in a small saucepan. Reserve.

8. Roll the dough out on a lightly floured surface into a 15 x 9-inch rectangle. Cut into fifteen 3-inch squares. Place 1 or 2 plumped apricots and prunes in the center of each square. Bring the opposite corners together; pinch to seal, making a square.

9. Dip the filled squares in the melted butter, then in the sugar-almond mixture to coat. Stand the squares on edge, side by side in spoke fashion, in the prepared pan. Cover and let rise in a warm place, away from drafts, until doubled in volume, for about 30 minutes.

10. Meanwhile, preheat the oven to moderate (375°).

11. Bake in a preheated moderate oven (375°) for 35 to 40 minutes or until browned. Invert onto a wire rack to cool slightly. Serve warm.

Fruity Saffron Bread

Since it takes about 75,000 flower blossoms to yield about 1 pound of saffron, this orange, pungent spice is very expensive. But a little goes a long way.

Bake at 350° for 30 to 35 minutes.
Makes 2 loaves (8 servings each).

Nutrient Value Per Serving: 325 calories, 7 gm. protein, 10 gm. fat, 206 mg. sodium, 50 mg. cholesterol.

 6 **cups unsifted all-purpose flour**
 ½ **cup currants**
 ½ **cup raisins**
 ½ **cup pecans, chopped**
 1 **tablespoon grated grapefruit rind**
 1 **tablespoon grated orange rind**
 1 **teaspoon grated lemon rind**
 1 **teaspoon salt**
 ½ **teaspoon ground nutmeg**
 2 **envelopes fast-rising dry yeast**
 ¾ **cup water**
 ½ **cup honey**
 ½ **cup (1 stick) butter or margarine**
 ⅓ **cup milk**
 ⅛ **teaspoon saffron threads**
 2 **eggs, slightly beaten**

1. Set aside 1 cup of the all-purpose flour. Mix together the remaining 5 cups of flour, the currants, raisins, pecans, grated grapefruit, orange and lemon rinds, salt, nutmeg and yeast in a large bowl.
2. Combine the water, honey, butter, milk and saffron in a medium-size saucepan. Heat to 130° (the mixture should feel comfortably hot to the touch). Stir into the dry ingredients. Mix in the eggs. Mix in just enough of the reserved flour to make a soft dough.
3. Turn the dough out onto a lightly floured surface. Knead until smooth and elastic, for 6 to 8 minutes. Cover; let rest for 10 minutes.
4. Divide the dough in half. Shape into loaves. Place in 2 greased 8½ x 4½ x 2½-inch baking pans. Cover; let rise in a warm place, away from drafts, until doubled in volume, for about 1 hour.
5. Meanwhile, preheat the oven to moderate (350°).
6. Bake in the preheated moderate oven (350°) for 30 to 35 minutes or until loaves are browned and sound hollow when tapped with the fingers. Remove the breads from the pans to wire racks to cool.

Pride O' California Fruit Bread

Bake at 350° for 35 minutes.
Makes 2 loaves (12 slices each).

Nutrient Value Per Slice: 237 calories, 6 gm. protein, 5 gm. fat, 265 mg. sodium, 9 mg. cholesterol.

  8 to 8½ cups **unsifted all-purpose flour**
  3 tablespoons sugar
2½ teaspoons salt
  1 envelope fast-rising dry yeast
  2 cups water
  1 cup milk
  6 tablespoons butter or margarine (¾ stick)
  1 cup finely chopped pitted prunes (6 ounces)
½ cup blanched almonds, finely chopped
¼ cup firmly packed dark brown sugar
  2 tablespoons grated orange rind

1. Combine 6 cups of the flour, the sugar, salt and yeast in a large bowl; stir to mix.
2. Combine the water, milk and butter in a small saucepan. Heat to 130° (the mixture should feel comfortably hot to the touch). Add to the flour mixture. Blend with an

electric mixer at low speed; then beat at medium speed for 3 minutes. Gradually stir in 1 cup of the remaining flour to make a soft dough.
3. Turn the dough out onto a well-floured surface. Knead until smooth and elastic, for about 5 minutes, adding up to 1½ cups of the remaining flour to prevent sticking. Place the dough in an oiled large bowl; turn to coat. Cover and let rise in a warm place, away from drafts, until doubled in volume, for about 1 hour.
4. Combine the prunes, almonds, brown sugar and orange rind in a small bowl; set aside.
5. Grease two 9 x 5-inch loaf pans.
6. Punch the dough down. Turn out onto a lightly floured surface. Cut into 2 equal pieces. Roll out one piece into a 12 x 9-inch rectangle. Sprinkle with half of the prune mixture. Roll up tightly from a 9-inch end. Pinch the seam to seal. Place, seam-side down, in the prepared loaf pan. Repeat with the second half of the dough. Cover and let rise in a warm place, away from drafts, until doubled in volume, for about 30 minutes.
7. Meanwhile, preheat the oven to moderate (350°).
8. Bake in the preheated moderate oven (350°) for 35 minutes or until browned and loaf sounds hollow when tapped on the bottom. Remove the loaves from the pans to wire racks to cool.

Honey-Graham Bread

Bake at 350° for 35 to 40 minutes.
Makes 2 loaves (8 servings each).

Nutrient Value Per Serving: 258 calories, 7 gm. protein, 4 gm. fat, 328 mg. sodium, 4 mg. cholesterol.

  5 cups **unsifted all-purpose flour**
  1 cup whole-wheat flour
  1 cup graham cracker crumbs
½ cup wheat germ
  2 tablespoons light brown sugar
  2 teaspoons salt
  2 envelopes fast-rising dry yeast
  2 cups water
  1 cup orange juice
¼ cup honey
  2 tablespoons butter or margarine
      Vegetable oil

1. Set aside 1 cup of the all-purpose flour. Mix together the remaining 4 cups of all-purpose flour, the whole-wheat flour, graham cracker crumbs, wheat germ, brown sugar, salt and yeast in a large bowl.
2. Combine the water, orange juice, honey and butter in a medium-size saucepan. Heat to 130° (the mixture should feel comfortably hot to the touch). Mix the liquid ingredients into the dry ingredients. Stir in just enough of the reserved 1 cup of all-purpose flour to make a soft dough.
3. Turn the dough out onto a lightly floured surface. Knead until smooth and elastic, for 8 to 10 minutes. Cover; let rest for 10 minutes.
4. Divide the dough in half. Shape into 2 loaves. Place in 2 greased 8½ x 4½ x 2½-inch baking pans. Cover; let the dough rise in a warm place, away from drafts, until it is doubled in volume, for about 45 to 55 minutes.
5. Meanwhile, preheat the oven to moderate (350°).
6. Bake in the preheated moderate oven (350°) for 35 to 40 minutes or until the loaves are browned and sound hollow when tapped with the fingers. Remove the breads from the pans to wire racks to cool. Brush the loaves with the oil while still warm.

European-Style Beer Bread

Bake at 375° for 30 to 35 minutes.
Makes 2 loaves (24 slices).

Nutrient Value Per Slice: 168 calories, 5 gm. protein, 2 gm. fat, 218 mg. sodium, 11 mg. cholesterol.

    2   cups flat beer
    ½   cup plus 2 tablespoons cornmeal
    2   teaspoons salt
    3½ cups unsifted bread flour
    2   cups whole-wheat flour
    ½   cup wheat germ
    ½   whole-bran cereal
    1   tablespoon sugar
    2   envelopes fast-rising dry yeast
    ½   cup plus 1 tablespoon water
    ½   cup molasses
    2   tablespoons margarine or vegetable
        shortening
    1   egg yolk

1. Heat the beer in a small saucepan over medium heat to simmering. Remove from heat; stir in the ½ cup of cornmeal and the salt. Cool to room temperature.
2. Combine 1½ cups of the bread flour, the whole-wheat flour, wheat germ, bran cereal, sugar and yeast in a large bowl; stir to mix.
3. Combine the ½ cup of water, the molasses and margarine in a small saucepan. Heat to 130° (the mixture should feel comfortably hot to the touch). Add to the flour mixture. Add the beer mixture. Blend with an electric mixer at low speed; then beat at medium speed for 3 minutes. Gradually mix in 1 cup of the remaining bread flour to make a soft dough.
4. Turn the dough out onto a well-floured surface. Knead for about 5 minutes, adding up to 1 cup of the remaining bread flour, until smooth and elastic. Place the dough in an oiied large bowl; turn to coat. Cover and let rise in a warm place, away from drafts, until doubled in volume, for about 30 minutes.
5. Punch the dough down; knead briefly. Let rise in the bowl again for 30 minutes.
6. Grease 2 baking sheets. Sprinkle with the remaining 2 tablespoons of cornmeal.
7. Punch the dough down; knead briefly. Divide the dough in half; shape into 2 balls. Place on the prepared baking sheets. Cover and let rise in a warm place, away from drafts, until almost doubled in volume, for about 25 minutes.
8. Meanwhile, preheat the oven to moderate (375°).
9. Make deep slashes with a floured, very sharp knife in a crisscross pattern on top

of the loaves. Mix the egg yolk and the 1 tablespoon of water in a small bowl. Brush over the top and sides of the loaves.

10. Bake the loaves in the preheated moderate oven (375°) for 30 to 35 minutes or until the bread is browned and sounds hollow when tapped on the bottoms with the fingers. Cool on wire racks.

Flowerpot Breads

Children can have fun decorating these individual holiday breads with Mom's help.

Bake at 375° for 30 minutes.
Makes 6 individual breads.

Nutrient Value Per Serving: 535 calories, 14 gm. protein, 23 gm. fat, 222 mg. sodium, 121 mg. cholesterol.

   3 cups **sifted** all-purpose flour
   ¼ cup sugar
   1 envelope fast-rising dry yeast
   ½ teaspoon salt
   ½ cup milk
   ⅓ cup unsalted butter or margarine
   2 eggs, slightly beaten
   ½ teaspoon vanilla
   ¾ cup raisins
   ¾ cup chopped blanched almonds
       Candy Flowers (instructions follow)

1. Combine 1¾ cups of the flour, the sugar, yeast and salt in a large bowl; stir to mix well.
2. Combine the milk and butter in a saucepan. Heat to 130° (should feel comfortably hot to the touch). Add to the flour mixture. Add the eggs and vanilla. Blend with a mixer on low speed; then beat on medium speed for 3 minutes. Stir in the raisins and almonds. Gradually stir in 1 cup of the flour to make a soft dough.
3. Turn the dough out onto a well-floured surface. Knead until soft and elastic, for 8 to 10 minutes, using the remaining ¼ cup of flour as necessary to prevent sticking.
4. Place the dough in an oiled large bowl; turn to coat. Cover with a cloth; let rise in a warm place, away from drafts, until doubled in volume, for 50 to 55 minutes.
5. Prepare six brand-new 3-inch clay flowerpots or 6-ounce custard cups: Gently press a 12-inch square of aluminum foil over the bottom of a glass spice jar; use the jar to

press the foil into the pot. Remove the jar. Press the foil to the sides of the pot. Grease the foil lightly. Repeat with the remaining pots. Do *not* use the clay pots without foil.

6. Punch the dough down. Turn out onto a lightly floured surface. Pat lightly into a 7-inch round; cut into 6 equal wedges. Place a wedge, point down, into each prepared pot. Place the pots on a jelly-roll pan. Cover; let rise in a warm place, away from drafts, until doubled in volume, for about 40 to 45 minutes.
7. Meanwhile, preheat the oven to moderate (375°).
8. Bake in the preheated moderate (375°) oven for 10 minutes. Cover the tops with foil to prevent overbrowning. Bake for another 20 minutes or until the breads sound hollow when lightly tapped. Remove the pots to a wire rack.
9. When cool, decorate with the Candy Flowers. Remember to remove the flowers and the foil before eating the bread.

Candy Flowers: Thinly slice large gumdrops, jellied orange section candies and jellied mint-leaf candies with a moistened knife (the knife should not be too wet). Press together to form flowers and leaves, as pictured below. Press onto the narrow wooden sticks. (The cut-side of the candies will stick together and to the wooden stick when firmly pressed.) Press the stick down into the bread to make a flower.

Flowerpot Breads

Quick Breads

Mixing Muffins

When adding the liquid to the dry ingredients, stir as little as possible, just enough to moisten the dry ingredients. The batter will be slightly lumpy. Overstirring will produce a muffin that is coarse-textured and full of tunnels. A good muffin should have straight sides, a rounded top and a uniform grain.

▚ ◁◁ ▢

Morning Spice Muffins

Lightly spiced and plump with raisins, perfect for breakfast with apple jelly.

Bake at 400° for 20 minutes.
Makes 12 muffins.

Nutrient Value Per Muffin: 160 calories, 3 gm. protein, 6 gm. fat, 192 mg. sodium, 37 mg. cholesterol.

- **1 cup sifted *all-purpose flour***
- **½ teaspoon salt**
- **1 teaspoon baking powder**
- **½ teaspoon baking soda**
- **½ teaspoon ground cinnamon**
- **½ teaspoon ground ginger**
- **¼ teaspoon ground nutmeg**
- **¾ cup stirred whole-wheat flour**
- **⅓ cup firmly packed light brown sugar**
- **1 egg**
- **1 cup buttermilk**
- **⅓ cup unsalted butter or margarine, melted**
- **½ cup raisins, plumped***

1. Preheat the oven to hot (400°). Grease the bottoms only of twelve 2½-inch muffin-pan cups.
2. Sift together the all-purpose flour, salt, baking powder, baking soda, cinnamon, ginger and nutmeg into a large bowl. Stir in the whole-wheat flour and sugar.
3. Lightly beat the egg in a small bowl. Beat in the buttermilk and butter; stir in the raisins. Pour all at once into the flour mixture. Stir briskly with a fork, just until all the dry ingredients are moistened; do not overstir. The batter will look lumpy.
4. Fill each prepared muffin-pan cup two-thirds full with batter, using a large spoon and rubber spatula.

5. Bake in the preheated hot oven (400°) for 20 minutes or until golden brown. Remove the pan to a wire rack. Loosen the muffins with the spatula and remove from the pan at once to prevent steaming. Serve piping hot.

* To plump the raisins, cover with hot water in a small bowl. Let stand for 5 minutes. Drain well.

Cultured Buttermilk Powder

This new product works like liquid buttermilk to give baked goods a lighter, fluffier texture. And it offers the convenience and economy of purchasing buttermilk in shelf-stable form. Use cultured buttermilk powder whenever a recipe calls for liquid buttermilk; mix ¼ cup of dry buttermilk powder for every cup of liquid buttermilk in a recipe, with other dry ingredients; then add 1 cup of water, when the recipe calls for the addition of liquid buttermilk.

▚ ◁◁ ▢

Citrus Muffins

Flavored with grated fresh lime and orange peels.

Bake at 400° for 20 minutes.
Makes 12 muffins.

Nutrient Value Per Muffin: 170 calories, 3 gm. protein, 10 gm. fat, 195 mg. sodium, 49 mg. cholesterol.

- **1¾ cups sifted *all-purpose flour***
- **3 tablespoons sugar**
- **2½ teaspoons baking powder**
- **½ teaspoon salt**
- **1 egg**
- **¾ cup milk**
- **⅓ cup unsalted butter or margarine, melted**
- **1 tablespoon grated fresh orange rind (1 orange)**
- **1 tablespoon grated fresh lime rind (2 limes)**
- **¼ cup unsalted butter or margarine, melted**
  Sugar for topping

1. Preheat the oven to hot (400°). Grease the bottoms only of twelve 2½-inch muffin-pan cups.
2. Sift together the flour, 3 tablespoons of sugar, the baking powder and salt into a large bowl.
3. Lightly beat the egg in a small bowl. Beat in the milk and the ⅓ cup of butter; stir in the orange and lime rind. Pour all at once into

the flour mixture. Stir briskly with a fork, just until all the ingredients are moistened; do not overstir. The batter will look lumpy.

4. Fill each prepared muffin-pan cup two-thirds full with batter, using a large spoon and rubber spatula.
5. Bake in the preheated hot oven (400°) for 20 minutes or until golden brown. Remove the pan to a wire rack. Loosen the muffins with the spatula and remove from the pan at once to prevent steaming.
6. While warm, brush the tops with the ¼ cup of melted butter and sprinkle with the sugar. Garnish the tops with strips of orange and lime peel, if you wish.

Ginger-Apricot Muffins

Delicious for breakfast, these muffins are also good with lunch or afternoon tea.

Bake at 400° for 25 muffins.
Makes 12 muffins.

Nutrient Value Per Muffin: 155 calories, 3 gm. protein, 6 gm. fat, 195 mg. sodium, 39 mg. cholesterol.

1¾ **cups** *sifted all-purpose flour*
  3 *tablespoons sugar*
2½ *teaspoons baking powder*
1½ *teaspoons ground ginger*
  ½ *teaspoon salt*
  1 *egg*
  ¾ *cup milk*
  ⅓ *cup unsalted butter or margarine, melted*
  ¾ *cup finely cut-up dried apricots*
1½ *teaspoons grated fresh lemon rind
      (1 lemon)*

1. Preheat the oven to hot (400°). Grease the bottoms only of twelve 2½-inch muffin-pan cups.
2. Sift together the flour, sugar, baking powder, ginger and salt into a large bowl.
3. Lightly beat the egg in a small bowl. Beat in

the milk and butter; stir in the apricots and lemon rind. Pour all at once into the flour mixture. Stir briskly with a fork, just until all the ingredients are moistened; do not overstir. The batter will look lumpy.

4. Fill each prepared muffin-pan cup two-thirds full with batter, using a large spoon and rubber spatula.
5. Bake in the preheated hot oven (400°) for 25 minutes or until golden brown. Remove the pan to a wire rack. Loosen the muffins with the spatula and remove from the pan at once to prevent steaming. Garnish with additional cut-up dried apricots, if you wish. Serve piping hot.

Applesauce Muffins

Wonderful with a bowl of fresh fruit.

Bake at 400° for 25 minutes.
Makes 12 muffins.

Nutrient Value Per Muffin: 213 calories, 4 gm. protein, 12 gm. fat, 211 mg. sodium, 66 mg. cholesterol.

  ½ *cup unsalted butter or margarine, softened*
  ⅓ *cup sugar*
  2 *eggs*
  1 *cup applesauce*
1¾ *cups* **sifted** *all-purpose flour*
  1 *tablespoon baking powder*
  ½ *teaspoon salt*
  ½ *cup chopped walnuts*

1. Preheat the oven to hot (400°). Grease the bottoms only of twelve 2½-inch muffin-pan cups.
2. Beat the butter and sugar in a large bowl until light and fluffy. Beat in the eggs, one at a time. Beat in the applesauce (the mixture may look separated).
3. Sift together the flour, baking powder and salt over the butter mixture. Add the nuts. Stir briskly with a fork, just until all the dry ingredients are moistened; do not overstir. The batter will look lumpy.
4. Fill each prepared muffin-pan cup two-thirds full with batter, using a large spoon and spatula.
5. Bake in the preheated hot oven (400°) for 25 minutes or until golden brown. Remove the pan to a wire rack. Loosen the muffins with the spatula and remove at once to prevent steaming. Serve piping hot.

◧◧◧

Blueberry-Bran Muffins

Nutritious bran fortifies these tender, cake-like muffins.

Bake at 425° for 23 minutes.
Makes 12 muffins.

*Nutrient Value Per Muffin: 164 calories, 3 gm. protein,
6 gm. fat, 195 mg. sodium, 39 mg. cholesterol.*

⅓ cup unsalted butter or margarine, softened
½ cup sugar
1 egg
¾ cup milk
¼ teaspoon vanilla
1⅔ cups **sifted** all-purpose flour plus
    1 tablespoon
2½ teaspoons baking powder
½ teaspoon salt
¼ cup unprocessed bran
1 generous cup fresh blueberries OR:
    1 generous cup unsweetened frozen
    blueberries, slightly thawed

1. Preheat the oven to hot 425°. Grease the bottoms only of twelve 2½-inch muffin-pan cups.
2. Beat together the butter and sugar in a large mixing bowl until light and fluffy. Beat in the egg, then the milk and vanilla; mix well (the mixture may look separated).
3. Sift together the 1⅔ cups of flour, the baking powder and salt into a medium-size bowl. Stir in the bran. Add to the butter mixture. Stir briskly with a fork, just until the dry ingredients are moistened; do not overstir. The batter will not be smooth.
4. Toss the berries with 1 tablespoon of the flour in a small bowl. Fold into the batter.
5. Fill each prepared muffin-pan cup two-thirds full with batter, using a large spoon and rubber spatula.
6. Bake in the preheated hot (425°) oven for 23 minutes or until golden brown. Remove the pan to a wire rack. Loosen the muffins with a spatula and remove from the pan at once to prevent steaming. Serve piping hot.

◧◧◧

Almond-Lemon Muffins

*Studded with chopped almonds and flavored with lemon
rind and vanilla.*

Bake at 400° for 25 minutes.
Makes 12 muffins.

*Nutrient Value Per Muffin: 184 calories, 4 gm. protein,
11 gm. fat, 195 mg. sodium, 39 mg. cholesterol.*

1¾ cups **sifted** all-purpose flour
3 tablespoons sugar
2½ teaspoons baking powder
½ teaspoon salt
1 egg
¾ cup milk
⅓ cup unsalted butter or margarine, melted
½ teaspoon lemon extract
⅛ teaspoon vanilla
¾ cup chopped unblanched almonds
2 teaspoons grated fresh lemon rind
    (1 lemon)

1. Preheat the oven to hot (400°). Grease the bottoms only of twelve 2½-inch muffin-pan cups.
2. Sift together the flour, sugar, baking powder and salt into a large bowl.
3. Lightly beat the egg in a small bowl. Beat in the milk, butter, lemon extract and vanilla. Stir in the nuts and lemon rind. Pour all at once into the flour mixture. Stir briskly with a fork, just until all the ingredients are moistened; do not overstir. The batter will look lumpy.
4. Fill each prepared muffin-pan cup two-thirds full with batter, using a large spoon and rubber spatula.
5. Bake in the preheated hot oven (400°) for 25 minutes or until golden brown. Remove the pan to a wire rack. Loosen the muffins with the spatula and remove from the pan at once to prevent steaming. Serve piping hot, garnished with almond slices, if you wish.

◧◧◧

Pumpkin-Nut Muffins

Bake at 350° for 20 minutes.
Makes 2 dozen muffins.

*Nutrient Value Per Muffin: 129 calories, 2 gm. protein,
5 gm. fat, 78 mg. sodium, 30 mg. cholesterol.*

2 cups **sifted** all-purpose flour
1 teaspoon baking soda

½ teaspoon baking powder
½ teaspoon ground cinnamon
½ teaspoon ground nutmeg
¼ teaspoon ground ginger
2 eggs, slightly beaten
⅓ cup buttermilk
⅓ cup butter or margarine, melted
1 tablespoon molasses
½ teaspoon vanilla
1 cup sugar
1 cup canned pumpkin
½ cup chopped pecans
½ cup raisins

1. Preheat the oven to moderate (350°). Grease 24 muffin-pan cups, 2¼ inches in diameter.
2. Sift together the flour, baking soda, baking powder, cinnamon, nutmeg and ginger onto wax paper.
3. Beat together the eggs, buttermilk, melted butter, molasses, vanilla, sugar and pumpkin in a large bowl. Stir in the dry ingredients, all at once, just until moistened. Fold in the nuts and raisins. Spoon into the prepared muffin-pan cups, filling almost to the top.
4. Bake in the preheated moderate oven (350°) for 20 to 25 minutes or until a wooden pick inserted in the centers comes out clean. Remove the muffins from the cups and cool on wire racks. Serve warm.

MICROWAVE DIRECTIONS
650 Watt Variable Power Microwave Oven
Directions: Place two 2½-inch paper cupcake liners into each of 18 microwave-safe muffin cups. Prepare the muffin batter as above. Divide the batter equally among the lined cups. Microwave 6 at a time at full power for 4½ minutes. Remove the muffins from the pans, peel off the outer paper liners and cool on wire racks. Makes 1½ dozen large muffins.
NOTE: Uncooked batter-filled cups can be frozen. To bake, place 6 frozen filled paper liners in microwave-safe muffin cups. Microwave at full power for 6 minutes.

Cranberry Bread

Bake at 350° for 1 hour and 5 minutes.
Makes 12 servings.

Nutrient Value Per Serving: 225 calories, 3 gm. protein, 8 gm. fat, 147 mg. sodium, 23 mg. cholesterol.

1 tablespoon all-purpose flour
1½ cups fresh or frozen cranberries, thawed if frozen, coarsely chopped
½ cup chopped walnuts

2 cups **sifted** all-purpose flour
1½ teaspoons baking powder
½ teaspoon salt
1 cup sugar
¼ cup vegetable shortening
1 egg, slightly beaten
¾ cup orange juice
1 tablespoon grated orange rind

1. Preheat the oven to moderate (350°). Grease an 8½ x 4½ x 2⅝-inch loaf pan.
2. Sprinkle the 1 tablespoon of flour over the cranberries and nuts on wax paper; toss to coat. Reserve.
3. Sift together the 2 cups of flour, the baking powder and salt into a large bowl; stir in the sugar.
4. Cut the shortening into the flour mixture with a pastry blender until crumbly. Beat the egg with the orange juice in a small bowl. Stir into the flour mixture, just until the dry ingredients are moistened. Stir in the cranberry-nut mixture and orange rind. Spoon into the prepared loaf pan.
5. Bake in the preheated moderate oven (350°) for 1 hour and 5 minutes or until a wooden pick inserted in the center comes out clean. Turn out onto a wire rack to cool. This bread cuts better the next day.

Make Ahead for a Great Gift

Wrap the cooled, baked loaf in freezer wrap or aluminum foil; freeze. Wonderful to have on hand for a holiday gift.

Store for up to 4 months in the freezer. Let stand at room temperature for 1 hour before serving.

Carrot-Raisin Bread

Here's a nutritious bread that has both flavor and lowfat appeal. Since it freezes well, it can be baked ahead.

Bake at 350° for 50 to 60 minutes.
Makes 1 loaf (12 slices).

Nutrient Value Per Serving: 165 calories, 2 gm. protein, 3 gm. fat, 113 mg. sodium, 0 mg. cholesterol.

- 1 cup finely grated carrots
- 1 cup seedless raisins
- 1½ cups water
- ½ cup firmly packed brown sugar
- ½ teaspoon ground cinnamon
- ¼ teaspoon ground nutmeg
- ¼ teaspoon ground cloves
- 2 tablespoons vegetable oil
- 2 cups **sifted, unbleached all-purpose flour**
- 1 teaspoon baking powder
- 1 teaspoon baking soda

1. Preheat the oven to moderate (350°). Grease a 9¼ x 5¼ x 2¾-inch loaf pan.
2. Combine the carrots, raisins, water, sugar, cinnamon, nutmeg and cloves in a large saucepan. Bring to boiling. Lower the heat and simmer, covered, for 5 minutes. Cool. Stir in the oil.
3. Combine the flour, baking powder and baking soda in a medium-size bowl. Stir into the carrot mixture until well mixed. Pour into the prepared loaf pan.
4. Bake in the preheated moderate oven (350°) for 50 to 60 minutes or until a cake tester inserted in the center comes out clean. Cool for 15 minutes in the pan on a wire rack. Turn the bread out onto the rack to cool completely.

Shortening vs. Butter or Margarine

Vegetable shortening and diet margarine are not substitutes for butter or margarine, unless called for in the recipe.

Date-Orange Coffee Cake

A scrumptious treat for Sunday brunch.

Bake at 325° for 50 minutes.
Makes 1 large coffee cake (10 slices).

Nutrient Value Per Slice: 484 calories, 7 gm. protein, 20 gm. fat, 235 mg. sodium, 58 mg. cholesterol.

- 1 package (8 ounces) pitted dates, cut up
- 1 cup walnuts, chopped
- 2½ cups **sifted all-purpose flour**
- 2 teaspoons baking powder
- ½ teaspoon baking soda
- ½ teaspoon salt
- ½ cup butter-flavored vegetable shortening
- 1 cup firmly packed light brown sugar
- 2 tablespoons grated orange rind
- 2 eggs
- 1 cup milk
  Fresh Orange Icing (recipe follows)

1. Preheat the oven to slow (325°). Grease and flour a 10-inch (10-cup) Kugelhopf or other fancy tube pan.
2. Combine the dates, walnuts and 2 tablespoons of the flour in a bowl; mix well. Sift the remaining flour, the baking powder, baking soda and salt onto wax paper.
3. Beat the shortening, brown sugar, orange rind and eggs in a large bowl until well blended.
4. Stir the flour mixture into the shortening mixture alternately with the milk, mixing after each addition, until smooth. Fold in the date mixture. Turn into the prepared pan.
5. Bake in the preheated slow oven (325°) for 50 minutes or until the top springs back when lightly touched with a fingertip. Remove the pan to a wire rack; cool for 5 minutes. Invert the cake onto the rack; lift off the pan. Cool completely.
6. Drizzle the top with the Fresh Orange Icing. Decorate with strips of orange zest, if you wish.

Fresh Orange Icing: Stir 2 tablespoons of fresh orange juice into 1 cup of *sifted* 10X (confectioners') sugar until smooth.

Blueberry-Sour Cream Coffee Cake

A tender, fruity coffee cake that is quick to make. Keep the recipe for the fresh blueberry season too!

Bake at 350° for 40 minutes.
Makes 1 coffee cake (9 slices).

Nutrient Value Per Slice: 364 calories, 6 gm. protein, 15 gm. fat, 265 mg. sodium, 95 mg. cholesterol.

>   **Brown Sugar Crumb Topping**
>   **(recipe follows)**
> 2   cups **sifted** all-purpose flour
> 2½ teaspoons baking powder
> ½   teaspoon baking soda
> ¼   teaspoon salt
> ¼   cup (½ stick) unsalted butter or margarine,
>   softened
> ¾   cup granulated sugar
> 2   eggs
> ¾   cup dairy sour cream
> ½   cup frozen or fresh blueberries
> 1   tablespoon all-purpose flour
>   10X (confectioners') sugar

1. Prepare and reserve the Brown Sugar Crumb Topping.
2. Preheat the oven to moderate (350°). Grease and flour a 9 x 9 x 2-inch baking pan.
3. Sift together the 2 cups of flour, the baking powder, baking soda and salt onto wax paper.
4. Beat the butter, granulated sugar and eggs in a medium-size bowl with an electric mixer until well blended.
5. Stir the flour mixture into the creamed mixture alternately with the sour cream, beating well after each addition until the batter is smooth. Turn into the prepared pan.
6. Toss the blueberries with the 1 tablespoon of flour in a small bowl; sprinkle over the batter. Rub the Brown Sugar Crumb Topping between the fingers to form crumbs; sprinkle evenly over the berries.
7. Bake in the preheated moderate oven (350°) for 40 minutes or until the center springs back when lightly pressed with a fingertip. Cool in the pan on a wire rack. Sprinkle with the 10X sugar pressed through a strainer. Cut into squares or rectangles; serve warm.

Brown Sugar Crumb Topping: Combine ¼ cup (½ stick) of softened butter or margarine with ¼ cup of firmly packed light brown sugar and

⅔ cup of *sifted* all-purpose flour in a small bowl; blend until smooth.

Orange-Nut Bread

A cake-like loaf to have on hand in the freezer, ready to bake when guests are coming for afternoon tea.

Bake at 350° for 1 hour and 10 minutes.
Makes 1 loaf (12 slices).

Nutrient Value Per Slice: 268 calories, 3 gm. protein, 15 gm. fat, 214 mg. sodium, 66 mg. cholesterol.

> 1½ cups **sifted** all-purpose flour
> 1¾ teaspoons baking powder
> ¼   teaspoon baking soda
> ¼   teaspoon salt
> ½   cup (1 stick) butter or margarine,
>   at room temperature
> ¾   cup sugar
> 1   tablespoon finely grated orange rind
> 2   eggs, separated
> ½   cup orange juice
> 1   cup coarsely chopped pecans or walnuts
>   (4 ounces)
>   **Orange Glaze (recipe follows)**

1. Line a 8½ x 4½-inch loaf pan with heavy-duty aluminum foil. (Or, use a double layer of regular foil.) Set aside.
2. Sift together the flour, baking powder, baking soda and salt onto wax paper.
3. Beat together the butter and sugar in a medium-size bowl until light and fluffy. Beat in the orange rind and egg yolks. Add the flour mixture, alternately with the orange juice, blending after each addition, beginning and ending with the flour mixture. Fold in the nuts.
4. Beat the egg whites in a medium-size bowl until stiff peaks form. Fold into the batter until no streaks of white remain. Spoon the batter into the prepared pan. Freeze, uncovered, until solid. Remove the frozen batter from the pan with foil; wrap tightly. Label and date the package. Freeze for up to 6 weeks.
5. To Bake: Preheat the oven to moderate (350°). Grease an 8½ x 4½-inch loaf pan.
6. Remove the frozen batter from the freezer. Peel off the foil and return the batter to the prepared pan. Bake in the preheated moderate oven (350°) for 1 hour and 10 ☞

minutes or until a wooden pick inserted in the center comes out clean. Cover with foil after the first 30 minutes of baking to prevent overbrowning.

7. Meanwhile, prepare the Orange Glaze.

8. Spoon the hot glaze over the bread as soon as it is removed from the oven. Cool the glazed bread in the pan for 15 minutes. Remove the bread to a wire rack to cool completely.

Orange Glaze: Combine ¼ cup of orange juice and ¼ cup of sugar in a small saucepan. Bring to boiling. Reduce the heat; simmer for 5 minutes or until slightly thickened.

Adding Baking Powder or Baking Soda

Be sure to thoroughly mix baking powder and baking soda with other dry ingredients by sifting or stirring with a wire whisk for uniform leavening and texture.

Whole-Wheat Cake Doughnuts

Makes about 2 dozen doughnuts.

Nutrient Value Per Serving: 151 calories, 3 gm. protein, 5 gm. fat, 164 mg. sodium, 29 mg. cholesterol.

    2 cups sifted all-purpose flour
    5 teaspoons baking powder
    ½ teaspoon salt
    ½ teaspoon ground nutmeg or mace
    2 cups whole-wheat flour
    ¼ cup (½ stick) butter or margarine, softened
    ¾ cup sugar
    2 eggs
    ¾ cup milk
    1 teaspoon vanilla
       Vegetable oil for frying
       10X (confectioners') sugar

1. Sift the all-purpose flour, baking powder, salt and nutmeg into a large bowl; stir in the whole-wheat flour.

2. Beat the butter, sugar and eggs in a large bowl with an electric mixer until well mixed. Beat in the milk and vanilla. Beat in about 1¼ cups of the flour mixture.

3. Stir in the remaining flour mixture with a spoon until the mixture forms a soft dough. If the dough is too sticky to handle, sprinkle with additional flour.

4. Wrap the dough in plastic wrap; chill for at least 2 hours or overnight.

5. Roll out the dough on a lightly floured surface to a ⅓-inch thickness; cut out with a lightly floured 3-inch doughnut cutter. Lift off dough around the doughnuts and in the center. The doughnut "holes" can be fried separately, if you wish. Reroll and cut out trimmings.

6. Fill a large saucepan or Dutch oven one-third full with oil. Heat to 370° on a deep-fat thermometer.

7. Transfer the doughnuts to the hot oil with a flexible spatula or pancake turner, frying 2 or 3 at a time. Fry, turning once, for 3 minutes or until golden. Drain on paper toweling. Cool.

8. Toss the doughnuts with the 10X sugar in a paper or plastic bag.

Chili Cornbread

Bake at 425° for 15 to 20 minutes.
Makes 8 servings.

Nutrient Value Per Serving: 211 calories, 6 gm. protein, 8 gm. fat, 354 mg. sodium, 79 mg. cholesterol.

    1   cup yellow cornmeal
    ¾   cup unsifted all-purpose flour
    2   tablespoons sugar
    ½   teaspoon baking soda
    2   teaspoon baking powder
    ½   teaspoon salt
    ½   teaspoon freshly ground pepper
    2   egg yolks
    ½   cup dairy sour cream
    ½   cup milk
    ½   cup chopped, canned mild green chilies
          (3 large)
    ⅛   teaspoon liquid red-pepper seasoning
    2½ tablespoons bacon drippings OR:
          2½ tablespoons unsalted butter or
          margarine, at room temperature
    3   egg whites

1. Preheat the oven to hot (425°).

2. Combine the cornmeal, flour, sugar, baking soda, baking powder, salt and pepper in a large bowl; stir to mix well.

3. Beat the egg yolks in a medium-size bowl until light. Beat in the sour cream and milk until well blended. Stir into the cornmeal mixture in a large bowl. Add the chilies, liquid red-pepper seasoning and 2 table-

spoons of the bacon drippings or butter.

4. Heat a heavy 8- or 9-inch ovenproof (cast iron is ideal) skillet over low heat. Add the remaining bacon drippings or butter to the skillet. Swirl to coat the bottom.

5. Beat the egg whites in a medium-size bowl until stiff, but not dry, peaks form. Stir one-quarter of the whites into the cornmeal mixture. Fold in the remaining whites. Pour into the hot skillet.

6. Bake in the preheated hot oven (425°) until golden and firm to the touch, for 15 to 20 minutes.

MICROWAVE DIRECTIONS
650 Watt Variable Power Microwave Oven
Ingredient Changes: Reduce the bacon drippings or unsalted butter to ½ tablespoon.
Directions: Use the bacon drippings to grease a round, clear-glass microwave-safe casserole, about 8½ x 2 inches (1½ quarts). Assemble the bread batter as directed in the above recipe. Pour into the prepared casserole. Center the casserole on an inverted saucer in the microwave oven. Cook at half power for 6 minutes, rotating one-quarter turn after 3 minutes. Microwave at full power for 2 to 4 minutes. Check for doneness after 2 minutes by looking through the bottom of the dish; no uncooked batter should appear in the center. Let stand for 10 minutes.

Savory Cream Puffs

Bake at 400° for 40 minutes.
Makes 6 servings.

Nutrient Value Per Serving: 426 calories, 24 gm. protein, 25 gm. fat, 658 mg. sodium, 271 mg. cholesterol.

Cream Puffs:
- 1   cup water
- ½   cup (1 stick) unsalted butter or margarine
- ⅛   teaspoon salt
- ¼   teaspoon leaf marjoram, crumbled
- ¼   teaspoon leaf thyme, crumbled
- 1   cup **sifted** all-purpose flour
- 4   eggs

Filling:
- ½   pound medium-size mushrooms, coarsely chopped
- 1   small onion, finely chopped
- ¼   teaspoon leaf thyme, crumbled
- 2   teaspoons unsalted butter or margarine
- ½   pound chicken breast cutlets, cut into ½-inch dice
- 1¼ cups dry white wine
- 2   tablespoons all-purpose flour
- ½   pound ½-inch-thick boiled ham, cut into ½-inch dice
- ¾   cup frozen small peas

1. Lightly grease a cookie sheet. Preheat the oven to hot (400°).

2. Prepare the Cream Puffs: Combine the water, butter, salt, marjoram and thyme in a saucepan. Bring to a full rolling boil. Add the flour all at once. Stir vigorously with a wooden spoon to form a thick, smooth ball that leaves the sides of the pan clean. Remove from the heat. Cool for 2 or 3 minutes.

3. Add the eggs, one at a time, beating well after each addition until the dough is shiny and smooth.

4. Spoon the dough into a large pastry bag fitted with a large star tip. Pipe onto the prepared cookie sheet in a solid 3-inch circle. Make a small circle of dough on top, ending in a point at the center. Repeat to make 5 more cream puffs.

5. Bake in the preheated hot oven (400°) for 40 minutes or until puffed and golden brown. Cool on a rack. Slice in half horizontally, three-quarters through. Remove any filaments of soft dough that remain.

6. Prepare the Filling: Sauté the mushrooms, onion and thyme in the butter in a large skillet until just tender and golden brown. Add the chicken and 1 cup of the white wine. Simmer until the chicken is just cooked through, for 5 to 8 minutes.

7. Stir the flour into the remaining ¼ cup of wine until smooth. Add to the simmering mixture. Cook, stirring, until thickened. Fold in the ham and peas; simmer for 1 minute. Spoon into the puffs.

To Make Ahead: The filling and the puffs may be made up to 24 hours ahead. Store the puffs in an airtight container in a cool, dry place; refrigerate the filling. To serve, spoon the filling into the puffs. Place on a cookie sheet. Bake in a preheated hot oven (400°) for 15 to 20 minutes or until heated through.

MICROWAVE DIRECTIONS
650 Watt Variable Power Microwave Oven
Ingredient Changes: Reduce the amount of wine from 1¼ cups to ¾ cup.
Directions: Prepare the puffs as directed above. To prepare the filling, combine the mushrooms, onion, thyme and butter in a 2-quart microwave-safe casserole. Microwave at full power for 4 minutes, stirring once. Add the chicken and ½ cup of the wine. Cover. Microwave at full power for 4 minutes, stirring once. Stir together the remaining ¼ cup of wine and the flour in a small cup until smooth. Stir into the casserole along with the ham and peas. Microwave at full power for 5 minutes, stirring once. Serve as directed above.
Nutrient Value Per Serving: 423 calories, 24 gm. protein, 25 gm. fat, 657 mg. sodium, 271 mg. cholesterol.

Best-Ever Biscuits

The secret to feather-light biscuits is to handle the dough as little as possible.

Bake at 425° for 12 minutes.
Makes 12 biscuits.

Nutrient Value Per Serving: 124 calories, 3 gm. protein, 5 gm. fat, 211 mg. sodium, 2 mg. cholesterol.

2 cups **unsifted all-purpose flour**
1 tablespoon baking powder
¼ cup powdered buttermilk
½ teaspoon salt
¼ cup vegetable shortening
¾ cup water

1. Preheat the oven to hot (425°).
2. Mix the flour, baking powder, powdered buttermilk and salt in a medium-size bowl.
3. Cut in the shortening with a pastry blender until the mixture is crumbly.
4. Add the water; stir lightly with a fork, just until a soft puffy dough forms.
5. Turn out onto a lightly floured pastry cloth. Knead lightly 8 times.
6. Roll or pat the dough to a ½-inch thickness. Cut into 2-inch rounds with a floured biscuit cutter, working neatly from the rim to the middle so there will be a few scraps to reroll. Place the biscuits, 1 inch apart, on an ungreased cookie sheet.
7. Bake in the preheated hot oven (425°) for 12 minutes or until golden brown.
Note: If you cannot find powdered buttermilk, substitute ¾ cup of buttermilk for the water in Step 3.

Suggested Variations—For Drop Biscuits: Prepare the Best-Ever Biscuits increasing the milk to 1 cup. Drop by tablespoons, 1 inch apart, on an ungreased cookie sheet. Bake, following the biscuit directions. For Sesame Fingers: Melt ¼ cup (½ stick) of butter or margarine in a 9 x 9 x 2-inch pan in the oven while preheating. Put ½ cup of sesame seeds on a large plate. Prepare the Best-Ever Biscuits. Roll or pat the dough to an 8-inch

square on a lightly floured pastry cloth or board. Cut the square in half. Cut each half into nine 4-inch strips. Dip each strip into the melted butter, then dip one side into the sesame seeds. Arrange the strips in 2 rows in the baking pan. Bake for 15 minutes or until golden brown.

Leavening Action

Baking powder reacts first on contact with liquid, then on contact with heat.

Whole-Wheat Pancakes

Makes about 8 pancakes.

Nutrient Value Per Serving: 539 calories, 14 gm. protein, 29 gm. fat, 348 mg. sodium, 193 mg. cholesterol.

½ cup **unsifted all-purpose flour**
1 tablespoon sugar
½ teaspoon baking powder
½ cup whole-wheat flour
1 egg
1 cup milk
1 tablespoon vegetable oil
2 to 3 tablespoons butter or margarine, softened

1. Sift together the all-purpose flour, sugar and baking powder into a medium-size bowl. Stir in the whole-wheat flour until thoroughly blended.*
2. Beat together the egg, milk and oil in a 4-cup measure. Pour into the dry ingredients; mix just until moistened (the batter will not be perfectly smooth).
3. Heat a heavy griddle or skillet; brush with the butter. Ladle the batter by ¼ cupfuls onto the griddle, forming 5-inch circles. When the edges begin to brown, turn the pancakes over and cook the other side until golden.
4. Stack the pancakes on top of each other and keep warm. Repeat until all the batter is used up. You should have about 8 pancakes. Serve with syrup, honey or preserves. Garnish with orange sections, if you wish.

*Note: To save time in the morning, mix the dry ingredients together the night before and store in a tightly covered container.

Teddy Bear Pancakes

4. Cook until the edges begin to brown and bubbles appear on top. Carefully turn the whole bear over. Cook until the other side is golden.
5. Transfer to an individual serving plate and keep warm. Repeat to make 7 more teddy bears. Decorate with the raisins for the eyes and nose, if you wish, and serve with maple syrup.

Griddle Test

Shake a few drops of water from your fingers over the hot griddle. If the drops sizzle, sputter and jump around over the surface, the griddle is ready.

Teddy Bear Pancakes

A special breakfast treat to make for your daughter's friends after the next slumber party.

Makes about 8.

Nutrient Value Per Serving: 185 calories, 7 gm. protein, 6 gm. fat, 460 mg. sodium, 71 mg. cholesterol.

2   cups **sifted** *all-purpose flour*
1   *tablespoon sugar*
1   *teaspoon baking soda*
1   *teaspoon salt*
2   *eggs*
2   *cups buttermilk*
2   *tablespoons vegetable oil*
    Raisins (optional)

1. Sift together the flour, sugar, baking soda and salt onto wax paper.
2. Beat together the eggs and buttermilk in a medium-size bowl. Add the dry ingredients to the buttermilk mixture; beat until smooth. Stir in the oil.
3. To form the teddy bear, use ¼ cup of the batter for the body, 2 tablespoons for the head and 1 teaspoon for each ear, arm and leg. Pour the batter in this order, onto a lightly greased medium-hot griddle, or an electric fry pan preheated to moderate (350°), to form overlapping circles in the shape of the bear.

Waffles

The word "waffle" comes from the German word, "wabe," which means honeycomb.

Makes 6 waffles.

Nutrient Value Per Serving: 327 calories, 8 gm. protein, 16 gm. fat, 374 mg. sodium, 98 mg. cholesterol.

2   cups **sifted** *all-purpose flour*
3   *tablespoons sugar*
2   *teaspoons baking powder*
½   *teaspoon salt*
2   *eggs, separated*
1¼ *cups milk*
⅓   *cup vegetable oil*

1. Sift the flour with the sugar, baking powder and salt onto a large piece of wax paper.
2. Beat the egg whites until stiff, but not dry, in a small bowl; set aside.
3. Beat the egg yolks well in a medium-size bowl and stir in the milk.
4. Add the sifted dry ingredients and mix just enough to blend; add the vegetable oil. Fold in the egg whites.
5. Bake in a moderately hot waffle iron, for 4 to 5 minutes, until crisp and brown or as the iron manufacturer directs. Serve hot with butter and syrup or honey.

Turkey and Pistachio Terrine (page 62) Cassis Punch Royale (page 250)

F irst impressions are often the most memorable ones, so why not guarantee a memorable first impression at your next gathering? The secret word is appetizers!

Whether you've planned a small dinner party for close friends or an all-out bash, appetizers have a way of setting things in motion, no matter how plain or fancy they are. A sampling of appetizers can range from a simple Bread Pot Fondue (page 58) served with fresh vegetables to bite-size hors d'oeuvres such as Bacon-Wrapped Scallops in Dijon Sauce (page 61) to tidbit nibblers such as Sugared and Salted Pecans (page 60).

To whet appetites at a sit-down dinner, plan a separate soup or salad course. Depending on the occasion and the time of year, you might want Autumn Bisque Soup (page 66) to ward off the chill, or, when the mercury rises, a cool Chilled Fruit Soup (page 67) might really "hit the spot."

A concern for healthier eating habits as well as a genuine interest in reducing calorie intake have made salads a regular feature on daily menus. They can simply be a mixture of leafy greens topped with a tablespoon of Russian Dressing (page 71) or a colorful mix of assorted vegetables.

If you're looking for appetizers that will have your guests begging for more of your "great cooking"—read on!

Finger Foods

Bread Pot Fondue

Bake at 350° for 1 hour and 10 minutes.
Makes 10 servings.

*Nutrient Value Per Serving: 472 calories, 17 gm. protein,
28 gm. fat, 787 mg. sodium, 71 mg. cholesterol.*

- 1 *round, firm loaf of bread (1½ pounds,
    8 to 10 inches in diameter)*
- 2 *cups shredded sharp Cheddar cheese
    (8 ounces)*
- 2 *packages (3 ounces each) cream cheese,
    softened*
- 1½ *cups dairy sour cream*
- 1 *cup diced cooked ham (5 ounces)*
- ½ *cup chopped green onions*
- 1 *can (3 ounces) whole mild or hot green
    chilies, drained and chopped*
- 1 *teaspoon Worcestershire sauce*
- 2 *tablespoons vegetable oil*
- 1 *tablespoon butter or margarine, melted
    Assorted raw vegetables for dipping, such
    as broccoli flowerets, radish roses, sweet
    red and yellow pepper strips, mushroom
    caps, cauliflower flowerets and celery
    sticks*

1. Preheat the oven to moderate (350°).
2. Slice off the top of the bread; reserve the top. Hollow out the inside with a small paring knife, leaving a ½-inch shell. Cut the removed bread into 1-inch cubes; you should have about 4 cups. Reserve for toasting.
3. Combine the Cheddar, cream cheese and sour cream in a bowl. Stir in the ham, green onions, chilies and Worcestershire.
4. Spoon the cheese filling into the bread shell; replace the top of the bread. Tightly wrap the loaf with several layers of heavy-duty aluminum foil; set on a cookie sheet.
5. Bake in the preheated moderate oven (350°) for 1 hour and 10 minutes or until the cheese filling is melted and heated through.
6. Meanwhile, stir together the bread cubes, oil and melted butter in a bowl. Arrange on a cookie sheet. Bake in the moderate oven (350°), turning occasionally, for 10 to 15 minutes or until golden brown. Remove from the oven and reserve to serve with the fondue.

7. When the bread is done, remove from the oven. Unwrap. Transfer to a platter. Remove the top of the bread. Stir the filling before serving. Use the toasted bread cubes and assorted vegetables as dippers for the fondue.

Tapenade Crisps

Puff-pastry spirals flavored with anchovy.

Bake at 400° for 15 to 18 minutes.
Makes 4½ dozen.

*Nutrient Value Per Crisp: 26 calories, 0 gm. protein,
2 gm. fat, 40 mg. sodium, 0 mg. cholesterol.*

- ½ *can (2 ounces) flat anchovy fillets, drained*
- 1 *can (3 ounces) pitted black olives, drained*
- 2 *tablespoons capers, drained*
- 1 *teaspoon dry mustard*
- 2 *teaspoons lemon juice*
- 2 *tablespoons olive or vegetable oil*
- ½ *of a 17½-ounce package frozen puff pastry,
    thawed according to package directions*
    All-purpose flour for dusting work surface

1. Coarsely chop the anchovies and olives. Place in an electric blender or food processor with the capers, mustard and lemon juice. Whirl until a purée. With the motor running, gradually add the oil to make a smooth paste. Reserve.
2. Roll out the unfolded pastry on a floured surface to a 15 x 11-inch rectangle. Spread the tapenade over the pastry, leaving a ½-inch border. Roll up from a long side, but not too tightly. Cut the roll in half crosswise. Place in the freezer for 1 hour or until firm enough to slice.
3. Preheat the oven to hot (400°).
4. Slice the rolls with a thin-bladed knife into ¼-inch-thick slices. Place 1½ inches apart on cookie sheets.
5. Bake in the preheated hot oven (400°) for 15 to 18 minutes or until golden brown. Serve slightly warm.

To Make Ahead: Bake and cool the crisps completely. Tightly wrap and freeze for up to several weeks. Reheat in a moderate oven (350°) for 5 to 10 minutes.

* Frozen puff pastry can be found in the freezer section of your supermarket.

CLOCKWISE, FROM LEFT: Belgian Endive with Herbed Cheese (page 289), Tapenade Crisps (for anchovy lovers) (page 58), Cherry Tomatoes with Pesto (page 283), Bacon-Wrapped Scallops in Dijon Sauce (page 61), Pork Balls en Brochette (page 61), Tortellini Pick-Ups (page 282), Hot Crab and Mushroom Puffs (page 59), Vegetable Sushi with Egg (page 62).

Hot Crab and Mushroom Puffs

Bake at 375° for 15 to 20 minutes.
Makes about 4 dozen.

Nutrient Value Per Puff: 55 calories, 1 gm. protein, 4 gm. fat, 71 mg. sodium, 14 mg. cholesterol.

- 3 *tablespoons chopped shallots or green onions*
- 1 *cup (2 sticks) butter or margarine*
- 1 *cup chopped mushrooms*
- 1 *teaspoon lemon juice*
- ¼ *cup all-purpose flour*
- ¾ *cup milk*
- 1 *package (6 ounces) frozen crabmeat, thawed, well drained and broken into pieces*
- 1 *tablespoon dry sherry*
- 1 *tablespoon chopped parsley*
- ½ *teaspoon salt*
- ¼ *teaspoon pepper*
- 8 *phyllo or strudel leaves*

1. Sauté the shallots in 4 tablespoons of the butter in a saucepan for 3 to 4 minutes. Toss the mushrooms with the lemon juice; add to the saucepan. Cook over medium-high heat, stirring often, until lightly browned, for about 5 minutes. Remove from the heat. Stir in the flour until well blended. Gradually stir in the milk until smooth. Return to the heat. Cook, stirring constantly, until the mixture thickens and bubbles; cook for 1 minute. Stir in the crabmeat, sherry, parsley, salt and pepper. Cool.
2. Preheat the oven to moderate (375°).
3. Melt the remaining butter in a small saucepan. Place the phyllo leaves between 2 dampened towels. Remove 1 leaf to a flat work surface. Brush with the melted butter. Cut lengthwise into six 2-inch-wide strips. Place a rounded teaspoon of the filling on one end of a strip. Fold one corner over the filling to the opposite side to form a triangle. Continue folding like a flag, keeping the triangle shape, to the other end of the strip. Repeat with the remaining strips and filling. Arrange the puffs on lightly buttered cookie sheets. Repeat with the remaining sheets and filling.
4. Bake in the preheated moderate oven (375°) for 15 to 20 minutes or until golden and puffed. Cool on racks. Serve hot or warm.

To Make Ahead: Fill and shape the puffs for several hours or a day ahead; refrigerate, unbaked. Or, wrap and freeze for up to 1 week. Remove from the freezer 1 hour before baking.

Sugared and Salted Pecans

Give your guests a choice.

Roast nuts at 350° for 20 minutes.
Makes ½ pound sugared pecans and ½ pound
salted pecans.

*Nutrient Value Per ⅛ Cup Salted Pecans: 443 calories,
5 gm. protein, 46 gm. fat, 334 mg. sodium, 16 mg. cholesterol.*

*Nutrient Value Per ⅛ Cup Sugared Pecans: 470 calories,
5 gm. protein, 46 gm. fat, 334 mg. sodium, 16 mg. cholesterol.*

¼ **cup (½ stick) butter or margarine**
1 **pound pecan halves**
1 **teaspoon salt**
2 **teaspoons 10X (confectioners') sugar**
½ **teaspoon ground cinnamon**
   10X (confectioners') sugar

1. Preheat the oven to moderate (350°).
2. Melt the butter in a 13 x 9 x 2-inch baking
   pan in the oven. Add the pecans; sprinkle
   with the salt and mix well. Return to the
   oven for 20 minutes, stirring the nuts
   occasionally.
3. Remove half of the nuts to a sheet of
   aluminum foil to cool.
4. Stir together the 2 tablespoons of 10X sugar
   and the cinnamon in a small bowl. Sprinkle
   the mixture over the remaining nuts in
   the pan. Toss well to coat. Cool the nuts in
   the pan.
5. Store the pecans separately in two airtight
   containers at room temperature.
6. Just before serving the sugared pecans,
   lightly dust with the 10X sugar.

Sweet 'n' Sour Meatballs

This saucy dish is even better if made a day ahead.

Makes 12 appetizer servings (4 meatballs per
serving).

*Nutrient Value Per Serving: 263 calories, 15 gm. protein,
17 gm. fat, 306 mg. sodium, 76 mg. cholesterol.*

1 **pound lean ground beef**
½ **pound ground pork**
½ **pound ground veal**
½ **cup fresh bread crumbs (1 slice)**
¼ **cup chopped parsley**
¾ **teaspoon salt**
½ **teaspoon ground nutmeg**
1 **egg**
¼ **cup milk**
2 **tablespoons vegetable oil**
1½ **cups chopped onions**
1 **can (16 ounces) whole tomatoes, broken up**
½ **cup tomato sauce**
⅓ **cup raisins**
2 **tablespoons light brown sugar**
3 **tablespoons lemon juice**

1. Combine the beef, pork, veal, bread
   crumbs, parsley, salt, nutmeg, egg and
   milk in a large bowl. Mix together well.
   Shape the mixture into meatballs, using
   1 tablespoon for each.
2. Heat 1 tablespoon of the oil in a large
   skillet. Brown the meatballs in two batches.
   As the meatballs brown, remove from the
   skillet with a slotted spoon to a plate.
3. Add the remaining 1 tablespoon of oil to
   the skillet. Add the onions; sauté until
   tender, for 2 to 3 minutes. Stir in the tomatoes, tomato sauce, raisins, brown sugar
   and lemon juice. Return the meatballs to
   the skillet. Bring to boiling. Lower the heat;
   cover and simmer for 15 minutes. Uncover;
   cook, stirring occasionally, for 10 minutes
   longer or until slightly thickened.

MICROWAVE DIRECTIONS
650 Watt Variable Power Microwave Oven
Ingredient Changes: Drain the canned tomatoes, saving
⅔ cup of the juice for another use and reserving the
remainder for this recipe. Reduce the oil from 2
tablespoons to 1 tablespoon.
Directions: Mix and shape the meatballs as directed in the
above recipe. Place the meatballs in a single layer in a
shallow microwave-safe baking dish, about 13 x 9 inches.
Cover with wax paper. Microwave at full power for 10
minutes; rearrange the meatballs after 5 minutes, placing
the less cooked ones around the outside edge of the dish.
Remove the meatballs with a slotted spoon; reserve. Drain
the liquid from the dish. Place the oil and onions in the
same dish. Cover with wax paper. Microwave at full
power for 3 minutes. Add the meatballs. Break up the
tomatoes in a medium-size bowl. Stir in the tomato sauce,
reserved drained tomato juice, raisins, brown sugar and
lemon juice. Pour over the meatballs. Cover with wax
paper. Microwave at full power for 7 minutes, stirring after
4 minutes. Remove from the oven. Let stand for 5 minutes.

Thawing Frozen Ground Meat

Frozen ground meat should be removed from
the freezer and placed, wrapped, in the
refrigerator to thaw the night before you wish
to serve it.

Pork Balls en Brochette

Bake at 400° for 15 minutes.
Makes 24 servings.

Nutrient Value Per Serving: 96 calories, 3 gm. protein, 4 gm. fat, 170 mg. sodium, 21 mg. cholesterol.

24 pitted prunes
½ cup port wine
¾ pound ground pork
¼ cup bread crumbs
¼ cup finely chopped walnuts
¼ cup chopped green onions
¾ teaspoon salt
¼ teaspoon ground pepper
1 egg
½ cup chili sauce
½ cup red currant jelly
1 tablespoon Worcestershire sauce
1 orange, peeled, cut into 24 equal pieces, seeded

1. Soak the prunes in the port wine in a small bowl for several hours or overnight. Drain, reserving the liquid and prunes separately.
2. Preheat the oven to hot (400°).
3. Combine the pork, bread crumbs, walnuts, green onions, salt, pepper and egg in a medium-size bowl; mix well. Shape into about 24 equal balls. Arrange on an oiled rack in a broiler pan.
4. Bake in the preheated hot oven (400°) for 15 minutes or until browned and no longer pink in the center. Place on a pie plate.
5. Combine the chili sauce, currant jelly, Worcestershire and 2 tablespoons of the port wine from the prunes in a small saucepan. Bring to boiling, stirring, until the jelly is melted. Add just enough sauce to the pork balls to coat.
6. Thread the orange, prunes and pork balls onto 24 short bamboo skewers. Serve hot or warm. Pass the sauce for dipping.

To Make Ahead: Prepare the pork balls, prunes, sauce and orange a day ahead; refrigerate. Bake the pork balls, reheat the sauce and assemble the brochettes 30 minutes before serving.

Peeling an Orange

For more colorful orange pieces, peel an orange with a small, sharp paring knife, removing the thin, white pith layer as you peel.

Bacon-Wrapped Scallops in Dijon Sauce

Broil for 4 to 5 minutes.
Makes 20 servings.

Nutrient Value Per Serving: 82 calories, 4 gm. protein, 6 gm. fat, 109 mg. sodium, 23 mg. cholesterol.

10 slices bacon
1 papaya, peeled, seeded and cut into 1-inch chunks
6 green onions, cut into 1½-inch lengths
1 pound sea scallops, halved, or quartered if large
¾ cup heavy cream
1 tablespoon Dijon-style mustard
1 teaspoon finely chopped parsley

1. Broil the bacon in a preheated broiler until partially cooked, but not crisp. Cut the pieces in half.
2. Thread a piece of papaya, green onion and scallop, with the bacon intertwining, onto each of the 20 short bamboo skewers. Arrange in a single layer on a rack in a broiler pan.
3. Combine the cream and mustard in a saucepan. Heat gently until slightly thickened, for 5 minutes. Add the parsley. Brush on the skewers.
4. Broil 6 inches from the heat until the scallops are firm, for 4 to 5 minutes, turning once and brushing with the sauce. Serve hot.

To Make Ahead: The bacon can be partially cooked and the skewers threaded and refrigerated early in the day.

Bay/Sea Scallops

Bay—the tiny, tender, pink- or tan-colored scallop. It is considered more of a delicacy and is usually more expensive.
Sea—the larger, whiter, more common mollusk.

Vegetable Sushi with Egg

Sushi refers to vinegared-rice preparations that are popular in Japanese cuisine. Here we've replaced the often-used seaweed wrapping with a thin omelet and blanched spinach leaves.

Makes about 30 pieces.

Nutrient Value Per Piece: 41 calories, 1 gm. protein, 0 gm. fat, 125 mg. sodium, 27 mg. cholesterol.

18 to 24 large spinach leaves
2 carrots, trimmed and cut lengthwise into ¼-inch-thick sticks
1 cup uncooked long-grain white rice
1¼ cups cold water
¼ cup rice vinegar
2 tablespoons sugar
1 teaspoon salt
3 eggs
3 tablespoons water
½ teaspoon salt
2 tablespoons finely chopped green onions
Vegetable oil
Pickled ginger (optional)

1. Blanch the spinach leaves, in batches, in a large quantity of boiling water in a large saucepan just until wilted, for 30 seconds. Remove with a slotted spoon to a colander. Rinse under cold water. Drain.
2. Steam the carrots until crisp-tender. Drain; rinse under cold water.
3. Rinse the rice in several changes of water until the water is clear. Combine the rice and the 1¼ cups of cold water in a 2-quart saucepan with a tight-fitting lid. Let soak for 15 minutes.
4. Bring the rice to boiling over high heat. Lower the heat; cover; cook for 10 minutes. Do not stir. Remove the pan from the heat. Allow the rice to steam, tightly covered, for 15 minutes.
5. Combine the vinegar, sugar and salt in a small bowl; stir to dissolve the sugar.
6. Transfer the rice to a deep platter or a shallow bowl. Toss for a few minutes with a fork to release steam. Sprinkle the vinegar dressing over the rice, 1 tablespoon at a time, tossing with a fork. Cool to room temperature.
7. Combine the eggs, the 3 tablespoons of water, the salt and green onions in a small bowl; beat with the fork until blended.
8. Heat a 10-inch omelet or other shallow skillet over medium heat. Brush with the vegetable oil to coat lightly. Pour a third of the egg mixture, about ¼ cup, into the skillet, swirling the skillet to spread the mixture evenly into an 8-inch circle. Cook until firm, for about 1 minute. Flip the "omelet" over; cook a few seconds. Slide onto a cookie sheet. Repeat with the remaining egg mixture to make 2 more "omelets." Cut each in half.
9. To assemble the sushi: Place an omelet half on a bamboo mat or heavy cloth napkin with the straight side facing you. Unfold and arrange 3 to 4 spinach leaves, overlapping slightly, over the omelet, leaving a ½-inch border of omelet around the spinach. With moist hands, spread ⅓ cup of rice in the center of the spinach leaves into a 5 x 3-inch rectangle; pat down neatly. Arrange 1 or 2 carrot sticks across the length of rice. Trim the omelet and spinach to within ½ inch from the edge of the rice.
10. Roll the mat, with the sushi inside, away from yourself, 1 or 2 turns, to enclose the carrot in the center of the rice; the omelet and spinach will form the outside of the roll. Squeeze gently to make the roll firm. Let rest in the mat for a few minutes. Repeat to make 5 more rolls.
11. Unroll the sushi from the mat. Transfer to a board. Cut into five 1-inch pieces. Arrange the slices in a flower-petal design on a serving plate. Repeat with the other rolls. Garnish with the pickled ginger, if you wish.

To Make Ahead: Prepare and dress the rice several hours ahead. Keep in a cool place, covered with a damp towel and plastic wrap; do not refrigerate or else the rice will harden. The rolls can be assembled 1 to 2 hours ahead; store, covered with damp towels, in a cool place.

Turkey and Pistachio Terrine

Bake at 300° for 2½ hours.
Makes about 24 servings.

Nutrient Value Per Serving: 212 calories, 9 gm. protein, 18 gm. fat, 259 mg. sodium, 90 mg. cholesterol.

⅓ cup chopped shallots or green onions
2 tablespoons butter or margarine
½ pound chicken livers, connective tissue removed

2   *teaspoons salt*
½   *teaspoon pepper*
½   *cup dry vermouth*
1¼ *pounds ground turkey*
¾   *pound ground pork*
¾   *pound ground fatback*
1   *egg*
½   *teaspoon leaf thyme, crumbled*
½   *teaspoon leaf marjoram, crumbled*
½   *teaspoon ground allspice*
⅓   *cup shelled whole pistachio nuts*
¾   *pound sliced bacon*
2   *bay leaves*

1. Sauté the shallots in the butter in a medium-size skillet for 3 minutes. Add the chicken livers, ½ teaspoon of the salt and ¼ teaspoon of the pepper. Sauté just until the livers are tender but still pink inside, for about 5 minutes. Stir in the vermouth. Bring to boiling, scraping up any browned bits from the bottom of the pan with a wooden spoon. Remove from the heat. Cool.
2. Combine the turkey, pork, fatback, egg, the remaining salt and pepper, thyme, marjoram, allspice and pistachio nuts in a bowl; mix well. Drain the wine with the shallots from the livers into the bowl with the meat; mix well.
3. Preheat the oven to slow (300°).
4. Line a 6- to 8-cup loaf pan or terrine with the bacon, allowing the ends to overhang the sides by 2 inches. Reserve 2 or 3 pieces to cover the top. Press a third of the meat mixture into the bottom of the pan. Arrange half of the chicken livers over the meat; gently press into the meat mixture. Top with another layer of the meat, then the remaining livers, and a final layer of meat. Smooth the top. Gently rap the pan on a counter to pack. Bring the ends of the bacon up and over the top. Cover the top with the remaining bacon; add the bay leaves. Cover tightly with foil. Place the loaf pan in a deep roasting pan. Place on the oven rack. Pour boiling water into the roasting pan so it comes halfway up the sides of the loaf pan.
5. Bake in the preheated slow oven (300°) for 2 hours. Remove the foil; bake until a meat thermometer registers 160°, for another 30 minutes. Remove the pan from the water bath. Cool on a rack for 1 hour. Replace the foil over the top. Weight the terrine with another pan filled with cans.

Refrigerate overnight.
6. Unmold the terrine. Carefully scrape off the fat and any jellied liquid. Wrap the terrine in plastic wrap. Refrigerate until serving time. Garnish with thyme sprigs, if you wish, and serve with toasted French bread and cornichons.

To Make Ahead: Refrigerate the terrine, wrapped, for 3 to 4 days.

Soups

Lemon-Chicken Egg Drop Soup

Can be prepared ahead through Step 2; reheat gently and complete Step 3 just before serving or filling a thermos to take to work.

Makes 9 servings (about ¾ cup each).

Nutrient Value Per Serving: 99 calories, 12 gm. protein, 2 gm. fat, 82 mg. sodium, 110 mg. cholesterol.

6   **cups broth prepared from low-sodium chicken bouillon powder or cubes, following label directions**
¼   **cup long-grain white rice**
1   **whole chicken breast (1 pound), all skin and visible fat removed**
3   **eggs, lightly beaten**
¼   **cup lemon juice**
2   **leaves chicory or escarole, torn into bite-size pieces**
    Salt

1. Bring the chicken bouillon broth to boiling in a large saucepan. Add the rice and chicken breast. Cover; lower the heat; simmer for 18 minutes or until the chicken is no longer pink near the bone. Remove from the heat.
2. Carefully remove the chicken breast from the broth, using a fork or tongs. When cool enough to handle, remove the bones from the chicken. Cut the meat into bite-size pieces. Return the pieces to the broth. Place over very low heat.
3. Holding a large strainer over the hot soup, pour the eggs through a strainer into the broth. Stir in the lemon juice and chicory. Ladle into individual soup bowls. Add the salt to taste.

Tex-Mex Potato Soup

Makes 6 servings (about 4 cups).

Nutrient Value Per Serving: 226 calories, 10 gm. protein, 14 gm. fat, 708 mg. sodium, 93 mg. cholesterol.

- 2 **large all-purpose potatoes (½ pound), peeled and cubed**
- 1 **medium-size onion, finely chopped (½ cup)**
- 1 **medium-size sweet green pepper, halved, seeded and chopped**
- 1 **medium-size sweet red pepper, halved, seeded and chopped**
- 2 **to 3 tablespoons butter or margarine**
- 4 **ounces cooked ham, cut into ½-inch cubes**
- 1 **tablespoon chopped mild or hot green chilies**
- ¼ **teaspoon white pepper**
- ⅛ **to ¼ teaspoon cayenne pepper**
- 1 **can (13¾ ounces) chicken broth**
- 1 **egg yolk, slightly beaten**
- ¼ **cup heavy cream**
- ½ **cup shredded sharp Cheddar cheese (optional)**

1. Cook the potatoes in boiling water to cover in a medium-size saucepan until tender, for about 15 minutes. Drain. Reserve.
2. Sauté the onion and green and red peppers in the butter in a skillet for 10 minutes or until softened. Stir in the ham, chilies, white pepper and cayenne; cook for 1 minute longer. Reserve.
3. Combine the potatoes and chicken broth in the container of an electric blender. Cover; whirl until a smooth purée. Return to the saucepan. Add the sautéed vegetable mixture.
4. Heat the soup just to boiling. Beat the egg yolk with the heavy cream in a small bowl. Stir in ½ cup of the hot soup; stir the yolk mixture back into the saucepan. Gently heat the soup; do not boil. Garnish with the shredded Cheddar cheese, if you wish.

Cheddar Cheese Soup

Makes 10 to 12 servings.

Nutrient Value Per Serving: 250 calories, 11 gm. protein, 15 gm. fat, 423 mg. sodium, 46 mg. cholesterol.

- 1 **large onion, thinly sliced**
- 1 **cup chopped celery**

Cheddar Cheese Soup

- ¼ **cup (½ stick) butter or margarine**
- ¼ **cup all-purpose flour**
- ¾ **teaspoon dry mustard**
- 2 **teaspoons Worcestershire sauce**
- 2 **cups chicken broth***
- 2 **medium-size carrots, chopped (1 cup)**
- 2 **large potatoes, pared and cubed (about 3 cups)**
- 3 **cups milk**
- 3 **cups shredded sharp Cheddar cheese (12 ounces)**
- ¼ **teaspoon pepper**
  Salt (optional)

1. Sauté the onion and celery in the butter in a kettle or Dutch oven for 3 minutes or until soft. Stir in the flour, mustard and Worcestershire sauce. Cook, stirring, for 2 minutes or until the vegetables are evenly coated and the mixture is bubbly.
2. Stir in the broth, carrots and potatoes. Bring to boiling. Lower the heat; cover; simmer, stirring occasionally, for 25 minutes or until the potatoes are tender.
3. Add the milk. Cook over medium heat until almost boiling; do not boil. Reduce the heat to low; stir in the cheese until melted.
4. Add the pepper and salt, if you wish. Ladle into a soup tureen or heated soup bowls. Garnish with extra cheese, if you wish.

* *Note:* To reduce the mg. of sodium per serving, use a reduced-sodium bouillon cube, bouillon powder or broth.

▨ ⦀ ▢
Mama's Chicken Soup with Fluffy Matzo Balls

Prepare this soup a day ahead so you can chill it and then easily remove the fat.

Makes 8 servings (plus chicken for another meal).

Nutrient Value Per Serving: 130 calories, 4 gm. protein, 4 gm. fat, 356 mg. sodium, 103 mg. cholesterol.

  1 *stewing chicken, about 4 pounds*
  2 *quarts water*
  1 *whole onion, peeled*
  2 *whole carrots, scraped*
  4 *celery stalks, including tops, cut into*
      3-inch lengths
  1 *large parsnip, trimmed, scrubbed and*
      quartered
  2 *sprigs fresh dill*
  ½ *teaspoon salt*
  ¼ *teaspoon pepper*
      Fluffy Matzo Balls (see recipe below)

1. Wash the chicken. Place in a deep pot; add the water, onion, carrots, celery, parsnip, parsley, dill, salt and pepper. Bring to boiling; lower the heat and simmer, covered, until the chicken is tender, for about 2 hours.
2. Remove the chicken and refrigerate for another use. Strain the soup into a large bowl, reserving cooked carrots. Chill the broth. Thinly slice the carrots and reserve.
3. To serve, skim the fat from the soup. Reheat the soup in a saucepan with the reserved carrots. Transfer to a tureen. Add the matzo balls.

▢
Fluffy Matzo Balls

Beaten egg white is used to make a fluffier matzo ball. There is no need to add chicken fat, which is high in cholesterol.

Makes 8 servings (2 per serving).

Nutrient Value Per Serving: 79 calories, 4 gm. protein, 2 gm. fat, 199 mg. sodium, 103 mg. cholesterol.

  3 *eggs, separated*
  ¼ *cup seltzer*
  1 *tablespoon chopped parsley*
      Salt
  ⅛ *teaspoon white pepper*
  ¾ *cup matzo meal*

1. Beat the egg yolks in a medium-size bowl with a fork until lemon-colored. Stir in the seltzer, parsley, ½ teaspoon of salt and the pepper.
2. Beat the egg whites in a small bowl until stiff peaks form; fold into the egg yolk mixture. Gently stir in the matzo meal. Chill for at least 1 hour.
3. Pour water into a Dutch oven or large saucepan to a depth of at least 2 inches; add ¼ teaspoon of salt. Bring to boiling.
4. Form the matzo mixture into sixteen 1-inch balls. Drop into the boiling water. Lower the heat and simmer for 20 minutes or until cooked through.

Cleaning Leeks

Trim the green leafy ends and cut off the roots. Cut the leeks in half lengthwise. Rinse thoroughly under running cold water to remove sand.

▨ ⦀ ▧
Creamy Watercress and Leek Soup

Makes 6 servings.

Nutrient Value Per Serving: 236 calories, 3 gm. protein, 21 gm. fat, 458 mg. sodium, 70 mg. cholesterol.

  1 *cup sliced washed leeks*
  3 *tablespoons butter or margarine*
  4 *cups water*
  2 *medium-size potatoes, pared and sliced*
      (about 2 cups)
  1 *small onion, chopped (¼ cup)*
  2 *tablespoons finely chopped fresh parsley*
  1 *bay leaf*
  1 *teaspoon salt*
  ¼ *teaspoon pepper*
  1 *bunch watercress*
  1 *cup heavy cream*
      Croutons
      Chopped fresh parsley

1. Sauté the leeks in the butter in a large saucepan until soft, but not brown, for about 5 minutes.
2. Add the water, potatoes, onion, parsley, bay leaf, salt and pepper. Bring to boiling; lower the heat; cover. Simmer for 30 minutes or until the potatoes are soft. Discard the bay leaf.
3. Wash and dry the watercress; remove the leaves. (You should have about 1 cup of ☞

leaves.) Add to the potato mixture. Cook
for 5 minutes.

4. Purée the soup, a part at a time, in an
electric blender. Chill for several hours. Stir
in the cream. Serve with the croutons and
additional chopped fresh parsley.

Curry Powder Components

Curry powder is actually a blend of spices,
such as cinnamon, cumin, mustard, turmeric,
cardamom, cayenne and ginger.

Curried Apple-Tomato Soup

Makes 4 servings.

*Nutrient Value Per Serving: 216 calories, 3 gm. protein,
13 gm. fat, 738 mg. sodium, 31 mg. cholesterol.*

 3 **medium-size apples, such as McIntosh,
     Rome Beauty or Cortland, cored and
     coarsely chopped (about 3 cups)**
 1 **medium-size onion, coarsely chopped
     (½ cup)**
 1 **medium-size carrot, sliced**
 ¼ **cup (½ stick) butter or margarine**
 3 **medium-size ripe tomatoes, cored and
     coarsely chopped**
 1 **tablespoon curry powder**
 1 **cup chicken broth**
 ¾ **teaspoon salt**
 ¼ **teaspoon pepper**
    **Apple slices, raisins and grated coconut
     for garnish**

1. Sauté the apples, onion and carrot in the
butter in a large saucepan until softened,
for about 5 minutes. Stir in the tomatoes
and curry. Cover; cook over low heat,
stirring occasionally, for 30 minutes or until
the vegetables are tender.
2. Purée the vegetable mixture in an electric
blender or food processor in two batches.
Force the purée through a sieve into a
saucepan. Stir in the chicken broth, salt and
pepper. Reheat the soup to a gentle boil.
3. Ladle the soup into soup bowls. Garnish
with the apple slices, raisins and coconut.

Autumn Bisque Soup

Makes 6 servings (6 cups).

*Nutrient Value Per Serving: 166 calories, 6 gm. protein,
7 gm. fat, 1,124 mg. sodium, 105 mg. cholesterol.*

 1 **pound butternut squash, pared, halved,
     seeded and cubed**
 2 **tart apples, pared, cored, cubed**
 1 **medium-size onion, chopped (½ cup)**
 2 **slices white bread, trimmed and cubed**
 4 **cups chicken broth**
1½ **teaspoons salt**
 ¼ **teaspoon pepper**
 ¼ **teaspoon ground rosemary**
 ¼ **teaspoon ground marjoram**
 2 **egg yolks, slightly beaten**
 ¼ **cup heavy cream**
    **Apple slices and fresh rosemary sprig for
     garnish (optional)**

1. Combine the squash, apples, onion, bread,
chicken broth, salt, pepper, rosemary and
marjoram in a large saucepan. Bring to
boiling. Lower the heat; simmer, uncovered,
for 35 minutes or until the squash and
apples are tender. Remove from the heat.
Cool to lukewarm.
2. Working in batches, spoon the soup into
the container of an electric blender or food
processor. Cover; whirl until puréed.
Return the soup to the saucepan. Reheat
the soup gently over very low heat.
3. Mix together the egg yolks and the cream in
a small bowl. Beat in a little of the hot
soup; return the yolk mixture to the saucepan, stirring. Heat gently to serve; do not
boil, or the eggs will curdle. Transfer to a
soup tureen. Garnish with the thin apple
slices, with the skin left on, and a fresh
rosemary sprig, if you wish.

Chilled Fruit Soup

Chilled Fruit Soup

A traditional Scandinavian dish served as a first course or dessert.

Makes 6 servings.

Nutrient Value Per Serving: 262 calories, .78 gm. protein, .45 gm. fat, 8 mg. sodium, 0 mg. cholesterol.

- 1 **quart cranberry juice cocktail**
- 2 **cups cold water**
- ¾ **cup sugar**
- 3 **tablespoons quick tapioca**
  Rind of 1 medium-size lemon
- 1 **three-inch stick cinnamon**
- 1 **pint strawberries, hulled and halved**
- 2 **medium-size bananas, peeled and sliced diagonally**

1. Bring the cranberry juice and water to boiling in a large saucepan; lower the heat to simmer.
2. Stir in the sugar and tapioca. Add the lemon rind and cinnamon stick. Cover; simmer for 15 minutes or until thickened.
3. Remove the lemon rind and cinnamon stick. Cool the soup to lukewarm.
4. Stir in the strawberries and bananas. Refrigerate for 2 hours or until the soup is thoroughly chilled.

Note: Fresh raspberries and green grapes can be used in this recipe.

Salads

Most Popular Salad Greens

- *Iceberg*, the best-known lettuce, has a nice crisp texture and stores well. After purchasing, wash, dry well and store the lettuce in a large, loosely packed (allows cool air to circulate) plastic bag or a tightly covered plastic container, with a drainage space, in the refrigerator.
- *Romaine lettuce* has long, dark green outside leaves with lighter, almost yellow inside leaves. The darker green leaves have the higher vitamin content, so use as many of these leaves as possible, discarding only the bruised parts.
- *Boston*, or *butterhead (cabbage), lettuce* has a delicate flavor and tender, velvety leaves that separate easily. Wash in a bowl of very cold water just before serving and blot dry on paper towels.
- *Leaf lettuce*, also known as *red-tipped* or *oak-leaf lettuce*, grows in large leafy bunches. The tender long leaves are delicate and should be washed just before serving.

Nice Salad Additions

- *Belgian endive*, an imported salad ingredient, is more expensive than other greens and, therefore, used sparingly in salads. Sliced lengthwise, the long slender leaves add an elegant touch.
- *Curly endive*, or *chicory*, has long, narrow, curly dark green outer leaves and pale green inner leaves. A slightly bitter taste makes it a good choice to combine with other, milder greens.
- *Green* and *red cabbage*, shredded into a salad, add color and texture.
- *Spinach* has a crisp texture, slightly biting taste and lots of vitamins in its dark green leaves.

Washing Spinach

To insure the removal of all sand from fresh spinach, wash several times in a basin filled with cool water. Lift leaves from water (the sand will fall to the bottom of the basin). Change the water each time the spinach is washed.

◪ ◄◄ ◻
Spinach Salad

Makes 6 servings.

Nutrient Value Per Serving: 169 calories, 5 gm. protein, 14 gm. fat, 289 mg. sodium, 4 mg. cholesterol.

- 1 **pound fresh spinach, washed and stems removed**
- ¼ **cup olive or vegetable oil**
- 1 **clove garlic, finely chopped**
- ¼ **teaspoon salt**
  Dash cayenne pepper
- 12 **small romaine lettuce leaves**
- 4 **ounces alfalfa sprouts**
- ¼ **cup sliced mushrooms (about 4 ounces)**
- 5 **plum tomatoes, cut in wedges**
- 1 **red onion, sliced**
- ½ **cup pitted black olives**
- 4 **slices bacon, cooked, crumbled**
  Bottled avocado dressing

1. Tear the spinach into bite-size pieces. Place in a large bowl. Combine the oil, garlic, salt and cayenne in a small bowl. Pour over the spinach; toss to coat.
2. Stand the romaine leaves on one side of the large salad bowl. Add the spinach. Arrange the alfalfa sprouts, mushrooms, tomatoes, onion, olives and bacon in the bowl. Serve with the avocado dressing.

To Make Ahead: Prepare the spinach, cover the bowl and refrigerate until ready to serve. Prepare the oil mixture, cover and refrigerate until ready to serve. When ready to serve, proceed as the recipe directs.

◪ ◄◄ ◻
Spinach and Red Cabbage Salad

Makes 12 servings.

Nutrient Value Per Serving: 168 calories, 3 gm. protein, 14 gm. fat, 335 mg. sodium, 20 mg. cholesterol.

- 2 **pounds spinach, trimmed and washed**
- ½ **small head red cabbage, finely shredded (2 cups)**
- 1 **large white onion, cut into rings**
- 2 **small yellow squash (½ pound), cut into ¼-inch-thick slices**
- 1 **bottle (16 ounces) creamy garlic and herb salad dressing**

1. Tear the spinach coarsely into large pieces. Line a salad bowl with the spinach.
2. Arrange the red cabbage, onion and yellow squash in the center. Cover and refrigerate.
3. To serve, pour the dressing over the salad; toss to mix well.

◪ ◄◄ ⊻
Herbed Walnut, Mushroom and Orange Salad

Makes 8 servings.

Nutrient Value Per Serving: 508 calories, 9 gm. protein, 46 gm. fat, 462 mg. sodium, 0 mg. cholesterol.

- ½ **pound shelled walnuts (2 cups)**
- 2 **cans (13¾ ounces each) chicken broth**
- 2 **bay leaves**
- ¼ **cup chopped onion**
- ¼ **cup chopped carrots**
- ¼ **cup chopped parsley**
  Leaf lettuce
- 4 **navel oranges, peeled and sliced**
- 1 **pound mushrooms, sliced**
- 6 **green onions, trimmed and sliced**
  Red Wine Vinegar Dressing (recipe follows)

1. Cook the walnuts in boiling water to cover in a saucepan, for 5 minutes. Drain. Rub in paper toweling to remove the skins. Remove any remaining skins with the point of a sharp knife.
2. Return the nuts to the saucepan. Add the broth, bay leaves, onion, carrots and parsley. Simmer for 20 minutes. Drain; chill the nuts and vegetables. (Save the broth for a soup or other uses.)
3. To serve, line a platter with the lettuce. Arrange the orange slices, mushrooms, green onions and walnuts over the lettuce. Pour the dressing over all.

To Make Ahead: The walnuts and dressing can be prepared a day ahead. The salad can be assembled, without the dressing, several hours before; tightly cover and refrigerate.

Red Wine Vinegar Dressing: Combine 1 cup of olive oil, 2 tablespoons of lemon juice, 2 tablespoons of red wine vinegar, 1 teaspoon of dry mustard, 1 teaspoon of leaf basil, crumbled, 2 cloves garlic, finely chopped, ½ teaspoon of salt and ¼ teaspoon of pepper in a jar with a tight-fitting lid. Cover; shake well. Reserve. Shake well again before serving.

Winter Fruit Salad with Honey-Lemon Dressing

Makes 6 servings.

Nutrient Value Per Serving: 241 calories, 3 gm. protein, 10 gm. fat, 220 mg. sodium, 0 mg. cholesterol.

- 3 large red apples
- 1 tablespoon lemon juice
- 1 pound red grapes
- 1 large red onion
- 2 bunches watercress, stems removed
- 2 tablespoons honey
- ⅔ cup lemon juice
- ¼ cup vegetable oil
- ½ teaspoon salt
- ⅛ teaspoon pepper
- ¼ cup finely chopped red onion

1. Wash, core and slice the apples. Toss with the 1 tablespoon of lemon juice in a bowl. Divide the grapes into clusters. Peel the onion; thinly slice.
2. Arrange the watercress around the outside edge of a large platter or serving bowl. Arrange the apples, grapes and onion on the platter. Reserve.
3. Combine the honey, the ⅔ cup of lemon juice, the oil, salt, pepper and chopped red onion in a large jar with a tight-fitting lid. Shake until the honey has dissolved. Spoon 3 tablespoons of the dressing over the apples and onion. Cover the salad tightly with plastic wrap. Refrigerate both the salad and dressing until ready to serve. Pass the dressing.

To Make Ahead: The dressing can be made a day ahead; the salad, several hours.

Flavor Enhancer

Allow salads to stand briefly at room temperature before serving.

Eggplant Garden Salad

Bake eggplant at 375° for 1 hour.
Makes 4 servings (about 1¾ cups).

Nutrient Value Per Serving: 121 calories, 2 gm. protein, 9 gm. fat, 596 mg. sodium, 4 mg. cholesterol.

- 1 small eggplant (1 pound)
- 1 medium-size tomato, cored and chopped
- ¼ cup chopped sweet green pepper
- 2 tablespoons chopped fresh parsley OR: cilantro*
- 2 tablespoons mayonnaise
- 2 tablespoons fresh lemon juice
- 1 tablespoon grated onion
- 1 tablespoon olive oil
- 1 teaspoon salt
- ¼ teaspoon pepper

1. Preheat the oven to moderate (375°). Prick the eggplant skin with a fork and set in a shallow baking dish.
2. Bake in the preheated moderate oven (375°) for 1 hour or until very soft, turning the eggplant over after 30 minutes. Remove and let cool.
3. Cut off the stem end and pare the eggplant. Cut the eggplant pulp into chunks. Chop in a blender, food processor or by hand. Transfer to a bowl.
4. Add the tomato, green pepper, parsley, mayonnaise, lemon juice, onion, oil, salt and pepper. Spoon into a serving dish. Refrigerate until ready to serve. Serve with pita bread, if you wish.

*** Note:** Cilantro, or Chinese parsley, is a pungent herb used in American Southwestern, Mexican, Middle Eastern and some Oriental cooking.*

Russian Salad

Try this salad as part of a light springtime buffet.

Makes 10 servings.

Nutrient Value Per Serving: 202 calories, 3 gm. protein, 15 gm. fat, 838 mg. sodium, 9 mg. cholesterol.

- 1 pound potatoes (3 medium-size), peeled and quartered
- 1 pound cauliflower (half a small head), separated into large flowerets
- 1 pound carrots, pared and quartered crosswise
- ½ pound untrimmed green beans
- 1 can (16 ounces) whole beets, drained
- ⅔ cup mayonnaise
- 4 to 5 tablespoons red wine vinegar
- 2 tablespoons vegetable oil
- 1 tablespoon salt
- ¼ teaspoon pepper

Russian Salad

1. Cook the potatoes in boiling water in a saucepan, for 10 minutes. Add the cauliflower; cook for 10 minutes longer or until the potatoes and cauliflower are tender. Drain; rinse under cold water.
2. Meanwhile, in a second large saucepan, cook the carrots in boiling water to cover, for 15 minutes. Add the beans; cook for 5 minutes longer or until the carrots and beans are tender.
3. Coarsely dice the potatoes, cauliflower, carrots and beets into ½-inch pieces. Slice the green beans into 1-inch lengths. Arrange the vegetables in circular bands in a large serving bowl.
4. Stir together the mayonnaise, vinegar, oil, salt and pepper. Pour over the salad; mix well.

To Make Ahead: Cook and cut the vegetables as the recipe directs; wrap the cut vegetables in individual plastic-wrap packages and refrigerate until ready to serve. Prepare the salad dressing as the recipe directs, cover and refrigerate until time to serve the salad.

Mixed Vegetable Salad

Makes 8 servings.

Nutrient Value Per Serving: 238 calories, 3 gm. protein, 22 gm. fat, 178 mg. sodium, 0 mg. cholesterol.

¼ cup red wine vinegar
1 teaspoon prepared mustard
½ teaspoon salt
⅔ cup olive or vegetable oil
2 tablespoons chopped parsley
  Lettuce leaves
1 red onion, sliced

1 cup sliced radishes
1 bunch watercress
3 cups cauliflower flowerets (1 small head)
1 cup sliced cooked beets, fresh or canned
1 ripe avocado

1. Combine the vinegar, mustard, salt and oil in a jar with a tight-fitting lid; shake well to blend. Add the chopped parsley. Refrigerate the dressing until ready to use.
2. Line a serving platter or shallow salad bowl with the lettuce leaves. Arrange the sliced onion, radishes, watercress, cauliflower flowerets and cooked beets over the lettuce in an attractive arrangement. Cover; refrigerate the salad for several hours or until ready to serve.
3. Just before serving, halve, pit, peel and slice the avocado. Add to the salad. Serve the dressing separately.

Couscous Salad

Serve this salad with barbecued or roast chicken, pork or beef.

Makes 8 to 10 servings.

Nutrient Value Per Serving: 379 calories, 8 gm. protein, 18 gm. fat, 36 mg. sodium, 0 mg. cholesterol.

1 box (1 pound) couscous*
2½ cups boiling water
5 tablespoons white wine vinegar
1 teaspoon grated orange rind
1 teaspoon grated lemon rind
2 tablespoons orange juice
1½ tablespoons lemon juice
1 teaspoon finely chopped garlic
¾ teaspoon ground ginger
⅛ teaspoon ground cinnamon
⅛ teaspoon ground cloves
⅛ teaspoon ground nutmeg
⅛ teaspoon turmeric
¾ cup olive oil
3 celery stalks, sliced (1¼ cups)
2 carrots, pared and cut into 2 x ¼-inch strips (1½ cups)
2 medium-size zucchini, cut into 2 x ¼-inch strips (2 cups)
1 medium-size onion, halved and thinly sliced (1⅓ cups)
2 medium-size tomatoes, cored, seeded and cut into large dice (2 cups)
1 cup chopped fresh coriander or parsley

1. Place the couscous in a large bowl. Add the boiling water. Stir gently with a fork to separate the grains, being careful not to mash the grains. Continue to stir, breaking up any lumps, until the water is absorbed and the couscous has cooled. Set aside.
2. Combine the vinegar, orange rind, lemon rind, orange juice, lemon juice, garlic, ginger, cinnamon, cloves, nutmeg and turmeric in a medium-size bowl. Gradually whisk in the olive oil until well blended. Set aside.
3. Toss together the celery, carrots, zucchini, onion, tomatoes and coriander in a medium-size bowl. Gently mix the vegetables into the couscous until thoroughly combined. Add the dressing and mix again. Refrigerate until 30 minutes before serving time.

Note: Couscous, sometimes referred to as "Moroccan pasta," is coarsely ground wheat granules. It can be found in the rice and grain section of your supermarket.

Chopping Coriander or Parsley

Remove the leaves from the stems and place the leaves in a 2-cup liquid measure. Using kitchen scissors, cut up the greens inside the cup.

Green Goddess Dressing

Green Goddess Dressing

Use on seafood salads and romaine lettuce.

Makes 2½ cups.

Nutrient Value Per 2 Tablespoons: 165 calories, 1 gm. protein, 18 gm. fat, 142 mg. sodium, 14 mg. cholesterol.

8 *anchovy fillets, mashed*
2 *green onions, finely chopped*
¼ *cup finely chopped parsley*
1 *teaspoon leaf tarragon, crumbled*
2 *cups mayonnaise or salad dressing*
2 *tablespoons white wine vinegar*
3 *tablespoons finely chopped chives*

Combine the anchovies, green onions, parsley and tarragon in a small bowl; mix well. Fold into the mayonnaise. Stir in the vinegar and chives. Refrigerate until ready to use.

Russian Dressing

Makes 3½ cups.

Nutrient Value Per Serving: 65 calories, 0 gm. protein, 7 gm. fat, 100 mg. sodium, 15 mg. cholesterol.

1 *small onion, coarsely chopped (¼ cup)*
1 *small sweet green pepper, halved, seeded and diced*
2 *hard-cooked eggs, coarsely chopped*
4 *sweet pickles, coarsely chopped*
1 *clove garlic*
2 *cups mayonnaise or salad dressing*
¼ *cup bottled chili sauce*
1 *teaspoon cayenne pepper*
½ *teaspoon Worcestershire sauce*
½ *teaspoon liquid red-pepper seasoning*
½ *teaspoon salt*
¼ *teaspoon pepper*

Combine the onion, green pepper, eggs, pickles and garlic in the container of an electric blender or food processor. Cover; whirl until chopped. Add the mayonnaise, chili sauce, cayenne, Worcestershire, liquid red-pepper seasoning, salt and pepper. Whirl until very smooth. Transfer to a cruet. Refrigerate until ready to serve.

Quick Vegetable Salad

Layer chilled fresh vegetables in a glass bowl and drizzle with vinaigrette for a fresh cold salad.

Basic Vinaigrette Dressing

Two parts of oil to one part of vinegar make a simple, standard vinaigrette—a light salad dressing and marinade. Add your favorite fresh herbs, a clove of garlic or a touch of honey, depending on the salad you're tossing with dressing.

Experiment with the many new oils and vinegars now available: different virgin olive oils, walnut oil, sesame oil, fruit and herb vinegars.

Fruits for Tossed Salads

Here are the fruits that go best in tossed salads:
- Sliced strawberries
- Seedless grapes
- Peach slices*
- Diced avocado*
- Pineapple chunks
- Nectarine slices*
- Melon balls or cubes
- Plum slices
- Blueberries
- Pear slices*
- Orange and grapefruit sections
- Apple wedges or slices*
- Banana slices
- Fruit cocktail, drained
- Papaya slices
- Figs
- Cherries, pitted
- Persimmons
- Blackberries
- Dates, pitted
- Prunes, pitted
- Raisins

Toss with a little lemon juice and water to prevent darkening.

Make Your Own Salad Bar

A salad bar is the perfect solution for keeping guests satisfied, but not filled, when the steaks need more time on the grill. It is also a great way to break the ice when all your guests don't know each other.

Even if you and your guests prefer a less varied combination for your salads, you should always plan a few surprises to encourage creativity.

The first step in planning your salad bar is to check the number of guests. Plan on a minimum of 1 cup of salad greens for each one. You might like to break an assortment—iceberg, leaf, romaine, chicory and spinach—into a large salad bowl.

It is best to buy the salad greens early on the party day. Wash them well in cool water until all sand is rinsed out. Then dry well, first draining in a colander, then rolling in Turkish towels; then place in plastic bags and refrigerate for at least 3 hours to crisp.

Greens may then be broken into bite-size pieces and placed in a large plastic bag. Refrigerate until the last minute.

Spoon accompaniments (see below) into smaller bowls and offer a variety of dressings in individual containers. The finishing touches are crunchy toppers—such as crumbled bacon pieces, sunflower seeds and seasoned croutons.

Suggestions for a Salad Bar

Vegetables—fresh, frozen, canned or dried; served separately or in combination: asparagus spears; avocado; marinated green beans; cooked garbanzos or lima beans; 3-bean salad; bean sprouts; alfalfa sprouts; cooked potato or potato salad; shredded carrots; raw cauliflower; sliced celery; sliced cucumbers; raw onions; sliced green onion; fried onion rings; chopped chives; fresh mushrooms; raw Brussels sprouts; marinated artichokes; pickled beets; raw peas; Chinese snow pea pods; tomatoes; cherry tomatoes; radishes; sauerkraut; turnips; raw zucchini; chopped sweet green peppers; water chestnuts.

Protein Foods—Meat: roast beef strips; meatballs; beef taco filling; salami, bologna, liverwurst and other cold cuts; frankfurters; ham; bacon; roast lamb strips; roast veal strips.

Fish: lobster; shrimp; crab, Alaska King crab; smoked oysters; anchovies; tuna; salmon, fresh, smoked or canned; pickled herring; sardines.

Poultry and poultry products: chicken strips; turkey strips; eggs, hard-cooked, deviled, egg salad.

Nuts, toasted: almonds; macadamia; peanuts; pecans; pistachios; pine nuts; walnuts; sesame seeds; coconut; roasted soy beans.

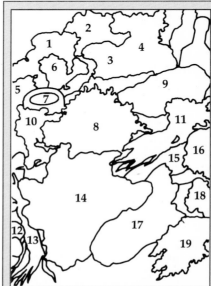

Variety of vegetables to make your own salad bar party:
1. Red cabbage
2. Red oak-leaf lettuce
3. Royal oak-leaf lettuce
4. French oak-leaf lettuce
5. Broccoli
6. Flowering Chinese broccoli
7. Borage blossoms
8. Tres Fin Frisee chicory
9. Green cabbage
10. Japanese turnips
11. Baby carrots
12. Brussels sprouts
13. Japanese long turnip
14. Chinese black flat cabbage
15. Bok choy
15. Choi sum
17. Shanghai green stalk bok choy
18. Greek oregano
19. Dill

Magyar Beef Paprikash (page 83)

*Choice suggestions for beef,
pork and lamb, poultry,
fish and shellfish.*

L ike any well thought-out project, planning a good meal begins with a central theme. Usually, this is the main course—the "heart of the meal." Once you have decided what that is to be, the accompanying foods seem to fall into place naturally.

In this chapter, we offer you a host of main-course ideas, featuring beef, pork, lamb, poultry, fish or shellfish, prepared in many styles and using a variety of cooking techniques from stewing to grilling.

Meat recipes range from elegant dinner party suggestions, such as Crown Roast of Pork with Wild Rice Stuffing (page 94), to a backyard barbecue of Tulsa Ribs (page 126).

Penny-wise and calorie-conscious poultry favorites, such as Roast Holiday Turkey and Giblet Gravy (page 111) with Savory Thanksgiving Stuffing (page 183) and Orange-Glazed Baked Chicken (page 100), are sure to be hits with your wallet as well as your diet.

Seafood is always a good choice for those who have little time for food preparation and cooking. Many recipes offer the option of using either convenient, frozen or canned seafood products from your local supermarket, or fresh varieties from your region. For instance, our Broiled Saucy Fish Fillets (page 120), which take only about 5 minutes from start to finish, call for fresh or frozen flounder fillets.

There are seasonal specialties, too. Chilled Chicken Rolls Marengo-Style (page 108) and Salmon en Papillote (page 118) lend themselves to the warmer months, while Hearty Beef Chili with Beans and Cheddar Cheese (page 78) is bound to help chase away "cabin fever" on a blustery winter day.

With the dozens of recipes to choose from, you already have more than a month's worth of menu starters, to say nothing of party ideas!

**Cheese-Stuffed Vegetables (page 150),
Cold Confetti Meatloaf (page 80).**

Beef

Selecting Meats

Cost: The most accurate way to determine meat cost is to base your calculations on price per serving, rather than price per pound. Cuts which contain a large amount of bone and fat may not be as economical as higher-priced cuts which contain less waste.

Do not confuse the number of servings with the number of people you can serve. A hearty eater can consume 3 servings at a meal!

To find the cost per serving, divide the price per pound by the number of servings per pound the cut will provide. For example, if a roast costs $1.79 a pound and that gives you 2½ servings a pound, your cost per serving would be 71¢.

Cut: Tender cuts come from muscles which are not used in movement and which have the least connective tissue. These muscles are found along the back of the animal and are called rib, loin or sirloin. The remaining muscles are used in movement and are less tender.

Many stores use a standardized meat-labeling system on their prepackaged meats. The label tells you the kind of meat (beef, pork, lamb, etc.), the primal or wholesale cut (chuck, rib, loin, round, etc.) which is where the cut comes from on the animal and the retail cut (blade, arm, short rib, etc.) which tells you from what part of the primal cut the meat comes.

Ground beef, or hamburger, contains not less than 70% lean. Use it for burgers, chili, sloppy Joes and casseroles. Lean ground beef, or ground chuck, has not less than 77% lean. Use it for meatloaf, meatballs and chopped steaks. Extra-lean ground beef, or ground round or sirloin, has not less than 85% lean. Use it as you would ground chuck or when you're watching calorie and fat consumption.

The color of meat is an important indication of tenderness. For example, beef can vary from dark pink to dark red. The lighter the color, the younger the animal and more tender the meat.

Watch out for liquid loss in a package. The drier the package, the fresher tasting the meat. The presence of liquid also indicates that the meat may have been frozen or is of a lower grade.

Meat Cooking Methods

Dry-Heat Methods for Tender Cuts
To Panbroil: For small, tender pieces cut 1 inch thick or less. Place the steak or patty in a heavy frying pan. Don't add fat or water and do not cover pan. Cook slowly, turning often; pour off any fat as it collects. Brown or cook to desired degree; season and serve.
To Panfry: For very thin, tender cuts or cuts made tender by pounding or cubing. They may be dusted with flour or crumbs. Heat a small amount of fat in the frying pan. Add meat and brown on both sides over high heat, turning occasionally. Stir-frying is a form of panfrying used in Oriental-style cooking. A wok, large pan or electric skillet can be used. Ingredients must be cut into uniform sizes before cooking. Sautéing is the French term for panfrying.
To Broil: For tender steaks or patties at least 1 inch thick. Place the meat on the broiler rack over a pan. Broil the meat, which is 1 inch thick, 2 to 3 inches from the preheated heat source. Broil thicker cuts 3 to 5 inches from the heat. Turn the meat with tongs rather than a fork, as a fork will pierce the meat, releasing juices. A charcoal, electric or gas grill can be used for broiling.
To Roast: For large, tender roasts. Season with salt, pepper or herbs. Place the meat, fat-side up, on a rack in an open, shallow pan. The fat on top bastes the meat, and the rack holds it out of the drippings. Insert a meat thermometer in the center of the largest muscle; do not let it touch bone or rest in fat. Do not add water or cover meat. Roast in a slow oven (300° to 325°F.). When the thermometer reads 5°F. below the desired degree of doneness, remove the meat roast from the oven and let stand for 15 minutes for easier carving. Rotisserie cooking is a form of roasting. Use large, uniformly shaped cuts. Insert the rotisserie rod lengthwise through the center of the roast; fasten securely. Place a drip pan under the turning meat to prevent flare-ups.
To Microwave: For tender roasts that are compact and uniform in shape. Boneless roasts are ideal. Place the roast on a rack and cover with wax paper. Use a low-power setting for a longer cooking time to get the most uniform doneness. If a roast is irregular in shape and a portion is cooking too fast, cover that area with a bit of foil to retard cooking. To assure even cooking, turn the roast or rotate the dish at intervals during the cooking time. To enhance the appearance of meat cooked by microwave, try brushing the surface with soy sauce, Worcestershire or a browning sauce. Or coat the surface with bread crumbs or glaze. You can also prebrown the roast in a frying pan or use the browning dish of the microwave. The cooking time will vary depending on the shape and size of the meat.

Moist-Heat Methods for Less-Tender Cuts
To Braise: Brown the meat, which may be coated with flour, in its own rendered fat or in a small amount of added fat in a heavy pan. Brown on all sides slowly; add onions, herbs and about ¼ to ½ cup of liquid, such as water, broth, vegetable juice or a marinade. Cover and cook over low heat until tender. Braising can be done on top of the range or in a slow oven (300° to 325°F.).
To Cook in Liquid: Coat the meat with flour and brown on all sides in its own fat or added fat in a heavy pan. Or, omitting the step above, cover the meat with liquid and cover the pan. Cook over low heat until the meat is just tender. If you like, add vegetables and cook along with the meat until tender.

To Pressure-Cook: Follow the manufacturer's directions.
To Slow-Cook: Follow the manufacturer's or recipe directions.

Tenderizing Meat

Less-tender cuts may be tenderized, then cooked using dry-heat methods. Tenderize by pounding the meat with a meat mallet or by using a marinade or commercial tenderizing mixture.

Manually pounding cuts, such as round steak, with a meat mallet tenderizes by breaking down the fibers and tissue. Cube steak is round steak that a butcher has put through a special machine which tears the fiber structure and creates a flattened steak.

Marinades are usually made of an acidic liquid, such as vinegar, wine, citrus or tomato juice. The acid helps soften the meat fibers and connective tissue, and adds flavor. Marinades also often contain flavoring ingredients, such as garlic, pepper, etc.

Commercial tenderizing mixtures are sold in various forms and contain enzymes which break down the connective tissue. Enzymes such as papain from papaya and bromelain from pineapple are usually used in these tenderizers.

Beef

The wide variety of fresh beef cuts offers an almost unlimited selection for any meal and menu. Beef supplies complete protein with 8 essential amino acids. One serving of cooked ground beef (3 ounces) provides 21.8 grams of protein, or 50 percent of the recommended daily amount, along with 225 calories, .15 milligrams of riboflavin, 4.8 milligrams of niacin and 1.1 micrograms of vitamin B_{12}. Beef is also a good source of iron and zinc.

Approximate Time for Broiling Beef

Cut	Approximate Weight	Approximate Thickness	Approximate Total Cooking Time in Minutes	
			Rare	Medium
Chuck Blade Steak	1¼ to 1¾ lbs.	¾ inches	14	20
(U.S. Prime and Choice)	1½ to 2½ lbs.	1 inch	20	25
	2 to 4 lbs.	1½ inches	35	40
Rib Eye Steak	8 to 10 ozs.	1 inch	15	20
	12 to 14 ozs.	1½ inches	25	30
	16 to 20 ozs.	2 inches	35	45
Rib Steak	1 to 1½ lbs.	1 inch	15	20
	1½ to 2 lbs.	1½ inches	25	30
	2 to 2½ lbs.	2 inches	35	45
Porterhouse Steak	1¼ to 2 lbs.	1 inch	20	25
	2 to 3 lbs.	1½ inches	30	35
	2½ to 3½ lbs.	2 inches	40	45
Tenderloin Steak	4 to 6 ozs.	1 inch	10	15
	6 to 8 ozs.	1½ inches	15	20
Top Loin Steak	1 to 1½ lbs.	1 inch	15	20
	1½ to 2 lbs.	1½ inches	25	30
	2 to 2½ lbs.	2 inches	35	45
Sirloin Steak	1½ to 3 lbs.	1 inch	20	25
	2¼ to 4 lbs.	1½ inches	30	35
	3 to 5 lbs.	2 inches	40	45
Top Round Steak	1¼ to 1¾ lbs.	1 inch	20	30
	1½ to 2 lbs.	1½ inches	30	35
Flank Steak	1 to 1½ lbs.	—	12	14
Ground Beef Patty	4 ozs.	1 inch	8	12

Onion Burgers

Add sautéed onions to ground beef to make 4 fat hamburgers from ½ pound of meat.

Makes 4 servings.

Nutrient Value Per Serving: 178 calories, 11 gm. protein, 11 gm. fat, 299 mg. sodium, 38 mg. cholesterol.

  2 **cups finely chopped onions (2 large onions)**
  2 **teaspoons vegetable oil**
  ½ **pound lean ground beef**
  ½ **teaspoon salt**
  ¼ **teaspoon pepper**
  2 **tablespoons all-purpose flour**
     Shredded Cheddar cheese (optional)
     Toasted hamburger buns (optional)

1. Sauté the onions in 1 teaspoon of the oil in a large heavy skillet, stirring frequently, until tender and lightly colored, for about 10 minutes. Cool to room temperature.
2. Combine the beef, sautéed onions, salt and pepper in a medium-size bowl. Shape into 4 equal patties, pushing onions firmly into the patties.
3. Place the flour on a piece of wax paper. Coat the patties with the flour.
4. Panfry the burgers in the remaining teaspoon of oil in a skillet, until crisp and golden brown on one side, for about 3 minutes. Turn; cook for another 1 or 2 minutes or until desired doneness. For cheeseburgers, sprinkle the shredded cheese over the burgers after turning; cover the skillet for the last 1 or 2 minutes. Serve on the toasted hamburger buns, if you wish.

To Make Ahead: Prepare the burgers as the recipe directs through Step 2. Wrap well and refrigerate until ready to serve. About 30 minutes before ready to serve, remove the patties from the refrigerator and allow them to come to room temperature. Proceed as the recipe directs.

Make and Freeze Ground Beef Patties

To freeze a large number of ground beef patties, shape the patties, place them on wax paper on a cookie sheet, cover with wax paper and place in the freezer. When frozen, remove from the cookie sheet, store in a plastic bag or wrap in aluminum foil with 2 pieces of wax paper between the patties. Return to the freezer.

Hearty Beef Chili with Beans and Cheddar Cheese

Makes 6 servings.

Nutrient Value Per Serving: 649 calories, 39 gm. protein, 40 gm. fat, 530 mg. sodium, 113 mg. cholesterol.

  2 **pounds beef chuck, cut into ½-inch cubes**
  3 **tablespoons vegetable oil**
  1 **cup chopped onion (1 large onion)**
  2 **cloves garlic, finely chopped**
  1 **can (16 ounces) no-salt-added whole tomatoes, broken up, drained and juice reserved**
     Cold water
  1 **can (6 ounces) no-salt-added tomato paste**
 1¼ **teaspoons chili powder**
  ¾ **teaspoon leaf oregano, crumbled**
  ½ **teaspoon ground cumin**
  ¼ **to ½ teaspoon crushed red pepper flakes**
  ¼ **teaspoon salt**
  1 **can (15 or 16 ounces) red kidney beans, drained and rinsed**
     Grated Cheddar cheese

1. Brown the beef in several batches in the oil in a large saucepan over medium-high heat, adding additional oil as needed. As the beef browns, remove to a plate.
2. Add the onion and garlic to the pan. Cook for 2 minutes, stirring, until lightly colored. Return the beef to the pan. Add the tomatoes, drained tomato liquid plus enough cold water to equal 1½ cups, the tomato paste, chili powder, oregano, cumin, red pepper flakes and salt. Lower the heat; simmer, partially covered, for 1 hour or until the meat is tender.
3. Stir in the beans. Simmer for 20 minutes longer.
4. Cool the chili slightly, sprinkle with the cheese and serve immediately. For future meals, divide among 6 freezer containers. Seal airtight and freeze.

Chili Beef

If you put the zippy meat mixture in a crisp corn tortilla, it's a taco; in a soft flour tortilla, it's a burrito; in a chewy pita, a taco burger.

Make 8 servings.

Nutrient Value Per Serving: 468 calories, 28 gm. protein, 29 gm. fat, 646 mg. sodium, 84 mg. cholesterol.

2   pounds ground chuck
1   large onion, grated (⅓ cup)
2   cloves garlic, finely chopped
2   tablespoons vegetable oil
1   can (8 ounces) tomato sauce
¾   cup water
2   tablespoons chili powder
1   tablespoon ground cumin
2   teaspoons leaf oregano, crumbled
½   teaspoon salt
½   teaspoon pepper
8   taco shells, flour tortillas or pita bread, heated
1   can (16 ounces) refried beans, heated
1   cup Monterey Jack or Cheddar cheese, shredded (4 ounces)
1   cup shredded iceberg or romaine lettuce, or a combination
1   large tomato, cored and diced (1 cup)
½   small unpared cucumber, diced and/or 8 radishes, diced (½ cup)
1   medium-size onion, diced (½ cup)
    Salsa (recipe, page 259)

1. Brown the beef, onion and garlic in the oil in a large skillet; drain off the excess fat. Add the tomato sauce, water, chili powder, cumin, oregano, salt and pepper; blend thoroughly. Bring the mixture to boiling; lower the heat; simmer for 30 minutes, stirring occasionally, until most of the liquid has evaporated.
2. For the tacos: Spoon some meat mixture into the taco shell; top with 1 to 2 tablespoons of the heated refried beans, the shredded cheese and an assortment of lettuce, tomato, cucumber and onion. Garnish with the Salsa. For the burritos: Fill the center of a large flour tortilla as above; fold to enclose the mixture. For the taco burgers: Cut off ½ inch from the top of the pita bread; fill the same as the taco.
Note: Any leftover meat filling can be frozen.

Stuffed Cabbage Rolls

Another great beef stretcher. Use the leftover cabbage for other recipes.

Makes 4 servings.

Nutrient Value Per Serving: 358 calories, 18 gm. protein, 17 gm. fat, 785 mg. sodium, 107 mg. cholesterol.

1   medium-size green cabbage (2½ to 3 pounds)
⅓   cup long-grain rice
½   teaspoon salt
½   pound lean ground beef
1   egg
1   medium-size onion, chopped (½ cup)
2   cloves garlic, finely chopped
2   teaspoons paprika
¾   teaspoon dillweed
¼   teaspoon pepper
1   can (16 ounces) stewed tomatoes

1. Bring 2 quarts of water to boiling in a large heavy kettle or Dutch oven.
2. Discard any tough or discolored outer leaves from the cabbage. Place the cabbage in the boiling water. Cover; cook for 10 minutes or until the outer leaves are tender.
3. Meanwhile, bring 3 cups of water to boiling in a medium-size saucepan. Add the rice and salt; cook for 15 minutes. Drain well.
4. When the outer cabbage leaves are tender, carefully remove the cabbage to a colander. Remove 8 outer leaves. (If not enough leaves are tender, return the cabbage to the boiling water.) Drain the leaves and the remaining head of cabbage.
5. Combine the ground beef, egg, onion, garlic, paprika, ½ teaspoon of the dillweed, pepper, ¼ cup of the liquid from the stewed tomatoes and the cooked rice in a medium-size bowl; stir to mix well.
6. Lay the 8 cabbage leaves, outer-side up, on a flat surface. Trim off and discard the raised portion of the center vein. Chop enough of the remaining cabbage from the head to make 2 cups; place in a large heavy saucepan or Dutch oven.
7. Divide the filling among the cabbage leaves, about ¼ cup per leaf, placing the filling near the stem ends. Fold the stem end of the leaf over the filling; tuck in the sides and roll up. Place the rolls, seam-side down, on the chopped cabbage in the saucepan. Pour the stewed tomatoes with ☞

the remaining liquid over the rolls. Sprinkle with the remaining ¼ teaspoon of dillweed.

8. Bring the cabbage roll mixture to boiling. Cover tightly; lower the heat; simmer for 60 minutes or until tender. Let stand for 15 minutes before serving. Spoon the sauce and chopped cabbage over the rolls.

To Make Ahead: Complete the recipe through placing the filled rolls in the saucepan in Step 7. Cover securely and refrigerate along with the stewed tomatoes until ready to cook. When ready to cook, allow the pan to come to room temperature and complete as the recipe directs.

Ground Meat Tips

Buy the meat the day you plan to use it, whenever possible. If ground meat must be saved until the next day, wrap it in wax paper and store it in the coldest part of your refrigerator.

To freeze ground meat, wrap it in serving-size portions in plastic wrap or aluminum foil soon after purchasing and place in the freezer.

Herbed Meatloaf

Great meatloaf for take-along lunches for kids, dads, dieters.

Bake at 350° for 1¼ hours.
Makes 1 loaf (eighteen ½-inch-thick slices).

Nutrient Value Per Serving: 270 calories, 22 gm. protein, 17 gm. fat, 337 mg. sodium, 130 mg. cholesterol.

2 pounds lean ground beef
1 cup fresh bread crumbs moistened with 2 tablespoons water
1 medium-size onion, coarsely grated
2 eggs, slightly beaten
2 tablespoons catsup
1 tablespoon Dijon-style mustard
1 tablespoon Worcestershire sauce
2 cloves garlic, finely chopped
1 teaspoon leaf thyme, crumbled
½ teaspoon salt
½ teaspoon black pepper

1. Preheat the oven to moderate (350°).
2. Combine the beef, bread crumbs, onion, eggs, catsup, mustard, Worcestershire sauce, garlic, thyme, salt and pepper in a large bowl. Shape into a 10 x 4-inch loaf in

a shallow baking pan.

3. Bake in the preheated moderate oven (350°) for 1¼ hours. Cool.

Cold Confetti Meatloaf

Serve in a hard-roll sandwich, if you wish.

Bake at 375° for 50 minutes.
Makes 4 servings.

Nutrient Value Per Serving: 505 calories, 33 gm. protein, 33 gm. fat, 702 mg. sodium, 180 mg. cholesterol.

1 tablespoon vegetable oil
¾ cup chopped carrot
¼ cup chopped sweet red pepper
¼ cup chopped sweet green pepper
½ cup chopped onion (1 medium-size onion)
1 teaspoon chopped fresh sage OR:
   ¼ teaspoon leaf sage, crumbled
¾ pound lean ground beef
½ pound lean ground pork
1 egg, slightly beaten
⅓ cup prepared chili sauce
1 cup fresh bread crumbs
¼ teaspoon salt
   Dash pepper
½ cup cubed (¼ inch) Cheddar cheese (about 4 ounces)

1. Heat the oil in a medium-size skillet over very low heat. Add the carrot, red and green peppers, onion and sage. Cover and cook over very low heat for 10 minutes; the mixture should be tender, but not browned.
2. Preheat the oven to moderate (375°). Lightly grease an 8½ x 4 x 2⅝-inch loaf pan. Fold a piece of aluminum foil to line the long sides and bottom of the pan, but not the short ends, leaving a 1-inch overhang on each side. Lightly grease the foil.
3. Combine the beef, pork, egg, chili sauce, bread crumbs, salt and pepper in a large bowl. Gently stir in the vegetables and cheese. Spoon into the prepared pan; pack lightly and smooth the top.
4. Bake in the preheated moderate oven (375°) for 50 minutes or until the juices run clear when pierced with a fork. Remove the pan to a wire rack to cool for 10 minutes.
5. Grasp the foil overhang and gently lift the loaf from the pan, allowing the juices to drain back into the pan. Place the loaf on a plate; refrigerate.
6. When the loaf is cold, carefully peel off the

foil. Cut into ¼-inch-thick slices and serve. If planning for a picnic, reform the loaf and wrap tightly in aluminum foil. Refrigerate overnight or until serving time.

7. To pack for a picnic, place in an insulated bag with a frozen ice pack.

Meatballs Stroganoff

Bake at 400° for 25 to 30 minutes.
Makes 12 servings.

Nutrient Value Per Serving: 404 calories, 30 gm. protein, 25 gm. fat, 437 mg. sodium, 175 mg. cholesterol.

3 **pounds ground round**
4 **slices soft whole-wheat bread, crumbled**
⅔ **cup milk**
1 **tablespoon Worcestershire sauce**
1 **teaspoon salt**
¼ **teaspoon pepper**
3 **eggs**
12 **ounces small mushrooms, thinly sliced**
2 **onions, finely chopped**
¼ **cup (½ stick) butter or margarine**
¼ **cup unsifted all-purpose flour**
4 **cups milk**
1 **cup dairy sour cream**
2 **tablespoons spicy brown mustard**
1 **teaspoon lemon juice**

1. Preheat the oven to hot (400°).
2. Combine the beef, bread, milk, Worcestershire, salt, pepper and eggs in a large bowl; mix well. Shape into 48 meatballs, using a heaping tablespoon for each.
3. Arrange the meatballs in a single layer in two 13 x 9 x 2-inch baking pans.
4. Bake, uncovered, in the preheated hot oven (400°) for 25 to 30 minutes or until the meatballs are no longer pink in the center.
5. Meanwhile, prepare the sauce: Sauté the mushrooms and onions in the butter in a large saucepan until tender, for about 5 minutes. Sprinkle the flour over the vegetables; cook, stirring, for 1 minute. Gradually stir in the milk. Cook, stirring, until the sauce thickens and no longer tastes floury, for 5 minutes.
6. Stir together the sour cream, mustard and lemon juice in a small bowl. Stir a little of the hot sauce into the sour cream mixture. Stir the mixture back into the saucepan. Keep warm over very low heat; do not let boil. Serve over the meatballs.

To Make Ahead: Prepare the meatballs as the recipe directs through Step 3. Cover the pans with aluminum foil and refrigerate. About 1 hour before serving the meatballs, remove from the refrigerator and allow them to come to room temperature. Proceed as the recipe directs.

MICROWAVE DIRECTIONS FOR COOKING MEATBALLS
650 Watt Variable Power Microwave Oven
Directions: Mix and shape the meatballs as in the above recipe. Evenly space half of the meatballs in a shallow microwave-safe baking dish, about 13 x 9 inches. Cover with wax paper. Microwave at full power for 9 to 10 minutes. After 4 minutes, rearrange the meatballs, placing the less cooked ones around the outside of the dish. Remove the meatballs with a slotted spoon. Pour off the pan liquid. Repeat with the remaining meatballs. Prepare the sauce on the stovetop, as directed in Steps 5 and 6, above.

Beef with Bean Curd and Vegetables

Beef with Bean Curd and Vegetables

Makes 6 servings.

Nutrient Value Per Serving: 231 calories, 19 gm. protein, 12 gm. fat, 958 mg. sodium, 39 mg. cholesterol.

¼ **cup soy sauce**
¼ **cup dry sherry**
1 **tablespoon cornstarch**
1 **teaspoon white vinegar**
1 **teaspoon sugar**
3 **tablespoons peanut or vegetable oil**
¾ **pound flank steak, thinly sliced on the diagonal**
2 **squares (8 ounces) firm bean curd (tofu), cubed**
½ **pound spinach, stemmed, torn in bite-size pieces**
¼ **pound mushrooms, sliced**
¼ **pound snow peas**
3 **green onions, cut into ½-inch slices**
1 **can (8 ounces) sliced bamboo shoots, drained**

1. Combine the soy sauce, sherry, cornstarch, vinegar and sugar in a small bowl. Mix well. Reserve.
2. Heat the oil in a wok or large skillet. Add the beef; stir-fry for 3 minutes. Add the bean curd, spinach, mushrooms, snow peas, green onions and bamboo shoots; stir-fry for 1 minute or until the spinach wilts. Stir the sauce into the wok; cook for 1 minute.

Stir-Fried Beef and Vegetables

Makes 4 servings.

Nutrient Value Per Serving: 415 calories, 18 gm. protein, 32 gm. fat, 773 mg. sodium, 58 mg. cholesterol.

2 tablespoons peanut or vegetable oil
1 clove garlic, pressed
12 ounces boneless sirloin steak, thinly sliced across the grain
1 large onion, cut into thin wedges
2 celery stalks, sliced
1 sweet red pepper, halved, seeded and cut into ¼-inch-wide strips
4 ounces mushrooms, washed and thinly sliced
3 tablespoons mild soy sauce
3 tablespoons water
2 tablespoons cornstarch
1 can (13¾ ounces) beef broth
4 ounces snow peas, trimmed
Cooked vermicelli (optional)

1. Heat 1 tablespoon of the oil in a large skillet or wok over high heat. Add the garlic and beef. Stir-fry until browned. Remove from the skillet with a slotted spoon.
2. Heat the remaining oil in the skillet. Stir-fry the onion, celery and the red pepper until the onion is tender, for about 4 minutes. Add the mushrooms; stir-fry for 2 minutes.
3. Combine the soy sauce, water and cornstarch in a small bowl. Stir into the skillet with the reserved beef and beef broth. Cook until the sauce thickens and becomes clear, for about 2 minutes.
4. Lower the heat. Add the snow peas; cook for 1 minute. Serve with the cooked vermicelli, if you wish.

Slicing Meat for Stir-Frying

To make slicing meat for stir-frying easier, wrap the meat in freezer wrapping paper, aluminum foil or plastic wrap and partially freeze just until slightly firm, but not frozen solid.

ONE LARGE CHUCK ROAST... FIVE MAIN-DISH MEALS

1. Cut around the blade bone of a 10-pound 7-bone chuck roast and remove the blade pieces. Turn; cut away the bone. Divide pieces into center and top.

2. Tie the center piece with kitchen string to make a savory pot roast.

3. Cut the top section into four thick slices to use for pepper steaks, after treating with instant meat tenderizer.

4. Use one blade meat section and make a braised beef dish. Cut the remaining blade piece into cubes and chop the meat in an electric food processor for a casserole. Use the bones and trims to make a hearty soup.

◣ ◀◀◀ ▢

Magyar Beef Paprikash

A Hungarian specialty featuring beef strips, mushrooms and sour cream.

Makes 8 servings.

Nutrient Value Per Serving: 572 calories, 36 gm. protein, 25 gm. fat, 986 mg. sodium, 163 mg. cholesterol.

2 *pounds boneless top sirloin or top round,*
   thinly sliced into bite-size pieces
1 *teaspoon salt*
¼ *teaspoon pepper*
   About 6 tablespoons butter or margarine
12 *ounces mushrooms, thickly sliced*
2 *large onions, thinly sliced*
3 *tablespoons Dijon-style mustard*
3 *tablespoons tomato paste*
3 *cups beef broth or stock*
¼ *cup dry sherry*
1 *tablespoon sweet Hungarian paprika*
1 *cup dairy sour cream*
1 *pound wide egg noodles, cooked*
   Dill sprigs (optional)

1. Pat the meat dry with paper toweling. Season with the salt and pepper.
2. Heat 2 tablespoons of the butter in a large skillet or wide pot. Quickly sauté the pieces of meat in a single layer until browned on both sides. Transfer to a platter. Brown the remaining meat, adding more butter as necessary.

3. Sauté the mushrooms in the same skillet over low heat, adding additional butter, if necessary, for about 5 minutes. Transfer to a separate plate.
4. Melt the additional 1 tablespoon of butter in the same skillet. Sauté the onions until tender, but not browned, for about 5 minutes. Add to the mushrooms.
5. Add the mustard and tomato paste to the skillet; stir to mix. Slowly stir in 2 cups of the beef broth to make a smooth sauce, scraping up any browned bits from the bottom of the skillet. Stir in the sherry and paprika. Return the mushrooms and onions to the skillet. Simmer, uncovered, for 10 minutes.
6. Gradually stir the remaining 1 cup of beef broth into the sour cream in a small bowl until the mixture is smooth. Pour into the skillet, stirring constantly. Simmer for 3 minutes.
7. Add the beef and noodles. Gently heat to serving temperature—do not boil. Garnish with the fresh dill sprigs, if you wish. Serve immediately.

To Make Ahead: Prepare through Step 5. Cover and refrigerate the meat and the remaining beef broth. Transfer the mushroom-onion mixture to a large bowl, cover and refrigerate. About 30 minutes before serving, remove from the refrigerator and proceed as the recipe directs.

Approximate Time for Braising Less-Tender Beef

Cut	Approximate Weight or Thickness	Approximate Total Cooking Time in Hours
Chuck Blade Roast	3 to 5 lbs.	2 to 2½
Chuck Arm Pot Roast	3 to 5 lbs.	2½ to 3½
Chuck Shoulder Roast, Boneless	3 to 5 lbs.	2½ to 3½
Round Steak	¾ to 1 inch	1 to 1¾
Chuck or Round Cubes (1½-inch)	1½ lbs.	1½ to 2½
Short Ribs (2 x 2 x 4-inch pieces)	3 lbs.	1½ to 2½

Approximate Time for Cooking Less-Tender Beef in Liquid

Cut	Approximate Weight or Thickness	Approximate Total Cooking Time in Hours
Fresh or Corned Beef	4 to 6 lbs.	3 to 4
Shank Cross Cuts	¾ to 1¼ lbs.	2 to 3

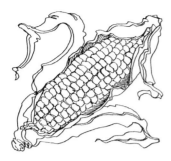

Easy Wine Cooking

Wine in cooking adds subtle flavor. Everyday stew becomes ragoût, and pot roast turns into Beef à la Mode. Wine rounds out the flavors, tenderizes tougher cuts of meat and gives distinction to your cooking. Remember that the alcohol content of wine boils off during cooking. All that remains is the flavor. Here are a few tips for successful casserole cooking with wines:
• Use the same wines you drink for cooking. Don't buy inferior wines for cooking; it's poor economy.
• Dry sherry and Madeira go well in shellfish and creamed dishes.
• Dry white wines are for poultry and veal casseroles. Rhine wine goes well with cheese and a variety of seafood casseroles.
• Hearty red wines are best for beef, game and some fish, plus some chicken and duck dishes.
• Dry vermouth can be used in place of white wine and stores for months.
• Flat champagne may be used for poaching fish or poultry. The cooking liquid will make a delicious sauce.
• Ham may be basted with port or Marsala wine. The drippings may then be used for a flavorful sauce.

Hearty Beef Stew

A savory stew with an abundance of spring vegetables.

Makes 8 servings.

Nutrient Value Per Serving: 453 calories, 42 gm. protein, 18 gm. fat, 875 mg. sodium, 111 mg. cholesterol.

   3 tablespoons olive or vegetable oil
   3 pounds lean chuck or round, cut into
         1½- to 2-inch cubes
   3 tablespoons finely chopped shallots
   1 clove garlic, finely chopped
   3 tablespoons unsifted flour
   1 can (10 ounces) condensed beef broth
   1 can (16 ounces) tomatoes OR: 1 cup peeled
         and chopped fresh tomatoes
   1 teaspoon salt
   ½ teaspoon leaf thyme, crumbled
 12 small white onions, peeled
   4 small turnips, pared and quartered
   3 to 4 carrots, pared and cut into 2-inch
         lengths
 12 small new potatoes, peeled (1 pound)
   1 package (10 ounces) frozen peas
   2 tablespoons chopped parsley

1. Heat the oil in a large saucepot or Dutch oven; brown the beef, a few pieces at a time. Remove pieces as they brown to a bowl.
2. Remove all but 1 tablespoon of the drippings from the kettle; add the shallots and garlic; sauté, stirring often, for 2 minutes or until golden brown. Sprinkle the flour over the shallots; cook over moderate heat, stirring constantly.
3. Stir in the beef broth and tomatoes; bring to boiling, stirring constantly to loosen the browned bits. Return the beef to the kettle. Stir in the salt and thyme. Bring to boiling; lower the heat, cover and simmer for 1 hour. Skim off the fat, if any.
4. Add the onions, turnips, carrots and potatoes to the beef, pushing them down under the liquid; cover; simmer for 45 minutes longer or until the beef and vegetables are tender. Stir in the peas; cover; simmer for 5 to 10 minutes longer. Sprinkle with the parsley.

Peeling Onions

To peel onions more quickly, immerse 2 to 3 at a time in a saucepan of boiling water for a few seconds. The skins will slip off easily.

Baked Brisket with Horseradish-Walnut Sauce

Prepare this hearty dish a day or two ahead and cut down on cooking time when company's coming.

Bake at 325° for 3 hours.
Reheat at 325° for 45 to 60 minutes.
Makes 8 servings.

Nutrient Value Per Serving: 600 calories, 54 gm. protein, 30 gm. fat, 347 mg. sodium, 155 mg. cholesterol.

- 1 **beef brisket (4 pounds), first cut*, trimmed**
- 1 **can (13¾ ounces) beef broth**
- 1 **bay leaf**
- 2 **whole cloves**
- 1 **small onion, sliced**
- 2 **cups Brussels sprouts, trimmed, OR:**
  1 package (10 ounces) frozen Brussels sprouts
- 4 **leeks, trimmed, split lengthwise and washed**
- 8 **small new potatoes, scrubbed**
- 2 **sweet potatoes, scrubbed and sliced**
- 2 **ears corn, cut into chunks**
  Horseradish-Walnut Sauce (recipe follows)

1. Preheat the oven to slow (325°).
2. Place the brisket in a large casserole or Dutch oven, just large enough to hold the meat snugly. Add the broth, bay leaf, cloves and onion. Cover tightly.
3. Bake in the preheated slow oven (325°) for 3 hours or until the meat is tender. Cool the brisket in the broth slightly. Refrigerate the meat and broth for 1 to 2 days.
4. Prepare the parboiled vegetables: Bring a large saucepan of salted water to boiling. Cook the Brussels sprouts for 8 to 10 minutes or until barely tender, or the frozen Brussels sprouts according to the label directions. Remove with a slotted spoon to a colander. Repeat with the remaining vegetables: Cook the leeks for 10 to 12 minutes. Cook the new potatoes for 20 minutes. Cook the sweet potatoes for 10 to 15 minutes. Cook the corn for 5 minutes. Rinse the vegetables with cold water as you place them in the colander. Refrigerate.
5. To reheat and serve: Remove the meat from the broth. Cut across the grain into thin slices. Arrange the slices, overlapping, in a large baking dish or roasting pan. Arrange the vegetables around the meat. Heat the broth in a medium-size saucepan. Pour through a sieve over the meat and vegetables. Cover the pan with foil. Reheat in a preheated slow oven (325°), basting once or twice, for 45 to 60 minutes or until heated through. Spoon a little broth over each serving. Pass the Horseradish-Walnut Sauce.

* Note: The flat, oblong first cut has less fat than other cuts of brisket.

Horseradish-Walnut Sauce

Serve this flavorful sauce on cold leftover roast beef.

Makes 1½ cups.

Nutrient Value Per Serving: 135 calories, 1 gm. protein, 14 gm. fat, 27 mg. sodium, 37 mg. cholesterol.

- ½ **cup dairy sour cream**
- 1 **to 2 tablespoons prepared horseradish**
- ½ **teaspoon lemon juice**
- 1 **teaspoon prepared mustard**
- 1 **teaspoon sugar**
- ¾ **cup heavy cream, whipped**
- ¼ **cup chopped toasted walnuts**

Combine the sour cream, horseradish, lemon juice, mustard and sugar in a small bowl; stir to mix. Fold in the whipped cream and walnuts. Cover; refrigerate for one to several hours.

Horseradish

An herb, root possessing a sharp flavor and frequently resembling a horse's hoof.

Temperature and Time for Roasting Beef

Cut	Approximate Pound Weight	Oven Temperature	Internal Meat Temperature When Done	Minutes Per Pound Roasting Time
Standing Rib (Ribs 6 to 7 inches long)	6 to 8	300° to 325°F.	140°F. (rare)	23 to 25
			160°F. (med.)	27 to 30
			170°F. (well)	32 to 35
	4 to 6	300° to 325°F.	140°F. (rare)	26 to 32
			160°F. (med.)	34 to 38
			170°F. (well)	40 to 42
Rolled Rib	5 to 7	300° to 325°F.	140°F. (rare)	32
			160°F. (med.)	38
			170°F. (well)	48
Delmonico (Rib Eye)	4 to 6	350°F.	140°F. (rare)	18 to 20
			160°F. (med.)	20 to 22
			170°F. (well)	22 to 24
Tenderloin, whole	4 to 6	425°F.	140°F. (rare)	45 to 60*
Tenderloin, half	2 to 3	425°F.	140°F. (rare)	45 to 60*
Rolled Rump (U.S. Prime and Choice)	4 to 6	300° to 325°F.	140° to 170°F.	25 to 30
Sirlion Tip (U.S. Prime and Choice)	3½ to 4	300° to 325°F.	140° to 170°F.	35 to 40
	4 to 6	300° to 325°F.	140° to 170°F.	30 to 35

* *Total roasting time.*

Marbling in Meats

"Marbling," the fine flecks of fat within the lean of the meat, is the key to selecting top-quality meat. The fat cooks away, leaving a tender, juicy piece of meat.

◄◄◄

Marinated Fillet of Beef

Other cuts can also be used in this recipe.

Roast at 425° for 45 to 50 minutes.
Makes 12 servings.

Nutrient Value Per Serving: 212 calories, 32 gm. protein, 8 gm. fat, 510 mg. sodium, 79 mg. cholesterol.

  1 fillet of beef (about 4 pounds) OR:
      1 rolled, boned rib roast of beef, or
      eye-round roast, or sirloin tip roast
      (about 4 pounds)
  1 cup soy sauce
  ½ cup medium or dry sherry
  ⅓ cup olive oil
  3 cloves garlic, finely chopped
  2 teaspoons ground ginger

1. Preheat the oven to hot (425°).

2. Trim the fillet if needed. In a large bowl (not aluminum), mix the soy sauce, sherry, olive oil, garlic and ginger. Place the roast in the mixture. Refrigerate for 4 hours or overnight, turning the roast several times, to season.

3. Remove the roast from the refrigerator 1 hour before cooking, and let stand at room temperature.

4. Place the roast on a rack in a roasting pan. Insert a meat thermometer into the center of the thickest part.

5. Roast in the preheated hot oven (425°), brushing with the soy mixture 3 or 4 times, for 45 to 50 minutes or until the thermometer registers 140° for rare. For medium rare, continue roasting to 150°. Do not overcook.

6. Remove the roast to a deep platter; pour the pan juices over the top. Slice and serve.

Prevent Shrinkage

Avoid overcooking meat. This causes dry-tasting, less-tender meat and makes for more shrinkage and, therefore, fewer servings.

Pork

There is a wide selection of pork cuts that can add variety to your family's meals. Pork is available fresh or cured and/or smoked. The most tender pork cuts are from the rib, the loin and the leg. (In butcher's terms, a leg is a ham, and a fresh ham is simply one that has not been cured or smoked.) These tender cuts require nothing more than gentle, slow roasting or panfrying. They can be cooked by one of the dry-heat methods described on page 76.

The not-so-tender cuts—those from the shoulder—are better when braised, that is, browned and then cooked in a covered pot on the range or in the oven with vegetables and liquid added.

Cured and/or smoked pork include ham, bacon, smoked pork shoulder rolls and picnics.

Sausage Pilaf with Lemon

Serve as a side dish with baked chicken or a roast leg of lamb, or with a salad and crusty bread for lunch.

Makes 4 servings.

Nutrient Value Per Serving: 567 calories, 19 gm. protein, 34 gm. fat, 1,035 mg. sodium, 62 mg. cholesterol.

- ½ **pound Italian sweet sausage, casings removed**
- 2 **tablespoons olive or vegetable oil**
- 2 **tablespoons butter or margarine**
- 1 **medium-size onion, finely chopped (½ cup)**
- 1 **clove garlic, finely chopped**
- ½ **medium-size sweet green pepper, chopped (¼ cup)**
- ½ **medium-size sweet red pepper, chopped (¼ cup)**
- 1 **small celery stalk, diced (⅓ cup)**
  Grated rind of 1 large lemon (1 tablespoon)
  Juice of 1 large lemon (about 3 tablespoons)
- 2 **cups chicken broth**
- 1 **cup long-grain rice**
- ½ **cup grated Parmesan or Romano cheese**
- ¼ **cup finely chopped green onions**

1. Sauté the sausage in the oil in a 10-inch skillet, breaking up with a wooden spoon, until the meat loses its pink color. Remove the sausage with a slotted spoon to paper toweling to drain. Drain off all but 2 table-spoons of the drippings from the skillet.
2. Add the butter to the remaining drippings in the skillet. Add the onion, garlic, green and red peppers and celery; sauté until

tender, for about 5 minutes.
3. Return the sausage to the skillet. Reserve the lemon rind. Add the lemon juice and chicken broth to the sausage. Bring to boiling; stir in the rice with a fork. Lower the heat; cover and cook for 20 minutes or until the liquid is absorbed and the rice is tender.
4. Stir in the cheese. Top with the green onions and reserved lemon rind.

Sausage-Cheese Tortanos (Filled Bread Rings)

These individual whole-wheat "doughnuts" are filled with a lightly seasoned mixture of sausage, cheese and spinach. Make a day ahead and keep refrigerated.

Bake at 375° for 25 minutes.
Makes 4 servings.

Nutrient Value Per Serving: 762 calories, 47 gm. protein, 38 gm. fat, 1,250 mg. sodium, 305 mg. cholesterol.

- 1¼ **cups unsifted all-purpose flour**
- ¾ **cup whole-wheat flour**
- 1 **envelope fast-rising dry yeast**
- 2 **tablespoons grated Parmesan cheese**
- ¼ **teaspoon salt**
- ⅔ **cup milk**
- 1 **tablespoon butter or margarine**
- 1 **egg, slightly beaten**
- 1 **pound fresh spinach, trimmed, OR:**
  1 package (10 ounces) frozen chopped spinach
- ½ **pound Italian sweet sausage**
- 1 **cup chopped onion (1 large onion)**
- ¼ **pound Provolone, cut into ¼-inch cubes**
- 1 **package (8 ounces) part-skim mozzarella cheese, cut into ¼-inch cubes**
- 1 **egg, slightly beaten**
- 1 **egg yolk combined with 1 tablespoon water**

1. Reserve 1 cup of the all-purpose flour. Combine the remaining all-purpose flour, whole-wheat flour, yeast, Parmesan cheese and salt in a large bowl.
2. Heat together the milk and butter in a small saucepan until hot to the touch (125° to 130°).
3. Stir the hot milk mixture into the dry ingredients. Stir in 1 slightly beaten egg. Gradually stir in enough of the reserved flour, about ½ cup, to make a soft dough. ☞

4. Turn the dough out onto a lightly floured surface. Knead until smooth and elastic, for about 10 minutes, adding flour only as necessary to prevent sticking.

5. Press the dough into a buttered large bowl; bring the buttered-side up. Let rise, covered, in a warm place, away from drafts, for 50 minutes or until doubled in volume.

6. Meanwhile, wash the trimmed fresh spinach. Place in a large pot. Cook, covered, over medium heat with only the water that clings to the leaves, just until wilted, for about 5 minutes. Drain. Or, cook the frozen spinach according to the package directions.

7. Remove the sausage from the casings. Sauté in a medium-size skillet, breaking up with a wooden spoon, for 5 minutes. Drain off all but 1 tablespoon of the fat. Add the onion; cook for 10 minutes or until the onion is tender and the sausage is no longer pink. Transfer with a slotted spoon to a bowl; let cool.

8. Squeeze all the excess water from the spinach. If using fresh spinach, coarsely chop. Add to the sausage. Stir in the Provolone, mozzarella and remaining egg. Set aside.

9. Punch the dough down. Cut into 4 equal pieces. Roll out each piece on a lightly floured surface to a 9 x 5-inch rectangle.

10. Spoon the spinach filling, lengthwise, down the center of each rectangle. Fold one long side of the dough over, overlapping the egg-brushed edge. Pinch together to seal. Brush the ends of the dough with the egg wash. Gently shape the roll into a ring; pinch the ends together to seal. Repeat with the remaining rectangles. Place on a large lightly greased cookie sheet, allowing room for rising. Cover; let rise in a warm place, away from drafts, for 45 minutes; the dough should almost double in volume.

11. Brush the tortanos with the egg yolk and water mixture. Bake in the preheated moderate oven (375°) for 25 minutes or until golden. Remove to a wire rack to cool for 15 minutes and serve immediately. Or, refrigerate for a picnic.

12. If preparing for a picnic, when chilled, wrap and refrigerate until time for the trip.

13. To pack, place in an insulated bag with a frozen ice pack.

Slivered Pork and Egg with Fried Noodles

Makes 4 servings.

Nutrient Value Per Serving: 630 calories, 32 gm. protein, 31 gm. fat, 1,871 mg. sodium, 188 mg. cholesterol.

½ *pound thin spaghetti*
2 *eggs*
1 *tablespoon water*
5 *tablespoons peanut or vegetable oil*
¾ *pound lean boneless pork, cut into matchstick-size pieces*
6 *green onions, sliced diagonally into 1-inch pieces*
1 *pound Chinese cabbage or romaine lettuce, coarsely chopped*
¼ *pound mushrooms, sliced*
1 *can (8 ounces) sliced bamboo shoots, drained and cut into thin strips*
⅓ *cup soy sauce*
2 *tablespoons dry sherry*
1 *teaspoon sugar*

1. Cook the spaghetti in 3 quarts of unsalted boiling water for 10 minutes; drain well. Dry completely on paper toweling.

2. Beat the eggs with the water in a small bowl until well mixed.

3. Heat 1 tablespoon of the oil in a medium-size skillet; pour in the eggs. Cook over medium heat, without stirring, until set, but still soft. Carefully turn over to lightly brown the other side. Slide the omelet onto a cutting board. Slice into thin shreds. Keep warm.

4. Heat 2 tablespoons of the oil in a wok or large skillet. Add the pork and green onions; stir-fry for 2 minutes. Add the cabbage, mushrooms, bamboo shoots, soy sauce, sherry and sugar; stir-fry for 3 minutes. Transfer the mixture to a platter; keep warm.

5. Heat the remaining 2 tablespoons of oil in a wok. Add the cooked spaghetti; stir-fry for 3 minutes. Add the pork mixture; stir-fry for 1 minute. Transfer to a warmed serving platter; sprinkle with the egg shreds. Serve immediately.

Sweet and Sour Pork

You can marinate the pork and prepare the batter and sauce ahead of time.

Makes 6 servings.

Nutrient Value Per Serving: 647 calories, 24 gm. protein, 27 gm. fat, 785 mg. sodium, 74 mg. cholesterol.

1½ **pounds boneless loin of pork, cut into ¾-inch cubes**
2 **tablespoons dry sherry**
2 **tablespoons soy sauce**
1 **can (20 ounces) pineapple chunks in pineapple juice**
1 **tablespoon cornstarch**
¾ **cup firmly packed light brown sugar**
¾ **cup cider vinegar**
3 **tablespoons catsup**
3 **cups peanut oil**
1 **large sweet red pepper, cut into 1-inch pieces**
1 **large sweet green pepper, cut into 1-inch pieces**
1 **large onion, slivered lengthwise**
  Crispy Batter (recipe follows)
  Hot cooked rice (optional)

1. Place the pork in a medium-size bowl. Add the sherry and 1 tablespoon of the soy sauce. Stir to mix well. Cover and marinate for at least 1 hour at room temperature or refrigerate, covered, overnight.
2. Drain the pineapple, reserving ¾ cup of the juice.
3. Place the cornstarch in a small bowl. Gradually stir in the reserved pineapple juice until smooth. Add the brown sugar, vinegar, catsup and the remaining 1 tablespoon of soy sauce; reserve.
4. Heat 2 tablespoons of the oil in a wok or large skillet. Stir-fry the peppers and onion until crisp-tender, for about 2 minutes. Stir the sauce in the bowl; pour into the skillet. Cook over medium heat, stirring constantly, until the mixture bubbles and thickens and becomes translucent. Remove from the heat. Add the reserved pineapple chunks. Set aside.
5. Heat the remaining oil in another wok or electric skillet until the oil reaches 375°.
6. Drain the meat; pat dry with paper toweling, if necessary. Working with about a quarter of the meat at a time, dip the chunks into the Crispy Batter. Fry in the hot oil until crisp, golden brown and cooked throughout, for about 3 minutes. Cut through a large piece to check for doneness. Drain on paper toweling. Keep warm. Repeat with the remaining meat.
7. Gently reheat the sauce. Stir in the pork. Serve over hot cooked rice, if you wish.

Crispy Batter: Stir together 1 cup of cornstarch, ½ cup of *sifted* all-purpose flour and ½ teaspoon of salt in a small bowl. Gradually mix in 1 cup of cold water until the mixture is smooth. Let stand for at least 15 minutes before using. If the batter is too thick, stir in a little more water to make a good coating consistency.

Braised Stuffed Pork Chops

Braised Stuffed Pork Chops

Makes 4 servings.

Nutrient Value Per Serving: 564 calories, 24 gm. protein, 41 gm. fat, 535 mg. sodium, 92 mg. cholesterol.

4 **double-thick loin pork chops (about 6 ounces each)**
1 **small tart apple, peeled, cored and diced**
1 **small onion, finely chopped (¼ cup)**
2 **tablespoons butter or margarine**
1¾ **cups soft bread crumbs**
¼ **cup raisins, chopped**
½ **teaspoon salt**
¼ **teaspoon powdered sage**
⅛ **teaspoon pepper**
  All-purpose flour
2 **tablespoons vegetable oil**
¼ **cup chicken broth**
  Apple slices and parsley for garnish

1. Cut a pocket in each chop. Set aside.
2. Sauté the apple and onion in the butter in a medium-size skillet until soft, for 4 minutes. Mix in the crumbs, raisins, salt, sage and pepper. Spoon the stuffing in the chop pockets. Close the openings with wooden picks. Dredge the chops in the flour.
3. Brown the chops on both sides in the oil in a heavy skillet. Pour off the drippings. Add the broth to the skillet. Cover; cook over medium-low heat for about 45 minutes or until the chops are tender. Remove the wooden picks before serving. Garnish with the apple slices and parsley.

To Make Ahead: Cut the pockets in the chops; wrap the chops in aluminum foil and refrigerate until ready to stuff and cook. Prepare the stuffing mixture, place it in a medium-size bowl, cover and refrigerate until ready to stuff and cook the chops. When ready to stuff and cook, proceed as the recipe directs.

Mustard-Glazed Pork with Apples and Cabbage

Bake at 350° for 1½ hours.
Makes 8 servings.

Nutrient Value Per Serving: 308 calories, 26 gm. protein, 16 gm. fat, 1,951 mg. sodium, 78 mg. cholesterol.

1 *boneless smoked pork butt (3 pounds)*
1 *medium-size green cabbage (2 pounds), cut into 8 wedges*
2 *large apples, such as McIntosh, Cortland or Rome Beauty, cored and each cut into 8 wedges*

¾ *cup dry white wine OR: chicken broth*
1 *bay leaf*
½ *teaspoon caraway seeds*
¼ *teaspoon pepper*
1 *tablespoon currant jelly*
1 *teaspoon Dijon-style mustard*
¼ *cup (½ stick) butter or margarine, melted Chopped parsley (optional)*

1. Preheat the oven to moderate (350°).
2. Soak the pork butt in a pan of warm water to cover for 15 minutes. Remove the netting.
3. Place the pork in a roasting pan. Pour in water to a ¼-inch depth. Cover the pan tightly with aluminum foil.
4. Bake in the preheated moderate oven (350°) for 1 hour.
5. Meanwhile, cook the cabbage in a large pot of boiling salted water until tender, for about 10 minutes. Drain.
6. Discard the water from the roasting pan. Arrange the cabbage and apple wedges around the pork. Add the wine, bay leaf, caraway seeds and pepper to the pan. Cover; bake for another 20 minutes.
7. Prepare the mustard glaze: Combine the jelly and mustard in a small cup.
8. Remove the foil from the pan. Brush the pork with the glaze. Brush the cabbage and apple with the melted butter. Continue baking, uncovered, until the apples are tender, for about 10 minutes.
9. To serve, cut the pork into ¼-inch-thick slices and arrange on a serving platter with the cabbage and apple wedges. Garnish with the chopped parsley, if you wish.

Temperature and Time for Roasting Cured and Smoked Pork

Cut	Approximate Pound Weight	Oven Temperature	Internal Meat Temperature When Done	Total Roasting Time
Ham (cook before eating)				
Bone in, half	5 to 7	325°F.	160°F.	2½ to 3 hours
Ham (fully cooked)				
Bone in, half	5 to 7 lbs.	325°F	140°F.	1½ to 2¼ hours
Boneless, half	3 to 4 lbs.	325°F	140°F.	1¼ to 1¾ hours
Arm Picnic Shoulder				
Bone in	5 to 8 lbs.	325°F	170°F.	2½ to 4 hours
Shoulder				
Boneless roll	2 to 3 lbs.	325°F	170°F.	1½ to 1¾ hours

SEVERAL MEALS FROM ONE PORK LOIN

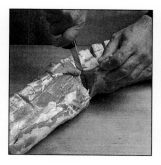

1. Cut a 12-pound whole pork loin at the 8th loin chop with a paring knife.

2, 3. Loosen the meat from the bones, using short strokes with a knife. Tie the meat for a pork loin roast.

4. Cut 4 chops from the remaining section.

5. Cut the remaining meat into cubes for a pork ragoût.

6. Cut the rib bones remaining from the pork loin and section from the ragoût for barbecued ribs.

7. Cut a pocket into the center of the pork chops and make stuffed pork chops. Freeze all in family or individual servings.

Temperature and Time for Roasting Pork

Cut	Approximate Pound Weight	Oven Temperature	Internal Meat Temperature When Done	Minutes Per Pound Roasting Time
Loin				
Center	3 to 5	325° to 350°F.	170°F.	30 to 35
Half	5 to 7	325° to 350°F.	170°F.	35 to 40
Blade Loin or Sirloin	3 to 4	325° to 350°F.	170°F.	40 to 45
Rolled	3 to 5	325° to 350°F.	170°F.	35 to 45
Picnic Shoulder	5 to 8	325° to 350°F.	170°F.	30 to 35
Rolled	3 to 5	325° to 350°F.	170°F.	35 to 40
Cushion Style	3 to 5	325° to 350°F.	170°F.	30 to 35
Boston Shoulder	4 to 6	325° to 350°F.	170°F.	40 to 45
Leg (Fresh ham)				
Whole (Bone in)	12 to 16	325° to 350°F.	170°F.	22 to 26
Whole (Rolled)	10 to 14	325° to 350°F.	170°F.	24 to 28
Half (Bone in)	5 to 8	325° to 350°F.	170°F.	35 to 40
Spareribs	3	325° to 350°F.	Well done	1½ to 2½ hrs. (total)

Crown Roast of Pork (page 94), Green Beans
and Herbed Walnut, Mushroom and Orange
Salad (page 68).

Crown Roast of Pork with Wild Rice Stuffing

This succulent pièce de résistance is an unforgettable combination of tastes.

Bake at 400° for 10 minutes;
then at 325° for 3 to 3½ hours.
Makes 8 servings.

Nutrient Value Per Serving: 1,033 calories, 55 gm. protein, 60 gm. fat, 352 mg. sodium, 190 mg. cholesterol.

1 crown roast of pork (6 to 7 pounds)*
2 packages (6 ounces each) wild rice mix
½ cup chopped onion (1 medium-size onion)
⅓ cup chopped celery
1 clove garlic, finely chopped
¼ cup (½ stick) butter or margarine
½ cup pine nuts
1 package (8 ounces) dried apricots, chopped
6 tablespoons chopped, drained, preserved ginger**
½ teaspoon ground allspice
6 whole cloves
2 bay leaves
¾ cup to 1 cup Madeira wine
1 can (13¾ ounces) beef broth
Kumquats (optional)

1. Preheat the oven to hot (400°). Place the roast on a rack in a large, shallow roasting pan.
2. Cook the rice according to label directions.
3. Sauté the onion, celery and garlic in butter in a skillet just until tender, for about 5 minutes.
4. Combine the sautéed vegetables, rice, pine nuts, ginger and allspice in a bowl; mix well. Spoon lightly into the center of the roast. (Spoon any extra stuffing into a buttered, shallow baking dish; bake during the last 20 minutes of roasting.) Cover the ends of bones and top of the stuffing with foil.
5. Roast in the preheated hot oven (400°) for 10 minutes. Lower the oven temperature to slow (325°). Roast for 30 minutes per pound of meat, 3 to 3½ hours, or until a meat thermometer registers 170° when inserted in the thickest part of the roast; do not let the thermometer touch bone or fat.
6. Remove the roast to a heated serving platter. Keep warm while preparing the gravy.
7. To prepare the gravy: Skim off and discard the fat from the pan drippings. Add the cloves, bay leaves, Madeira and broth to the juices in the pan. Cook over medium heat, scraping up any browned bits from the pan. Increase the heat to high; cook until the gravy is reduced by a third. Strain into a sauce boat. Serve with the roast and any extra stuffing. Garnish the rib ends with the kumquats, if you wish.

To Make Ahead: The stuffing can be made early in the day.

* *Order the roast several days ahead and ask your butcher to assemble and tip the crown roast.*

** *Preserved ginger is packed in syrup under the Raffetto label and can be found in the gourmet section of the supermarket.*

Kumquat

A small citrus fruit possessing a rather sweet edible rind and a somewhat tart flesh. Kumquats can be eaten raw or cooked.

Lamb

Meat of young sheep under 1 year in age, usually 6 months. Lamb is tender, lean meat with a delicate but distinctive flavor. Mutton is the meat from mature sheep.

Buying lamb: Lamb is available fresh or frozen. Frozen lamb is usually imported from New Zealand. Fresh lamb is pink to light red in color with firm, fine textured flesh. Some cuts of lamb have a thin, papery skin, called "fell," surrounding the fat. If it has not been removed, pull it off steaks and chops before cooking; leave it on roasts to help hold their shape during cooking.

Some cuts of lamb, such as the rib or loin chops, have given lamb an expensive reputation, but there are many cuts that are economical and are excellent to use in everyday meals. For example, buy cuts from the shoulder, such as a shoulder arm roast or shoulder steaks.

Cooking lamb: Most cuts of lamb are tender and can be cooked by one of the dry-heat methods. (See *Meat Cooking Methods*, page 76). Some cuts should be braised or cooked in liquid.

Crescent Lamb Triangles (page 95), Orange-Ambrosia Cake (page 195), Rice Dressing (page 291).

Crescent Lamb Triangles

Serve these lamb- and spinach-filled Middle-Eastern pastry triangles with a green salad.

Bake at 350° for 20 minutes.
Makes 8 servings.

Nutrient Value Per Serving: 557 calories, 25 gm. protein, 37 gm. fat, 1,507 mg. sodium, 152 mg. cholesterol.

- 1 **pound ground lamb**
- 1 **medium-size onion, chopped**
- 1 **can (16 ounces) mixed vegetables, drained**
- 1 **can (8 ounces) tomato sauce**
- 1 **teaspoon garlic powder**
- 1 **teaspoon ground cumin**
- ½ **teaspoon ground cloves**
- ½ **teaspoon ground ginger**
- ½ **teaspoon ground coriander**
- ¼ **teaspoon cayenne pepper**
- ¼ **teaspoon salt**
- ⅛ **teaspoon ground cinnamon**
- 2 **cans (8 ounces each) refrigerated crescent dinner rolls**
- 1 **can (15 ounces) spinach, drained**
- 12 **ounces Cheddar cheese, shredded (3 cups)**
- 2 **egg yolks, lightly beaten with 2 teaspoons water for egg wash**

1. Brown the lamb in a large skillet over medium heat until no longer pink, for about 5 minutes. Drain off the fat. Add the onion; cook for 5 minutes. Add the mixed vegetables, tomato sauce, garlic powder, cumin, cloves, ginger, coriander, cayenne, salt and cinnamon. Simmer for 5 minutes.
2. Separate 1 can of the crescent rolls into 8 individual crescents. Roll out each on a lightly floured surface into an 11 x 7 x 7-inch triangle. Transfer to ungreased cookie sheets.
3. When cool enough to handle, divide the lamb filling equally among the 8 triangles, about ½ cup for each. Spread evenly over the dough, leaving a ½-inch border around the edges. Place a mound of spinach in the center of each triangle; mound the shredded cheese on top of the spinach. Spread evenly over the lamb, leaving a ½-inch border.
4. Preheat the oven to moderate (350°).
5. Separate the second package of rolls into 8 individual crescents. Roll each out on a lightly floured surface into triangles slightly larger than the first batch. Top each of the filled smaller triangles with a larger one. Press the edges together firmly to form a tight seal. Brush the tops with the egg wash. Cut 1 or 2 steam vents into the top of each triangle.
6. Bake in the preheated moderate oven (350°) for 20 minutes or until golden brown.

Morroccan Lamb Stew

Moroccan Lamb Stew

An exotic but simple platter of mixed appetizers would be an exciting way to start an evening of Moroccan fare: Stuffed grape leaves skewered with a sliver of lemon; pita bread quarters filled with eggplant salad or seasoned chick-pea purée; wedges of feta cheese drizzled with olive oil and sprinkled with pepper; and olives, sweet green pepper rings and cherry tomatoes. For dessert, offer baked apples, served with cinnamon and honey-sweetened yogurt.

Makes 10 servings.

Nutrient Value Per Serving: 562 calories, 29 gm. protein, 31 gm. fat, 498 mg. sodium, 97 mg. cholesterol.

- 3 **pounds boneless leg of lamb, cut into large cubes**
- 1 **teaspoon salt**

- ¼ *teaspoon pepper*
- ¼ *cup unsifted all-purpose flour for coating, or as needed*
- ¼ *cup olive or vegetable oil, or as needed*
- 3 *large sweet green peppers, halved, seeded and cut into thin strips*
- 2 *large onions, sliced*
- 1 *teaspoon finely chopped garlic*
- ½ *teaspoon ground cinnamon*
- ¼ *teaspoon ground cardamom*
- ¼ *teaspoon ground coriander*
- ¼ *teaspoon ground cumin*
- ¼ *teaspoon ground ginger*
- ⅛ *teaspoon cayenne pepper*
- 2 *cups beef broth*
- 2 *tablespoons tomato paste*
- 1 *cup golden raisins*
- 4 *cups hot cooked saffron or white rice*
- ½ *cup slivered almonds*

1. Pat the lamb dry with paper toweling. Season with the salt and pepper. Coat lightly with the flour, shaking off the excess.
2. Heat 2 tablespoons of the oil in a large flameproof casserole. Brown the lamb in batches, adding more oil as necessary. As the meat browns, remove to a plate.
3. Sauté the green peppers in the oil remaining in the casserole, stirring often, for 2 minutes. Remove; reserve.
4. Sauté the onions and garlic in the same casserole until tender, but not browned, for about 5 minutes. Add the cinnamon, cardamom, coriander, cumin, ginger and cayenne; cook for 30 seconds, stirring constantly.
5. Add the beef broth, scraping up any browned bits from the bottom of the casserole with a wooden spoon. Stir in the tomato paste. Return the lamb and a third

Temperature and Time for Roasting Lamb

Cut	Approximate Pound Weight	Oven Temperature	Internal Meat Temperature When Done	Minutes Per Pound Roasting Time
Leg	5 to 9	300° to 325°F.	140°F. (rare)	20 to 25
			160°F. (med.)	25 to 30
			170°-180°F. (well)	30 to 35
Leg, shank half	3 to 4	300° to 325°F.	140°F. (rare)	25 to 30
			160°F. (med.)	30 to 35
			170°-180°F. (well)	35 to 40
Rib	2 to 3	300° to 325°F.	140°F. (rare)	25 to 30
			160°F. (med.)	30 to 35
			170°-180°F. (well)	35 to 40

of the peppers to the casserole. Bring to boiling. Lower the heat; cover; simmer for 1 hour.

6. Add the raisins; continue cooking, covered, for 30 minutes or until the lamb is tender. Stir in the remaining peppers.

7. Serve with the rice, sprinkled with the almonds.

To Make Ahead: Prepare the stew as the recipe directs through Step 5. Cool the stew and transfer to a bowl. Cover and refrigerate the stew and remaining peppers. When ready to serve, remove from the refrigerator, bring to room temperature, transfer to a flameproof casserole and proceed with Step 6.

Leg of Lamb Piquant

Baste the roast with a no-fat sherry mixture and serve with our unusual coffee gravy.

Roast at 325° for about 2¼ hours.
Makes 8 servings.

Nutrient Value Per Serving: 263 calories, 40 gm. protein, 10 gm. fat, 98 mg. sodium, 141 mg. cholesterol.

1 leg of lamb (5 pounds), well trimmed
½ cup dry sherry
1 tablespoon lemon juice
1 clove garlic, finely chopped
¼ teaspoon ground ginger
⅛ teaspoon white pepper
½ cup boiling water
1 teaspoon instant coffee

1. Preheat the oven to slow (325°). Wipe the lamb with damp paper toweling. Place on a rack in a roasting pan.

2. Combine the sherry, lemon juice, garlic, ginger and pepper in a small bowl. Brush half of the mixture over the lamb.

3. Roast, uncovered, in a preheated slow oven (325°) for 2¼ hours or until a meat thermometer inserted in the thickest part of the meat, without touching bone or fat, registers 140° for rare or 150° for medium. Baste the roast several times with the remaining sherry mixture.

4. Remove the roast to a heated platter. Pour off any excess fat from the drippings in the roasting pan. Place the pan over medium heat on top of the stove. Add the boiling water, scraping up any browned bits from the bottom of the pan. Add the instant coffee. Strain the gravy into a heated gravy boat.

Buy a Whole Leg of Lamb

When they are on sale, buy a whole leg of lamb and ask the butcher to cut it into 1-inch-thick chops. You will get about 10 tender chops for broiling and shank meat for braising.

Meat and Poultry Refrigerator Storage

Meat and poultry should be stored, wrapped, in the coldest part of the refrigerator. For the best flavor and nutritive value, meat should be used in 2 to 3 days. (Ground meat should be used within 24 hours to prevent spoilage.) Poultry should be used within 1 or 2 days. Information on the recommended maximum length of time meat and poultry should be stored in the refrigerator may be found below.

Fresh, Uncooked Meat	Storage Time
Beef	
roasts	4 days
steaks	3 days
stew meat, liver, kidney	2 days
ground	1 day
Veal	
roasts	3 days
chops, slices, liver, kidney	2 days
ground	1 day
Lamb	
roasts	3 days
chops, shanks, kidney	2 days
ground	1 day
Pork	
fresh roasts, chops, spareribs	3 days
fresh ground	1 day
salt pork	30 days
slab bacon	14 days
sliced bacon	7 days
hams, whole, picnic	7 days
ham steak	4 days
Poultry	
chicken, whole or cut up	2 days
chicken livers	2 days
turkey, whole or cut up	3 days
Cornish game hens	2 days
duck	2 days
goose	2 days

Poultry

Types of Chicken

- **Broiler-Fryers:** These weigh 1½ to 3½ pounds and are about 2 months old. The meat is tender, moist and perfect for broiling, grilling, sautéing, poaching and baking. Sold whole and in parts.
- **A Roaster** is a slightly larger and older chicken. It weighs between 4½ to 6 pounds and is best roasted as its name implies.
- **A Stewing Chicken** is a plump meaty bird, a year or a little older. It weighs around 4½ to 6 pounds. Because it is older, this chicken is tougher than either the roaster or broiler-fryer and is best when stewed.
- **A Capon** is a young male chicken that has been desexed. It is fleshy and tender with a high proportion of white meat. Capons can weigh from 6 to 9 pounds. It can be cooked many ways but is superb roasted.
- **A Rock Cornish Game Hen** is a special breed developed by crossing a Cornish game cock with a white Rock hen. It is marketed at 4 to 6 weeks and weighs 1½ pounds or less. It's popular with white-meat lovers.

Buying Chicken...Quality and Quantity

Look for chicken that has moist skin without any dry spots. Avoid packages where blood or juice has accumulated in the bottom—a sign that the chicken has been out for too long or may have been frozen. Chicken should smell fresh. This can mean no smell at all or a pleasant chicken aroma. If upon opening the package at home you find a slight chicken odor, rinse the chicken under cold water and rub with a lemon half or dip briefly in vinegar-water.

- Chicken for frying: Allow ¾ to 1 pound per serving.
- Chicken for roasting: Allow ¾ to 1 pound per serving.
- Chicken for stewing: Allow ½ to 1 pound per serving.
- Chicken livers: Allow ¼ pound per serving.
- Rock Cornish Game Hen: Allow 1 small game hen per person.
- Turkey: If you think of turkey only at Thanksgiving, think again. Though turkey is a perfect choice to feed a large gathering, the many new varieties of turkey products make tasty, economical and nutritious meals.

Chicken with Wild Rice Dressing

Chicken with Wild Rice Dressing

This easy but elegant dish is especially tasty with the sweet-nutty flavor of the wild rice.

Bake at 375° for 1¼ hours.
Makes 4 servings.

Nutrient Value Per Serving: 682 calories, 54 gm. protein, 34 gm. fat, 1,181 mg. sodium, 163 mg. cholesterol.

- 2 **cans (13¾ ounces each) chicken broth**
- 1 **bay leaf**
- 1 **cup wild rice***
- ½ **cup chopped celery**
- ½ **cup chopped onion (1 medium-size onion)**
- ½ **cup chopped carrot**
- 1 **pound medium-size mushrooms, sliced**
- ¼ **cup (½ stick) butter or margarine**
- ½ **teaspoon salt**
- ¼ **teaspoon pepper**
- ⅛ **to ¼ teaspoon poultry seasoning**
- 1 **broiler-fryer (3 pounds)**

1. Bring the chicken broth to boiling in a medium-size saucepan. Add the bay leaf and wild rice. Lower heat. Cover and simmer for 30 minutes or until the rice has absorbed the broth.
2. Preheat the oven to moderate (375°).
3. Sauté the celery, onion, carrot and mushrooms in the butter in a medium-size skillet over medium heat just until tender, for about 5 minutes. Add the salt, pepper and poultry seasoning. Mix well with the wild rice.
4. Stuff the chicken loosely with the dressing. The extra dressing can be baked in a small baking dish during the last 30 minutes of roasting time. Cover the cavity of the chicken with aluminum foil.

5. Roast in the preheated moderate oven (375°) for 1¼ hours or until the leg moves easily in its joint and the meat is no longer pink near the bone.

To Make Ahead: Prepare the wild rice dressing through Step 3, omitting Step 2. Transfer the dressing mixture to a medium-size bowl, cover and refrigerate until ready to roast the chicken. Proceed with Step 4.

* Note: Wild rice is widely available in supermarkets.

Vegetable-Herb Stuffing

For a calorie-saving stuffing for roast poultry, use a mixture of vegetables and herbs, rather than a bread or rice mixture. Then baste with chicken broth, rather than fat, while cooking.

Broiled Marinated Chicken with Lemon Glaze

This chicken is also tasty when served cold.

Bake at 350° for 1 hour; broil for 6 minutes. Makes 4 servings.

Nutrient Value Per Serving: 547 calories, 45 gm. protein, 36 gm. fat, 408 mg. sodium, 143 mg. cholesterol.

> **Grated rind of 1 large lemon
> (1 tablespoon)**
> **Juice of 1 large lemon (about
> 3 tablespoons)**
> ¼ **cup olive or vegetable oil**
> 1 **teaspoon leaf tarragon, crumbled**
> 1 **teaspoon finely chopped garlic**
> ½ **teaspoon salt**
> ¼ **teaspoon white pepper**
> 1 **broiler-fryer (3 to 3½ pounds)**
> 1 **tablespoon lemon juice**
> 2 **tablespoons honey**

1. Reserve the grated lemon rind and 1 tablespoon of the lemon juice. To make the marinade, combine the remaining lemon juice, the olive oil, tarragon, garlic, salt and pepper in a small bowl; set aside.
2. Place the chicken on a cutting board with the back bone facing up. Remove the back bone by cutting down either side of the bone with a heavy knife, being careful not to cut through the breast. Discard the backbone. Twist the wing tips back of the

second joint so the wings lie flat. To secure the legs, make 1-inch slits in the thigh skin close to the edge and push the ends of the legs through. Gently press on the chicken with open hands to flatten the chicken as much as possible. Place the chicken in a shallow glass or ceramic baking dish just large enough to hold the chicken.

3. Pour the marinade over the chicken, making sure to coat the entire surface. Marinate for 3 to 4 hours at room temperature or overnight, covered, in the refrigerator, basting occasionally with the marinade.
4. When ready to cook, preheat the oven to moderate (350°). Place the chicken on a broiler rack in the broiler pan.
5. Combine the reserved lemon rind, 1 tablespoon of lemon juice and honey in a small bowl; mix well. Set the glaze aside.
6. Roast the chicken in the preheated oven (350°) for 30 minutes, basting every 10 minutes with the marinade. Gently turn the chicken over with 2 wide spatulas, being careful not to tear the skin. Continue roasting until the juices run clear and the meat is no longer pink near the bone, for about 30 minutes, basting every 10 minutes.*
7. Broil 6 inches from the source of heat for 3 minutes, basting once with half the lemon-honey glaze. Turn the chicken over. Broil for 3 minutes longer or until nicely browned, brushing once with the remaining lemon-honey glaze.

To Grill: Grill the chicken over moderately hot coals for 20 to 30 minutes per side or until the juices run clear and the meat is no longer pink near the bone; baste every 10 minutes with the marinade. During the last 10 minutes of cooking, brush each side with the lemon-honey glaze and grill just enough to set the glaze.

* Note: If the chicken browns too quickly in the oven, cover the wing tips or other parts with aluminum foil.

Fat in Chicken

Chicken is lower in fats than most red meats. Three ounces of broiled chicken with skin yield about 9 grams of fat; that amount is doubled or tripled in equal portions of other meats. Chicken skin contains about 17% fat, a small amount compared to the flavor it offers. Interestingly, the fat that is present is two-thirds unsaturated. This is good news, especially for people watching their cholesterol intake.

Orange-Glazed Baked Chicken

To reduce cholesterol intake, remove all visible fat from the chicken.

Bake at 350° for 1 hour.
Makes 8 servings.

Nutrient Value Per Serving: 440 calories, 36 gm. protein, 29 gm. fat, 135 mg. sodium, 145 mg. cholesterol.

- 2 **broiler-fryers (2½ pounds each), cut into quarters**
- 1 **clove garlic, crushed**
- 1 **cup orange juice**
- 1 **tablespoon grated orange rind**
- ½ **teaspoon dry mustard**
- ¼ **teaspoon ground nutmeg**
- 1 **orange, thinly sliced**

1. Preheat the oven to moderate (350°).
2. Wash the chicken; pat dry. Place in a large roasting pan. Rub the chicken skin with the garlic.
3. Combine the orange juice, orange rind, mustard and nutmeg; pour over the chicken.
4. Bake, uncovered, in the preheated moderate oven (350°), basting frequently, until tender and well browned, for about 1 hour. Garnish with the orange slices.

Chicken Livers

Keep a container in the freezer for chicken livers. This way, you can save them up until you have enough for a meal.

Chicken Parmesan with Noodles and Cheese

Serve with garlic bread, Italian-style green beans and almond-macaroon cookies for dessert.

Makes 4 servings.

Nutrient Value Per Serving: 895 calories, 57 gm. protein, 33 gm. fat, 1,054 mg. sodium, 286 mg. cholesterol.

- 1 **package (12 ounces) egg noodles**
- 1 **cup bottled spaghetti sauce**
- ¼ **cup unsifted all-purpose flour**
  Pinch pepper
- 1 **egg, slightly beaten**
- 1 **tablespoon water**
- ½ **cup packaged seasoned bread crumbs**
- ¼ **cup grated Parmesan cheese**
- ½ **teaspoon leaf oregano, crumbled**
- 4 **boneless, skinned chicken breast halves (1¼ pounds), lightly flattened**
- 2 **tablespoons olive or vegetable oil**
- 1 **cup shredded mozzarella cheese (4 ounces)**
- 1 **tablespoon butter or margarine**
- ¼ **cup heavy cream**
  Dash white pepper

1. Cook the noodles following the package directions.
2. Heat the spaghetti sauce in a small saucepan over low heat.
3. Combine the flour and pepper on wax paper. Combine the egg and water in a shallow dish. Combine the bread crumbs, 2 tablespoons of the Parmesan and the oregano on a second piece of wax paper.
4. Turn the chicken in the flour mixture to coat both sides evenly. Dip the chicken in the egg mixture, then the crumbs, turning to coat all sides.
5. Heat the oil in a large skillet over high heat. Sauté the chicken on one side for 3 minutes in the hot oil or until lightly browned. Turn and sauté for 2 minutes longer.
6. Lower the heat to medium. Sprinkle the mozzarella over the chicken. Cover the skillet and cook for 2 minutes or until the cheese is melted and the chicken is firm to the touch.
7. Meanwhile, drain the noodles. Add the butter and cream to the pot used to cook the noodles. Heat over medium heat until the butter is melted and the cream is bubbly. Add the noodles, remaining Parmesan and white pepper; toss to combine.
8. Pour the noodles onto a serving platter; sprinkle with additional Parmesan, if you wish. Arrange the chicken over the noodles and spoon the spaghetti sauce over the chicken.

Chicken Cutlets Tampa

Serve this with dinner rolls, broccoli and chocolate ice cream with vanilla wafers.

Makes 4 servings.

Nutrient Value Per Serving: 646 calories, 45 gm. protein, 22 gm. fat, 589 mg. sodium, 139 mg. cholesterol.

1½ cups couscous*
1½ cups chicken broth
2 tablespoons butter or margarine
1 tablespoon vegetable oil
4 boneless, skinned chicken breast halves (1¼ pounds), flattened slightly
1 bunch green onions, trimmed, green and white parts sliced separately
¾ cup orange juice
½ cup heavy cream
¼ teaspoon salt
1 orange, thinly sliced

1. Cook the couscous using the chicken broth and 1 tablespoon of the butter, following the package directions.
2. Melt the remaining tablespoon of butter and the oil together in a large skillet over medium-high heat. Sauté the chicken, turning once, until golden and firm to the touch, for 5 to 6 minutes. Remove the chicken to a plate. Cover with aluminum foil to keep warm.
3. Add the white part of the green onions, the orange juice, cream and salt to the skillet. Boil over high heat, scraping up any browned bits from the bottom of the pan, for 2 minutes to reduce the sauce. Add the orange slices and remove from the heat.
4. Stir the green part of the green onions into the cooked couscous. Spoon onto a serving platter. Arrange the chicken with an orange slice on the couscous. Spoon the orange sauce over the chicken.

* *Note:* Couscous, sometimes referred to as "Moroccan pasta," is coarsely ground wheat granules; it can be found in the rice and grain section of your supermarket.

Chicken Picante

Once marinated in a taco sauce, mustard and lime juice marinade, this winning recipe can be prepared in minutes. Yogurt and chopped cilantro are the final touch.

Makes 6 servings.

Nutrient Value Per Serving: 255 calories, 36 gm. protein, 7 gm. fat, 548 mg. sodium, 100 mg. cholesterol.

½ cup medium-chunky taco sauce
¼ cup Dijon-style mustard
2 tablespoons fresh lime juice
6 boneless, skinned chicken breast halves (about 1¾ pounds)
2 tablespoons butter or margarine
6 tablespoons plain yogurt
1 lime, peeled and sectioned
Chopped cilantro*

1. Combine the taco sauce, mustard and lime juice in a large bowl. Add the chicken, turning once to coat; marinate for at least 30 minutes.
2. Melt the butter in a large skillet over medium heat until foamy. Remove the chicken from the marinade and place in the skillet. Reserve the marinade. Cook the chicken, turning once, for about 10 minutes or until brown on both sides.
3. Add the marinade and cook until the chicken is firm to the touch and the marinade is slightly reduced and beginning to form a glaze, for about 5 minutes. Remove the chicken to a warm serving platter.
4. Raise the heat to high; boil the marinade for 1 minute. Pour over the chicken. Place 1 tablespoon of the yogurt on each breast half and top each with a lime segment. Sprinkle the cilantro over the chicken.

* *Note:* Cilantro, or Chinese parsley, is a pungent herb used in American Southwestern, Mexican, Middle-Eastern and Oriental cuisines.

MICROWAVE DIRECTIONS
650 Watt Variable Power Microwave Oven
Ingredient Changes: Eliminate the 2 tablespoons of butter.
Directions: Combine the taco sauce, mustard and lime juice in a microwave-safe 10-inch pie plate. Arrange the chicken in the pie plate, placing the meatier parts toward the outside of the plate. Spoon some sauce over the chicken. Cover with plastic wrap and refrigerate for at least 30 minutes. Turn back one side of the plastic wrap to vent. Microwave at full power for 6 minutes. Rearrange the chicken in the pie plate; spoon the sauce over the top. Cover, venting the plastic wrap. Microwave at full power for 4 to 5 minutes or until the chicken is firm to the touch. Let stand for 5 minutes. Remove the wrap. Garnish and serve as above.
Nutrient Value Per Serving: 221 calories, 36 gm. protein, 3 gm. fat, 509 mg. sodium, 90 mg. cholesterol.

Microwaving Chicken

To Microwave: Chicken cooks quickly on the high-power setting and retains its natural juices. In general, a 3-pound whole chicken takes 1 to 1½ hours to roast in a regular oven, but it will cook in less than 30 minutes in a microwave. Here are some tips for cooking chicken in a microwave oven:

• To brown chicken, coat with butter (not margarine) or use soy sauce, paprika, herbs or a commercial browning sauce.

• Do not salt chicken before cooking. Add salt during the standing time.

• Chicken parts cook best on high power, but use medium power for whole birds.

• When cooking parts, place the larger, thicker parts near the outside and the thinner parts toward the center of the baking dish. Place the giblets under the breast.

• When in doubt about whether chicken is done, undercook rather than overcook. It's easy to return the chicken for more cooking. Remember, chicken will continue to cook during the standing time.

• Because chicken cooks so quickly, added flavors are absorbed more fully if chicken is marinated before cooking.

▮▮ Lemon Chicken

Crispy-coated chicken and colorful vegetables combine with a delicate lemon sauce in this delicious Chinese dish.

Makes 4 servings.

Nutrient Value Per Serving: 393 calories, 35 gm. protein, 14 gm. fat, 444 mg. sodium, 82 mg. cholesterol.

     2 *tablespoons sugar*
    1½ *teaspoons cornstarch*
     ½ *cup chicken broth*
     1 *teaspoon soy sauce*
     ¼ *teaspoon grated lemon rind*
     1 *small sweet green pepper, cut into thin strips, 1½ inches long*
     1 *small sweet red pepper, cut into thin strips, 1½ inches long*
     1 *small carrot, pared and cut into thin strips, 1½ inches long*
     3 *cups vegetable oil*
     1 *large green onion, cut into thin strips, 1½ inches long*
     4 *chicken cutlets, pounded to ¼-inch thickness (about 1¼ pounds)*

     ½ *recipe Crispy Batter (see Sweet and Sour Pork recipe, page 89)*
     2 *tablespoons lemon juice*

1. Combine the sugar and cornstarch in a small bowl. Gradually stir in the chicken broth, soy sauce and lemon rind until smooth. Set aside.
2. Stir-fry the peppers and carrot in 1 tablespoon of the oil in a small skillet for 1 minute. Add the green onion; stir-fry for 1 minute longer.
3. Stir the chicken broth mixture; pour into the skillet. Cook over medium heat, stirring constantly, until the mixture thickens and bubbles. Set the sauce aside.
4. Heat the remaining oil in a wok or an electric skillet until the oil reaches 375°.
5. Dip the chicken in the Crispy Batter. Fry 2 pieces of the batter-coated chicken at a time in the hot oil, turning once or twice, until lightly browned, for 3 to 5 minutes. Drain on paper toweling. Keep the chicken warm while frying the remaining pieces.
6. Arrange the chicken on a serving plate. Add the lemon juice to the sauce. Heat gently to serving temperature. Pour over the chicken.

▮ Stir-Fry Chicken with Chinese Noodles

In this lightly spiced Oriental dinner, frozen vegetables eliminate chopping and reduce preparation time. Serve with a spinach, Mandarin orange and red onion salad, and almond cookies with coffee for a leisurely dessert.

Makes 4 servings.

Nutrient Value Per Serving: 589 calories, 46 gm. protein, 12 gm. fat, 1,299 mg. sodium, 149 mg. cholesterol.

     1 *package (10 ounces) Chinese noodles OR: 12 ounces quick-cooking capellini spaghetti*
     2 *tablespoons peanut or vegetable oil*
     4 *boneless, skinned chicken breast halves (1¼ pounds), cut crosswise into ½-inch strips*
     1 *slice pared fresh gingerroot (⅛ inch thick)*
     ⅛ *teaspoon red pepper flakes*
     1 *package (10 ounces) frozen Oriental-style mixed vegetables*
     1 *cup chicken broth*
     4 *green onions, trimmed and both green and white parts cut into 2-inch lengths*
     3 *tablespoons soy sauce*

3 tablespoons dry sherry or dry vermouth
2 tablespoons cornstarch
1 can (8 ounces) water chestnuts, drained

1. Half-fill a large saucepan with water. Bring to boiling over high heat. Add the noodles and cook following the package directions. Drain.

2. Meanwhile, heat the oil in a wok or large skillet over high heat. Stir-fry the chicken with the ginger and red pepper flakes until the chicken turns white all over, for about 3 minutes. Remove with a slotted spoon to a bowl. Discard the ginger.

3. Add the frozen vegetables to the skillet and stir-fry over high heat for 1 minute. Add the chicken broth; cook for 3 minutes. Add the reserved chicken. Lower the heat to medium; cover the wok and cook, stirring once or twice, for 3 minutes. Add the green onions; cook for 1 minute longer or until the vegetables are tender-crisp.

4. Combine the soy sauce, sherry and cornstarch in a small bowl. Add to the wok along with the water chestnuts. Simmer until the mixture thickens and bubbles.

5. Add the reserved noodles; cook for 30 seconds longer tossing gently.

Vegetable Oil

Most main-dish recipes call for a few tablespoons of oil in which to brown the protein source. Any of the versatile "salad" oils will work fine.

Chicken with Broccoli and Fried Walnuts

Makes 4 servings.

Nutrient Value Per Serving: 521 calories, 33 gm. protein, 37 gm. fat, 758 mg. sodium, 66 mg. cholesterol.

1   cup walnut halves or pieces (4 ounces)
½   cup peanut or vegetable oil
2   whole chicken breasts, halved, skinned and boned
2   tablespoons cornstarch
⅛   teaspoon cayenne pepper
2   tablespoons soy sauce
2   tablespoons dry sherry
3   tablespoons water

1   teaspoon sugar
1   clove garlic, finely chopped
1   teaspoon finely chopped gingerroot
2   cups broccoli flowerets (reserve stalks for another use)

1. Drop walnuts into 2 quarts of boiling water; cook for 30 seconds. Drain. Rinse with cold water. Rub the walnuts in paper toweling to dry and rub off the loosened skins.

2. Heat the oil in a wok or large skillet until hot but not smoking. Add the walnuts; sauté, stirring constantly, until golden brown, for about 1 minute. Remove the walnuts with a slotted spoon to paper toweling to drain. Let the oil cool slightly. Pour off all the oil, reserving ¼ cup.

3. Cut the chicken into bite-size pieces. Place in a small bowl. Sprinkle with 1 tablespoon of the cornstarch and the cayenne; toss to coat well. Reserve. Combine the remaining 1 tablespoon of cornstarch, the soy sauce, dry sherry, water and sugar in another small bowl; stir to mix well. Reserve.

4. Heat 2 tablespoons of the reserved oil in the wok. Add the chicken; stir-fry for 2 minutes. Transfer the chicken to a plate. Heat the remaining 2 tablespoons of oil in the wok. Add the garlic and gingerroot; stir-fry for 10 seconds. Add the broccoli; stir-fry for 3 minutes. Stir the soy sauce mixture. Add to the wok; cook for 1 minute or until bubbly. Add the chicken and walnuts; stir-fry for 1 minute. Serve immediately.

Poultry Substitutions

You can substitute slices of raw turkey fillet for the boneless chicken in any recipe for stir-fry chicken.

Chicken Versatility

Chicken is a versatile meat that's compatible with many foods. A little chicken will go a long way when you combine it with economical extenders, like rice, pasta, dried beans and sauce, for a hearty, hot casserole.

Chicken Enchiladas in Cheese Cream

Extra chicken breasts stored in your freezer? Put them to good use in this rich Tex-Mex main dish.

Bake at 400° for 20 minutes.
Makes 12 servings.

Nutrient Value Per Serving: 297 calories, 16 gm. protein, 19 gm. fat, 354 mg. sodium, 73 mg. cholesterol.

 2 **whole boneless, skinned chicken breasts (about 1 pound), halved**
 ½ **cup water**
 2 **cloves garlic, thinly sliced**
 1 **large onion, finely chopped (1 cup)**
 3 **tablespoons butter or margarine**
 1 **clove garlic, finely chopped**
 2 **cans (3½ ounces each) whole green chilies, seeded, rinsed and chopped**
 1 **tablespoon chili powder**
 ½ **teaspoon ground cumin**
 ½ **teaspoon salt**
 ¼ **teaspoon leaf oregano, crumbled**
 ¼ **teaspoon pepper**
 ¼ **cup all-purpose flour**
 1 **cup chicken broth**
 1 **cup heavy cream**
 ½ **pound Monterey Jack cheese, shredded (2 cups)**
 ¼ **to ⅓ cup vegetable oil**
 12 **corn tortillas (6-inch)**
 6 **green onions, trimmed and sliced**

1. Place the chicken breasts in a medium-size saucepan. Add the water and sliced garlic. Cover. Bring to a simmer. Cook just until tender, for about 15 minutes. Cool. Remove the chicken and reserve the broth. Cut the chicken into thin julienne strips. Set aside in a bowl.
2. Sauté the onion in the butter in a medium size skillet just until soft, for about 5 minutes. Add the chopped garlic; sauté for 1 minute. Add the chilies, chili powder, cumin, salt, oregano and pepper; cook for 1 minute. Stir in the flour until well combined; cook for 1 minute, stirring.
3. Stir in the reserved cooking broth, the 1 cup of chicken broth and heavy cream. Cook over medium heat, stirring frequently, until the mixture thickens, for about 10 minutes. Remove from the heat. Stir in 1 cup of the shredded cheese until melted.
4. Combine 1 cup of the cheese sauce with the reserved chicken.
5. Preheat the oven to hot (400°).
6. Heat the vegetable oil in a small skillet until hot. Dip the tortillas, one at a time in the hot oil, just until limp, for about 5 to 10 seconds on each side; do not let them become crisp. Place on a work surface.
7. Divide the chicken filling equally along the center of each tortilla. Top each with the sliced green onions. Roll up the tortillas and place, seam-side down, in 2 rows in a 13 x 9 x 2-inch baking dish. Pour the remaining cheese sauce evenly over the tortillas. Sprinkle with the remaining 1 cup of cheese.
8. Bake in the preheated hot oven (400°) for 20 minutes or until bubbly. Garnish with extra sliced green onions, if you wish.

Storing Cooked Chicken

Cooked chicken can be safely refrigerated for no more than 2 to 3 days in the coldest part of your refrigerator. It can also be frozen, packaged the same way as fresh chicken, but the recommended freezing period is only 2 months.

Hot Chicken Salad

A tasty old-fashioned casserole.

Bake at 350° for 45 minutes.
Makes 10 servings.

Nutrient Value Per Serving: 506 calories, 17 gm. protein, 37 gm. fat, 801 mg. sodium, 62 mg. cholesterol.

 3 **cups cooked bite-size chicken pieces (about ¾ pound)***
 3 **cups thinly sliced celery**
 3 **cups cooked rice**
 1 **medium-size onion, chopped (½ cup)**
 1 **box (10 ounces) frozen peas, thawed**
 1½ **cups mayonnaise or salad dressing**
 3 **tablespoons lemon juice**
 1 **teaspoon salt**
 ¼ **teaspoon pepper**
 ¼ **cup (½ stick) butter or margarine**
 ⅓ **cup all-purpose flour**

3   cups chicken broth
½   cup sliced almonds

1. Preheat the oven to moderate (350°). Grease a 13 x 9 x 2-inch baking pan.
2. Combine the chicken pieces, celery, rice, onion and peas in a large bowl. Stir in the mayonnaise, lemon juice, salt and pepper; mix well.
3. Melt the butter in a medium-size saucepan over medium heat. Stir in the flour. Cook, stirring constantly, for 1 minute or until the mixture is thickened and bubbly. Gradually pour in the chicken broth. Cook, stirring constantly, until the sauce is thick and smooth, for about 2 minutes.
4. Pour the sauce over the chicken mixture; stir to combine thoroughly. Spoon into the prepared pan. Sprinkle with the almonds.
5. Bake in the preheated moderate oven (350°) for 45 minutes or until bubbly hot.

To Make Ahead: Complete Step 2 of the recipe, cover the bowl and refrigerate until ready to bake. About 30 minutes before ready to bake, remove from the refrigerator and allow to come to room temperature. Proceed with the recipe.

* Note: About 2 pounds of whole chicken breasts or a 3-pound broiler-fryer will yield 3 cups of cooked chicken pieces.

MICROWAVE DIRECTIONS (For Cooking Chicken)
650 Watt Variable Power Microwave Oven
Directions: Place 2 pounds of whole breasts, halved, skin-side up, in a 10-inch microwave-safe pie plate, arranging the meatier sides toward the outside of the plate. Sprinkle lightly with salt and pepper. Pour in ¼ cup of dry white wine or water. Cover with wax paper. Microwave at full power for 9 to 11 minutes. Remove the skin and bones. Cut the chicken into bite-size pieces. Use in the Hot Chicken Salad recipe, above.

Creole-Style Chicken Stew

Use a large, shallow saucepan to bring the liquids in this stew to a quick boil. Serve with corn muffins, a green salad and chocolate-fudge cake for dessert.

Makes 4 servings.

Nutrient Value Per Serving: 431 calories, 41 gm. protein, 16 gm. fat, 1,075 mg. sodium, 91 mg. cholesterol.

1   can (13¾ ounces) chicken broth
1   can (14½ ounces) stewed tomatoes
1   bag (16 ounces) frozen vegetables for stew

1   teaspoon leaf thyme
¼   teaspoon liquid red-pepper seasoning
      Pinch pepper
4   sprigs parsley
2   tablespoons vegetable oil
4   boneless, skinned chicken breast halves
      (1¼ pounds), each cut into 6 pieces
5   brown-and-serve sausage links
      (½ package; wrap and freeze remainder
      for another use), each cut in half
2   cloves garlic, pressed
1   tablespoon all-purpose flour
1   package (10 ounces) frozen cut okra
1   tablespoon chopped parsley (optional)

1. Combine the chicken broth, tomatoes, frozen vegetables, thyme, red-pepper seasoning, pepper and parsley in a large saucepan. Bring to boiling over high heat. Lower the heat. Cook, covered, over medium heat for 5 minutes (the mixture should be gently boiling).
2. Meanwhile, heat the oil in a medium-size skillet over high heat. Add the chicken, sausage and garlic and stir-fry until the chicken turns white on all surfaces, about 2 minutes. Remove from the heat. Sprinkle the flour over the chicken, stirring to coat the chicken.
3. When the vegetable mixture has cooked for 5 minutes, add the okra, breaking up gently with a fork. Cover and cook for 3 minutes.
4. Stir the chicken and sausage into the stew. Cover and simmer for 5 minutes or until the vegetables are tender. Garnish with the chopped parsley, if you wish.

How to Defrost Frozen Poultry

It's best to thaw chicken in the refrigerator. Don't unwrap it because the skin tends to dry out and toughen when exposed to air. Allow 12 to 16 hours for thawing whole birds under 4 pounds, 4 to 9 hours for thawing chicken parts. For more rapid thawing, place the chicken, still wrapped, in cold water. Do not refreeze thawed raw chicken. Instead, prepare the chicken, then freeze.

Country Vegetable Soup

This hearty, chunky soup is an excellent way to use frozen vegetables. And for added goodness, stir in any dried pasta and canned beans you have in the cupboard. Serve with grilled cheese sandwiches or Cheddar-topped garlic toast.

Makes 8 servings.

Nutrient Value Per Serving: 292 calories, 24 gm. protein, 3 gm. fat, 730 mg. sodium, 48 mg. cholesterol.

2½ **pounds chicken parts, thawed if frozen,**
        OR: 1 broiler-fryer (2½ pounds), cut into
        eight pieces*
  6 **cups water**
  1 **large onion, chopped (1 cup) (optional)**
  3 **carrots, pared and sliced (optional)**
  3 **celery stalks, sliced (optional)**
  3 **cloves garlic, sliced**
  6 **whole cloves**
  1 **bay leaf**
  1 **teaspoon salt**
 ½ **teaspoon leaf thyme, crumbled**
 ½ **teaspoon leaf basil, crumbled**
 ½ **teaspoon pepper**
  1 **can (2 pounds, 3 ounces) Italian-style plum**
        tomatoes
  1 **cup small elbow macaroni**
  1 **package (10 ounces) frozen sweet corn**
  1 **package (10 ounces) frozen mixed**
        vegetables
  1 **can (16 ounces) red kidney beans, drained**
        and rinsed
  2 **tablespoons butter or margarine, melted**
        (optional)
  3 **tablespoons all-purpose flour (optional)**

1. Combine the chicken parts, water, optional onion, carrots and celery, if using, and garlic in a large kettle or Dutch oven; add the cloves, bay leaf, salt, thyme, basil and pepper. Heat slowly to boiling; lower the heat; simmer for 30 minutes or until the chicken is tender. Remove the chicken parts to a platter. Let cool. Pour the broth through a strainer into a large bowl. Reserve for the soup. Discard the contents in the strainer. (When the chicken is cool enough to handle, remove the meat from the bones; cut into bite-size chunks. Reserve and use for a chicken salad.)
2. Skim any fat from the broth. Add the tomatoes, breaking up with a wooden spoon. Bring to boiling. Add the macaroni; boil for 3 minutes. Add the corn, mixed vegetables and kidney beans. Lower the

heat; simmer for 5 minutes or until the pasta is tender.
3. If you wish a slightly thicker soup, combine the melted butter and flour in a small cup; stir until smooth and well blended. Stir a small amount of the hot soup into the flour mixture; mix well. Add the flour mixture to the soup; blend in well. Cook, stirring constantly, until the soup thickens.

* Note: Substitute 6 cups of chicken broth for the chicken parts and 6 cups of water, if you wish. Add the onion, carrots and celery, if using, and proceed with Step 1.

Chicken Pot Pies

The sage-flavored crusts for these pies are baked separately and can be made into any shape you wish.

Bake crusts at 425° for 10 minutes.
Reheat pies at 375° for 30 minutes.
Makes 4 servings (4 individual pies).

Nutrient Value Per Serving: 964 calories, 48 gm. protein, 56 gm. fat, 1,451 mg. sodium, 225 mg. cholesterol.

  1 **chicken (about 3½ pounds), cut up**
        into 6 to 8 pieces
  2 **cups water**
  1 **medium-size onion, quartered**
  1 **stalk celery with leaves, chopped**
  1 **teaspoon salt**
 ¼ **teaspoon pepper**
  1 **bay leaf**
 ¾ **teaspoon leaf thyme, crumbled**
  4 **carrots, sliced (1 cup)**
  1 **cup frozen pearl onions**
  1 **cup frozen peas**
  2 **cups quartered mushrooms**
        (about 6 ounces)
  2 **teaspoons lemon juice**
 ¼ **cup (½ stick) butter or margarine**
 ¼ **cup unsifted all-purpose flour**
 ¼ **cup chopped parsley**
  1 **teaspoon leaf sage, crumbled**
  1 **package (11 ounces) piecrust mix**
  1 **egg yolk, mixed with 1 tablespoon water**

1. Place the chicken pieces in a large saucepan. Add the water, onion and celery. Bring slowly to boiling. Lower the heat. Skim off the fat. Add the salt, pepper, bay leaf and thyme. Simmer gently for 30 to 40 minutes or until the chicken can be easily removed from the bones. Remove the chicken pieces from the broth with a slotted

HOW TO CUT UP A CHICKEN

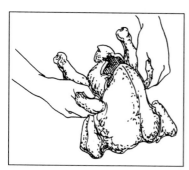

Step 1. Breaking the joints: Using a sharp knife, cut through the skin between the body and thighs; bend the legs away from the body to break the joints.

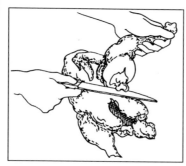

Step 2. Removing the legs: Turn the bird on its side. Remove the leg and thigh from the body by cutting from the tail toward the shoulder between the joints.

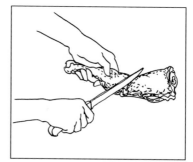

Step 3. Separating the thighs and drumsticks: Locate the knee joint by bending the thigh and drumstick together. Cut through the joints of each leg.

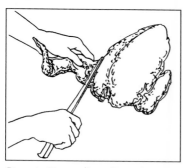

Step 4. Removing the wings: With the chicken on its back, remove the wings by cutting down through the skin at the base of the wing and through the joint.

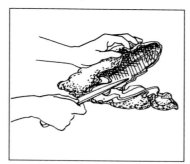

Step 5. Separating the backbone from the carcass: Place the bird on its back; put the knife in the cavity from the tail end. Cut through the rib cage on one side next to the backbone. Repeat on the other side of the backbone.

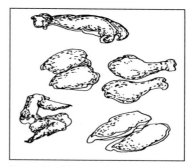

Parts: Backbone (for soups), thighs, drumsticks, wings and breasts are now ready to use in recipes that require chicken parts.

Instructions courtesy of the National Broiler Council.

---

spoon to a bowl. Discard the onion and celery.

2. Add the carrots and pearl onions to the broth. Simmer, covered, for 20 minutes. Add the peas. Remove from the heat.

3. Meanwhile, toss the mushrooms with the lemon juice in a bowl. Sauté the mushrooms in the butter in a medium-size saucepan until they start to turn light golden. Stir in the flour; cook for 1 minute, stirring. Gradually stir in the broth-vegetable mixture. Cook, stirring constantly, until the sauce thickens and bubbles, for 2 minutes. Stir in the parsley; remove from the heat.

4. Remove the chicken from the bones; remove and discard the skin. Cut the meat into bite-size pieces. Return to the bowl. Add the sauce; mix well. Divide equally among four 2-cup baking dishes or casseroles. Cover with aluminum foil; refrigerate for 1 to 2 days.

5. Preheat the oven to hot (425°).

6. To prepare the crust: Add the sage to the piecrust mix. Prepare the crust with the water following the label directions. Divide the dough into quarters. Roll each piece into a circle, 1-inch larger than the top of the baking dishes. Trim to make the circles slightly smaller than the tops.* Place the dough circles on a cookie sheet. Reroll the trimmings. Cut the leaf designs.

7. Brush the pastry rounds with the egg yolk wash. Prick all over with a fork. Arrange ☞

the pastry cutouts on top of each circle. Brush the decorations with the wash.

8. Bake in the preheated hot oven (425°) for 10 to 12 minutes or until golden. Remove to a wire rack to cool. Wrap in aluminum foil and keep in a cool place until ready to use.

9. To assemble and reheat: Remove the baking dishes from the refrigerator and let stand for 15 minutes. Place on a cookie sheet. Reheat, covered with foil, in a preheated moderate oven (375°) for 20 minutes. Remove the foil; stir the mixture. Place the pastry rounds on top of each bowl. Bake for 10 minutes or until bubbly hot.

Note: Dough may be cut in different shapes, such as squares, triangles or crescents.

MICROWAVE DIRECTIONS
650 Watt Variable Power Microwave Oven
Ingredient Changes: Reduce the ¼ cup of butter to 1 tablespoon and the 2 cups of water to 1 cup.
Directions: Arrange the chicken pieces, bony-side up, in a 13x9x2-inch microwave-safe baking dish with the meatiest parts toward the outside of the dish. Add ½ cup of the water, the onion, celery, salt, pepper, bay leaf and thyme. Cover tightly. Microwave at full power for 8 minutes. Rearrange the chicken pieces so the less-done parts are toward the outside of the dish. Add the carrots, pearl onions, peas, 1 tablespoon of butter, the mushrooms, lemon juice and the flour stirred into the remaining ½ cup of water. Cover tightly. Microwave at full power for 8 minutes longer. Remove the chicken pieces to a plate. Stir the sauce until smooth. Fold in the parsley. Remove the chicken from the bones. Assemble the pot pies as directed in Step 4. Just before serving, prepare the crusts as directed in Steps 6 and 7. Add a little browning liquid to the egg wash, if you wish. Place the pastry circles on pieces of wax paper. Microwave, two at a time, at full power for 3 minutes. Place on top of the pot pies. Microwave the 4 pot pies at full power for 5 to 6 minutes or until the chicken mixture is heated through. Microwave 1 pot pie at full power for 3 minutes. Let stand for 5 minutes before serving.
Nutrient Value Per Serving: 889 calories, 48 gm. protein, 47 gm. fat, 1,365 mg. sodium, 202 mg. cholesterol.

Marengo-Style Dishes

These types of dishes were originated by Napoleon's chef after the battle of Marengo in 1800. Originally served with fried eggs and crayfish.

Chilled Chicken Rolls Marengo-Style

Make these chicken rolls the day before. Preslice and arrange them on individual servings of Wild Rice Salad (page 175). This recipe is easily doubled to serve 4.

Bake at 375° for 25 minutes.
Makes 2 servings.

Nutrient Value Per Serving: 488 calories, 56 gm. protein, 23 gm. fat, 915 mg. sodium, 166 mg. cholesterol.

¼ cup packaged unseasoned bread crumbs
1 tablespoon grated Parmesan cheese
   Dash pepper
2 large, boned, skinless chicken breast halves
   (6 ounces each)
2 thin slices cooked ham (about 4x4 inches)
2 thin slices Monterey Jack cheese
   (about 4x4 inches)
1 small tomato, chopped
1 teaspoon chopped fresh basil OR:
   ¼ teaspoon leaf basil, crumbled
1 teaspoon chopped parsley
1½ tablespoons butter or margarine, melted

1. Lightly grease an 8x8x2-inch-square baking pan.
2. Combine the crumbs, Parmesan and a dash of pepper on wax paper. Set aside.
3. Gently pound the chicken breasts, smooth-side down, between 2 pieces of wax paper to a ¼-inch thickness. Remove the top piece of wax paper. Place a slice of ham and cheese on each breast, folding ½ inch smaller than the flattened breasts.
4. Sprinkle half the tomato, the basil, parsley and a dash of pepper over each. Roll up egg-roll style, tucking the ends in as you roll.
5. Brush each roll all over with the melted butter; roll in the crumb mixture to coat completely. Place in the prepared pan, seam-side down. Let stand for 15 minutes to set the crumbs. Meanwhile, preheat the oven to moderate (375°).
6. Bake the rolls in the preheated moderate oven (375°) for 25 minutes or until light golden and slightly firm to the touch. Let cool in the refrigerator. Cover and chill for several hours or overnight.

Chicken Breasts with Curry Chutney Butter

Tips for Cooking in Foil Packets

- Use 12-inch-wide regular-weight aluminum foil, or as otherwise specified in the recipe.
- Measure the size of the foil carefully.
- Arrange the ingredients as directed in each recipe. Fold the upper half of the foil over the ingredients, matching up the edges evenly to enclose the filling. Turn the long double edge of the foil up to create ½-inch double folds. Fold the foil over again. Fold the two shorter sides in the same manner to create two ½-inch double folds.
- Make sure there are no holes in the foil packet and that it is carefully sealed to prevent any steam leakage.
- Double-check the oven temperature with an oven thermometer. Do not use a toaster oven.
- Place the packets in a single layer on a preheated baking sheet.
- Time carefully. The high cooking temperature can cause food to be underdone or overdone in a matter of one minute. Start timing as soon as the packets go into the oven.
- To serve, lift each packet off the sheet with a metal spatula and set on a large dinner plate. Take care not to rip the foil. Cut an X that goes from side to side in the top of the packet. Carefully fold back the edges of the cut foil and serve immediately.

Chicken Breasts with Curry-Chutney Butter

Bake at 500° for 10 minutes.
Makes 4 servings.

Nutrient Value Per Serving: 366 calories, 36 gm. protein, 11 gm. fat, 515 mg. sodium, 98 mg. cholesterol.

- 1 cup very thinly sliced carrot
- 1 cup very thinly sliced zucchini
- 4 teaspoons cold water
- 4 skinned, boned chicken breast halves (5 ounces each)
- ½ teaspoon salt
- ¼ teaspoon pepper
- ½ cup mango chutney
- 2 tablespoons butter or margarine
- 1 tablespoon curry powder
- ¼ cup chopped unsalted peanuts
- 1 tablespoon flaked coconut

1. Preheat the oven to very hot (500°).
2. Tear off four 14 x 12-inch sheets of regular-weight aluminum foil. Lightly butter the center of the lower half of each sheet.
3. Place one-quarter of the carrot and zucchini slices on the buttered portion of each foil sheet. Sprinkle each with 1 teaspoon of the cold water. Set a chicken breast half on the ☞

109

vegetables in each packet; sprinkle with the salt and pepper.

4. Mix the chutney, butter and curry powder in a small bowl. Spoon over the chicken, dividing equally. Sprinkle each with the peanuts and coconut. Seal the packets tightly.

5. Place a large baking sheet in the very hot oven for about 2 minutes.

6. Bake the packets on the hot baking sheet in one layer in the preheated very hot oven (500°) for 10 minutes. Serve immediately.

Herbed Tomato Chicken with Pimiento-Garlic Sauce

Bake at 500° for 10 minutes.
Makes 4 servings.

Nutrient Value Per Serving: 388 calories, 43 gm. protein, 18 gm. fat, 605 mg. sodium, 167 mg. cholesterol.

½ *pound fresh green beans, halved lengthwise, cut into 1½-inch lengths*
4 *teaspoons cold water*
4 *chicken cutlets, lightly pounded (about 1½ pounds)*
1 *can (16 ounces) whole tomatoes, drained and broken up*
¼ *cup chopped onion (1 small onion)*
2 *tablespoons chopped fresh parsley*
1 *tablespoon dry red wine or white wine (optional)*
½ *teaspoon leaf basil, crumbled*
½ *teaspoon leaf thyme, crumbled*
¼ *teaspoon grated orange rind*
¼ *teaspoon salt*
⅛ *teaspoon pepper*
⅛ *teaspoon fennel seed*
Pimiento-Garlic Sauce:
1 *egg yolk*
2 *tablespoons drained pimiento*
2 *cloves garlic, finely chopped*
1 *slice white bread, crumbled*
¼ *cup corn or olive oil*
½ *to 1 teaspoon distilled white vinegar*
¼ *teaspoon salt*
⅛ *teaspoon pepper*
⅛ *teaspoon liquid red-pepper seasoning*

1. Preheat the oven to very hot (500°).
2. Tear off four 14 x 12-inch sheets of regular-weight aluminum foil. Arrange a quarter of the green beans in the center of the lower half of each foil sheet. Sprinkle each vegetable portion with 1 teaspoon of cold

water. Top with the chicken.

3. Combine the tomatoes, onion, parsley, wine, if using, basil, thyme, orange rind, salt, pepper and fennel seed in a medium-size bowl. Spoon the mixture over the chicken. Seal the packets tightly.

4. Place a large baking sheet in the very hot oven for about 2 minutes.

5. Bake the packets on a hot baking sheet in the preheated very hot oven (500°) for 10 minutes.

6. Meanwhile, prepare the Pimiento-Garlic Sauce: Whisk together the egg yolk, pimiento and garlic in a small bowl until blended. Beat in the bread crumbs. Add the oil in a thin stream, whisking constantly, to form a mayonnaise-like sauce. Whisk in the vinegar, salt, pepper and red-pepper seasoning. Serve the sauce on the side with the chicken.

Freezing Chicken

When wrapping chicken for the freezer, be sure the package is airtight to prevent freezer burn. Do not rinse the chicken before freezing. For best results, wrap in freezer bags, wax-coated freezer paper or heavy-duty aluminum foil, separating parts with wax paper to allow easy removal and quicker thawing.
● Storage time for home-frozen, fresh chicken is 4 to 6 months.
● Commercially frozen chicken, wrapped and stored under the most favorable conditions, can be safely stored in the freezer for up to 12 months.
● The best way to thaw chicken to retain flavor and texture is to place the package on a tray or roasting pan in the refrigerator. Separated parts thaw in 7 to 8 hours; allow 12 hours for every 2 pounds of whole chicken. Duckling, large roasters, capons and small turkeys (4 to 12 pounds) will take 1 to 2 days to thaw; turkeys (12 to 20 pounds) will take 2 to 3 days; and a large turkey weighing up to 24 pounds will take 3 to 4 days.

Stuffing Poultry

Don't stuff poultry until you are ready to roast it. The stuffing can be made ahead and refrigerated until you are ready to use it. Always remove the stuffing from the bird immediately after the meal and store it in a separate container in the refrigerator.

Roast Holiday Turkey

Roast at 325° for 4½ to 6 hours.
Makes 12 servings.

Nutrient Value Per Serving: 443 calories, 77 gm. protein, 12 gm. fat, 195 mg. sodium, 203 mg. cholesterol.

> 1 **turkey, 12 to 16 pounds, giblets removed and reserved for Giblet Gravy**
> **Savory Thanksgiving Stuffing (see recipe, page 183)**
> **Melted butter or margarine**
> **Giblet Gravy (recipe follows)**

1. Preheat the oven to slow (325°).
2. Stuff the turkey and neck cavity with the Savory Thanksgiving Stuffing. Sew the cavities closed. Place the turkey, breast-side up, on a rack in a shallow roasting pan. Brush the turkey all over with the melted butter.
3. Roast in the preheated slow oven (325°) for 4½ to 6 hours, depending on the size of the bird, or until the drumstick joint moves easily or the meat thermometer registers 180° to 185° with the bulb in the thickest part of the thigh, not touching the bone. Remove the turkey from the oven. Let stand for at least 20 minutes before carving. Serve with the Giblet Gravy.
4. To store leftovers, remove the stuffing from the turkey; refrigerate separately from the turkey.

Giblet Gravy

Makes about 2½ cups.

Nutrient Value Per Serving: 65 calories, 5 gm. protein, 4 gm. fat, 139 mg. sodium, 74 mg. cholesterol.

> **Turkey giblets**
> 2 **cups water**
> 1 **bay leaf**
> ½ **teaspoon salt**
> ¼ **teaspoon pepper**
> 2 **tablespoons butter or margarine**
> 2 **tablespoons all-purpose flour**
> 1 **cup milk**

1. Combine the turkey giblets, except the liver, the water, bay leaf, salt and pepper in a medium-size saucepan. Bring to boiling. Lower the heat; cover; simmer for 1 hour or until tender. Add the liver; simmer for 15 minutes longer. Drain the mixture, reserving 1 cup of the broth. Discard the bay leaf. Finely chop the giblets and reserve.
2. Melt the butter in a medium-size saucepan; stir in the flour until smooth. Add the reserved 1 cup of turkey broth. Cook over medium heat, stirring constantly, until the mixture thickens and boils. Stir in the milk and the chopped giblets. Gently heat to serving temperature. Season to taste with the salt and pepper.

Types of Turkey

A *Roaster*, the traditional big bird, comes in sizes that range from about 10 pounds to 30 pounds. Big birds look most festive on the groaning board and are the most economical in cost per serving; however, they take longer to roast. If you have a family that goes for drumsticks and wings, you'll double the number by substituting with two smaller turkeys.

A *Fryer-Roaster* is a small, meaty turkey weighing from 4 to 9 pounds. Perfect for smaller families.

A *Boneless Turkey Roast* is a plump roast weighing from 2 to 5 pounds and provides an easy-to-carve combination of white and dark meat. Perfect to slice for sandwiches.

A *Frozen Prestuffed Turkey* can go directly from the freezer to the oven with no thawing. Available in a broad range of sizes.

A *Frozen Self-Basting Turkey* is injected with butter before being frozen and bastes itself as it cooks. Available in a wide range of sizes.

A *Frozen Boneless Turkey Roll* can come raw, fully cooked or smoked, and also as all-dark or all-white meat or as a combination. Sizes range from 3 to 10 pounds.

Frozen Turkey Steaks are turkey minute steaks that come either plain or breaded.

Turkey Parts, drumsticks, wings, thighs and breasts, are marketed just like chicken parts. Legs and wings especially offer good eating at relatively low cost.

Smoked Turkey is a gourmet item, ready to slice and eat.

How Much to Buy
When buying turkeys under 12 pounds, allow ¾ to 1 pound per serving; when buying birds weighing more than 12 pounds, allow ½ to ¾ pound per serving (big birds have proportionately more meat).

Clockwise, from right top: Pumpkin-Nut Muffins (page 48), Autumn Bisque (page 66), Cranberry Bread (page 49), Marinated Vegetables (page 166), Candied Yams (page 172), creamed onions, whole-cranberry sauce, Cranberry-Orange Relish (page 185), Roast Holiday Turkey with Savory Stuffing and Giblet Gravy (page 111) garnished with Acorn Squash Rings and Green Beans (page 167).

HOW TO CARVE A ROAST TURKEY

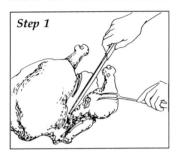

Step 1. Removing the legs: Press the leg away from the body. The joint connecting the leg may snap free; if not, sever it with a knife. Carefully cut the dark meat completely from the body contour with a knife.

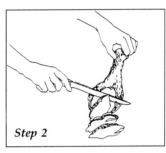

Step 2. Slicing the dark meat: Separate the drumstick from the thigh by cutting through the connecting joint. Tilt the drumstick and cut off even slices.

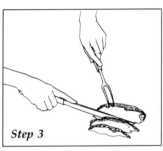

Step 3. Slicing the thigh: Hold the thigh firmly with a fork. Cut off even slices parallel to the bone.

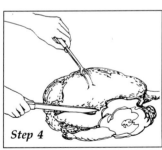

Step 4. Preparing the breast: In preparing the breast for easy slicing, place the knife parallel and as close to the wing as possible. Make a deep cut into the breast, cutting right to the bone to create your base cut. All the breast slices will stop at this vertical cut.

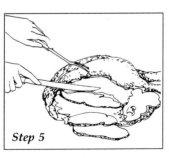

Step 5. Carving the breasts: After the base cut, begin to slice the breast. Carve downward, ending at the base cut. Start each new slice slightly up on the breast. Keep the slices thin and even.

A Turkey Is Cooked

● When a meat thermometer, inserted in the thickest part of the thigh, without touching the bone, reads 185°.
● When the drumstick moves up and down freely. (Grasp, using several thicknesses of paper toweling to protect your fingers.)
● When the thick part of the thigh feels soft when pressed.
● When the juices are yellow or almost colorless. (Pierce the inner thigh with a fork tine.)

Turkey Roll Florentine

This rolled turkey breast, stuffed with a savory spinach stuffing, cuts easily into thin slices for a dramatic presentation. The basting sauce is a combination of apple juice, bourbon and fresh ginger. This dish would work well for any buffet.

Bake at 325° for 2½ hours.
Makes 12 servings.

Nutrient Value Per Serving: 363 calories, 44 gm. protein, 12 gm. fat, 327 mg. sodium, 170 mg. cholesterol.

- 3 eggs, lightly beaten
- 3 packages (10 ounces each) frozen chopped spinach, thawed and well drained
- ¼ cup grated onion
- ¼ cup chopped parsley
- ¼ cup chicken broth
- 1 teaspoon leaf thyme, crumbled
- 1 teaspoon leaf marjoram, crumbled
- ½ teaspoon salt
- ⅛ teaspoon pepper
- 3½ cups soft bread crumbs (7 slices)
- 2 large carrots, pared
- 1 whole turkey breast (about 6 pounds)
- 1 can (6 ounces) frozen apple juice concentrate, thawed
- 1 teaspoon grated, pared fresh gingerroot
- 2 tablespoons bourbon

1. Combine the eggs, spinach, onion, parsley, chicken broth, thyme, marjoram, salt, pepper and bread crumbs in a large bowl. Set aside.
2. Cook the whole carrots in ½ inch of water in a medium-size skillet, covered, until just

tender. Drain. When cool enough to handle, trim the whole carrots lengthwise into decorative shapes, such as triangles or diamonds. Set aside.

3. Place the turkey breast, skin-side down, on the work surface. With a sharp, thin-bladed knife, carefully remove the breastbone and ribs from the meat without piercing the skin. Partially cut through the thickest part of the meat, but not all the way through. Press the breast flat on the surface. Pound lightly to flatten the breast slightly. (This will give you a larger and more uniform amount of breast meat in which to enclose the stuffing.)

4. Preheat the oven to slow (325°).

5. Spoon half of the stuffing down the center of the boned breast. Press the carrots, end to end, down the center of the stuffing, trimming the ends if necessary to make a neat fit. Cover with the remaining stuffing.

6. Wrap the meat around the stuffing to form a roll. Fasten the skin together with wooden picks. Gently pull the skin to cover all the meat. Place the roll, seam-side down, on a rack in a roasting pan.

7. Combine the apple juice concentrate, gingerroot and bourbon in a small bowl. Brush over the roll. Cover the roll loosely with an aluminum foil tent.

8. Bake in the preheated slow oven (325°) for 2½ hours, basting occasionally with the sauce. Remove the foil tent during the last 30 minutes of baking time so the roll browns.

9. Let the roll stand for 10 minutes. Remove the wooden picks. Place the roll, seam-side down, on a serving platter. Cut into slices. Garnish the platter with watercress or parsley and the top of the roll with thin carrot slices, if you wish.

Sicilian-Style Hot Turkey Sausage

Makes 2 pounds (16 patties).

Nutrient Value Per Patty: 92 calories, 10 gm. protein, 5 gm. fat, 180 mg. sodium, 36 mg. cholesterol.

  2 *pounds ground turkey, thawed if frozen*
  1 *teaspoon whole fennel seed*
  1 *teaspoon crushed fennel seed*
  1 *teaspoon crushed red pepper flakes*
  1 *teaspoon salt*
  1 *teaspoon pepper*
  ½ *teaspoon garlic powder OR: 1 clove garlic, finely chopped*
     Vegetable oil for cooking

1. Combine the turkey, whole and crushed fennel seed, red pepper flakes, salt, pepper and garlic in a large bowl. Mix thoroughly with the hands to distribute the spices evenly.

2. Shape the mixture into 16 equal patties. Refrigerate, covered, for up to several hours.

3. To cook the patties: Lightly oil the bottom of a large skillet. Add just enough water to cover the bottom. Add the patties to the skillet, making sure they do not touch. Cook, uncovered, over medium heat, turning once, until browned and cooked through for 10 to 15 minutes.

Garlic Turkey Sausage

A garlicky, low-calorie sausage for breakfast or a light luncheon with breadsticks and a green salad.

Makes 2 pounds (16 patties).

Nutrient Value Per Patty: 91 calories, 10 gm. protein, 5 gm. fat, 180 mg. sodium, 36 mg. cholesterol.

  2 *pounds ground turkey, thawed if frozen*
1½ *teaspoons ground coriander*
  1 *teaspoon salt*
  1 *teaspoon pepper*
  ½ *teaspoon garlic powder OR: 1 clove garlic, finely chopped*

1. Combine the turkey, coriander, salt, pepper and garlic in a large bowl. Mix thoroughly with your hands to distribute the spices evenly.

2. Shape the mixture into 16 equal patties. Refrigerate, covered, for up to several hours.

3. To cook the patties: Lightly oil the bottom of a large skillet. Add just enough water to cover the bottom. Add the patties to the skillet, making sure they do not touch. Cook, uncovered, over medium heat, turning once, until browned and cooked through, for 10 to 15 minutes.

FIVE TURKEY DISHES WITH ONE BIRD

1. Remove the skin from the raw, chilled 12-pound turkey by cutting with a sharp, long boning knife from the center of the cavity to the neck. Pull the skin back gently, loosening with the knife.

2. Cut the breast into long, thin slices at the middle of the breast. Continue until all the breast meat is removed.

3. Remove the thigh and leg section from the carcass by working the knife into the socket at the joining and cutting the meat from the bone; pull the thigh away; repeat.

4. Separate the thigh from the leg at the joint by cutting the meat away; cut into the socket. Trim the meat from the thigh bone; cube to use in a sweet and sour dish.

5. Break up the remaining carcass and place in a large kettle with the remaining bones and skin to make a turkey broth, turkey salad and a turkey tetrazzini.

6. Use a rolling pin or meat pounder to pound turkey slices between layers of wax paper into thin cutlets to use as a substitute for veal in any classic dish.

Sausage Skillet Supper

Makes 4 servings.

Nutrient Value Per Serving: 413 calories, 26 gm. protein, 21 gm. fat, 678 mg. sodium, 76 mg. cholesterol.

- 1 *pound (8 patties) Sicilian-style Hot Turkey Sausage patties (see recipe, page 115)*
- 2 *tablespoons vegetable oil*
- 1½ *pounds sweet green and red peppers, halved, seeded and thickly sliced*
- 2 *large onions, sliced*
- 1 *pound potatoes, pared and cut into ⅛-inch-thick slices*
- ⅓ *cup dry white wine*
- 1 *teaspoon leaf oregano, crumbled*
- ½ *teaspoon salt*
- ¼ *teaspoon pepper*

1. Brown the patties on both sides in 1 tablespoon of the oil in a large skillet over medium heat. Remove from the skillet and reserve.
2. Add the remaining tablespoon of the oil to the skillet. Stir-fry the peppers and onions until softened, for about 5 minutes. Add the potato slices to the skillet, pushing them to the bottom of the skillet with a wooden spoon. Add the sausage patties. Pour in the wine; sprinkle with the oregano, salt and pepper. Bring to boiling. Lower the heat; cover tightly; simmer for 15 minutes or until the potatoes are tender.

Sausage Skillet Supper

MICROWAVE DIRECTIONS
650 Watt Variable Power Microwave Oven

Ingredient Changes: Eliminate the 2 tablespoons of vegetable oil. Decrease the wine from ⅓ cup to 2 tablespoons. Decrease the pepper from ¼ teaspoon to ⅛ teaspoon.

Microwave Directions: Place the sausage patties, evenly spaced, in a microwave-safe baking dish, about 13 x 9 x 2 inches. Microwave at full power for 5 minutes, turning the patties once. Pour off the pan liquid. Add the green and red peppers, onions and potatoes. Pour in the wine; sprinkle with the oregano, salt and pepper. Cover tightly. Microwave at full power for 16 minutes or until the potatoes are tender, stirring well after 5 minutes and 10 minutes. Let stand for 3 minutes before serving.

Fish

These cold-blooded water animals can be divided into two groups: saltwater and freshwater. Saltwater fish include striped or sea bass, cod, haddock, halibut, herring, mackerel, pompano, salmon, shad, sole, sturgeon, swordfish and tuna. Freshwater fish include large- or small-mouth bass, catfish, perch, pike and trout. Fish is low-calorie and contains high-quality protein. It is also a good source of the B vitamins and fluorine, iron and calcium. Saltwater fish also provides iodine.

Buying and Storing: Whenever you buy fish, choose those that are clear-eyed, red-gilled, bright-skinned and sweet-smelling.

The forms of fresh fish available—

Whole Fish: This is, of course, the entire fish, no different from what is was when just pulled from the water. Hence, the most work has to be done with this form before it is cooked. It must be cleaned, dressed, scaled and finned.

Drawn Fish: This form of fish has already been eviscerated, but it still must be scaled and finned before it is cooked.

Pan-dressed Fish: In this form, the fish is completely cleaned and dressed, so all you have to do is cook it.

Fish Fillets: These are sides of fish, skinned and boned, that are ready to cook.

Fish Steaks: Crosscut slices of large fish containing the backbone and vertebrae; ready to cook.

How much to buy? As a general rule, allow 1 pound of whole or drawn fish for 1 serving or ½ pound of pan-dressed fish, fillets or steaks for 1 serving.

For Fresh Fish, Look for

- Firm flesh that springs back when pressed with your fingertip.
- Shiny scales that adhere firmly to the skin (they should not be slimy).
- Reddish-pink gills, free of odor or discoloration.
- Bulging, clean and clear eyes.

To Freeze Fish

Fresh fish is highly perishable. It should be used within one day. Keep it refrigerated. For freezing, wrap fish in moisture-proof paper and store it up to 6 months at 0°F.

Thaw frozen fish in the refrigerator, but remember, it is really better to cook the fish frozen. This takes a little longer, but there is less loss of liquid, which means better flavor and texture. Store-bought frozen fish should be solidly frozen when purchased. If thawed, use immediately. Do not refreeze.

To Cook Fish

Fresh or frozen fish may be cooked in a number of ways. But whichever way you choose, keep in mind that it takes very little time to cook. Most often, people overcook fish. You need only to cook it until the flesh is firm and has lost its translucent appearance.

To test for doneness, insert a fork into the thickest part and gently separate the flesh. It should fall into thick flakes or layers; with whole fish, the flesh should easily be freed from the backbone.

Most fresh or frozen fish can be baked, pan-fried, broiled, grilled, poached or steamed.

Salmon en Papillote

Serve with peas and garnish the plate with greens and sweet yellow pepper rings.

Bake at 500° for 5 to 7 minutes.
Makes 4 servings.

Nutrient Value Per Serving: 524 calories, 27 gm. protein, 43 gm. fat, 547 mg. sodium, 132 mg. cholesterol.

- 1 lime
- 6 tablespoons butter or margarine, softened
- 1 salmon fillet without skin (1 pound), cut into 4 equal portions

½ teaspoon salt
¼ teaspoon pepper
1 teaspoon grated fresh, pared gingerroot
¼ cup chopped shallots OR: ¼ cup chopped
 green onions, white part only
½ cup white port wine
½ cup heavy cream
 Dash cayenne pepper
 Fresh dill sprigs (optional)

1. Remove the outer green rind, with no white pith, from the lime with a vegetable peeler. Cut the rind into ⅛-inch-wide strips. Cook in boiling water for 2 minutes to remove the bitter taste. Drain; rinse under cold water. Reserve.
2. Remove 8 sections from the lime. Squeeze ½ teaspoon of the juice from the remaining lime. Reserve the juice and sections separately.
3. Preheat the oven to very hot (500°).
4. Cut four large heart shapes (15 inches long, 14 inches wide) from heavy-duty foil. Brush one-half of each heart with ½ teaspoon of the butter. Arrange a portion of the salmon on each buttered half of the foil. Combine the salt, pepper, lime rind and ¾ teaspoon of the gingerroot. Sprinkle over each salmon portion, dividing equally. Top each with 2 lime sections. Fold the foil over the fish; fold the edges together; fold over and pleat to form a tight seal. Place on a baking sheet.
5. Bake in the preheated very hot oven (500°) for 5 to 7 minutes or until the packets begin to puff. To test for doneness, carefully open the corner of the packet; the fish should just begin to flake when touched with a fork.
6. Meanwhile, prepare the sauce: Sauté the shallots in 2 tablespoons of the butter in a small saucepan until softened for 3 minutes. Pour in the wine. Cook over medium-high heat until the liquid is reduced by half and is syrupy, for about 8 minutes. Stir in the cream, reserved lime juice, remaining ¼ teaspoon of gingerroot and the cayenne. Keep warm. Whisk in the remaining butter just before serving.
7. To serve, spoon the sauce onto each of 4 plates. Remove the salmon from the packets and place 1 portion in each pool of sauce. Garnish with the dill sprigs, if you wish.

Herb-Baked Scallops

Bake at 350° for 25 minutes.
Makes 6 servings.

Nutrient Value Per Serving: 192 calories, 23 gm. protein, 8 gm. fat, 832 mg. sodium, 74 mg. cholesterol.

2 pounds fresh or thawed frozen sea scallops
½ cup (1 stick) butter or margarine
3 tablespoons chopped fresh parsley
1½ teaspoons leaf basil, crumbled
1 teaspoon salt
¼ teaspoon pepper

1. Preheat the oven to 350°. Wash the scallops in cold water and drain thoroughly between sheets of paper toweling.
2. Place the scallops in a single layer in a large, shallow baking dish; dot with the butter; sprinkle with the parsley, basil, salt and pepper.
3. Bake in the preheated moderate oven (350°) for 5 minutes. Stir the scallops to coat well with the butter mixture. Bake for 20 minutes longer or until tender. Serve the buttery sauce for the dish over mashed potatoes or rice, if you wish.

Flounder Florentine

Put this dish together in less than 15 minutes for a quick dinner.

Bake at 350° for 20 minutes.
Makes 2 servings.

Nutrient Value Per Serving: 351 calories, 44 gm. protein, 17 gm. fat, 629 mg. sodium, 144 mg. cholesterol.

1 package (10 ounces) frozen chopped
 spinach, thawed
½ cup shredded mozzarella cheese
1 tablespoon grated Parmesan cheese
½ teaspoon lemon juice
¼ to ½ teaspoon pepper
⅛ teaspoon salt
⅛ teaspoon leaf oregano, crumbled
2 fresh flounder fillets (about 7 ounces each)
4 teaspoons butter or margarine
2 teaspoons packaged Italian-style bread
 crumbs (optional)

1. Preheat the oven to moderate (350°). Grease a small, shallow baking dish.
2. Stir together the spinach, mozzarella, Parmesan, lemon juice, pepper, salt and ☞

119

oregano in a medium-size bowl.

3. Halve each flounder fillet lengthwise. Spread the filling over each, dividing equally. Roll up jelly-roll fashion; secure each with a wooden pick. Arrange, seam-side down, in the prepared dish. Dot each roll with 1 teaspoon of the butter. Sprinkle with the bread crumbs, if using.

4. Bake, covered, in the preheated oven (350°) for 20 minutes or until the fish in the center of the roll just begins to flake when touched with a fork and the filling is hot. Carefully transfer the rolls with a metal spatula to a serving plate. Discard the wooden picks. Serve with baby carrots and wilted spinach leaves, if you wish.

Broiled Saucy Fish Fillets

Makes 6 to 8 servings.

Nutrient Value Per Serving: 155 calories, 23 gm. protein, 6 gm. fat, 279 mg. sodium, 77 mg. cholesterol.

2   pounds fresh or thawed frozen flounder or sole fillets
2   tablespoons drained prepared horseradish
2   tablespoons Dijon-style mustard
2   tablespoons lemon juice
3   tablespoons grated Parmesan cheese
⅓   cup plain yogurt
2   tablespoons unsalted butter or margarine, melted

1. Preheat the broiler.
2. Arrange the fish in a single layer in a foil-lined broiler pan.
3. Combine the horseradish, mustard, lemon juice, Parmesan cheese and yogurt in a small bowl. Add the butter; stir until smooth. (The mixture should be firm, but spreadable.) Spread the mixture over the fillets in a thin even layer.
4. Broil for about 4 minutes or until the fish is just cooked through and the sauce is bubbly and slightly glazed. (Timing depends on the thickness of the fillets. Do not overcook.)

Don't Overcook Fish

Fish is cooked when it changes from a translucent off-white to a solid opaque-white and when the flesh just begins to separate easily when touched with a fork.

Fish Fillets with Green Onion-Lime Butter

Bake at 500° for 8 minutes.
Makes 4 servings.

Nutrient Value Per Serving: 245 calories, 29 gm. protein, 13 gm. fat, 824 mg. sodium, 116 mg. cholesterol.

4   tablespoons (½ stick) butter or margarine, at room temperature
3   tablespoons finely chopped parsley
¼   teaspoon grated lime rind
2   teaspoons lime juice
1   teaspoon finely chopped, pared fresh gingerroot
¼   teaspoon pepper
¼   pound spinach, stemmed, rinsed
4   fish fillets (6 ounces each), such as flounder, sole, scrod or perch
1   teaspoon salt
1   green onion, green part only, thinly sliced

1. Preheat the oven to very hot (500°).
2. Tear off four 15 x 12-inch sheets of regular-weight aluminum foil.
3. Mash together the butter, parsley, lime rind and juice, gingerroot and pepper with a fork in a small bowl until blended.
4. Place a quarter of the spinach in the center of the lower half of each foil sheet. Sprinkle the fish with the salt. Place 1 fillet on top of the spinach in each packet, folding the narrow ends of the fish under. Dot with the seasoned butter and sprinkle with the onion. Seal the packets tightly.
5. Place a large baking sheet in a very hot oven for about 2 minutes.
6. Bake the packets on the hot baking sheet in the preheated very hot oven (500°) for 8 minutes. Serve hot.

Tuna-Mushroom Batter Bake

A golden brown yeast-batter topping covers a moist filling of tuna, sour cream, black olives and hard-cooked eggs.

Bake at 350° for 45 minutes.
Makes 12 servings.

Nutrient Value Per Serving: 426 calories, 19 gm. protein, 26 gm. fat, 764 mg. sodium, 240 mg. cholesterol.

1   cup long-grain brown rice
1   package (10 ounces) frozen peas

4 ounces (half 8-ounce package) cream
      cheese, at room temperature
3 eggs, at room temperature
1 cup grated Parmesan cheese
1 teaspoon salt
¼ teaspoon pepper
1 pint dairy sour cream, at room temperature
2 cans (4 ounces each) mushroom slices,
      drained
2 tablespoons all-purpose flour
1 teaspoon dried dillweed
2 cans (7 ounces each) solid white tuna,
      drained and flaked
4 hard-cooked eggs, sliced
1 can (7 ounces) pitted black olives,
      quartered
¼ cup (½ stick) butter or margarine, melted
1½ teaspoons active dry yeast
1 teaspoon sugar
2 tablespoons very warm water
1¼ cups all-purpose flour
1 egg yolk
½ teaspoon cold water
2 tablespoons sesame seeds

1. Cook the rice, according to the package
   directions, just until tender, for about 40
   minutes. Stir in the frozen peas. Drain, if
   necessary. Transfer to a bowl. Add the
   cream cheese; stir until melted. Let cool for
   5 minutes.
2. Add 2 of the eggs, one at a time, blending
   well after each addition. Stir in ⅓ cup of the
   grated Parmesan cheese, the salt and pepper. Turn the rice mixture into a buttered
   13 x 9 x 2-inch baking pan, spreading evenly.
3. Combine 1¼ cups of the sour cream,
   mushrooms, the 2 tablespoons of flour and
   the dillweed in a medium-size bowl; blend
   well. Stir in the tuna until well blended.
   Spread over the rice mixture evenly. Top
   with the hard-cooked egg slices and
   quartered olives. Drizzle with 2 tablespoons
   of the melted butter.
4. Sprinkle the yeast and sugar over the very
   warm water in a small bowl. ("Very warm
   water" should feel comfortably warm when
   dropped on the wrist.) Stir to dissolve the
   yeast. Let stand until bubbly, for about
   10 minutes.
5. Combine the remaining egg, sour cream,
   remaining melted butter and yeast mixture
   in a large bowl. Reserve 2 tablespoons of
   the Parmesan. Add the remaining cheese
   and 1 cup of the flour to the bowl. Beat with

an electric mixer on high speed for 3 minutes.
Beat in the remaining ¼ cup of flour until
well blended; the mixture will be sticky.
6. Spoon the batter by tablespoonfuls over the
   mixture in the baking pan. Spread out
   evenly with a spoon dipped in warm water.
   Cover the pan loosely with aluminum foil.
   Let stand in a warm place until the batter
   has doubled in volume, for about 1 hour.
7. When the batter has risen, preheat the oven
   to moderate (350°).
8. Combine the egg yolk and water in a small
   bowl. Brush the egg wash gently over the
   batter. Sprinkle the batter evenly with the
   sesame seeds and the reserved 2 tablespoons of Parmesan.
9. Bake in the preheated moderate oven (350°)
   for 45 minutes or until the top is puffed and
   golden brown. Let stand at room
   temperature for 10 minutes before cutting
   into serving-size squares.

Alaskan Newburg

Salmon, soup and peas star in this inviting cold-weather casserole.

Bake at 350° for 20 minutes.
Makes 4 servings.

*Nutrient Value Per Serving: 404 calories, 20 gm. protein,
9 gm. fat, 995 mg. sodium, 26 mg. cholesterol.*

1 can (10¾ ounces) condensed cream of
      shrimp soup
1 cup milk
½ cup dry vermouth
1 tablespoon Worcestershire sauce
1 can (about 7 ounces) salmon, drained and
      flaked
3 cups cooked rice
1 package (10 ounces) frozen peas, cooked
      and drained

1. Preheat the oven to moderate (350°).
2. Combine the soup, milk, vermouth and the
   Worcestershire sauce in a large saucepan;
   heat slowly, stirring often, until bubbly.
   Fold in the salmon and rice. Spoon into a
   6-cup shallow casserole.
3. Bake in the preheated moderate oven (350°)
   for 20 minutes or until bubbly hot.
4. Spoon the cooked peas around the edge of
   the dish; garnish with twists of lemon, if
   you wish.

Shellfish

Shrimp Creole

Makes 8 to 10 servings.

Nutrient Value Per Serving: 288 calories, 23 gm. protein, 16 gm. fat, 652 mg. sodium, 190 mg. cholesterol.

- 3 pounds sweet green peppers, seeded and chopped
- 1 pound onions, chopped
- 2 celery stalks, thinly sliced
- ½ cup (1 stick) butter or margarine
- ¼ cup olive or vegetable oil
  Flavorful Broth (recipe follows)
- ½ cup tomato purée
- ⅓ cup Worcestershire sauce
- ⅓ cup dry white wine
- 1½ to 2 tablespoons liquid red-pepper seasoning
- 1 teaspoon salt
- 3 pounds large shrimp, shelled and deveined

1. Sauté the peppers, onions and celery in the butter and oil in a large pot until tender, for 10 minutes. Stir in the Flavorful Broth and tomato purée. Bring to boiling. Lower the heat; simmer, uncovered, for 15 minutes.
2. Add the Worcestershire, wine, red-pepper seasoning and salt; simmer for 5 minutes. Add the shrimp; simmer for 10 minutes more. Serve with rice and sprinkle with chopped parsley, if you wish.

To Make Ahead: Chop the green peppers and onions, and slice the celery; place in a large bowl, cover and refrigerate. Shell, devein and place the shrimp in a plastic bag. Tie the bag securely and refrigerate. When ready to serve the shrimp, proceed with the recipe.

Flavorful Broth: Combine 2½ cups of water, 1 tablespoon of vinegar, 2 bay leaves and 2 whole cloves in a saucepan. Bring to boiling. Lower the heat; simmer for 5 minutes. Remove the bay leaves and cloves.

Baked Parsley-Stuffed Lobster

If you can buy ready-cooked lobsters, the preparation is speedy.

Bake at 425° for 15 minutes.
Makes 4 servings.

Nutrient Value Per Serving: 464 calories, 32 gm. protein, 29 gm. fat, 760 mg. sodium, 200 mg. cholesterol.

- 4 small live lobsters (about 1¼ pounds each)
- ½ cup (1 stick) butter or margarine, melted
- 2⅔ cups unsalted soda-cracker crumbs (32 crackers)
- 1 cup chopped fresh parsley
- 2 teaspoons paprika

1. Drop the live lobsters into a very large saucepot of boiling salted water; cover. Lower the heat; simmer for 10 minutes or until the lobsters turn red. Remove at once with tongs; drain; let cool enough to handle.
2. Place each lobster on its back and cut down the middle with scissors, being careful not to cut through the hard shell of the back. Press the lobster open so it will lie flat. (If necessary, crack the shell of the back in a few places.)
3. Lift out the pink coral (roe), if any, and the green tomalley (liver).* Discard the stomach sac or "lady" from the back of the head, the black vein running from head to tail and the spongy gray tissue. Brush the meat with some of the melted butter or margarine. Place the lobsters on cookie sheets. Preheat the oven to 425°.
4. Mix the cracker crumbs, parsley, paprika and salt in a medium-size bowl; drizzle with the remaining melted butter or margarine; toss lightly to mix. Pack into the opened lobsters, dividing evenly.
5. Bake in the preheated hot oven (425°) for 15 minutes or until the meat is hot and the topping is golden. Place on large, individual platters.

* Add the pink coral and tomalley to the cracker mixture or serve separately on Pilot crackers.

Barbecue

Barbecue Methods

The two most popular methods of outdoor grilling are open brazier, or barbecuing, and covered cooking.
● Open brazier, or barbecue cooking, uses an uncovered grill to cook foods requiring quick searing such as burgers, steaks and chops. The food should be no more than 5 inches from the coals.
● Covered cooking, like roasting in the oven, cooks food by heat reflected down from the grill cover as well as by heat from the coals underneath. Roasts, whole poultry, whole fish and vegetables are better, more tender and juicier, when cooked by this method.

Types of Heat

Food may be cooked using direct or indirect heat.
● Direct heat: Hot coals are spread directly under the food to be cooked.
● Indirect heat: Hot coals are spread to either side of the grill, and a drip pan is placed directly under the food. A cover is placed over the grill.

Starting the Fire

● For fast cleanup, line the grill basin with heavy-duty aluminum foil.
● Store the charcoal tightly closed in a cool, dry place. Charcoal is difficult to light if it gets wet or absorbs a lot of moisture from the air.
● To light charcoal quickly and evenly, stack the charcoal in a pyramid in the center of the grill.
● Douse the coals with liquid starter. (Caution: *Never use kerosene or gasoline.*) Wait for 2 minutes for the starter to soak in before igniting.
● Let the coals burn for 20 to 30 minutes or until covered with a light gray ash, before carefully spreading them with a poker over the bottom of the grill.
● Spread the coals with a long fork in a tight, even layer. Food should be completely underlined with hot coals.
● For extended periods of grilling, add new charcoal to the outside edge of the fire so the charcoal touches the burning coals. When covered with a light gray ash, carefully move the charcoal to the center of the fire and add more charcoal to the outside edge as needed.

Temperature of the Fire

To check the fire temperature, carefully place your hand, palm-side down, at cooking height over the coals. Count off the number of seconds you can hold that position before you have to pull your hand away.
● 4 seconds equals medium heat.
● 3 seconds equals medium-high heat.
● 2 seconds equals high heat.
To regulate the fire temperature—
● Adjust the vent holes: Open to increase the temperature; close to decrease the temperature.
● Adjust the grid height: Lower the grid to increase the temperature and raise the grid to decrease the temperature.
● Arrange the coals: Push closer together to increase the temperature; spread apart to decrease the temperature.

More Pointers for a Successful Barbecue

● Be Charcoal Wise: If you barbecue often, save money by purchasing the largest bag of charcoal available.
● Equipment: Make sure you have the right tools—they'll make cooking outdoors easier and safer. Always choose long-handled equipment and protective mitts to shield your hands from heat and grease spatters. Check out the following suggestions for specific items.
● *Metal spatula:* Turning meats with a fork can pierce them, letting juices escape, so use a spatula. (For large pieces of meat, however, a fork gives you a firmer hold.)
● *Tongs:* For hard-to-grip pieces, such as chicken legs, potatoes and corn. The best ones open and close like scissors.
● *Large basting brush:* Use for putting sauces or butters on foods.
● *Skewers:* For kabobs. Best ones are 16-inch-long skewers with large, easy-to-grip handles. Avoid skewers which come in fours, attached at the handle; you can't turn these skewers individually on the grill.
● *Hinged grill basket:* Handy for cooking small items, such as vegetables or foods that crumble when turned, such as fish fillets. Comes in many shapes. *Tip:* To make it easier to remove grilled food from the basket, heat the basket over the coals before putting the food inside and brush lightly with oil.

Added Flavoring

● To give grilled foods a special taste, sprinkle a handful of soaked aromatic wood chips over the glowing coals. You can find chips at home centers, mail-order concerns and gourmet shops.
Hickory: Gives a pronounced smoky taste to all foods. Use sparingly—it's strong!
Apple, cherry and alder: These add a mild fruity flavor.
Mesquite: Derived from a shrub from the Southwest. Has a pungent taste. Use in small quantities for pork, beef and lamb or stronger-flavored fish, such as salmon.

Preparation/Cooking

● Marinate less-tender cuts of meat like chuck, rump and shoulder and round steaks to tenderize them.
● Score the fat around the edges of steaks and chops at 1-inch intervals, cutting just to the edge of the meat, to prevent curling.
● For best results, cook thin steaks close to the coals, about 3 inches, for a higher heat, and thicker steaks further from the coals, about 5 inches, for a medium heat.

Charcoal Fire Safety

● Always use long-handled implements and pot holders.
● Keep a water-filled spray container handy to use in case of fat flare-ups with an open-style grill.
● Never add charcoal starter to the fire after it has been lighted.
● Never use a charcoal grill indoors or in an enclosed area. Avoid open, windy areas.

Cleanup

● Lightly oil the grill to prevent food from sticking and move the food several minutes after placing on the grill.
● To clean the grill once it has cooled down: Use a stiff, narrow wire or special grill brush to scrape the rack and inside of the grill—no water needed!

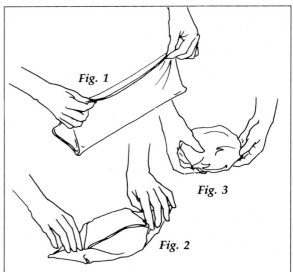

Fig. 1

Fig. 3

Fig. 2

THE DRUGSTORE WRAP

This is a great way to wrap and seal packets of food for the barbecue (or meats for the freezer). It is essential that the seal be tight, so that the juices of the cooking food won't spill over into the fire (and the air won't get into the meat and cause freezer-burn). Start by placing the item to be wrapped in the center of a piece of heavy-duty aluminum foil that is large enough to go around the food and allow for folding at the top and sides. Bring the two long sides up and over the food and fold them over about 1 inch (Fig. 1). Make a crease the entire length; make one more tight fold to bring the wrapping down to the level of the food surface. Press out the air toward the ends (Fig. 2). Fold the ends up and over, pressing out the air and shaping to the contours of the food (Fig. 3).

TO MAKE A GRILL COVER OR DOME FOR A BARBECUE GRILL

When the recipe calls for a covered grill, an open-style grill may be used by constructing your own dome from a wire coat hanger frame, and then covering it with aluminum foil. Snip the hooks off of several hangers and open them out into straight pieces. With pliers, twist together the ends of 2 or 3 hanger pieces to make a ring the size of your grill.

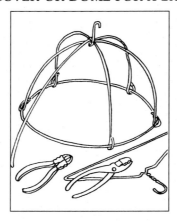

Use 5 or 6 more to fashion a dome. Twist the ends of the hangers forming the dome around the ring base (left). Then cover the dome with several sheets of overlapping aluminum foil, gathering the foil at the top of the dome and twisting it together to form a topknot for a handle. Cut several flaps for vents near the top (right).

124

Top left: Mediterranean Onion Relish (tops the burger, also) (page 184), Polynesian Spareribs (below).

Polynesian Spareribs

Cook these luscious, gooey spareribs over charcoal or in the oven. We also give you two different methods for precooking.

Bake at 300° for 1 hour, or grill for 45 minutes to 1 hour.
Makes 6 servings.

Nutrient Value Per Serving: 716 calories, 48 gm. protein, 49 gm. fat, 816 mg. sodium, 196 mg. cholesterol.

5   to 6 pounds pork spareribs, cut into 2-rib sections
Polynesian Sauce:
2   teaspoons cornstarch
1   can (6 ounces) frozen pineapple juice concentrate, thawed
½   cup apricot nectar
3   tablespoons soy sauce
1   tablespoon distilled white or cider vinegar

1. Precook the ribs using one of the following methods: (a) Place the ribs in a Dutch oven or large pot. Cover with cold water. Bring to boiling. Lower the heat and simmer, partially covered, for 45 minutes. Drain. Or (b), place the ribs in a large, shallow baking pan, curved-side up. Add 2 cups of water. Bake in the preheated very hot oven (450°) for 30 minutes. Drain.
2. Meanwhile, prepare the Polynesian Sauce: Place the cornstarch in a small saucepan.

Gradually stir in the juice concentrate until smooth. Stir in the apricot nectar, soy sauce and vinegar. Cook over medium heat, stirring constantly, until thickened and bubbly. Remove from the heat.
3. To Bake Ribs: Preheat the oven to slow (300°). Place the precooked ribs in a large, shallow baking pan. Brush with the sauce. Bake in the preheated slow oven (300°), for about 1 hour or until the meat is very tender, basting occasionally with the sauce. Or, grill for 45 minutes to 1 hour or until the meat is very tender, turning the ribs often and brushing with the sauce.
Note: For the photograph, we precooked an uncut rack of spareribs in the oven, then finished baking the rack in the oven, brushing often with the sauce.

Ribs Tip

Home-cooked ribs taste best if precooked, either by oven roasting or parboiling, before saucing and baking.

Know Your Ribs

Baby backs, cut from a porker's back, include the rib bone and meat from the eye of a loin. They are generally meatier but more expensive.

Spareribs are the larger variety and include the breast bone, rib bones and rib cartilage.

> ### Buying Ribs
>
> Pork ribs shrink slightly in cooking, so plan on ¾ to 1 pound per serving.

Tulsa Ribs

Remember to replenish the coals in the charcoal grill when barbecuing over a long period of time.

Grill for 1½ hours to 2 hours.
Makes 6 to 8 servings.

Nutrient Value Per Serving: 622 calories, 21 gm. protein, 52 gm. fat, 482 mg. sodium, 97 mg. cholesterol.

- 6 **pounds meaty beef ribs, cut into 4- to 5-inch-long pieces**
- **Barbecue Sauce:**
- 2 **tablespoons unsalted butter or margarine**
- 1 **cup chopped onion (1 large onion)**
- 1 **clove garlic, finely chopped**
- 1 **can (16 ounces) tomato sauce**
- 1 **cup cider vinegar**
- 1 **cup tomato-vegetable juice**
- ½ **cup prune juice**
- 1 **generous tablespoon slivered lemon peel (½ lemon)**
- 3 **tablespoons lemon juice (1 large lemon)**
- 1 **bay leaf**

- 6 **crushed juniper berries (optional)**
- ½ **teaspoon cayenne pepper**
- 2 **tablespoons brown sugar OR: honey**

1. Prepare the charcoal for grilling or preheat the gas unit.
2. To precook the ribs, divide the ribs up and wrap in 3 heavy-duty aluminum foil packets. Place on the grid. Cover with the dome.* Cook over high heat for 1 hour. (If cooking over coals, replenish with new charcoal as needed.)
3. Meanwhile, prepare the Barbecue Sauce: Melt the butter in a large saucepan over medium heat. Stir in the onion; cook for 2 minutes. Add the garlic; cook for 1 minute longer. Add the tomato sauce, vinegar, tomato-vegetable juice, prune juice, lemon peel, lemon juice, bay leaf, juniper berries, if using, cayenne and brown sugar. Bring to boiling. Lower the heat and simmer until the sauce has thickened, for about 30 minutes.
4. Remove the rib packets from the grid. Carefully open and place the ribs back on the grid. Place the hood on the grill. Cook until tender, for 30 minutes to 1 hour, basting with the barbecue sauce and turning, if necessary. Pass the extra barbecue sauce.

* Note: To make a barbecue cover or dome, see page 124.

> ### KETTLE-ROASTING
>
> This technique can be used to cook large cuts of meat, such as pork shoulder or beef eye roast or leg of lamb, or turkey, large chickens or ducklings. Try also to cook or heat casseroles by this method.
>
> **To Grill Meat:** Arrange gray coals around a drip pan. (See drawing.) Cover the kettle and arrange the vents, following the manufacturer's directions; follow the individual recipe directions for cooking times.
>
> **To Cook Casseroles:** Arrange gray coals in a ring around the edge of the barbecue; place the casserole inside the ring on the grill. Cover the kettle and arrange the vents, following the manufactuer's directions, and follow the individual recipes for cooking times.

Buttermilk-Soused Rosemary-Scented Lamb

This succulent lamb is first grilled over a drip pan in a covered grill. The pan is then removed, the coals rearranged and the lamb browned directly over the coals. Be sure to protect your hands with heavy barbecue mitts and tongs when removing the grid and the drip pan.

Grill for 43 to 48 minutes.
Makes 6 servings (with enough leftovers for another meal).

Nutrient Value Per Serving: 396 calories, 60 gm. protein, 15 gm. fat, 186 mg. sodium, 204 mg. cholesterol.

- 1 **leg of lamb (5 to 6 pounds), trimmed, boned and butterflied***
- 2 **cloves garlic, crushed**
- 2 **or 3 sprigs of fresh rosemary OR: 2 teaspoons leaf rosemary, crumbled, for marinade and 1 teaspoon for fire**
- 1 **quart buttermilk**
- ¼ **teaspoon freshly ground pepper**
  Salt

1. Pat the lamb dry with paper toweling. Place in a shallow, 4-quart ceramic or glass dish. Add the garlic and rosemary sprigs or leaf rosemary. Pour the buttermilk over the lamb. Sprinkle with the pepper. Cover and refrigerate overnight.
2. Prepare the charcoal for grilling with a drip pan in the center under the grid, or preheat the gas unit with a drip pan. Remove the garlic and fresh rosemary, if using, from the marinade and reserve.
3. If using charcoal, place fresh charcoal around the outside edge of the hot coals. Place the lamb on the grid. Cover the grill with the dome. Cook over medium-high heat with the vents about three-quarters open, if using a grill with vents, for 15 minutes. Then baste with some of the remaining buttermilk marinade. Cook, covered, for 10 minutes longer.
4. Turn the lamb over and baste. (If cooking over coals, rearrange the newer coals from the outside so they are evenly distributed.) Cook, covered, until the lamb is almost done, for 10 to 15 minutes longer if you want the lamb to be medium-rare.
5. Remove the dome and the grid with the lamb on it. Remove the drip pan and carefully push the coals to the center. Place the reserved garlic and reserved fresh or 1 teaspoon of the leaf rosemary directly on the coals.
6. Return the grid and the lamb to the grill. Continue to cook, uncovered, over high heat, until lightly browned on all sides, for about 4 minutes per side for medium-rare, or longer for desired doneness. (A meat thermometer inserted in the thickest part of the meat should register 145° for medium-rare.) Sprinkle with the salt to taste.

* Note: Ask your butcher to trim, bone and butterfly the leg of lamb. Or, to do it yourself, trim all but a thin layer of fat from the lamb. Place the lamb, fat-side down, on a cutting board. Cut through the meat alongside the bones. Scrape the meat from around the bones; remove the bones. Cut thicker sections of meat almost in half and open the leg, like a book, into one flat piece; meat should be an even thickness.

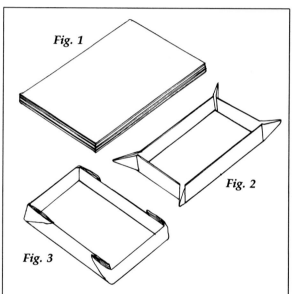

Fig. 1

Fig. 2

Fig. 3

HOW TO MAKE A DRIP PAN

Fat flare-ups will be a problem of the past when you place a custom-size drip pan under the meat you are kettle-grilling or -roasting on the rotisserie. Tear off three 24-inch pieces of 18-inch-wide heavy-duty aluminum foil. Fold in half to make a double thickness (Fig. 1). Turn up the edges 2 inches on each side and press edges firmly together to form mitered corners (Fig 2). Press mitered corners inward, toward pan sides, to make a firm pan (Fig. 3). *Note:* This will give you an 8 x 14-inch drip pan. If this is not the right size for your needs, begin with the size pan you will need and then add 4 inches to both the length and the width and then double the measurement of the width.

This Alaska seafood combo of Grilled King
Crab Legs, Grilled Alaska Salmon and
Wine-Marinated Halibut (all on page 130) is
a whopper of a catch any day.

Wine-Marinated Halibut

Firm fish, such as halibut, is excellent for grilling whole or as kabobs.

Grill for 16 minutes.
Makes 6 servings.

Nutrient Value Per Serving: 255 calories, 36 gm. protein, 11 gm. fat, 461 mg. sodium, 85 mg. cholesterol.

 6 **halibut steaks, cut about 1 inch thick**
 ½ **cup dry white wine**
 ¼ **cup olive or vegetable oil**
 1 **tablespoon white wine vinegar**
 1 **tablespoon lime juice**
 1 **tablespoon minced green onion**
 1 **tablespoon minced parsley**
 1 **clove garlic, crushed**
 ½ **teaspoon salt**
 ½ **teaspoon leaf oregano, crumbled**
 ⅛ **teaspoon freshly ground pepper**

1. Place the halibut steaks in a single layer in a large, shallow glass dish.
2. Combine the wine, oil, vinegar, lime juice, green onion, parsley, garlic, salt, oregano and pepper in a small bowl. Pour over the halibut; cover with plastic wrap; refrigerate for several hours or overnight. Drain and reserve the marinade.
3. Build a medium-hot fire, or set an electric or a gas grill to medium-hot following the manufacturer's directions.
4. Grill, 3 inches from the heat, basting often, for 8 minutes per side or until the fish flakes easily when tested with a fork.

Note: You may substitute another firm fish, such as red snapper or cod, for the halibut in this recipe.

Suggested Variation: Halibut Kabobs—Makes 6 servings. Cut the halibut into chunks; discard the skin and bones. Proceed with the recipe above. Just before grilling, thread the halibut on six long metal skewers, alternating with cherry tomatoes, green pepper squares and fresh mushrooms. Grill over medium-hot coals for 8 to 10 minutes, turning once and basting frequently with the marinade.

Grill Fish by the Thickness

For perfectly cooked salmon or any other firm fish, grill 10 minutes per inch of thickness measured at its thickest part.

Grilled King Crab Legs

Excellent eaten alone or in combination with salmon and halibut.

Grill for 8 minutes.
Makes 6 servings.

Nutrient Value Per Serving: 345 calories, 26 gm. protein, 26 gm. fat, 553 mg. sodium, 213 mg. cholesterol.

 ¾ **cup (1¼ sticks) butter or margarine, melted**
 1 **clove garlic, crushed**
 4 **teaspoons lemon juice**
2½ **pounds Alaskan King Crab split legs, thawed if necessary**

1. Build a hot fire, or set an electric or a gas grill to high, following the manufacturer's directions.
2. Combine the melted butter or margarine, garlic and lemon juice in a small bowl.
3. Grill the crab, shell-side down, 5 inches from the heat, 8 minutes or until thoroughly cooked, brushing occasionally with the mixture.
4. Shell the crab; cut the meat into bite-size pieces; dip into the remaining butter.

Grilled Alaska Salmon

Here's an easy and flavorful way to prepare salmon.

Grill for 10 minutes.
Makes 6 servings.

Nutrient Value Per Serving: 535 calories, 45 gm. protein, 38 gm. fat, 269 mg. sodium, 108 mg. cholesterol.

 6 **salmon steaks (about 7 ounces each), cut 1 inch thick**
    Salt and pepper
 6 **tablespoons butter or margarine, melted**
 ¼ **cup lemon juice**
 1 **tablespoon grated onion**
 1 **teaspoon grated lemon rind**
 ½ **teaspoon liquid red-pepper seasoning**
    Fresh dill sprigs (optional)
    Lemon wedges (optional)

1. Build a hot fire, or set an electric or a gas grill to high, following the manufacturer's directions.
2. Rinse the salmon steaks and pat dry with paper toweling. Season lightly with the salt and pepper. Place the steaks on a sheet of

greased heavy-duty aluminum foil on the grill rack.

3. Combine the melted butter or margarine, lemon juice, onion, lemon rind and red pepper sauce in a small bowl; brush the steaks with some of the butter mixture.

4. Grill, 4 inches from the heat, for 5 minutes on each side or until the fish flakes easily when tested with a fork, basting often. Garnish with the fresh dill and the lemon wedges, if you wish.

Silo Chicken

Grill for 40 minutes.
Makes 6 servings.

Nutrient Value Per Serving: 590 calories, 49 gm. protein, 25 gm. fat, 1,060 mg. sodium, 154 mg. cholesterol.

3 **small chickens or large Cornish game hens (1½ to 2 pounds each)**
½ **lemon**
1½ **teaspoons coarse salt**
1 **teaspoon finely chopped fresh sage OR: ⅓ teaspoon leaf sage, crumbled**
½ **teaspoon snipped fresh chives**
¼ **teaspoon mild paprika OR: ¼ teaspoon mild ground chilies**
⅛ **teaspoon cayenne pepper**
1 **jar (12 ounces) apricot preserves**
½ **cup chicken broth**
1 **tablespoon soy sauce**
1 **tablespoon Dijon-style mustard**
½ **teaspoon chopped fresh thyme OR: ⅛ teaspoon leaf thyme**
1 **teaspoon grated lemon rind**
½ **teaspoon black pepper**
 Vegetable oil

1. Remove the back bones from the chickens or hens. Cut each chicken in half through the breast. Wipe the chicken with damp paper toweling. Pound gently with the flat side of the cleaver or the bottom of a heavy saucepan to flatten the chicken as much as possible.

2. Squeeze the lemon over the chicken. Sprinkle with the salt, sage, chives, paprika and cayenne. Wrap the chicken in wax paper and place in a 13 x 9 x 2-inch baking pan. Refrigerate overnight.

3. Let the chicken stand at room temperature for 1 hour before grilling.

4. Combine the apricot preserves, chicken broth, soy sauce, mustard, thyme, lemon rind and pepper in a saucepan. Bring to boiling. Lower the heat and simmer for 5 minutes. Let cool.

5. Prepare the charcoal for grilling, or preheat the gas unit.

6. Place the chicken halves, skin-side down, on the grid. Sear over high heat until browned, for 2 to 3 minutes. Turn the chicken over and brown the other side. Remove the chicken from the grid.

7. Cover the grid with heavy-duty aluminum foil; punch ventilation holes every 2 inches. Brush the foil lightly with the oil.

8. Return the chicken to the foil, skin-side up. Baste well with the apricot mixture. Cover the grill with the dome*. Cook, basting about every 5 minutes with the apricot mixture, until the juices run clear when the chicken is pierced with a fork and the meat is no longer pink near the bone, for about 40 minutes.

* *Note:* To make a barbecue cover or dome, see page 124.

How to Grill Turkey

● Marinades help tenderize, lubricate and flavor turkey cuts; allow meat to marinate for at least 4 hours or overnight, covered and refrigerated. See page 135 for recipes.
●Baste sparingly while grilling. Dripping sauce may cause coals to burst into flames and dry the cuts.
● Never flip turkey cuts with a fork; it pierces the meat, allowing valuable juices to escape.
● Serve immediately after cooking. If held too long in a warming oven, turkey tends to dry and toughen.

Be careful not to overcook turkey cuts. Lower temperatures and frequent basting seal in juices and flavor. Fresh white-meat cuts and ground turkey meat are cooked and safe for consumption when the internal cooking temperature has reached 165°, and dark meat when the internal temperature has reached 175°. Cook fresh turkey tenderloins, ground turkey and drumstick steaks until the meat springs back when touched and the inside is no longer pink.

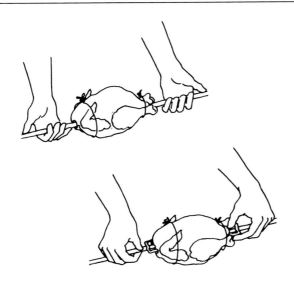

TO TRUSS POULTRY

Secure the neck skin with a metal skewer; push the tail into the cavity and secure with a metal skewer. Press the wings against the side of the breast and wrap a long piece of cotton twine twice around the bird and tie securely; loop a second long piece of twine several times around the drumsticks and tie. If the poultry is stuffed, be sure to secure the opening with small metal skewers and lace it closed with twine.

POINTS ON ROTISSERIE COOKING

Roasts, chickens, turkeys and Rock Cornish hens are more moist and flavorful when cooked over the coals, turning slowly on a rotisserie. In Fig. 1 you see how the roast or poultry should balance evenly on the rotisserie rod for even cooking. Fig. 2 shows how the holding forks should be inserted securely to prevent the meat from slipping while roasting. Fig. 3 illustrates how the gray coals should be piled to the back of the grill with the drip pan directly under the grilling poultry to prevent flare-ups that give a burnt, rather than a charcoal, taste to foods.

Turkey Cuts At-A-Glance

Cut	Grilling Conditions	Suggested Preparations	Complementary Seasonings
Breast Roll	medium-hot coals, 6"-8" from heat, covered, about 35 minutes per pound	Glaze roasts, marinate or rub meat with spices before grilling, or cut into cubes for kabobs.	Thyme, basil, mustard, marjoram, garlic salt, rosemary, dill, ginger, Worcestershire sauce, tarragon, sage, horseradish, poultry seasoning.
Breast Tenderloin	hot coals, 6" from heat, 10 minutes per side	Marinate, cut pockets in side and fill with cheese or favorite dressing, wrap with bacon before grilling, or cut into cubes or slices for kabobs.	Basil, mustard, marjoram, garlic, rosemary, dill, ginger, Worcestershire sauce, horseradish, poultry seasoning, chili powder, lemon juice, red pepper flakes.
Ground Turkey	burger (½" thick), hot coals, 4 minutes per side	Top with cheese or place layers of cheese in middle of patty, or combine seasonings with meat before shaping into patty.	Thyme, basil, mustard, marjoram, parsley, pimiento, garlic, nutmeg, dill, summer savory, red pepper flakes, liquid red-pepper seasoning, chili powder, ginger, oregano, tarragon, sage, curry, poultry seasoning, lemon juice.
Drumstick Steaks	hot coals, 6" from heat, 6 minutes per side	Slice or cut into cubes and skewer onto kabobs and brush with glaze.	Thyme, basil, marjoram, garlic, dill, mustard, parsley, summer savory, red pepper flakes, liquid red-pepper seasoning, chili powder, ginger, oregano, Worcestershire sauce, tarragon, sage, horseradish sauce, poultry seasoning, cranberry relish.

Times & Temperatures for Rotisserie-Cooking Beef Roasts on Charcoal Grills

Important! The grilling times below may differ according to the amount of coals used, weather conditions, type of grill. We recommend these times be used only as a guide. For best results, use a meat thermometer and remove the roast when the thermometer reaches 10° below desired doneness.

Cut of Meat	Rare 130°F.	Medium 145°F.	Well-Done 160°F.
Beef Rib, 6½ pounds	1½ - 1¾ hrs.	2 - 2½ hrs.	1½ - 1¾ hrs.
Rib Eye Roast, 6 pounds	1½ - 1¾ hrs.	2 - 2½ hrs.	3 - 3½ hrs.
Tenderlion Roast, 4 pounds	45 minutes	1 hour	1¼ - 1½ hrs.
Beef Round Tip Roast, 6 pounds	1½ - 1¾ hrs.	2 - 2½ hrs.	2¾ - 3½ hrs.
Eye Round Roast, 6 pounds	1½ - 1¾ hrs.	2 hours	2½ hours
Cross Rib Pot Roast (boneless) or **Rump Roast,** 6 pounds	1¾ - 2¼ hrs.	2½ - 3 hrs.	3¼ - 3¾ hrs.

Grilling the Perfect Steak

Meat	Thickness	Doneness	Fire	Distance	Time
Beef	1 inch	rare	medium-hot	4 inches	5 minutes
		medium	medium-hot		7 minutes
		well-done	medium-hot		10 minutes
Beef	2 inches	rare	medium	5 inches	15 minutes
		medium	medium		20 minutes
		well-done	medium		25 minutes
Ham	1 inch	medium	medium	5 inches	8 minutes
Lamb	¾ inch	rare	medium-hot	6 inches	5 minutes
		medium	medium-hot		7 minutes
		well-done	medium-hot		9 minutes
Pork*	1 inch	well-done	medium	5 inches	14 minutes

* All fresh pork must be grilled to well-done. Allow steaks to come to room temperature before grilling.

Barbecued Vegetables

Vegetables should be grilled 6 inches above coals that have been allowed to burn until they are covered with white ash (about 30-45 minutes); if using a gas grill, preheat on medium setting. Cooking times for grilling will vary depending on the size and type of vegetable. Eggplant, for instance, will cook in 30 minutes; root vegetables, like carrots and potatoes, need at least 45 minutes. Cooked directly on the grill, sliced vegetables or vegetable kabobs will take approximately 15 minutes. Vegetables wrapped in foil are thoroughly cooked when they yield to gentle pressure. Vegetable slices and kabobs are done when easily pierced with a fork.

Foil Grilling

First, rinse the vegetables thoroughly and *do not* dry. The water that clings will help steam-cook them in their packets. Place no more than four servings of vegetables on a single sheet of heavy-duty aluminum foil. When combining vegetables either in foil packets or on kabobs, cut them into similar sizes for even cooking. Corn on the cob should be wrapped separately. Dot vegetables evenly with butter or margarine, or sprinkle with vegetable or olive oil or Italian dressing before sealing the foil. Most vegetables are done when just fork-tender.

Direct Grilling

Grilling vegetables directly imparts that wonderful barbecue flavor, though it is a bit trickier than foil-roasting. Zucchini, summer squash, eggplant and onion should be sliced 1 inch thick and brushed with basting sauce, melted butter or margarine or oil. Vegetables prepared for kabobs should be cut into equal sizes so that they cook evenly. Lightly grease the grill and turn the vegetables occasionally to prevent sticking.

Coal Roasting

Hearty vegetables like potatoes, carrots and onions may be wrapped whole in foil and cooked in the coals...great for campfire cooking. Place the foil-wrapped vegetables on the edge of the fire or place directly into a low, low flame.

The cooking time varies greatly, depending on the intensity of the heat.

133

Vegetable Grilling

Vegetable	Serving Size (about 4 oz.)	Preparation Tips	Grilling Time	Suggested Seasonings
Asparagus	4-6 medium-size spears.	Snap off and discard tough ends, remove scales with vegetable scraper, plunge in cold water and drain.	15-20 minutes or until just tender.	Butter or margarine, tarragon, lemon, dill.
Beans (Green, Italian, Wax)	10-15 green or wax, about 8-12 Italian.	Rinse, snap off and discard ends. Leave whole or cut in half.	15-20 minutes or until fork-tender.	Butter or margarine, chives, fresh dill, lemon, Italian dressing; add a little to the foil packet before grilling.
Broccoli	About 2 stalks, ½ cup flowerets.	Rinse, cut and discard base; leave whole and slash through bottom inch of stalks or slice stalk and cut into flowerets.	20-25 minutes or until fork-tender.	Butter or margarine, lemon, dill, fresh ginger, curry.
Carrots	2-5, depending on size.	Trim tops and root ends and scrub with a vegetable peeler.	20-25 minutes or until fork-tender.	Butter or margarine, mustard, horseradish mixed with mayonnaise, fresh mint and nutmeg.
Cauliflower	½ cup flowerets.	Trim away green leaves, core and cut or break into flowerets.	20-25 minutes or until fork-tender.	Butter or margarine, tarragon, lemon juice, soy, dill.
Corn on the Cob	1 ear.	Remove the husk and silk, wrap in aluminum foil; or peel back husk, remove silk, and replace husk to cover cob. Do not wrap in foil.	15-20 minutes until just tender.	Butter or margarine and bacon.
Eggplant	¼ large or ½ medium.	Slice into ½-inch slices or 1-inch cubes.	15-20 minutes per side or until brown; or use on kabobs.	Italian dressing or olive oil with oregano, parsley, garlic.
Mushrooms	5-7, depending on size.	Wipe with damp towel or mushroom brush, trim stem end, leave whole.	10-15 minutes.	Italian dressing, olive oil with oregano, lemon, butter, dill.
Onions (Dry)	¼-½ medium or 1 small, depending on strength.	Peel away dry skin and slice; or chop and use with other vegetables; or leave skin on and use directly on grill.	20-25 minutes, sliced; cubed for kabobs; 45-50 minutes, whole unskinned.	Butter or margarine, Italian dressing, or olive oil with oregano, lemon butter, basil or nutmeg.
Peppers (Red or Green Sweet)	½ large or 1 whole medium.	Core and remove seeds. Cut in half; or in cubes for kabobs; or leave whole.	15-20 minutes until tender.	Italian dressing, olive oil with oregano, lemon butter, basil.
Potatoes	1 large or 2-3 small.	Scrub and pierce with a fork. Leave whole or slice lengthwise or horizontally.	50-60 minutes or until tender or 15 minutes per side, until brown.	Butter or margarine, chives, dill sour cream, yogurt, cheese. Baste with oil and seasonings or Italian dressing.
Squash (Summer)	½ medium or 1 small.	Slice lengthwise or horizontally.	20-25 minutes or until tender.	Butter or margarine, chives, basil, Italian dressing.
Squash (Winter)	¼ to ½, depending on size.	Remove seeds, place cut-side down on grill.	40-45 minutes until tender.	Butter or margarine, nutmeg, brown sugar.
Tomatoes (Whole, Cherry)	1 medium, ½ large or 3-5 cherry.	Cut leaves from stem and core. Quarter or use cherry tomatoes for kabobs.	20-25 minutes or until soft.	Drizzle with salad oil or olive oil and basil, dill, oregano; add grated cheese 5 minutes before removing from grill.

Marinades, Bastes and Butters
Add delicious character to any cut of beef, poultry or seafood with marinades, bastes and butters.

	Makes	Ingredients	Directions
Onion-Tomato Baste	2½ cups	1 can (15 oz.) tomato sauce with tomato bits; ½ cup chopped onion; 1 clove minced garlic; ¼ cup soy sauce; 2 tablespoons sugar; 1 teaspoon dry mustard; ⅛ teaspoon cayenne pepper.	Combine tomato sauce with tomato bits, onion, garlic, soy sauce, sugar, dry mustard and cayenne in a large jar with a screw top; shake to blend.
Zippy Barbecue Sauce	1 cup	½ cup catsup; ¼ cup water; 2 tablespoons light brown sugar; 2 tablespoons grated onion; 2 tablespoons Worcestershire sauce; 2 tablespoons cider vinegar; ½ teaspoon salt; ¼ teaspoon chili powder; ⅛ teaspoon garlic powder; ⅛ teaspoon pepper; dash liquid red-pepper seasoning.	Combine catsup, water, brown sugar, onion, Worcestershire sauce, cider vinegar, salt, chili powder, garlic powder, pepper and red-pepper seasoning in a small saucepan. Simmer 15 minutes.
Hot Pepper Baste	⅔ cup	½ cup (1 stick) butter or margarine; 2 tablespoons lime or lemon juice; few drops liquid red-pepper seasoning.	Melt butter or margarine in a small metal pan with a flameproof handle over grill; stir in lime or lemon juice and red-pepper seasoning. Push to side of grill and keep warm.
Super Beer Baste	3½ cups	1 bottle (16 oz.) barbecue sauce; 1 can (12 oz.) beer; 2 tablespoons Worcestershire sauce; few drops liquid red-pepper seasoning.	Combine barbecue sauce, beer, Worcestershire sauce and red-pepper seasoning in a 4-cup glass jar with a screw top. Store at least 1 day to develop flavors. Brush meat, for the last 15 minutes of grilling.
Almond-Cheese Butter	1 cup	½ cup crumbled blue cheese; ¼ cup (½ stick) softened butter or margarine; ¼ cup ground almonds; 2 tablespoons sherry, white wine, brandy or cream.	Allow crumbled cheese and butter to stand at room temperature for about 1 hour. Mash cheese with softened butter in a small bowl with a fork. Stir in almonds and sherry, wine, brandy or cream and mix to a smooth paste. Turn into a bowl. Serve at room temperature.
Sauce Chablis	2 cups	¼ cup (½ stick) butter or margarine; ¼ cup chopped green onions; ¼ cup all-purpose flour; 1½ cups beef broth; ½ cup Chablis wine; 1 teaspoon salt; 1 teaspoon crumbled leaf thyme; ¼ teaspoon white pepper.	Melt butter in a metal saucepan with a flameproof handle over grill; stir green onions and sauté until soft, about 3 minutes. Stir in flour and cook, stirring constantly, until mixture bubbles; stir in broth, wine, salt, thyme and pepper. Cook, stirring constantly, until sauce thickens and bubbles, for 3 minutes; push to side of grill and simmer for 10 minutes. Serve warm over sliced steak.
Basic Barbecue Sauce	2 cups	1¼ cups catsup; ¼ cup chili sauce; ¼ cup red wine vinegar; 2 tablespoons lemon juice; 1½ tablespoons bottled steak sauce; 2 teaspoons Worcestershire sauce; 1 tablespoon prepared mustard; ¼ cup light brown sugar; ½ teaspoon soy sauce; 1 teaspoon vegetable oil; ⅔ cup beer; 1 teaspoon freshly ground black pepper; dash liquid red-pepper seasoning.	Combine catsup; chili sauce, red wine vinegar, lemon juice, steak sauce, Worcestershire sauce, mustard, brown sugar, soy sauce, oil, beer, pepper and red-pepper seasoning in a large jar with a screw top. Cover and shake to blend well. Refrigerate sauce for at least 2 hours to blend flavors. Brush on ribs, chops or chicken breasts during the last 20 minutes of grilling.

MAIN
COURSES

Salad Pizza (page 155)

Delectable entrées using pasta,
beans, eggs, cheese or vegetables
as a base.

T oday's health-conscious cooks have turned more and more to pasta and dried bean dishes to reduce saturated fat and cholesterol intake. Aside from being economical, varied and adaptable, pasta and beans are nutritious. Excellent as meat substitutes, as they are high in protein, they're also good sources of carbohydrates and fiber.

From whole-wheat pasta to Chinese cellophane noodles, the many combinations of flavors and textures and the different shapes of pasta add a new and exciting dimension to good home cooking.

Eggs and cheese are yet another way of putting variety into menus without including meat. Versatile and complete sources of protein, they offer change for the budget-conscious menu planner. You'll find two favorites in this chapter: Cheese Lasagne Rolls with Spinach (page 148) and French-Toasted Cheese (page 150).

One-dish meals that combine vegetables *and* meat, such as Eggplant Parmesan Stew (page 160), are ideal time-savers. Year-round availability of many delicious vegetables makes these meal-in-one creations especially popular and part of many cooks' "basic repertoire".

We've added main-dish soups and salads as other welcome alternatives in menu planning. Our fresh steaming Cabbage and Sauerkraut Soup (page 151) combines meat and vegetables in a savory broth. Our Salad Pizza (page 155) is a healthy meal that even the kids will love!

Pasta

Pasta Cooking Tips

- To cook pasta properly, at least 6 quarts of water should be used for each pound of pasta.
- Bring the water to boiling; then add 2 tablespoons of salt.
- Add the pasta gradually—in small amounts—to keep the water boiling. Stir frequently to keep the strands or pieces of pasta separate.
- Fresh pasta will cook much faster than dried pasta, in approximately 1 minute. For the proper cooking times for dried pasta, check the label directions.
- Do not rinse cooked hot pasta in cold water unless it is to be served cool in a pasta salad.

Simple Substitution

Zucchini, yellow crookneck and straightneck squash share many of the same cooking qualities and may be interchanged in most recipes.

Pasta Rustica

An ideal dish for a buffet supper.

Makes 8 servings.

Nutrient Value Per Serving: 365 calories, 14 gm. protein, 13 gm. fat, 743 mg. sodium, 41 mg. cholesterol.

- 1 **large onion, finely chopped (1 cup)**
- 2 **cloves garlic, finely chopped**
- 1 **leek OR: 1 bunch green onions with tops, finely chopped**
- 4 **radishes, finely chopped**
- 2 **medium-size carrots, finely chopped**
- 1 **bunch parsley, stems removed, finely chopped**
- 3 **tablespoons fresh basil leaves, finely chopped, OR: 1 teaspoon leaf basil, crumbled**
- ⅓ **cup olive or vegetable oil**
- 3 **large tomatoes (1¼ pounds), peeled, seeded and coarsely chopped**
- 1¾ **cups chicken or beef broth***
- 3 **cups shredded green cabbage**

- 2 **small zucchini, halved and cut into thin julienne strips**
- 1 **teaspoon salt***
- ½ **teaspoon pepper**
- 1 **can (15 ounces) red kidney beans, drained**
- 6 **cups cooked ziti (short tube pasta) (3 cups uncooked)**
- ¼ **cup (½ stick) butter or margarine (optional)**
- ½ **cup freshly grated Parmesan cheese**
Meat (optional):
- ½ **pound salami, cut into ½-inch cubes**

1. Combine the onion, garlic, leek, radishes, carrots, parsley and basil in a small bowl.
2. Sauté the vegetables in the oil in a kettle or Dutch oven, stirring occasionally, for 8 to 10 minutes or until the vegetables just begin to brown. Add the tomatoes, chicken broth, cabbage, zucchini, salt and pepper. Bring to boiling. Lower the heat; cover; simmer, stirring frequently, for 10 minutes or until crisp-tender.
3. Stir in the beans and cooked ziti. Heat, stirring gently. Ladle into a large soup tureen. Stir in the butter, if using, and the Parmesan. Serve hot or at room temperature.

Optional Meat: Add the salami cubes along with the beans and ziti.
Nutrient Value Per Serving: 484 calories, 20 gm. protein, 23 gm. fat, 1,270 mg. sodium, 64 mg. cholesterol.

* Note: To reduce the mg. of sodium per serving, use a reduced-sodium bouillon cube, bouillon powder or broth, and eliminate or reduce the salt in the recipe.

Pasta Pronto

Makes 4 servings.

Nutrient Value Per Serving: 750 calories, 28 gm. protein, 40 gm. fat, 849 mg. sodium, 219 mg. cholesterol.

- 12 **ounces fettuccine**
- 1 **large onion, thinly sliced**
- ½ **pound fresh asparagus, trimmed and cut into ½-inch pieces***
- 1 **tablespoon butter or margarine**
- 6 **ounces sliced Canadian bacon, cut into ¼-inch-wide strips**
- 1¼ **cups heavy cream**
- ½ **cup grated Parmesan cheese**
  Pepper

(continues on page 140)

Rotelle with Shrimp and Lemon (page 140)

1. Cook the fettuccine following the label directions.
2. Sauté the onion and asparagus in the butter in a medium-size skillet until the onion is softened, for about 3 minutes. Add the bacon. Lower the heat; cook, covered, for 5 minutes or until the asparagus is tender.
3. Bring the cream to a rolling boil in a medium-size saucepan. Boil gently for 2 minutes to reduce slightly. Remove from the heat. Stir in the Parmesan.
4. Add the cream mixture to the asparagus-bacon mixture in the skillet. Add the pepper to taste. Simmer for 2 minutes, stirring once or twice.
5. Drain the fettuccine. Toss with the sauce. Serve with extra Parmesan, if you wish.

Note: If using frozen asparagus spears, add to the skillet along with the bacon.

Rotelle with Shrimp and Lemon

Makes 4 servings.

Nutrient Value Per Serving: 741 calories, 31 gm. protein, 37 gm. fat, 422 mg. sodium, 254 mg. cholesterol.

12 ounces rotelle, or other spiral or
     corkscrew-shaped pasta
 1 cup heavy cream
 4 tablespoons (½ stick) butter or margarine
⅛ teaspoon cayenne pepper
¼ cup grated Parmesan or Romano cheese
 1 clove garlic, halved
 1 pound medium-size fresh shrimp, shelled
     and deveined, OR: 1 pound frozen,
     thawed and drained
 1 cup finely chopped fresh herbs, such as
     parsley, basil, chives
     Grated rind of 1 large lemon (1 tablespoon)
     Juice of 1 large lemon (about 3 tablespoons)
 1 tablespoon capers, coarsely chopped if large
     Lemon wedges (optional)
     Basil leaves (optional)

1. Cook the rotelle in boiling salted water in a large saucepan, following the package directions. Drain.
2. Meanwhile, combine the cream, 2 tablespoons of the butter, the cayenne pepper and cheese in a small saucepan. Place over low heat to heat through.
3. Sauté the garlic in the remaining 2 table-spoons of butter in a medium-size skillet; remove the garlic when it begins to brown.
4. Increase the heat to medium-high. Add the shrimp and stir-fry until firm, pink and curled, for about 3 to 5 minutes. Quickly stir in the herbs, lemon rind and juice, and the capers. Remove from the heat.
5. Transfer to a warm serving bowl. Pour the hot cream sauce over the pasta; toss together until well blended. Spoon the shrimp mixture over the pasta; toss. Garnish with the lemon wedges and basil leaves, if you wish.

Pasta Salad with Tuna

Tired of tuna? Try this terrific combination of pasta and tuna. The dressing can be quickly prepared in a blender.

Makes 6 servings.

Nutrient Value Per Serving: 503 calories, 19 gm. protein, 34 gm. fat, 550 mg. sodium, 60 mg. cholesterol.

 2 teaspoons salt
 2 tablespoons vegetable oil
 8 ounces small shell pasta
 1 tablespoon plus ½ cup olive or vegetable oil
½ pound cherry tomatoes
 2 cans (6½ ounces each) tuna
 1 small clove garlic
 2 canned anchovy fillets
 1 tablespoon lemon juice
 1 egg yolk
½ teaspoon leaf marjoram, crumbled
½ teaspoon leaf basil, crumbled
¼ teaspoon pepper
 1 jar (2½ ounces) pitted green olives, drained

1. Bring 2 quarts water to a rapid boil in a pot. Add 1 teaspoon of the salt and the vegetable oil. Add the pasta. Return to the rapid boil and cook for 10 minutes or just until firm but tender. Drain in a colander; cool under cold running water. Toss the drained pasta with the 1 tablespoon of olive oil to prevent sticking.
2. Cut the tomatoes in half crosswise. Gently squeeze out and discard seeds. Reserve the tomatoes in a bowl.
3. Drain the tuna and break into medium-size chunks.
4. To prepare the dressing: Using a knife, chop and mash together the garlic and anchovies. Combine the garlic mixture,

lemon juice and egg yolk in a medium-size bowl. Slowly drizzle in the ½ cup of olive oil while whisking vigorously, as you would when making mayonnaise. (The dressing can also be made in a blender.) Mix in the marjoram, basil, pepper and the remaining 1 teaspoon of salt.

5. Combine the shells, tomatoes, tuna, olives and dressing in a large bowl; toss gently to mix well. Refrigerate, covered, for at least 30 minutes or overnight. Stir before serving.

Macaroni Salad

Macaroni Salad

Make this colorful salad for picnics, family gatherings and parties.

Makes 8 servings.

Nutrient Value Per Serving: 438 calories, 17 gm. protein, 20 gm. fat, 337 mg. sodium, 27 mg. cholesterol.

- **1 box (16 ounces) mostaccioli macaroni (large tubes)**
- **4 ounces fresh green beans**
- **1 small cucumber, sliced**
- **1 large ripe tomato, cored and coarsely chopped**
- **½ cup cubed cooked ham (4 ounces)**
- **½ cup cubed cooked turkey (4 ounces)**
- **½ cup cubed sharp Cheddar cheese (2 ounces)**
- **½ cup pitted black olives, halved**
- **½ cup vegetable oil**
- **7 tablespoons red wine vinegar**
- **2 tablespoons chopped parsley**
- **1 teaspoon dry mustard**
- **½ teaspoon sugar**
- **¼ teaspoon cayenne pepper**
- **¼ teaspoon paprika**
- **1 clove garlic, finely chopped**

1. Cook the macaroni following the label directions. Drain. Rinse briefly under cold water.
2. Cook the green beans in boiling water until crisp-tender. Drain. Rinse under cold water. Cut into 2-inch lengths. Place in a large salad bowl. Add the cucumber, tomato, ham, turkey, cheese and olives.
3. Whisk together the oil, vinegar, parsley, mustard, sugar, cayenne, paprika and garlic in a small bowl. Pour over the salad; toss well.
4. Stir the macaroni into the salad. Refrigerate for 1 hour or until serving time.

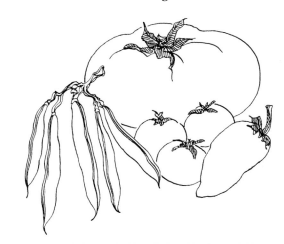

Cucumbers

A cucumber is classified as a fruit, not a vegetable. Cucumbers are refreshing additions to salads, crudité platters and sandwiches. They are wonderful marinated in vinegar or yogurt and fresh mint to serve along with barbecued lamb.

Look for bright green, well-shaped cucumbers. The flesh should be firm and the seeds soft.

Store washed and dried cucumbers in plastic bags in the refrigerator for up to five days. Beware of cucumbers that are withered or shriveled.

Peak season: June-July.

Rainbow Spaghetti with Basil and Pine Nuts

Long strips of zucchini, yellow squash and carrot add crunch to this pasta dish.

Makes 4 servings.

Nutrient Value Per Serving: 443 calories, 13 gm. protein, 21 gm. fat, 464 mg. sodium, 36 mg. cholesterol.

¼ cup (½ stick) butter or margarine
¼ cup pine nuts
2 cloves garlic, finely chopped
1 medium-size zucchini (about 6 ounces), trimmed and cut lengthwise into 3 x ⅛-inch sticks
1 medium-size yellow squash (about 6 ounces), trimmed and cut lengthwise into 3 x ⅛-inch sticks
1 tablespoon vegetable oil
1 large carrot, trimmed and cut lengthwise into 3 x ⅛-inch sticks
8 ounces thin spaghetti, broken in half
½ cup lightly packed fresh basil leaves, coarsely chopped
¼ cup grated Romano cheese
½ teaspoon salt
¼ teaspoon black pepper
⅛ teaspoon crushed red pepper flakes

1. Melt the butter in a small skillet over medium-low heat. Add the pine nuts; cook for 2 minutes. Add the garlic; cook for 2 minutes or until golden. Remove from the heat.
2. Place the zucchini and yellow squash in a colander. Bring a large pot of salted water, to which 1 tablespoon of oil has been added, to a rolling boil over medium-high heat. Place the carrot in a strainer. Lower the strainer into the boiling water and cook for 2 minutes. Lift the strainer and run carrot under cold water to stop the cooking. Add the carrot to the colander with the squash.
3. Cook the spaghetti in the same boiling water until firm but tender. Pour the spaghetti and spaghetti water into the colander over the vegetables. Transfer the spaghetti mixture to a large serving bowl. Add the pine nut mixture, basil, cheese, salt, black pepper and red pepper flakes. Toss until well mixed. Serve hot with additional cheese, if you wish.

Pine Nuts

This tasty morsel is the seed of a pine tree variety grown in the southwestern United States and southern Europe. It is delicious raw or roasted. It is also known as Indian nuts, pignoli or pignon.

Pasta Varieties

• Durum Wheat Pasta—Most pasta is made from durum wheat flour and water. Experiment with the enormous range of shapes and sizes, from barley-like orzo to tubular manicotti.
• Egg Noodles—A bit richer with egg yolk added; serve with assorted vegetables, cream sauce and top with grated cheese.
• Spinach Pasta—Adds garden-patch color and flavor. Toss with regular pasta, melted butter and grated cheese, for "straw and hay."
• Whole-Wheat Pasta—Available in the health food section of your market; a chewy pasta with a nutty flavor and whole-grain nutrients. Toss with tomato sauce and cheese chunks.
• High-Protein Pasta—The latest arrival to the world of pasta, this product was developed as a low-cost, low-cholesterol alternative to meat.
• Oriental Noodles—Found in Oriental food shops. They add exotic texture and taste to soups and main dishes. Chinese cellophane noodles, clear when cooked, are delicious in vegetable soup. Japanese buckwheat noodles are tasty when served with chopped green onions and soy sauce.

Reheating Pasta or Rice

Reheating and refreshing pasta or rice is simple: Place in a colander or strainer and set over boiling water in a pan; cover loosely with aluminum foil. Steam for 15 minutes. Toss with a bit of butter or oil, if not adding to a casserole immediately, to keep from sticking.

Dried Beans

⧉⧉⧉ ⬎ ▢
Spinach-Lentil Soup

A hearty, very thick stew-like soup.

Makes 6 servings.

Nutrient Value Per Serving: 408 calories, 28 gm. protein, 10 gm. fat, 1,032 mg. sodium, 0 mg. cholesterol.

Nutrient Value Per Serving With Meat: 529 calories, 32 gm. protein, 21 gm. fat, 1,455 mg. sodium, 19 mg. cholesterol.

- 2 **large onions, coarsely chopped (2 cups)**
- 3 **tablespoons vegetable oil or bacon fat**
- 7 **cups chicken broth***
- 1 **package (1 pound) dried lentils, picked over and rinsed**
- 1 **pound fresh spinach, trimmed and torn into bite-size pieces OR: 2 packages (10 ounces each) frozen chopped spinach, thawed**
- ⅛ **teaspoon pepper**
- ⅛ **teaspoon ground allspice**
   Salt (optional)
- ½ **pound frankfurters, sliced (optional), OR: 1 cup shredded Cheddar cheese (4 ounces) (optional)**

1. Sauté the onions in the oil in a kettle or Dutch oven, stirring, for 5 minutes or until soft.
2. Stir in the broth and lentils. Bring to boiling. Lower the heat; cover; simmer, stirring occasionally, for 45 minutes or until the lentils are tender. Add the spinach, pepper, allspice and frankfurters, if using. Taste and add salt, if you wish. Simmer for 10 minutes longer, stirring occasionally.
3. Ladle into a tureen or heated soup bowls. Sprinkle with the Cheddar cheese, if you wish.

* Note: To reduce the mg. of sodium per serving, use a reduced-sodium bouillon cube, bouillon powder or broth.

⬎ ⧉⧉⧉ ▢
Sweet and Sour Lima Beans with Lentils

Make this for your next contribution to a potluck supper or picnic. Try substituting Italian sausage, breakfast sausage or even cubes of ham for the kielbasa.

Bake at 325° for 2 hours.
Makes 12 servings.

Nutrient Value Per Serving: 424 calories, 18 gm. protein, 20 gm. fat, 709 mg. sodium, 34 mg. cholesterol.

- 1 **package (1 pound) large dried lima beans**
- 2 **quarts cold water**
- 3 **cloves garlic, thinly sliced**
- 4 **ounces (½ cup) dried lentils, picked over and rinsed**
- 3 **large onions, thinly sliced**
- 2 **tablespoons vegetable oil**
- 1 **pound kielbasa, cut into ½-inch-thick slices**
- 1 **can (16 ounces) peeled whole tomatoes, coarsely chopped and undrained**
- ⅓ **cup tomato paste**
- ⅓ **cup molasses**
- ⅓ **cup cider vinegar**
- 1½ **teaspoons leaf basil, crumbled**
- 1 **teaspoon salt**
- ½ **teaspoon pepper**
- 6 **slices uncooked bacon**

1. Combine the lima beans, cold water and garlic in a large kettle or Dutch oven. Bring to boiling. Lower the heat; simmer for 30 minutes. Add the lentils. Return to boiling. Cook for 10 minutes. Drain, reserving the liquid.
2. Sauté the onions in the oil in a large skillet over medium heat for 5 minutes. Lower the heat; cook, covered, for 5 minutes. Transfer to a large bowl. Set aside.
3. Preheat the oven to slow (325°).
4. Brown the kielbasa in the same skillet, turning frequently, until lightly browned, for about 5 minutes. Set aside.
5. Combine the sautéed onions, tomatoes, tomato paste, molasses, vinegar, basil, salt, pepper and ½ cup of the reserved bean cooking liquid; blend well. Add the lima beans and lentils; mix well. Pour into a 13 x 9 x 2-inch baking pan. Place the kielbasa on top. Arrange the bacon slices over the top.
6. Bake in the preheated slow oven (325°) for 2 hours or until the beans are tender. Add a little of the reserved bean cooking liquid if the bean mixture becomes too dry.

Classy Baked Beans

These zesty beans take about 8 hours to prepare, so start them very early in the morning or prepare them a day ahead.

Bake at 275° for 7 hours.
Makes 6 to 8 servings.

Nutrient Value Per Serving: 382 calories, 18 gm. protein, 9 gm. fat, 882 mg. sodium, 12 mg. cholesterol.

- 1 pound dry, small white (navy) beans
- 2 teaspoons unsalted butter or margarine
- 1 clove garlic, crushed
- 1 cup finely chopped onion (1 large)
- 3 strips bacon, cooked and crumbled
- 2 tablespoons dark brown sugar
- 2 teaspoons Worcestershire sauce
- 4 tablespoons molasses
- 5 tablespoons prepared chili sauce
- 1 tablespoon dry English mustard
- 1 teaspoon curry powder
- 1½ teaspoons salt
- ½ cup dark rum
- 1½ cups tomato juice, or more as needed
- 3 strips uncooked bacon

1. Place the beans in a large pot of boiling water over high heat. Return to boiling. Turn off the heat; let stand for 1 hour.
2. Preheat the oven to very slow (275°). Grease a 1¾-quart bean pot or casserole with the butter. Rub with the garlic.
3. Drain the beans. Place in a large mixing bowl. Add the onion, crumbled bacon, brown sugar, Worcestershire, molasses, chili sauce, dry mustard, curry powder, salt and rum. Mix well. Stir in ¼ cup of the tomato juice. Transfer to the prepared bean pot. Place the strips of bacon on top.
4. Bake, covered, in the preheated very slow oven (275°) for 7 hours or until the beans are tender, gently stirring in the additional tomato juice as the liquid is absorbed by the beans.

Dried Beans Expansion

One cup of dried beans expands to 2 to 2½ cups cooked, or enough to serve 3 to 4 people. Prepare a large batch and refrigerate leftovers for up to 1 week or freeze for 4 to 6 months. Reheat gently to retain shape.

Lentil Chili

To convert this delicious chili to a vegetarian main dish, simply omit the ground beef and second tablespoon of oil.

Makes 10 servings.

Nutrient Value Per Serving: 276 calories, 17 gm. protein, 7 gm. fat, 663 mg. sodium, 15 mg. cholesterol.

- 7 cups of water or chicken broth
- 1 package (1 pound) dried lentils, picked over and rinsed
- 2 large onions, chopped (2 cups)
- 2½ cups coarsely chopped celery
- 1 clove garlic, finely chopped
- 2 tablespoons vegetable oil
- ½ pound lean ground beef
- 2 teaspoons chili powder
- 1 tablespoon ground cumin
- 2 teaspoons leaf basil, crumbled
- 1½ teaspoons salt
- 1 can (8 ounces) tomato sauce
- 2 cans (3 ounces each) whole green chilies, drained, seeded and chopped
- 1 can (28 ounces) whole peeled tomatoes with their liquid, coarsely chopped

1. Combine the water, lentils, onions, celery, garlic and 1 tablespoon of the vegetable oil in a kettle or Dutch oven. Bring to boiling. Lower the heat; cover; simmer for 20 minutes or until the lentils are slightly tender.
2. Cook the ground beef slowly in the remaining 1 tablespoon of vegetable oil in a large skillet, breaking up the meat with a wooden spoon, until brown, for about 15 minutes. Remove the beef with a slotted spoon to the lentil mixture.
3. Add the chili powder, cumin, basil, salt, tomato sauce, green chilies and chopped tomatoes with their liquid; stir to combine. Bring the mixture to boiling. Lower the heat; cover; simmer for 15 minutes or until the lentils are tender and the flavors are well blended.
4. Ladle the chili into a soup tureen or individual heated soup bowls.

Prevent Boil-Overs

Starchy foods will not boil over if the top inch or two inside the pot is rubbed with oil.

Dried Bean Varieties

- Baby Limas—The dry form of the fresh bean; serve in main dishes, soups or simply buttered.
- Black Beans (Turtle Soup Beans)—Use in sauces and soups, especially those with an Oriental or Mediterranean flavor.
- Black-Eyed Peas—Oval with a black speck, a traditional ingredient in soul food; serve with rice for a balanced meal.
- Garbanzos (Chick-Peas)—Nutty in flavor; add to Italian dishes or marinate for a hearty salad.
- Great Northerns—Good baking beans; use in chowder or salads.
- Kidney Beans—Light or dark red, this bean stands up to the hottest meatless chili recipe! Use in salads and soups, too.
- Peas—Available split or whole, yellow or green. Use splits in soups, whole peas in casseroles.
- Pintos—Speckled and succulent; serve in Tex-Mex dishes, such as refried beans or spicy meatless chili.
- Soy Beans—The only beans to contain all 8 essential amino acids, they rival meat in high-quality protein. Mix their unusual flavor and texture with other, more familiar beans.

Eggs

Eggs are graded by the U.S. Department of Agriculture according to appearance. Grade AA or Fresh Fancy Eggs are the highest quality.

Eggshell color is determined by the breed of the hen and has no effect on the quality, taste or nutrient value of the egg.

Eggs should be stored in the refrigerator, large end up (this keeps the yolks centered), in their original carton for up to one week. Soiled eggs should be wiped clean with a dry cloth before storing. A wet cloth would wash off the natural protective film.

Keep eggs away from strong-smelling foods, as the shell is porous and will absorb odors.

If you're in doubt about an egg's freshness, break it into a saucer. A super-fresh egg has a cloudy white and a high-standing yolk. Older eggs will have less cloudy whites and flatter yolks. A "bad" egg will have a definite odor or "chemical" smell when sniffed.

"Eggspandable" Eggs with Apricot-Glazed Sausages

An easy-to-make dish for a Sunday brunch. Hard-cook the eggs and make the onion sauce the day before.

Bake at 400° for 20 minutes.

Nutrient Value Per Serving: 273 calories, 11 gm. protein, 20 gm. fat, 507 mg. sodium, 303 mg. cholesterol.

- 3 medium-size onions, thinly sliced
- 3 tablespoons butter or margarine
- ½ teaspoon dried dillweed
- ½ teaspoon salt
- ¼ teaspoon pepper
- ¼ cup unsifted all-purpose flour
- 1 cup chicken broth
- 1 cup milk
- 12 hard-cooked eggs, halved
- 3 tablespoons prepared mustard
- 2 tablespoons mayonnaise or salad dressing
- ¼ cup packaged unseasoned bread crumbs
- 2 tablespoons butter or margarine, melted
- 2 tablespoons chopped parsley
- 1 package (1 pound) breakfast-style sausage links
- 1 can (5½ ounces) apricot nectar (⅔ cup)
- 2 tablespoons apricot preserves

1. Sauté the onions in the butter in a large, heavy skillet over medium heat for 5 minutes. Lower the heat. Cover; cook for 5 minutes.
2. Stir in the dillweed, salt, pepper and flour. Cook over medium heat, stirring constantly, for 1 minute. Stir in the broth and milk; cook, stirring constantly, until thickened, for about 3 minutes.
3. Preheat the oven to hot (400°).
4. Spoon the onion sauce into each of twelve 3-inch baking dishes, dividing equally. Place 2 egg halves in each dish.
5. Combine the mustard and mayonnaise in a small bowl. Spoon evenly over the eggs. Combine the bread crumbs, butter and parsley in a small bowl; blend well. Sprinkle evenly over each dish.
6. Bake in the preheated hot oven (400°) for 20 minutes or until bubbly and light brown.
7. Meanwhile, combine the sausages and apricot nectar in a large skillet. Bring to simmering over medium heat. Cook the sausages, turning several times, until the sausages are browned and the nectar has evaporated, for about 10 minutes. ☞

Remove and discard any fat.

8. Add the preserves to the sausages; stir gently to coat the sausages. Cook over medium heat, turning the sausages frequently, until glazed, for about 5 minutes. Arrange on a platter and serve with the eggs. Garnish the eggs with parsley sprigs, if you wish.

About Omelet Skillets

● Any skillet with a rounded bottom, whether it's heavy aluminum, cast iron or stainless steel, can be used to make omelets. If it is your everyday skillet you plan to use, *do* clean it thoroughly with a soapy steel-wool pad, then rinse and dry. To season (which you must do each time), heat a ¼-inch depth of vegetable oil in the skillet over low heat for 10 minutes; pour off the oil and wipe out the skillet.

● You can skip the cleaning process if you use a skillet solely for making omelets or a skillet with a nonstick surface. You need to season only the first time you use the skillet. Simply wipe off—not wash—after each use, and it'll be ready for the next omelet.

● Omelets will stick to the skillet if you let the butter brown. If this happens, pour off the browned butter, wipe out the skillet with paper toweling and start again.

Potato-Beef Omelet

Potato-Beef Omelet

Prepare the filling in advance, then reheat while preparing the eggs.

Makes 4 omelets.

Nutrient Value Per Serving: 679 calories, 40 gm. protein, 47 gm. fat, 307 mg. sodium, 904 mg. cholesterol.

½ **pound sliced mushrooms**
1 **cup chopped onion**
⅔ **cup chopped sweet red pepper (1 small)**
3 **tablespoons vegetable oil**
1½ **cups frozen, unseasoned hash brown potato cubes**
½ **pound ground round**
¼ **teaspoon leaf thyme**
1 **cup grated Fontina cheese (4 ounces)**
4 **teaspoons butter or margarine**
12 **eggs**

1. Prepare the filling: Sauté the mushrooms, onion and red pepper in the oil in a medium-size skillet until soft, for about 5 minutes. Stir in the hash browns. Cook, stirring occasionally, for 8 minutes longer or until the potatoes are tender. Stir in the beef and thyme. Cook until the beef is no longer pink, for about 2 minutes. Stir in the cheese. Remove from the heat and reserve; keep warm.
2. Prepare the omelets: Heat 1 teaspoon of the butter in an 8-inch nonstick skillet. Beat 3 eggs lightly in a small cup. Pour into the skillet. Cook, stirring with the flat of a fork and shaking the pan back and forth, until the omelet is firm on the bottom and almost set on top. Spoon about ¾ cup of the filling in the center. Fold the omelet over the filling. Slide onto a heated serving plate. Keep warm in a very low oven while making the remaining omelets.

Dilled Pita Omelet

Makes 1 serving.

Nutrient Value Per Serving: 156 calories, 9 gm. protein, 7 gm. fat, 70 mg. sodium, 274 mg. cholesterol.

1 **small whole-wheat pita bread**
1 **large egg**
1 **teaspoon snipped fresh dill OR:**
    ½ **teaspoon dried dillweed**
    Salt and pepper to taste
2 **tablespoons dairy sour cream or plain yogurt (optional)**

1. Cut the pita bread in half to form 2 separate pockets. Beat the egg with the dill in a small bowl.
2. Heat a small, ungreased nonstick skillet over medium heat. Pour the egg mixture into the skillet. Cook, stirring, until the egg is almost set. Turn the omelet over. Cook until firm. Season with the salt and pepper.
3. Slice the omelet in half and scoop a half into each pita pocket. Spoon the sour cream over each, if you wish. Serve immediately, or wrap in aluminum foil to eat on the run within 30 minutes.

Deviled-Eggs Florentine

Stuffed eggs are covered with a mushroom sauce and baked on a bed of spinach.

Bake at 350° for 30 minutes.
Makes 4 servings.

Nutrient Value Per Serving: 342 calories, 15 gm. protein, 26 gm. fat, 1,039 mg. sodium, 421 mg. cholesterol.

1 **can (10¾ ounces) condensed cream of mushroom soup**
2 **tablespoons milk**
1 **can (3 or 4 ounces) sliced or chopped mushrooms, drained**
2 **packages (10 ounces each) frozen chopped spinach**
6 **hard-cooked eggs, shelled**
¼ **cup mayonnaise or salad dressing**
2 **teaspoons snipped chives**
2 **teaspoons prepared mustard**

1. Combine the soup and milk in a saucepan and heat slowly, stirring until blended; stir in the mushrooms. ☞

2. While the soup heats, cook the spinach, following the label directions; drain.

3. Halve each egg crosswise. Remove the yolks carefully; place in a small bowl; mash with a fork. Stir in the mayonnaise or salad dressing, chives and mustard. Pile back into the whites, mounding slightly.

4. Spoon the spinach into 4 small, shallow baking dishes. Place 3 stuffed egg halves on top of each; spoon the mushroom sauce over all. Cover each dish with plastic wrap.

5. Refrigerate for up to 24 hours; 35 minutes before serving time, remove from the refrigerator; uncover. Preheat the oven to moderate (350°).

6. Bake in the preheated moderate oven (350°) for 30 minutes or until hot. Garnish with additional chives, if you wish.

Cheese

◧ ◧ ◻

Cheese Lasagne Rolls with Spinach

If there is no Cheddar cheese in the refrigerator, any combination, such as Swiss and American, will serve equally well.

Bake at 325° for 20 minutes.
Makes 8 servings.

Nutrient Value Per Serving: 554 calories, 27 gm. protein, 25 gm. fat, 681 mg. sodium, 124 mg. cholesterol.

- ¼ cup (½ stick) butter or margarine
- ⅓ cup all-purpose flour
- ½ teaspoon salt
- ¼ teaspoon pepper
- ¼ teaspoon ground nutmeg
- 1 quart milk
- 3 packages (10 ounces each) frozen chopped spinach, thawed
- 1 cup grated Parmesan cheese
- ½ pound sharp Cheddar cheese, shredded (2 cups)
- 2 teaspoons paprika
- 2 teaspoons dry mustard
- 1 package (1 pound) lasagne noodles

1. Melt the butter in a large saucepan. Stir in

the flour, salt, pepper and nutmeg. Cook, stirring, for 1 minute. Remove from the heat. Gradually stir in the milk. Return to the heat and cook, stirring constantly, until the cream sauce is thickened and bubbly. Set aside.

2. Drain the thawed spinach in a colander, pressing against the sides to remove as much liquid as possible. Transfer to a bowl. Stir in 1 cup of the cream sauce and ½ cup of the Parmesan until well blended. Set aside.

3. Stir the shredded Cheddar, ¼ cup of the remaining Parmesan, the paprika and dry mustard into the remaining cream sauce until well blended. Set aside.

4. Preheat the oven to slow (325°).

5. Cook the lasagne noodles, following the label directions, just until tender. Drain.

6. Spread the spinach mixture over each lasagne noodle. Roll up the noodles jelly-roll fashion. Place, seam-side down, in a buttered 13x9x2-inch baking pan.

7. Spoon the remaining cheese sauce over the rolls. Sprinkle with the remaining Parmesan.

8. Bake in the preheated slow oven (325°) for 20 minutes or until thoroughly heated.

To Make Ahead: Prepare the recipe through Step 6. Cover the baking pan and the sauce-pan of sauce and refrigerate until ready to serve. About 1½ hours before serving, remove the baking pan and the sauce from the refrigerator and allow them to come to room temperature. Proceed as the recipe directs.

Chicken Enchiladas in Cheese Cream (page 104), Cheese Lasagne Rolls with Spinach (page 148), "Eggspandable" Eggs with Apricot-Glazed Sausages (page 145).

Summer Pizza with Sweet Peppers

This recipe makes two large rectangular pizzas. Bake the second while you eat the first.

Bake at 450° for 20 minutes.
Makes 12 servings.

Nutrient Value Per Serving: 386 calories, 16 gm. protein, 21 gm. fat, 474 mg. sodium, 112 mg. cholesterol.

Dough:
- 1   envelope active dry yeast
- ¼   cup very warm water
- 1   cup milk
- 2   tablespoons butter or margarine
- ½   teaspoon salt
- 1   egg
- 3½ cups **uns**ifted all-purpose flour

Topping:
-     Grated rind of 1 large lemon (1 tablespoon)
-     Juice of 1 large lemon (about 3 tablespoons)
- ¼   cup olive or vegetable oil
- ½   teaspoon salt
- ¼   teaspoon pepper
- 1   large sweet green pepper, halved, seeded and cut into 2 x ½-inch strips
- 1   large sweet red pepper, halved, seeded and cut into 2 x ½-inch strips
- 1   large onion, halved lengthwise and cut crosswise into ½-inch-thick strips
- ¾   pound mozzarella cheese, coarsely shredded (3 cups)
- 2   eggs, slightly beaten
- 1   cup dairy sour cream
- 1   cup grated Parmesan or Romano cheese
- ¼   cup thinly sliced green onions

Summer Pizza with Sweet Peppers

1. Prepare the Dough: Sprinkle the yeast over very warm water in a large bowl. ("Very warm water" should feel comfortably warm when dropped on the wrist.) Stir gently with a fork until the yeast is dissolved.
2. Meanwhile, heat the milk, butter and salt in a small saucepan until the butter is melted. Remove from the heat and let cool to lukewarm. Beat in the egg. Add the milk mixture to the yeast along with 1 cup of the flour; mix thoroughly with a wooden spoon. Add the second cup of flour; mix until the dough begins to form a soft sticky mass.
3. Scrape the dough out onto a floured board. Knead in the remaining flour, a little at a time, until the dough is no longer sticky. Continue to knead just until smooth and elastic, for 3 to 4 minutes.
4. Place the dough in a lightly oiled 2-quart bowl; turn to coat with the oil. Tightly cover the bowl with plastic wrap. Let rise in a warm place, away from drafts, until doubled in volume, for 30 to 45 minutes.
5. Meanwhile, prepare the Topping: Reserve the grated lemon rind. Combine half of the lemon juice, the olive oil, ¼ teaspoon of the salt, the pepper, green and red peppers and onion. Toss together to coat the vegetables; set aside.
6. Toss the mozzarella with the remaining lemon juice and reserved grated rind in a small bowl; set aside.
7. Combine the eggs, sour cream and remaining ¼ teaspoon of salt in a small bowl; beat until well blended. Stir in the grated Parmesan; set aside.
8. Preheat the oven to very hot (450°).
9. Punch the dough down. Turn out onto the board. Knead for 1 minute. Return half of the dough to the bowl; cover. Roll out the other half into a 15 x 10-inch rectangle. Fit into a 15 x 10 x 1-inch jelly-roll pan, pressing and shaping the dough ½ inch up the sides of the pan. Roll out the remaining dough to the same dimensions; cover.
10. Pour half of the sour cream mixture over the pizza dough in the pan, spreading to within ½ inch of the edges. Toss the vegetable mixture and evenly distribute half of it over the sour cream mixture. Sprinkle with half of the mozzarella mixture and half of the green onions.
11. Bake in the preheated very hot oven (450°) for 20 minutes or until puffed and the edges of the crust are golden brown. Remove from the oven. Gently loosen from the pan with two large metal spatulas. ☞

Slip the pizza onto a large cutting board.

12. Immediately fit the remaining dough in the pan as in Step 9. Repeat layering and baking as in Steps 10 and 11.

13. Cut the cooked pizza into 6 pieces.

French-Toasted Cheese

Makes 1 serving.

Nutrient Value Per Serving: 337 calories, 16 gm. protein, 21 gm. fat, 523 mg. sodium, 317 mg. cholesterol.

2 *slices whole-wheat bread*
1 *slice Muenster, Swiss, Monterey Jack or American cheese*
1 *large egg*
2 *teaspoons butter or margarine*

1. Make a sandwich with the bread and cheese, trimming the cheese to neatly fit the bread if necessary.

2. Beat the egg lightly in a shallow dish. Dip the sandwich into the egg, turning the bread to coat both sides.

3. Fry the sandwich in the butter in a skillet over medium heat until lightly browned on both sides, for about 1 minute. Gently press down the sandwich as it cooks to melt the cheese. Serve immediately, or wrap in aluminum foil to eat on the run within 30 minutes.

Cheese-Stuffed Vegetables

This refreshing first course may be made a day ahead.

Makes 4 servings.

Nutrient Value Per Serving: 166 calories, 6 gm. protein, 14 gm. fat, 310 mg. sodium, 42 mg. cholesterol.

1 *package (3 ounces) cream cheese, softened*
1 *package (2 ounces) blue cheese, softened*
1 *teaspoon finely chopped onion*
1 *teaspoon fresh lemon juice*
1 *small cucumber, pared and trimmed*
2 *medium-size celery stalks, washed and trimmed*
2 *ounces snow peas, washed, stem ends removed*

1. Combine the cheeses, onion and lemon juice in a small bowl.

2. Cut the cucumber into ⅓-inch-thick slices.

Remove some seeds from the center of each slice with a melon baller to form a small cavity. Spoon 1 teaspoon of the cheese filling into each cavity.

3. Fill the celery stalks with the filling. Cut into 1½-inch-long pieces.

4. Carefully cut open the snow peas on the curved edge. Spoon or pipe 1 teaspoon of the cheese mixture in each.

5. Place the vegetables in a shallow, airtight container lined with damp paper toweling. Cover with another piece of damp paper toweling, then seal with the container cover. Refrigerate for up to 24 hours.

6. Pack containers in an insulated bag with a frozen ice pack.

Ricotta Pie

Ricotta Pie

Bake at 350° for 1 hour and 15 minutes. Makes 8 servings.

Nutrient Value Per Serving: 539 calories, 22 gm. protein, 40 gm. fat, 516 mg. sodium, 349 mg. cholesterol.

1¾ *cups sifted all-purpose flour*
¼ *teaspoon salt*
¾ *cup (1½ sticks) unsalted butter or margarine*
3 *egg yolks, slightly beaten*
2 *to 3 tablespoons ice water*
4 *eggs*
1 *container (15 ounces) whole-milk ricotta cheese*
1 *package (8 ounces) smoked mozzarella, cut into ¼-inch cubes*
¼ *pound Genoa salami in one piece, cut into ¼-inch cubes*
1 *tablespoon grated Parmesan cheese*
½ *teaspoon pepper*

1. Sift the flour and salt into a large bowl. Cut in the butter until crumbly. Add the yolks and 2 tablespoons of the water, tossing with a fork. Work the dough until soft enough to gather into a ball; add the additional tablespoon of water, if necessary. Wrap; chill for 1 hour.
2. Beat the eggs and ricotta until smooth. Stir in the mozzarella, salami, Parmesan and pepper.
3. Reserve a third of the dough; cover. Roll the remaining dough on a lightly floured surface into a 12-inch round. Ease into a 9-inch springform pan. Press the dough over the bottom and sides. Prick with a fork. Spoon the filling into the pan.
4. Preheat the oven to moderate (350°).
5. Roll the reserved dough into a 10-inch round. Center on top of the filling. Moisten the edges of the top and bottom crusts with water; pinch together to seal. Set the pan on a cookie sheet.
6. Bake in the preheated moderate oven (350°) for 1 hour and 15 minutes. Cool in the pan on a rack for 35 minutes. Carefully remove the sides. Serve warm.

the bread-cheese mixture. Cover with plastic wrap.
3. Refrigerate for up to 24 hours; 1 hour before serving time, remove from the refrigerator; uncover. Preheat the oven to moderate (350°).
4. Bake in the preheated moderate oven (350°) for 1 hour or until puffed and golden. Garnish with the watercress and cherry tomatoes, if you wish.

Cheese Capitals

The reason some cheeses are spelled with initial capital letters is that they are named after towns or areas of their origin. Examples: Brie and Camembert, France; Cheddar, England; Parma and Gorgonzola, Italy.

Main-Dish Salads/ Vegetables

Cabbage and Sauerkraut Soup

Traditionally, this Russian specialty was made with fermented cabbage.

Makes 8 servings.

Nutrient Value Per Serving: 248 calories, 11 gm. protein, 14 gm. fat, 839 mg. sodium, 34 mg. cholesterol.

- 1 large onion, chopped (1 cup)
- 2 cloves garlic, finely chopped
- 1 tablespoon bacon fat, butter or margarine
- 1 can (28 ounces) low-sodium whole tomatoes with their liquid, coarsely chopped
- 2 celery stalks, chopped (½ cup)
- 2 medium-size carrots, cut into thin julienne strips (1 cup)
- 1 small cabbage (¾ to 1 pound), cut into wedges and cored
- 1 medium-size rutabaga (yellow turnip) (1½ pounds), peeled and cut into 1-inch cubes
- 4 cups low-sodium chicken broth
- ¾ pound kielbasa sausage, cut into ¼-inch slices
- 1 package (1 pound) sauerkraut, drained and squeezed dry ☞

Bacon and Cheese Strata

Bake at 350° for 1 hour.
Makes 4 servings.

Nutrient Value Per Serving: 501 calories, 24 gm. protein, 34 gm. fat, 696 mg. sodium, 483 mg. cholesterol.

- 6 slices day-old bread
- 3 tablespoons butter or margarine, softened
- 1 cup shredded Cheddar cheese (4 ounces)
- 4 slices bacon, crisply fried, drained and crumbled
- 6 eggs, slightly beaten
- 1½ cups milk
- 1 teaspoon dry mustard
- ⅛ teaspoon pepper
  Watercress (optional)
  Cherry tomatoes (optional)

1. Butter the bread on a wooden board; cut into small cubes. Alternate layers of the bread cubes, Cheddar cheese and the bacon in a buttered 8-cup casserole.
2. Blend the eggs, milk, dry mustard and pepper in a medium-size bowl; pour over

2 tablespoons lemon juice OR: distilled
    white vinegar
1 tablespoon sugar (optional)
2 bay leaves
    Salt (optional)
    Pepper
1 tablespoon minced fresh dill OR: parsley
½ cup dairy sour cream (optional)

1. Sauté the onion and garlic in the bacon fat in a kettle or Dutch oven, stirring, for 3 minutes. Add the tomatoes with their liquid, celery, carrots, cabbage, rutabaga and chicken broth; break up the tomatoes with a wooden spoon. Bring to boiling. Lower the heat; cover; simmer, stirring occasionally, for 30 minutes.
2. Stir in the sliced kielbasa, sauerkraut, lemon juice, sugar, if using, and bay leaves. Cover; simmer for 30 minutes longer. Season to taste with the salt and pepper.
3. Ladle into a soup tureen or heated soup bowls. Sprinkle with the dill; top each serving with a dollop of the sour cream, if you wish.

Kielbasa Sausage

A smoked sausage made from ground beef and pork, with garlic added for flavoring.

Tarragon Chicken Salad

Makes 2 servings.

Nutrient Value Per Serving: 436 calories, 34 gm. protein, 32 gm. fat, 652 mg. sodium, 112 mg. cholesterol.

2 boneless, skinned chicken breast halves
    (5 ounces each), lightly pounded
½ teaspoon leaf tarragon, crumbled
¼ teaspoon salt
¼ teaspoon pepper
1 tablespoon butter or margarine

1 tablespoon vegetable oil
⅓ cup chopped celery
¼ cup pitted black olives, quartered
¼ cup chopped sweet red pepper
2 tablespoons mayonnaise or salad dressing
2 tablespoons dairy sour cream
1½ teaspoons lemon juice

1. Sprinkle the chicken with ¼ teaspoon of the tarragon, ⅛ teaspoon of the salt and ⅛ teaspoon of the pepper.
2. Melt the butter with the oil in a medium-size skillet over medium heat. Place the chicken in the skillet; cover with a sheet of aluminum foil. Cook for 2 minutes or until lightly browned. Turn the chicken over. Cover with foil and cook for 3 minutes longer or until firm when lightly pressed with the finger. Remove and cool.
3. Cut the chicken into ½-inch pieces. Combine the chicken, celery, olives, red pepper, mayonnaise, sour cream, lemon juice, the remaining ¼ teaspoon of tarragon, ⅛ teaspoon of salt and ⅛ teaspoon of pepper in a medium-size bowl; stir until well mixed. Transfer to an airtight container. Cover and refrigerate until ready to serve.

New Moon Chicken Salad

Makes 8 servings.

Nutrient Value Per Serving: 430 calories, 22 gm. protein, 22 gm. fat, 642 mg. sodium, 123 mg. cholesterol.

2 eggs
¾ cup cornstarch
1 broiler-fryer (2½ pounds), quartered
1 tablespoon Oriental sesame oil (dark
    sesame oil)*
1¼ cups vegetable oil
2 tablespoons soy sauce
1½ tablespoons hoisin sauce*
1 tablespoon dry mustard
½ teaspoon salt
¼ teaspoon pepper
1 package (6¾ ounces) rice sticks*
1 bunch green onions, chopped
3 tablespoons chopped toasted almonds
2 tablespoons toasted sesame seeds
1 small head iceberg lettuce, finely shredded

1. Lightly beat the eggs in a small saucer. Spread the cornstarch on a piece of wax paper.

2. Dip the chicken into the beaten eggs, then into the cornstarch to evenly coat; shake off the excess.
3. Fry the coated chicken in the sesame oil and ¼ cup of the vegetable oil in a medium-size skillet until nearly tender, for about 25 minutes. Remove the chicken to a platter.
4. To prepare the dressing, combine the soy sauce, hoisin sauce, water, mustard, salt and pepper in a small bowl; mix well. Reserve.
5. Heat the remaining 1 cup of vegetable oil in a large, deep skillet until a deep-fat frying thermometer registers 375°. Fry the rice sticks, a few at a time, just until lightly golden brown, for 30 to 40 seconds. Remove with a slotted spoon to paper toweling to drain.
6. When cool enough to handle, remove the chicken from the bones, leaving the skin on. Cut into bite-size pieces. Combine the chicken in a large bowl with the chopped green onions, almonds, sesame seeds and shredded lettuce. Pour the reserved soy sauce dressing over and add the fried rice sticks. Toss gently to mix.

Note: Oriental sesame oil, hoisin sauce and rice sticks can be found in the Oriental food section in some supermarkets or in a specialty food shop.

Salmon Potato Salad

Makes 10 servings.

Nutrient Value Per Serving: 326 calories, 15 gm. protein, 19 gm. fat, 800 mg. sodium, 132 mg. cholesterol.

2½ pounds small, red new potatoes
2 teaspoons salt
1 package (10 ounces) frozen cut green beans or peas
1 clove garlic, finely chopped
½ teaspoon pepper
2 tablespoons Dijon-style mustard
¼ cup olive or vegetable oil
7 tablespoons cider vinegar
1 can (16 ounces) pink salmon, drained, boned, flaked and any skin removed
½ cup thinly sliced green onions (about 8 green onions)
¼ cup chopped parsley
4 hard-cooked eggs, coarsely chopped
½ cup mayonnaise or salad dressing
Lettuce leaves

1. Place the potatoes in a large pot. Cover with cold water and 1 teaspoon of the salt. Bring to boiling. Cook just until tender, for about 20 minutes. Drain. When cool enough to handle, cut into ¼-inch-thick slices. Place in a large bowl.
2. Cook the green beans or peas according to the label directions. Drain. Add to the potatoes.
3. Combine the garlic, remaining teaspoon of salt, the pepper, mustard, olive oil and vinegar in a small bowl; blend well. Pour over the potatoes and green beans; toss gently to mix well. Cover with plastic wrap. Cool to room temperature.
4. Add the salmon, green onions, parsley and hard-cooked eggs; toss gently. Stir in the mayonnaise.
5. To serve, arrange the lettuce leaves on a serving plate. Mound the salad on the lettuce. Serve chilled or at room temperature.

Steak and Broccoli Salad

Makes 4 servings.

Nutrient Value Per Serving: 478 calories, 40 gm. protein, 29 gm. fat, 435 mg. sodium, 107 mg. cholesterol.

1 bunch broccoli (about 1¼ pounds)
1 tablespoon prepared mustard
½ cup red wine vinegar
2 teaspoons sugar
6 tablespoons corn oil
3 tablespoons chopped fresh dill
2 tablespoons thinly sliced green onion
½ teaspoon salt
½ teaspoon black pepper
1 pound cooked and chilled flank steak, cut into 2 x ½-inch strips*
1 cup small cherry tomatoes
1 medium-size head romaine lettuce
Pimiento for garnish (optional)

1. Divide the broccoli into stems and flowerets. Peel the stems; cut ½-inch diagonal slices.
2. Cook the broccoli flowerets and stems in a large pot of boiling salted water until crisp-tender, for about 2 minutes. Drain and rinse under cold water to stop the cooking. Drain well. Set aside.

3. Whisk together the mustard, vinegar and sugar in a large bowl. Whisk in the oil. Stir in the dill, green onion, salt and pepper. Fold in the sliced steak, cherry tomatoes and reserved broccoli; toss to coat well. Refrigerate until 30 minutes before serving.
4. To serve, arrrange the romaine leaves on a serving platter or individual plates. Arrange the steak and broccoli mixture over the top. Drizzle with any remaining marinade. Garnish with the pimiento slices, if you wish.

* *Note:* A 1-pound, 6-ounce flank steak, cooked, will yield about 1 pound.

◀◀ ▼
Pork Teriyaki Salad

Makes 8 servings.

Nutrient Value Per Serving: 458 calories, 31 gm. protein, 25 gm. fat, 1,408 mg. sodium, 80 mg. cholesterol.

1½ *cups dry white wine*
½ *cup soy sauce*
¼ *cup honey*
3 *tablespoons chopped, pared fresh gingerroot*
2 *cloves garlic, crushed*
3 *tablespoons Oriental sesame oil**
2 *pounds fresh asparagus, trimmed and pared, OR: 2 packages (10 ounces each) frozen asparagus spears*
1 *pound snow peas, trimmed, OR: 1 pound green beans, trimmed*
5 *cups cooked pork loin** pieces (2 x 1½ inches)*
3 *sweet red peppers, halved, seeded and cut into 2 x ½-inch strips (2½ cups)*
1 *pound mushrooms, cut into ¼-inch-thick slices*
1 *small head romaine lettuce and 1 small head radicchio*** OR: 2 heads romaine lettuce OR: 2 heads radicchio*
2 *tablespoons toasted sesame seeds (optional)*

1. Combine the wine, soy sauce, honey, gingerroot and garlic in a medium-size saucepan. Cook over medium heat until the mixture is reduced to 1⅔ cups, for 10 to 15 minutes. Strain through a sieve into a medium-size bowl. Add the Oriental sesame oil. Set the marinade aside to cool.
2. Cook the fresh asparagus in a large quantity of boiling water for 3 minutes or until crisp-tender, or cook the frozen asparagus following the package directions. Drain. Rinse under cold water to stop the cooking. Refrigerate.
3. Cook the snow peas in a large quantity of boiling water for 1 minute, or the green beans until crisp-tender, for about 5 minutes. Drain. Rinse under cold water to stop the cooking. Refrigerate.
4. At least 4 hours before serving time, combine the pork and the red peppers in a large bowl. Add half of the mushrooms; toss to coat. Cover and refrigerate. Place the mushrooms in a medium-size bowl. Add the remaining marinade; cover and refrigerate. The mushrooms should marinate for at least 1½ hours or as long as the pork.
5. To serve, line a large serving platter with the leaves of the romaine and radicchio. Remove the pork and peppers from the marinade with a slotted spoon and pile in the center of the platter; reserve the marinade. Remove the mushrooms from the marinade with a slotted spoon and arrange, along with the asparagus and snow peas, around the meat. Drizzle the reserved marinade over all. Sprinkle with the toasted sesame seeds, if you wish.

Notes: * Oriental sesame oil has more flavor and is darker in color than regular sesame oil. It can be found in the Oriental section of your supermarket or a specialty food shop.
** A 2-pound boned loin of pork, when cooked, will yield about 5 cups of cooked pieces. The center cut is the leanest from the loin, but usually the most expensive.
*** Radicchio is a bitter-tasting Italian red chicory. Store, wrapped, in the refrigerator for only a day or two.

◣ ◀◀ ▼
Curried Chicken and Rice Salad

Makes 6 servings.

Nutrient Value Per Serving: 677 calories, 57 gm. protein, 32 gm. fat, 390 mg. sodium, 160 mg. cholesterol.

½ *cup mayonnaise*
½ *cup prepared mayonnaise-type salad dressing*
½ *cup raisins*
3 *tablespoons mango or other chutney*
2 *tablespoons curry powder*
1 *tablespoon lemon juice*

4½ cups cubed cooked chicken (2½ to 3 pounds whole chicken breasts)
2 cups cooked rice (¾ cup uncooked converted rice)
¼ cup thinly sliced green onions
1 banana, cut into ¼-inch-thick rounds (optional)
¼ cup peanuts
¼ cup flaked coconut

1. Combine the mayonnaise, salad dressing, 2 tablespoons of the raisins, the chutney, curry powder and lemon juice in the container of an electric blender. Cover; whirl until a smooth purée.
2. Combine the chicken pieces, rice, green onions and remaining raisins in a large bowl. Blend in the curry dressing. Cover and refrigerate until serving time.
3. To serve, arrange the salad in a serving bowl or on a platter. Garnish with the banana, if you wish, the peanuts and coconut.

MICROWAVE DIRECTIONS (For Cooking Chicken)
650 Watt Variable Power Microwave Oven
Directions: Cut 3 pounds of unboned chicken breasts in half. Arrange in a single layer in a microwave-safe dish, about 13 x 9 inches, placing the meatier portions toward the outside edge of the dish. Sprinkle with salt and pepper. Pour in ¼ cup of dry white wine or water. Cover with wax paper. Microwave at full power for 12 to 13 minutes or until the juices run clear and the meat is no longer pink near the bone, rotating one-half turn after 6 minutes. Cool; remove the bones and skin. Cut into cubes and use in the above recipe.

Curried Chicken and Rice Salad, Pork Teriyaki Salad (page 154) and Couscous Salad (page 70)

Salad Pizza

This main-dish salad is one of Family Circle's favorites—it'll wow any crowd!

Bake bread crust at 400° for 20 to 25 minutes.
Makes 6 servings

Nutrient Value Per Serving: 558 calories, 20 gm. protein, 32 gm. fat, 912 mg. sodium, 44 mg. cholesterol.

Pizza Bread (recipe follows)
¼ cup olive or vegetable oil
½ teaspoon leaf basil, crumbled
⅛ to ¼ teaspoon crushed red pepper flakes
8 ounces mozzarella cheese, cut into ½-inch cubes
¼ cup sliced, pitted black olives
1 jar (6 ounces) marinated artichoke hearts, undrained
3 cups broccoli flowerets and tender stems (about half a bunch)
½ cup green beans (about 2 ounces), cut into 1-inch lengths
2 tablespoons tarragon vinegar
2 teaspoons finely chopped shallots or onion
1 small sweet yellow or red pepper, halved, seeded and cut into ¼-inch-wide strips
3 radishes, thinly sliced
12 to 18 slices salami, cut into wedges
2 cups shredded crisp lettuce, such as romaine, escarole and/or iceberg
3 medium-size tomatoes, each cut into about 8 wedges
Alfalfa sprouts
Chopped parsley

1. Prepare the Pizza Bread.
2. Combine the oil, basil, pepper flakes, cheese, olives and undrained artichoke hearts in a medium-size bowl; stir to mix. Marinate in the refrigerator, stirring once or twice, for 2 to 3 hours.
3. Meanwhile, cook the broccoli and green beans in a large saucepan of boiling water for 1 minute. Drain; plunge into ice water to stop the cooking and chill. Drain; refrigerate.
4. About 30 minutes before serving, add the broccoli, green beans, vinegar, shallots, pepper, radishes, and salami to the marinated cheese mixture; toss to mix.
5. Spread the lettuce over the Pizza Bread. Arrange the tomato wedges around the outside edge, overlapping the rim slightly. Spoon the salad with a slotted spoon into ☞

the center. Drizzle any remaining dressing from the bowl over the tomatoes. Garnish with the alfalfa sprouts and sprinkle with the parsley. To serve, cut into wedges with a serrated knife.

Pizza Bread: Prepare 1 package (16 ounces) of country white or golden wheat yeast bread mix with water and oil, and knead following the label directions. Cover with a bowl; let rest for 5 minutes. Lightly grease a 14-inch pizza pan or large cookie sheet. Roll out half of the dough into a 14-inch round. Press into the pizza pan. Divide the remaining dough in half. Roll each half between your palms into a long strand about 48 inches long. Twist the strands together to form a rope. Moisten the edge of the dough round with water. Place the rope on the moistened edges; pinch the ends together. Using the end of a spoon, press the outside edges of the rope to the pizza base to firmly attach. Let rise in a warm place, away from drafts, for about 20 minutes or until doubled in volume. Meanwhile, preheat the oven to hot (400°). For a shiny crust, brush the rope with a slightly beaten egg. Bake in the preheated oven (400°) for 20 to 25 minutes or until the bread is golden brown and sounds hollow when tapped with the finger. Remove the bread from the pan to a wire rack to cool.

Seafood Salad

Makes 6 servings.

Nutrient Value Per Serving: 307 calories, 20 gm. protein, 22 gm. fat, 438 mg. sodium, 98 mg. cholesterol.

½ **pound sea scallops, sliced in half horizontally if large**
½ **pound shrimp, shelled and deveined**
½ **pound "sea legs"* or crabmeat**
2 **carrots, pared and cut into 2x¼-inch strips**
2 **celery stalks, cut into 2x¼-inch strips**
¼ **cup thinly sliced green onions, both white and tender green parts**
    Seafood Dressing (recipe follows)
½ **pound mushrooms, thinly sliced**
1 **small head green leafy lettuce**

1. Cook the scallops in gently simmering water in a skillet until opaque, for about 2 minutes. Remove with a slotted spoon to a colander. Keep the water simmering. Rinse gently under cold water to stop the cooking. Drain well. Transfer to a large bowl.
2. Cook the shrimp gently in the same simmering water until pink and firm, but not rubbery, for 2 to 2½ minutes. Drain in the colander. Rinse under cold water to stop the cooking. Drain well.
3. Combine the shrimp with the scallops, along with the sea legs or crabmeat, in the large bowl. Set aside.
4. Cook the carrots and celery in boiling water to cover in a medium-size saucepan until crisp-tender, for about 2 minutes. Drain in the colander and rinse under cold water to stop the cooking. Drain. Combine with the green onions in a medium-size bowl.
5. Pour one-third of the Seafood Dressing over the vegetables; toss to coat. Cover and refrigerate until serving time.
6. Combine the mushroom slices with the seafood in the large bowl. Add the remaining dressing; toss to coat. Cover and refrigerate until serving time.
7. To serve, arrange the lettuce leaves around the edge of a round or oval platter. Drain the seafood and vegetable mixtures separately, reserving the marinade. Mound the seafood mixture in the center of the platter. Surround with the vegetables. Sprinkle with the marinade to taste.

Seafood Dressing: Combine ½ teaspoon of dry mustard, ½ teaspoon of leaf tarragon, crumbled, ½ teaspoon of salt, ¼ teaspoon of pepper, 3 tablespoons of lemon juice, 1 tablespoon of tarragon vinegar, 1 tablespoon of tarragon vinegar, 1 tablespoon of walnut oil and ½ cup of olive or vegetable oil in a medium-size mixing bowl. Whisk to combine well. Makes ¾ cup of dressing.

* Note: "Sea legs" are usually a combination of pollack (a white fish), shell fish and other ingredients, and can be found in the seafood section of your supermarket.

Rolled Stuffed Eggplant

Savory Stuffed Tomatoes

Bake at 350° for 20 minutes.
Makes 6 servings.

Nutrient Value Per Serving: 179 calories, 8 gm. protein, 8 gm. fat, 699 mg. sodium, 19 mg. cholesterol.

6 large tomatoes
1 medium-size sweet green pepper, halved, seeded and finely chopped
2 tablespoons butter or margarine
⅓ cup dry white wine
½ to 1 teaspoon caraway seeds
1 can (8 ounces) sauerkraut, drained and chopped
1 can (4 ounces) mushrooms, stems and pieces, finely chopped
1 cup drained canned pinto beans
½ cup unseasoned bread crumbs
½ teaspoon salt
¼ teaspoon pepper
½ cup shredded Monterey Jack cheese (2 ounces)
   Dairy sour cream (optional)

1. Cut a thin slice from the bottom of the tomatoes so they stand upright. Carefully scoop out the insides with a grapefruit spoon or small paring knife, leaving a ½-inch shell. Reserve and chop ½ cup of the pulp. (Reserve the remaining pulp for soups and sauces.)
2. Sauté the green pepper in the butter in a medium-size skillet until softened, for 5 to 7 minutes. Add the wine and caraway seeds. Lower the heat; simmer for 5 minutes.
3. Stir in the sauerkraut, mushrooms, beans, crumbs, reserved tomato pulp, salt and pepper. Simmer for 32 minutes. Set aside.
4. Preheat the oven to moderate (350°).
5. Place the tomatoes in an ungreased 13 x 9 x 2-inch baking pan. Stir the cheese into the skillet. Fill the tomatoes with the sauerkraut mixture.*
6. Bake, uncovered, in the preheated moderate oven (350°) for 20 minutes or until the tomatoes are heated through. Top with a dollop of sour cream, if you wish.

* Note: The leftover filling can be baked separately.

Fresh Eggplant

Really a fruit, an eggplant should be firm and heavy in relation to size, with a uniformly dark, rich purple color. Use as quickly as possible after purchasing or, if necessary, store in a plastic bag in the refrigerator for a day or two.

Rolled Stuffed Eggplant

Take the work out of entertaining with this make-ahead main dish.

Bake at 450° for 30 minutes.
Makes 15 servings (30 rolls).

Nutrient Value Per Serving: 509 calories, 20 gm. protein, 26 gm. fat, 986 mg. sodium, 106 mg. cholesterol.

4 cloves garlic, finely chopped
1 cup vegetable oil
2 cans (28 ounces each) crushed tomatoes with purée
1 can (8 ounces) tomato sauce
½ teaspoooon salt
½ teaspoon pepper
4 cups plain bread crumbs
2 cups sifted all-purpose flour
4 eggs
¼ cup milk
2 eggplant (1 pound each)
2 containers (15 ounces each) ricotta cheese
1 package (8 ounces) mozzarella cheese, grated
½ cup grated Parmesan cheese
2 cups chopped parsley

☞

1. Sauté the garlic in 1 tablespoon of the oil in a large saucepan until golden brown, for about 4 minutes. Working in batches, combine the crushed tomatoes, tomato sauce, salt and pepper in a blender. Whirl until smooth. Pour into the saucepan. Bring to boiling. Lower the heat; simmer, partially covered, for 30 minutes. Reserve.
2. Combine the crumbs and flour in a large shallow pan. Beat the eggs and milk in a large bowl. Peel the eggplant; cut lengthwise into ⅛-inch-thick slices. Dip into the egg mixture; dredge with the flour mixture, shaking off the excess. Set on wax paper.
3. Working in batches and using about 3 tablespoons of oil per batch, sauté the eggplant in the large skillet until golden, 1 minute per side. Drain on paper toweling.
4. Preheat the oven to hot (450°).
5. Combine the ricotta, mozzarella, Parmesan and parsley in a bowl; mix well. Spread 2 to 3 tablespoons on one side of each slice of the eggplant. Roll up jelly-roll fashion. Spread 1 cup of the tomato sauce over the bottom of each of two 11¾ x 7-inch baking dishes. Arrange the rolls, seam-side down, in a single layer in the dishes. Spoon the sauce over the rolls; save the remainder to pass.
6. Bake, covered, in the preheated hot oven (450°) for 30 minutes or until the sauce is bubbly. Garnish with additional chopped parsley, if you wish.

To Make Ahead: Prepare the dough early in the day; bake just before serving. Or freeze. Defrost in the refrigerator overnight; bake as above.

Mexican Pizzettes

A packaged yeast bread mix cuts the preparation time for these individual pizzas.

Bake at 500° for 10 minutes.
Makes 4 servings.

Nutrient Value Per Serving: 710 calories, 26 gm. protein, 28 gm. fat, 166 mg. sodium, 41 mg. cholesterol.

1 medium-size eggplant (1¼ pounds), cut into ¼-inch-thick slices
3 tablespoons olive or vegetable oil
3 large, ripe plum tomatoes (about ½ pound), seeded and cut into ½-inch chunks
1 medium-size sweet green pepper, cored, seeded and cut into ½-inch chunks
½ cup fresh corn kernels or drained, canned whole corn kernels
3 cloves garlic, cut into slivers
1 package (14 or 16 ounces) white or whole-wheat yeast bread mix
3 tablespoons finely chopped canned green chilies
1 teaspoon leaf oregano, crumbled
¼ teaspoon pepper
1½ cups coarsely shredded Monterey Jack cheese (6 ounces)

1. Set the oven racks in the lower half of the oven. Preheat the oven to very hot (500°).
2. Lightly brush the eggplant on both sides with 2 tablespoons of the oil. Heat a large nonstick skillet over medium-high heat. Fry the eggplant in batches for 4 minutes on each side or until golden brown; do not add oil to the skillet. Remove the eggplant to paper toweling. Raise the heat to high.
3. Add the remaining 1 tablespoon of the oil to the skillet. Add the tomatoes, green pepper, corn and garlic. Cook for 2 minutes or until the moisture from the tomatoes is evaporated. Remove from the heat.
4. Prepare the bread dough following the package directions. After kneading, divide the dough into 4 pieces; cover and let rest for 5 minutes. Pat the dough down on a floured surface into 6-inch rounds. Set on a large baking sheet. Divide the eggplant among the dough rounds; spoon the tomato mixture over. Top with the green chilies, oregano and pepper. Cover with the shredded cheese.
5. Bake in the preheated very hot oven (500°) for 10 minutes or until the underside of the dough is golden and the topping is bubbly hot.

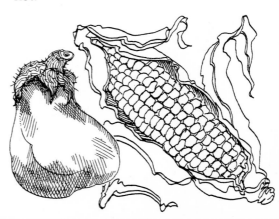

Clockwise, from top left: Collard Green Quiche (page 160), Piña Colada Down-Up Cake (page 191), Shrimp Creole (page 122).

Collard Green Quiche

Bake crust at 425° for 5 minutes;
then quiche at 350° for 40 minutes.
Makes 6 servings.

*Nutrient Value Per Serving: 378 calories, 14 gm. protein,
27 gm. fat, 509 mg. sodium, 229 mg. cholesterol.*

- 1 unbaked, 9-inch, homemade pie shell OR: 9-inch, store-bought frozen, deep-dish pie shell
- 1 package (10 ounces) frozen chopped collard greens
- 1 medium-size onion, chopped (½ cup)
- ½ cup chopped sweet green pepper
- 2 tablespoons butter or margarine
- ¼ teaspoon leaf tarragon, crumbled
- 1¼ cups half and half (half cream, half milk)
- 4 eggs
- ½ teaspoon salt
- ¼ teaspoon pepper
- 4 ounces Swiss cheese, grated (1 cup)
- ¼ teaspoon ground nutmeg

1. Preheat the oven to hot (425°).
2. Bake the pie shell in the preheated hot oven (425°) for 5 minutes. Remove to a wire rack. Lower the oven temperature to moderate (350°).
3. Cook the collard greens following the package directions. Drain well. Squeeze out the excess liquid.
4. Sauté the onion and green pepper in the butter in a large skillet until tender. Remove from the heat. Stir in the collard greens and tarragon.
5. Combine the half and half, eggs, salt and pepper in the container of an electric blender. Whirl until mixed.
6. Spread the collard green mixture into the bottom of the pie shell. Sprinkle with the cheese. Stir lightly to mix. Pour the egg mixture over. Sprinkle with the nutmeg.
7. Bake in the preheated moderate oven (350°) for 40 minutes or until the mixture is set and the quiche is lightly browned on top. Let stand for 5 minutes before slicing.

Eggplant Parmesan Stew

A rich stew with lots of vegetables and pasta.

Makes 10 servings.

*Nutrient Value Per Serving: 371 calories, 17 gm. protein,
9 gm. fat, 346 mg. sodium, 24 mg. cholesterol.*

- 6 cups low-sodium chicken broth
- 3 cups diced, pared potatoes (about 2 pounds)
- 2 large onions, chopped (2 cups)
- 1 bay leaf
- 1 small head cauliflower (about ¾ pound)
- 1 sweet red pepper, halved, seeded and coarsely chopped
- 1 sweet green pepper, halved, seeded and coarsely chopped
- 2 cups chopped celery
- 4 cups pared and cubed eggplant (about 1 pound)
- ½ pound Italian sausage, cut into ½-inch-thick slices
- 2 small zucchini (about ¾ pound), sliced
- 2 cups sliced mushrooms (½ pound)
- 1 can (15 ounces) low-sodium tomato sauce
- 2 cans (6 ounces each) low-sodium tomato paste
- 2 teaspoons leaf basil, crumbled
- ½ teaspoon garlic powder
- 6 cups cooked ziti (3 cups uncooked)
- ⅓ cup grated Parmesan cheese
  Salt to taste
- 1 cup shredded mozzarella cheese (4 ounces)

1. Combine the broth, potatoes, onions and bay leaf in a kettle or Dutch oven. Bring to boiling. Lower the heat; cover; simmer for about 20 minutes or until the potatoes are very soft.
2. Cut the cauliflower head into flowerets; finely chop the stems.
3. Add the cauliflower stems, red and green peppers, celery and eggplant to the kettle. Simmer, covered, for 10 minutes or until the eggplant is firm-tender.
4. Lightly brown the sausage in a large skillet over medium-high heat. Lower the heat; cook for 10 to 15 minutes or until cooked through. Remove with a slotted spoon to the stew. Add the cauliflower flowerets, zucchini, mushrooms, tomato sauce, tomato paste, basil and garlic powder. Simmer, covered, for 10 minutes or until the cauliflower is crisp-tender.

5. Reduce the heat to very low; stir in the cooked ziti and Parmesan cheese. Season with the salt to taste. Ladle into a large casserole dish or soup tureen. Garnish with the shredded mozzarella cheese.

Two Ways to Peel Tomatoes

1. Add the tomatoes, a few at a time, to a large pot of boiling water. When the water returns to boiling, boil very ripe tomatoes for 10 seconds and firmer tomatoes for 20 seconds. Remove with a slotted spoon. (If the skin splits, remove the tomato immediately.) Rinse under cold water to stop the cooking. Working from the bottom to the stem end, peel off the skin with a paring knife.
2. Stick a long, two-tined fork into the stem end of the tomato. Hold the tomato directly in a gas burner flame. Slowly rotate the tomato so all sides begin to show a speckled brown color. Set aside to cool. Peel as above.

Seeding a Tomato

Cut the tomato in half crosswise. Holding the tomato half in the palm of your hand, gently squeeze the tomato until the seeds loosen and fall. Gently scrape harder-to-remove seeds with a teaspoon.

Green Gnocchi with Sweet Red Pepper Sauce

Makes 4 generous servings (about 40 gnocchi).

Nutrient Value Per Serving: 540 calories, 25 gm. protein, 31 gm. fat, 1,145 mg. sodium, 189 mg. cholesterol.

> 2 **cups finely shredded zucchini (2 medium-size or about 1 pound), excess liquid squeezed out**
> 1 **clove garlic, finely chopped**
> 2 **tablespoons butter or margarine**
> 1 **cup grated Parmesan cheese**
> 1 **cup ricotta cheese**
> 1 **cup unsifted all-purpose flour**
> ¼ **cup finely chopped flat-leaf (Italian) parsley**
> 2 **eggs**
> ½ **teaspoon salt**
> ¼ **teaspoon pepper**
> 1 **tablespoon vegetable oil**
> **Sweet Red Pepper Sauce (page 183)**
> **Grated Parmesan cheese**

1. Sauté the zucchini and garlic in the butter in a medium-size skillet over medium heat for 3 minutes. Transfer to a large bowl; cool. Stir in the Parmesan, riccota, flour, parsley, eggs, salt and pepper.
2. Bring a large pot of salted water to boiling; add the vegetable oil.
3. Shape the gnocchi mixture with floured hands into small ovals, using 1 level measuring tablespoonful for each gnocchi. Set on a very lightly floured baking sheet. Carefully lower about 12 gnocchi, one at a time, with a slotted spoon into the gently boiling water. Cook until the gnocchi rise to the surface and are firm, for about 5 minutes. Remove with a slotted spoon to a paper toweling-lined tray. Continue to cook the remaining gnocchi.
4. To serve, cover the bottom of shallow soup bowls or plates with hot Sweet Red Pepper Sauce. Top with the gnocchi and sprinkle with the additional Parmesan cheese.

To Make Ahead: Prepare the Sweet Red Pepper Sauce and refrigerate. Prepare the gnocchi through placement on the baking sheet in Step 3, omitting Step 2. Loosely cover with plastic wrap and refrigerate until ready to cook. About 30 minutes before serving, remove the gnocchi from the refrigerator. Complete Step 2 and the remainder of Steps 3 and 4.

6 TASTY ACCOMPANIMENTS

Silo Chicken (page 131), Oh My! Potato Salad (page 171), Herbed Tomatoes and Onions (page 173).

*An assortment of vegetable and
fruit side dishes, stuffings and relishes —
to dress up your main course.*

W hat main course isn't made that much better with just the right side dishes as a complement? Of course, the most common of these are vegetable, but they needn't be. Fruits, stuffings and relishes, for example, are also wonderful additions that add a touch of elegance to your roast or fish.

Always purchase fresh vegetables in season for maximum flavor and nutritive value (prices will be lower then, too!) and use them within two or three days. And always keep in mind the one cardinal rule of vegetable cooking: Don't overcook! Vegetables are best when they're crisp-tender.

Fruits also make interesting accompaniments either alone or as ingredients in recipes such as Carrot-Yam Tzimmes (page 174), which include prunes and apricots.

Stuffings are an economical, easy and most ingenious way to stretch servings. They can be created from scratch with odds and ends of leftover breads, meats or vegetables. Different types of rices, potatoes, crackers or cornbread also provide a new twist—like our Tex-Mex Stuffing (page 180), which gets its punch from sweet and hot peppers.

When selecting accompaniments to accent the main course, be sure to consider compatibility, color and texture.

Vegetables

Fresh Fruit and Vegetable Availability

The following fruits and vegetables, thanks to refrigeration and efficient transportation, are usually available all year:

Apples	Cucumbers	Parsley and Herbs
Artichokes	Eggplant	Parsnips
Avocados	Escarole	Pears
Bananas	Garlic	Peas, green
Beans, green	Grapefruit	Peppers, sweet
Beets	Grapes	Pineapples
Broccoli	Greens	Plantains
Brussels Sprouts	Lemons	Potatoes
Cabbage	Lettuce	Radishes
Carrots	Limes	Spinach
Cauliflower	Mushrooms	Squash
Celery	Onions	Strawberries
Chinese Cabbage	Onions, green	Sweet Potatoes
Coconuts	Oranges	Tomatoes
Corn, sweet	Papayas	Turnips-Rutabagas

The following are widely available in the markets during the months indicated:

Apricots—June to August
Asparagus—March to July
Blueberries—June to August
Cantaloupes—April to October
Cherries—May to August
Cranberries—September to December
Honeydews—February to October
Mangoes—March to August
Nectarines—January and February, June to September
Okra—April to November
Peaches—May to September
Persimmons—October to February
Plums and Prunes—June to October
Pomegranates—September to December
Pumpkins—September to December
Tangelos—October to February
Tangerines—November to March
Watermelons—April to September

Refrigerating Fresh Fruits and Vegetables

Fruits and vegetables may be stored in the refrigerator for several days. The longer they are refrigerated the greater the vitamin loss, so it is best to eat them as soon after purchase as possible.

Asparagus, broccoli, cabbage, cauliflower, celery, cucumbers, green beans, green onions, green and red peppers, radishes, and greens (kale, spinach, turnip greens, chard and salad greens) should be promptly refrigerated in a covered container, moisture-proof bag or a vegetable crisper.

Apples, apricots, berries, cherries, corn (in husks), grapes, nectarines, peaches, pears, peas (in shell) and plums should be refrigerated loosely covered or in a plastic produce bag with air holes.

Vegetable Preparation

- **Don't overcook!** Vegetables should be cooked only until tender.
- **Boil:** Use a small amount of water, cover with a tight-fitting lid and cook over low heat to minimize loss of vitamins and minerals. Cook until tender.
- **Blanch:** Bring plenty of water to a rolling boil, immerse vegetables and bring water back to a boil for 2 to 4 minutes. Refresh vegetables under icy cold water and use in salads.
- **Steam:** Place a steaming basket, colander or bamboo steamer over 1½ to 2 inches of boiling water, then place prepared vegetables on the rack. Cover the pan, reduce the heat but keep the water boiling and cook until just tender.
- **Stir-Fry:** Place the wok or wide skillet over high heat; when hot, add salad oil and cut-up vegetables. Cook uncovered, stirring constantly, just until the vegetables have been lightly coated and slightly cooked (approximately 1 to 2 minutes). Add approximately ¼ cup of broth to 4 cups of vegetables; then cover and cook, stirring occasionally, until tender. Add more broth if necessary.
- **Microwave:** Cook all vegetables on 100% high power, following the manufacturer's directions. Cover the cooking dish with a casserole lid or heavy-duty plastic wrap. Cooking time depends on the freshness, moisture content and maturity of the vegetable. Remove the vegetables from the microwave after the shortest recommended time, let stand and test for doneness. If the vegetables are still too crisp, microwave further in one-minute segments.
- **Sauté:** Melt butter, margarine or oil in a large skillet. Try a combination of butter and corn oil or olive oil and corn oil. (Butter and olive oil impart flavor, and corn oil allows for cooking over high heat.) Add the prepared vegetables and cook, stirring constantly, until the vegetables are coated lightly, then cover, reduce the heat and cook just until tender.
- **Bake:** Prepare and cut vegetables into thick slices, arrange in a single layer in a baking pan or casserole or place on foil. Dot with butter or oil and bake uncovered until tender.

  Try tucking vegetables (*i.e.*, onions, squash and any of the root vegetables) in with the roast and increase the cooking time accordingly.
- **Testing for Doneness:** Cooking time depends on the freshness or maturity of the vegetables. They should be cooked until just tender, that is, until they give slightly, but remain firm when pierced. The color of the vegetable becomes intense when it is cooked until just tender.
- **Serving Suggestions:** Season vegetables *after* they have been cooked; do not salt the water first.

  Snip fresh garden herbs over vegetables before serving or sprinkle with fresh lemon or lime juice.

Top left: Mama's Chicken Soup with Fluffy
Matzo Balls (page 65), Orange-Glazed Baked
Chicken (page 100), Carrot-Yam Tzimmes
(page 174), Dilled Green Beans (page 166),
Matzo Honey Cake (page 190).

Steamed Asparagus Amandine

Here's an easy way to steam asparagus without having to purchase a special deep saucepan for the task.

Makes 8 servings.

Nutrient Value Per Serving: 45 calories, 3 gm. protein, 1 gm. fat, 4 mg. sodium, 0 mg. cholesterol.

- 2 **pounds fresh asparagus**
- 1 **cup water**
- 2 **tablespoons lemon juice**
- 2 **tablespoons slivered almonds**
- 1 **lemon, sliced paper-thin**

1. Wash and trim the asparagus. Tie loosely into a bundle with white string. Stand upright in the bottom of a double boiler. Add the water and lemon juice. Invert the top of the double boiler and place over the bottom to serve as a "cover."
2. Bring to boiling over high heat. Lower the heat and cook for 12 to 15 minutes or until tender; the thick bottoms will boil while the tender tips will steam.
3. Meanwhile, brown the slivered almonds in a small skillet over medium heat, stirring, until golden. Set aside.
4. Remove the string from the asparagus. Arrange on a platter and garnish with the almonds and thin slices of the lemon.

Dilled Green Beans

Choose crisp, fresh green beans. Remove only the stem end of the beans to reduce vitamin loss during cooking.

Makes 8 servings.

Nutrient Value Per Serving: 37 calories, 2 gm. protein, 0 gm. fat, 8 mg. sodium, 0 mg. cholesterol.

- 2 **pounds green beans, trimmed**
- 2 **tablespoons snipped fresh dill**
- 1½ **cups water**
  Fresh dill for garnish (optional)

Place the green beans flat in a large saucepan or skillet. Add the dill and water. Bring to boiling. Lower the heat and simmer, covered, for 10 minutes or until just tender. Drain. Serve with the additional fresh dill, if you wish.

Vegetable Leftovers

Use up leftovers: Toss steamed, boiled or blanched vegetables into salads. Purée leftover vegetables and add to a chilled cream soup.

Selecting and Storing Fresh Corn

Yellow or white, corn should have fresh green husks, plump and bright, firm kernels. Corn should be prepared immediately after purchase or wrapped in plastic and refrigerated for up to two days. Corn becomes less sweet as the natural sugar converts to starch. Peak season: July-September.

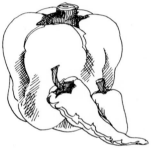

Marinated Vegetables

To preserve the brightness of the vegetables, prepare no more than a day ahead.

Makes 10 servings.

Nutrient Value Per Serving: 237 calories, 5 gm. protein, 17 gm. fat, 282 mg. sodium, 0 mg. cholesterol.

- 2 **pounds fresh green beans OR: 2 packages (10 ounces each) frozen whole green beans**
- 2 **cups cooked fresh corn (2 medium-size corn on cob) OR: 1 package (10 ounces) frozen kernel corn, thawed**
- 1 **package (10 ounces) frozen peas, thawed**
- 1 **cup thinly sliced celery (2 large stalks)**
- 1 **medium-size onion, chopped (½ cup)**
- 1 **sweet green pepper, halved, seeded and diced**
- 1 **jar (4 ounces) pimiento, sliced**
- ¾ **cup distilled white vinegar**
- ¾ **cup vegetable oil**
- 2 **tablespoons water**
- 1 **teaspoon salt**
- ½ **teaspoon pepper**
- ½ **teaspoon paprika**

1. Cook the fresh beans in boiling salted water to cover in a large pot for 7 minutes or until crisp-tender. Or, cook the frozen beans following the label directions. Drain. Rinse under cold water. Cut into 2-inch lengths.
2. Combine the beans, corn, peas, celery, onion, green pepper and pimiento in a large, shallow glass baking dish.
3. Combine the vinegar, oil, water, salt, pepper and paprika in a screw-top jar; shake until well blended. Pour over the vegetables; stir to coat well. Cover and marinate overnight in the refrigerator. Drain the marinade before serving, if you wish.

▧ ⧉ ⧠
Dilled Carrots

Serve chilled as a salad or side dish with roast or barbecued meats or deli sandwiches.

Makes 12 servings.

Nutrient Value Per Serving: 219 calories, 2 gm. protein, 10 gm. fat, 406 mg. sodium, 0 mg. cholesterol.

  3 **pounds carrots, pared and cut into ½-inch-thick slices**
  2 **large sweet green peppers, halved, seeded and cut into ¼-inch-wide strips**
  2 **large onions, thinly sliced into rings**
  1 **can (10¾ ounces) tomato soup**
  1 **cup sugar**
  ½ **cup vegetable oil**
  ½ **cup red wine vinegar**
  1 **teaspoon Worcestershire sauce**
  1 **teaspoon salt**
  ½ **teaspoon pepper**
  ¼ **cup snipped fresh dill OR: 4 teaspoons dried dillweed**

1. Cook the carrots in boiling salted water to cover in a large saucepan until crisp-tender, for about 5 minutes. Drain and cool.
2. Combine the carrots, green peppers and onions in a large bowl. Divide the vegetables between two 13½ x 8½ x 2-inch glass baking dishes.
3. Stir together the soup, sugar, oil, vinegar, Worcestershire, salt and pepper in a 4-cup glass measure. Pour half of the marinade over the vegetables in each dish. Stir gently to combine. Cover and refrigerate for 24 hours. Just before serving, drain the excess marinade, if you wish. Stir in the dill.

▧ ⧠
Acorn Squash Rings and Green Beans

Bake at 350° for 60 to 65 minutes.
Makes 6 servings.

Nutrient Value Per Serving: 153 calories, 4 gm. protein, 8 gm. fat, 114 mg. sodium, 21 mg. cholesterol.

  2 **acorn squash (1 pound each), trimmed**
  4 **tablespoons (½ stick) butter or margarine**
1½ **pounds green beans, trimmed**
  1 **tablespoon Worcestershire sauce**
  ¼ **teaspoon pepper**

1. Preheat the oven to moderate (350°).
2. Bake the squash in the preheated moderate oven (350°) for 30 minutes. Remove the squash from the oven; leave the oven on. Slice each squash into 3 equal rings, about 1 inch thick. Discard the seeds and pulp.
3. Melt 1 tablespoon of the butter in a small saucepan. Brush the squash slices with the butter. Arrange in a 13 x 9 x 2-inch baking dish.
4. Return to the moderate oven (350°) and bake for 30 to 35 minutes or until tender.
5. Meanwhile, cook the green beans in boiling salted water to cover in a large saucepan, for 5 to 10 minutes or until crisp-tender. Drain and transfer to a large bowl.
6. Melt the remaining 3 tablespoons butter in the same small saucepan. Stir in the Worcestershire sauce and pepper. Pour over the beans. Toss to coat well. Divide the beans into 6 equal bunches; stuff 1 bunch into the center of each squash ring.

Clockwise, from top center: Watermelon Basket (page 231), Sugared and Salted Pecans (page 60), Strawberry-Limon Punch (page 250), Cheese Rolls (page 286), Dilled Carrots (page 167), Hot Chicken Salad with Rice (page 104), Marinated Vegetables (page 166).

Sweet and Sour Cabbage

This wonderful and inexpensive vegetable dish is excellent with barbecued meats.

Makes 6 servings.

Nutrient Value Per Serving: 124 calories, 3 gm. protein, 8 gm. fat, 269 mg. sodium, 7 mg. cholesterol.

  4 **ounces sliced bacon, cut into ½-inch pieces**
1½ **cups chopped onion**
  1 **clove garlic, finely chopped**
  8 **cups coarsely chopped cabbage
     (about 1½ pounds)**
  1 **tablespoon sugar**
  5 **tablespoons distilled white or cider vinegar**
  ½ **teaspoon salt**
  ¼ **teaspoon pepper**

1. Cook the bacon in a large skillet until crisp and golden brown, stirring often. Remove with a slotted spoon to paper toweling to drain. Pour off all but 2 tablespoons of the bacon fat.
2. Add the onion and garlic to the skillet. Sauté until softened, for about 2 minutes. Add the cabbage. Cook, uncovered, over low heat, stirring often, for 15 minutes. Add half the bacon. Cook for 15 minutes longer or until the cabbage is tender. Stir in the sugar, vinegar, salt and pepper. Transfer the cabbage to a serving plate. Sprinkle with the remaining bacon.

MICROWAVE DIRECTIONS
650 Watt Variable Power Microwave Oven
Ingredient Change: Leave the bacon in slices.
Directions: Place the bacon slices in a single layer on a microwave-safe bacon rack in a large, shallow microwave-safe baking dish, about 13 x 9 inches. Cover with paper toweling. Microwave at full power for 3½ minutes. Remove the bacon; reserve. Remove the bacon rack from the pan. Pour off all but 2 tablespoons of the bacon fat. Add the onion and garlic. Microwave, uncovered, at full power for 3 minutes, stirring once. Add the cabbage. Cover with wax paper. Microwave at full power for 4 minutes. Crumble the reserved bacon; stir into the cabbage. Cover with wax paper. Microwave at full power for 4 minutes or until the cabbage is crisp-tender. Remove the dish from the oven. Stir the sugar, vinegar, salt and pepper into the cabbage mixture.

Pineapple Slaw

Makes 6 to 8 servings.

Nutrient Value Per Serving: 330 calories, 3 gm. protein, 27 gm. fat, 213 mg. sodium, 22 mg. cholesterol.

  1 **small green cabbage (2 pounds), coarsely shredded (about 12 cups)**
  ½ **cup grated carrot (1 large, pared)**
  ½ **cup finely chopped onion (1 medium-size)**
  ½ **cup finely chopped sweet red pepper
     (1 small)**
  1 **can (8 ounces) pineapple chunks packed in juice, drained and ¼ cup juice reserved**
  1 **cup mayonnaise or salad dressing**
  ¼ **cup dairy sour cream**
1½ **teaspoons tarragon vinegar**
  ¼ **teaspoon crushed red pepper flakes**
  1 **slice dried pineapple, slivered
     (about ⅓ cup)
     Sweet red pepper rings, for garnish
     (optional)**

1. Combine the cabbage, carrot, onion and red pepper in a large bowl.
2. Chop the pineapple chunks. Add to the cabbage mixture.
3. Mix the mayonnaise, sour cream, vinegar and red pepper flakes in a bowl. Whisk in the reserved pineapple juice. Pour over the cabbage mixture; mix thoroughly. Garnish with the dried pineapple and the sweet red pepper rings, if you wish.

Scalloped Potatoes

Scalloped Potatoes

Bake at 375° for 45 minutes.
Makes 8 servings.

Nutrient Value Per Serving: 209 calories, 6 gm. protein, 9 gm. fat, 367 mg. sodium, 24 mg. cholesterol.

- 3 **pounds all-purpose potatoes, pared and thinly sliced (about 6 cups)**
- 2 **large onions, thinly sliced**
- ¼ **cup (½ stick) butter or margarine**
- 3 **tablespoons unsifted all-purpose flour**
- 2 **cups milk**
- 1 **teaspoon salt**
- ¼ **teaspoon pepper**
- ½ **cup chopped parsley**
- 2 **tablespoons chopped pimiento**

1. Cook the potatoes and onions in lightly salted boiling water in a large saucepan for 5 minutes; drain. Set aside.
2. Preheat the oven to moderate (375°). Butter a 2-quart baking dish.
3. Melt the butter in a medium-size saucepan. Stir in the flour until smooth. Stir in the milk, salt and pepper. Cook over medium heat, stirring constantly, until the mixture thickens and boils, for about 2 minutes. Remove from the heat; stir in the parsley and pimiento.
4. Spoon half of the potato-onion mixture into the prepared baking dish; add half the sauce. Stir gently to mix well. Add the remaining potato-onion mixture and sauce; stir to mix.
5. Bake in the preheated moderate oven (375°) for 45 minutes or until browned on top. Garnish with additional parsley and pimiento, if you wish.

Oh My! Potato Salad

Apples give this salad special texture and taste.

Makes 6 to 8 servings.

Nutrient Value Per Serving: 396 calories, 4 gm. protein, 25 gm. fat, 721 mg. sodium, 19 mg. cholesterol.

- 2½ **pounds new potatoes (about 5 cups)**
- 3 **sweet apples, such as Red Delicious or McIntosh**
- 2 **tablespoons lemon juice (1 lemon)**
- 1 **cup finely chopped onion (1 large onion)**
- 1 **cup thinly sliced dill pickles (3 to 4 pickles)**
- 2 **tablespoons capers, drained**
- 1 **teaspoon caper juice**
- 1 **cup mayonnaise or salad dressing**
- ½ **teaspoon salt**
- ¼ **teaspoon pepper**
  Watercress (optional)

1. Cook the potatoes in their skins in boiling water in a large, covered saucepan until just tender, for about 20 to 25 minutes; the centers should not be soft. Drain. Rinse briefly under cold running water; drain.
2. Meanwhile, peel, core and slice the apples. Place in a large bowl, sprinkling with the lemon juice as you cut them. Add the onion, pickles, capers, caper juice and mayonnaise. Toss lightly to combine.
3. Peel the potatoes while still warm. Cut into thin slices. Fold into the apple mixture. Add the salt and pepper. Serve slightly warm or chilled. Garnish with the watercress, if you wish.

Caper

This is the bud of the flower of the caper bush. The caper bush grows in the Mediterranean region and parts of Central Asia.

Creamy Topped Potato

This lowcal treat makes a perfect portable lunch.

Bake at 375° for 1 hour.
Makes 1 serving.

Nutrient Value Per Serving: 273 calories, 19 gm. protein, 5 gm. fat, 524 mg. sodium, 7 mg. cholesterol.

- 1 **baking potato (6 ounces), washed and pricked with fork**
- ½ **cup lowfat cottage cheese**
- ¼ **cup coarsely grated carrot**
- ¼ **cup chopped celery**
- ¼ **cup chopped sweet red or green pepper**
- 2 **tablespoons Creamy Yogurt Dressing (recipe follows)**

1. Preheat the oven or toaster-oven to moderate (375°).
2. Bake the potato for 1 hour or until the potato gives when lightly squeezed, turning after 30 minutes. Remove and cool. Or, cook the potato in a microwave oven according to the manufacturer's directions.
3. Cut the potato in half lengthwise. Wrap tightly in plastic wrap or aluminum foil and refrigerate.
4. Combine the cottage cheese, carrot, celery and pepper in a small dish. Pack into an airtight container and refrigerate overnight.
5. Spoon 2 tablespoons of the Creamy Yogurt Dressing into a covered container and refrigerate.
6. Pack the baked potato, cottage cheese topping and dressing separately in a lunch box. At lunchtime, spoon the cottage cheese over the baked potato halves and drizzle with the dressing.

Creamy Yogurt Dressing: Combine ½ cup of plain yogurt, 1 tablespoon of vegetable oil, 1 tablespoon of minced dry onion, 1 teaspoon of lemon juice, ½ teaspoon of paprika, ½ teaspoon of sugar, ½ teaspoon of Worcestershire sauce and ⅛ teaspoon of pepper in a small bowl. Makes about ⅔ cup (5 servings).

Candied Yams

Bake at 375° for 30 minutes.
Makes 6 servings.

Nutrient Value Per Serving: 178 calories, 2 gm. protein, 4 gm. fat, 60 mg. sodium, 10 mg. cholesterol.

- 2 *large yams or sweet potatoes (about 1¼ pounds), scrubbed*
- ⅓ *cup light corn syrup*
- 2 *tablespoons light brown sugar*
- 2 *tablespoons bourbon*
- 2 *tablespoons butter or margarine*
  Chopped pecans (optional)

1. Preheat the oven to moderate (375°). Grease a shallow 1-quart baking dish.
2. Cook the yams in boiling salted water to cover in a large saucepan for 30 minutes or just until tender. Drain. When cool enough to handle, peel. Slice crosswise into ¼-inch-thick slices.
3. Arrange the yams in the prepared baking dish. Stir together the corn syrup, sugar and bourbon in a small bowl. Pour evenly over the yams. Dot with the butter.
4. Bake in the preheated moderate oven (375°), basting several times, for 30 minutes or until glazed and heated through. Sprinkle with the chopped pecans, if you wish.

To Make Ahead: Cook the potatoes in the boiling salted water, drain and refrigerate until ready to serve. When ready to serve, proceed as the recipe directs.

Tangy Vegetables

Makes 6 servings.

Nutrient Value Per Serving: 165 calories, 3 gm. protein, 12 gm. fat, 284 mg. sodium, 0 mg. cholesterol.

- ⅓ *cup olive or vegetable oil*
- ¼ *cup red wine vinegar*
- ¼ *cup chopped parsley*
- ¼ *cup chopped sweet red pepper*
- 1 *tablespoon chopped sweet pickle*
- 2 *teaspoons Dijon-style mustard*
- ½ *teaspoon salt*
- ¼ *teaspoon pepper*
- 3 *medium-size carrots, decoratively sliced crosswise*
- 1 *cup cauliflower flowerets*
- 1 *medium-size zucchini (about 1 cup) cut into ½-inch sticks*
- 1 *cup red onion rings*
- ½ *pound small or button mushrooms*

1. Combine the oil, vinegar, parsley, red pepper, sweet pickle, mustard, salt and pepper in a screw-top jar. Cover; shake until well blended. Reserve.
2. Cook the carrots and cauliflower in boiling water to cover in a saucepan for 3 minutes or just until the carrots brighten in color. Drain; run under cold water to stop the cooking.
3. Combine the carrots, cauliflower, zucchini, onion and mushrooms in a bowl. Shake the dressing and pour over the vegetables. Toss well to coat. Marinate, covered, in the refrigerator overnight.

Sliced Tomato with Tomato-Garlic Vinaigrette

Herbed Tomatoes and Onions

Makes 6 to 8 servings.

Nutrient Value Per Serving: 94 calories, 1 gm. protein, 8 gm. fat, 89 mg. sodium, 0 mg. cholesterol.

Green leafy lettuce
3 to 4 medium-size ripe tomatoes (1 to 1¼ pounds), cut into ¼-inch-thick slices
1 medium-size red onion, thinly sliced
2 tablespoons chopped fresh basil OR:
  2 teaspoons leaf basil, crumbled
1 small clove garlic, crushed
¼ teaspoon coarse kosher salt
1 teaspoon coarse-grained mustard
2 teaspoons lemon juice
¼ cup olive or vegetable oil
1 to 2 teaspoons wine vinegar
¼ teaspoon freshly ground pepper

1. Arrange the lettuce on a serving plate. Overlap the tomato slices with the onion slices over the lettuce. Sprinkle with the basil.
2. Mash the garlic with the salt in a small bowl with the back of a spoon to form a smooth paste. Stir in the mustard, lemon juice, oil and vinegar. Drizzle over the tomatoes. Sprinkle with the pepper.

To Make Ahead: Prepare the dressing the day before or several hours in advance to allow the flavor to develop.

Sliced Tomato with Tomato-Garlic Vinaigrette

Makes 4 servings.

Nutrient Value Per Serving: 138 calories, 1 gm. protein, 12 gm. fat, 264 mg. sodium, 0 mg. cholesterol.

3 medium-size tomatoes, sliced
5 Herb-Scented Oven-Dried Tomato halves (recipe below), diced
3 tablespoons olive or vegetable oil
1 tablespoon vinegar, preferably cider
1 clove garlic, finely chopped
¼ teaspoon salt
⅛ teaspoon pepper
⅛ teaspoon leaf oregano, crumbled
Pinch dry mustard

1. Arrange the sliced tomatoes in a serving dish. Sprinkle with the oven-dried tomatoes.
2. Whisk together the oil, vinegar, garlic, salt, pepper, oregano and mustard in a small bowl. Pour over the tomatoes. Marinate for 1 to 3 hours, occasionally spooning the dressing over the tomatoes.

Herb-Scented Oven-Dried Tomatoes

Use these in salads, pasta sauce, soups or any dish that would benefit from a sharp tomato flavor. Use sparingly since the flavor is very concentrated.

Bake at 150° for 14 to 17 hours.
Makes 4 half-pints.

Nutrient Value Per Dried Tomato Half: 19 calories, 0 gm. protein, 2 gm. fat, 100 mg. sodium, 0 mg. cholesterol.

6 pounds large, uniform-size ripe plum tomatoes, halved lengthwise
2 tablespoons coarse kosher salt
4 sprigs fresh herbs, such as rosemary, thyme or oregano
4 cloves garlic, split
16 whole black peppercorns
Olive and vegetable oils

☞

1. Preheat the oven to very slow (150°).
2. Arrange the tomatoes, cut-side up, on 2 wire racks set over jelly-roll pans; sprinkle with the salt.
3. Bake in the preheated very slow oven (150°) for 14 to 17 hours or until the tomatoes are very wrinkled, deep red and without signs of moisture. Begin checking the tomatoes every hour after 14 hours. (The size of the tomatoes will determine how long they will take to dry out completely.)
4. When ready to can, wash 4 half-pint canning jars and lids and bands in hot soapy water. Rinse. Leave the jars in hot water until needed. Place the lids and bands in a saucepan of simmering water until ready to use.
5. Pack the tomatoes into the clean, hot canning jars. Place 1 herb sprig, 2 pieces of garlic and 4 peppercorns in each jar. Cover with the oils. Seal. Refrigerate for up to 3 months.

Ripening of Pears

Pears ripen from the inside out. Choose pears that are a little firm and have a slight fruity aroma.

Poached Pears with Carrot and Pea Purées

Bake at 350° for 15 minutes.
Makes 8 servings.

Nutrient Value Per Serving: 228 calories, 4 gm. protein, 4 gm. fat, 137 mg. sodium, 13 mg. cholesterol.

8 firm pears (3½ pounds)
⅔ cup lemon juice
1 cup dry white wine
1 can (6 ounces) frozen orange juice concentrate, thawed
2 whole cinnamon sticks
8 whole cloves
6 whole allspice
¼ cup sugar (optional)*
Carrot Purée:
½ pound carrots, pared and cut into ¼-inch slices
2 tablespoons finely chopped dried apricots
3 tablespoons heavy cream
⅛ teaspoon ground nutmeg
Pea Purée:
1 package (10 ounces) frozen peas

2 tablespoons heavy cream
¼ teaspoon ground ginger

1. Pare the pears; leave the stem on. One third down from the top of each pear, cut through with a paring knife in a zigzag pattern. Gently remove the top. Core the bottom portion of the pear. Place the tops and bottoms in a bowl; toss with the lemon juice.
2. Combine the wine, thawed orange juice concentrate, cinnamon sticks, cloves, allspice and sugar, if using, in a large non-aluminum saucepan. Bring to a simmer. Add the pears; poach, turning frequently, just until tender, for 12 to 15 minutes. Let the pears stand in the poaching liquid for 15 minutes. Remove the pears with a slotted spoon to a shallow baking dish. Set aside. Reserve 1 tablespoon of the poaching liquid.
3. Prepare the Carrot Purée: Cook the carrots in boiling salted water to cover until tender, for about 8 minutes. Drain. Combine the carrots, apricots, reserved 1 tablespoon of poaching liquid, the cream and nutmeg in a bowl. Place in the container of a blender or food processor. Whirl until smooth. Scrape back into the bowl. Reserve.
4. Preheat the oven to moderate (350°).
5. Prepare the Pea Purée: Cook the peas according to the label directions. Drain. Combine the peas, cream and ginger in a blender or food processor. Whirl until smooth. Scrape into a bowl.
6. Spoon or pipe the Carrot Purée into 4 of the pears, and the Pea Purée into the other 4. Top with the pear tops.
7. Bake in the preheated moderate oven (350°) for 15 minutes or until thoroughly heated.
To Make Ahead: The pears can be poached early in the day and refrigerated in their poaching liquid. The purées can be made early in the day and refrigerated.

* Omit the sugar if using very sweet pears.

Carrot-Yam Tzimmes

There's nothing more delicious than this traditional mixture of vegetables and fruits, slightly sweetened with honey.

Bake at 350° for 30 minutes.
Makes 8 servings.

Nutrient Value Per Serving: 194 calories, 3 gm. protein, 0 gm. fat, 35 mg. sodium, 0 mg. cholesterol.

- 2 **pounds yams, pared and cut into**
  ¾-inch-thick slices
- 1 **pound carrots, scraped and cut into**
  ¾-inch-thick slices
- ½ **cup dried prunes**
- ½ **cup dried apricots**
- 1 **cup orange juice**
- 2 **tablespoons honey**
- 1 **tablespoon grated lemon rind**
- ¼ **teaspoon ground nutmeg**
- ¼ **teaspoon ground ginger**
  Orange rind (optional)

1. Cook the yams and carrots in 1 inch of simmering water in a covered saucepan until barely tender, for about 15 minutes. Drain.
2. Preheat the oven to moderate (350°).
3. Grease a 2½-quart casserole. Place the yams and carrots in the casserole; stir in the dried prunes and apricots.
4. Pour the orange juice over the vegetables and fruits. Dot with the honey; sprinkle with the lemon rind, nutmeg and ginger.
5. Bake in the preheated moderate oven (350°) for 30 minutes or until fork-tender, stirring gently once or twice. Garnish with the thin strips of orange rind, if you wish.

To Make Ahead: Complete Step 1, place in a large bowl, cover and refrigerate until ready to bake. Remove from the refrigerator and allow to come to room temperature before completing the recipe.

> *Root Vegetables*
>
> Root vegetables are those that mature underground, like potatoes and carrots.

Wild Rice Salad

This rice salad is best made a day ahead for a delicious blending of flavors.

Makes 2 servings.

Nutrient Value Per Serving: 614 calories, 12 gm. protein, 28 gm. fat, 547 mg. sodium, 0 mg. cholesterol.

- 1 **package (6 ounces) long-grain and**
  wild rice mix
- ¼ **teaspoon salt**
- 1 **jar (6 ounces) marinated artichoke hearts,**
  undrained

- 2 **tablespoons olive oil**
- 1 **tablespoon lemon juice**
- ½ **clove garlic, finely chopped**
- 3 **green onions with tender green parts,**
  thinly sliced
- 1 **small zucchini, halved lengthwise, then**
  sliced crosswise ¼ inch thick
- 1 **small tomato, chopped**
- ¼ **cup chopped sweet red pepper**
- 1 **small celery stalk, thinly sliced**

1. Remove the rice and seasoning packet from the long-grain and wild rice mix package. Reserve the seasoning packet for another use*. Prepare the rice following the label directions and adding the ¼ teaspoon of salt to boiling water; omit the butter if called for. When cooked, remove from the heat, spoon into a medium-size bowl, cover with plastic wrap and cool slightly, for about 15 minutes.
2. Combine the artichoke hearts with their marinade, the olive oil, lemon juice, garlic and green onion in a small bowl.
3. Add the zucchini, tomato, red pepper and celery to the rice. Pour the artichoke mixture over; toss to combine. Refrigerate, covered, for several hours or overnight.

* Note: If you prefer, prepare the rice using the flavor packet, following the label directions, but omitting the butter if called for. Omit the artichoke hearts and marinade, then continue with the remaining directions in Step 2.

Gingered Baked Acorn Squash and Apples

Serve with baked ham, roast pork or roast chicken.

Bake at 400° for 40 minutes.
Makes 6 servings.

Nutrient Value Per Serving: 213 calories, 2 gm. protein, 8 gm. fat, 264 mg. sodium, 20 mg. cholesterol.

- 1 **acorn squash (about 1½ pounds)**
- 1 **can (5½ ounces) apple juice**
- ¼ **cup firmly packed light brown sugar**
- ¼ **cup (½ stick) butter or margarine, melted**
- 2 **tablespoons slivered crystallized ginger**
- ½ **teaspoon salt**
- ¼ **teaspoon nutmeg**
- 2 **large red apples, such as Cortland or Rome**
  Beauty, cored
  Arugula (optional)

☞

1. Preheat the oven to hot (400°).
2. Cut the squash crosswise into ¾-inch-thick slices; remove the seeds. Arrange the slices in a shallow baking dish.
3. Combine the apple juice, brown sugar, butter, ginger, salt and nutmeg in a bowl. Pour over the squash.
4. Bake in the preheated hot oven (400°) for 20 minutes, basting once with the pan juices.
5. Cut the apples into ¾-inch-thick rounds. Arrange around the squash. Brush with the pan juices. Bake for 20 minutes longer or until the apples and squash are tender. Garnish with the arugula, if you wish.

MICROWAVE DIRECTIONS
650 Watt Variable Power Microwave Oven
Directions: Prepare the squash and arrange in a shallow microwave-safe baking dish as directed above. Prepare the apple juice mixture; pour over the squash. Cover tightly. Microwave at full power for 8 minutes. Prepare the apples and add to the squash as directed above. If any parts of the squash are still firm, turn them toward the outside of the dish. Cover tightly. Microwave at full power for 4 minutes longer or until the squash and apples are tender.

Baked Stuffed Mushrooms

Select large, firm white mushrooms, stuff them ahead and then bake just before serving.

Bake at 350° for 15 minutes.
Makes 8 servings (2 mushrooms per serving).

Nutrient Value Per Serving: 60 calories, 4 gm. protein, 1 gm. fat, 237 mg. sodium, 1 mg. cholesterol.

16 **large mushrooms (1¾ pounds)**
½ **cup packaged seasoned bread crumbs**
2 **tablespoons grated Parmesan cheese**
 Chopped parsley (optional)

1. Grease a 15 x 10 x 1-inch jelly-roll pan.
2. Wipe the mushrooms with a damp towel; pat dry. Remove the stems from the mushrooms.
3. Preheat the oven to moderate (350°).
4. Combine the chopped stems, bread crumbs and Parmesan cheese in a medium-size bowl. Mound the mixture into the mushroom caps. Place in the prepared pan.
5. Bake in the preheated moderate oven (350°) for 15 minutes or until cooked through and lightly browned on top. Garnish with the chopped parsley, if you wish.

Corn and Cheese Soufflé

Bake at 350° for 1 hour.
Makes 6 servings.

Nutrient Value Per Serving: 400 calories, 17 gm. protein, 29 gm. fat, 669 mg. sodium, 298 mg. cholesterol.

6 **tablespoons (¾ stick) butter or margarine**
¼ **cup unsifted all-purpose flour**
⅛ **teaspoon garlic powder**
⅛ **teaspoon cayenne pepper**
⅓ **cup milk**
1 **can (17 ounces) cream-style corn**
1½ **cups shredded sharp Cheddar cheese (6 ounces)**
½ **cup shredded Provolone**
5 **eggs, separated**
¼ **teaspoon cream of tartar**

1. Preheat the oven to moderate (350°). Prepare a collar for a 7-cup glass soufflé dish: Measure off a length of foil long enough to encircle the dish; fold in half lengthwise. Grease one side of the foil. Fasten around the dish, greased-side in, with tape or string; the collar should be about 2 inches higher than the rim of the dish.
2. Melt the butter in a medium-size saucepan over medium heat. Blend the flour, garlic powder and cayenne; cook, stirring constantly, for 1 minute, until well blended.
3. Stir in the milk until smooth. Cook, stirring, until thickened and bubbly, for about 1 minute. Remove from the heat. Stir in the corn, Cheddar cheese and Provolone. Cool slightly. Beat in the egg yolks, 1 at a time, mixing after each addition.
4. Beat the egg whites with the cream of tartar in a large bowl until soft peaks form. Stir one-quarter of the egg whites into the sauce. Fold in the remaining whites to lighten. Pour into the prepared dish.
5. Bake in the preheated moderate oven (350°) for 1 hour or until puffed and golden brown. Carefully remove the collar. Serve immediately.

To Make Ahead: Prepare the soufflé dish, grate the cheese and separate the eggs, allowing them to stand at room temperature for about 1 hour.

Winter Vegetable Stew

Makes 8 servings.

Nutrient Value Per Serving: 129 calories, 3 gm. protein, 3 gm. fat, 617 mg. sodium, 8 mg. cholesterol.

    7   cups water
    3   medium-size white turnips (about
        ¾ pound), pared and cut into bite-size
        pieces
    1   large red onion, chopped (1 cup)
    1   large yellow onion, chopped (1 cup)
    2   large potatoes (about 1 pound), cut into
        large chunks
    7   carrots, sliced into ¼-inch-thick rounds
        (2 cups)
    ½   small rutabaga, pared and chopped (1 cup)
    2   medium-size beets, unpeeled, well scrubbed
        and cut into small cubes
    ½   bunch green onions with tops, sliced
    1   clove garlic, finely chopped
    2   tablespoons chopped parsley
    1   tablespoon leaf basil, crumbled
    2   teaspoons salt
    ½   teaspoon pepper
    2   tablespoons butter or margarine
    ¼   cup snipped fresh chives OR: 1 tablespoon
        dried chives
    1   cup dairy sour cream (optional)
Meat (optional):
    ½   pound round steak
    2   tablespoons butter or margarine

1. Combine the water, turnips, and red and yellow onions in a kettle or Dutch oven. Bring to boiling. Lower the heat; cover; simmer, stirring occasionally, for about 60 minutes or until the vegetables become very soft and slightly thicken the broth.
2. Add the potatoes, carrots and rutabaga. Simmer, covered, for 15 minutes or until the potatoes are barely tender.
3. Add the beets, green onions, garlic, parsley, basil, salt and pepper. Simmer, covered, until the beets are tender, for about 15 to 20 minutes. The soup will be pink. Remove from the heat. Stir in the butter and chives.
4. Ladle into a soup tureen or heated soup bowls. Garnish each serving with a dollop of sour cream, if you wish.

Optional Meat: Slice the round steak into paper-thin slices. (For easier slicing, place the meat in the freezer for 10 minutes.) Stir-fry the meat in the 2 tablespoons of butter in a large skillet for 3 to 5 minutes or to desired doneness. Add to the hot stew.
Nutrient Value Per Serving: 210 calories, 9 gm. protein, 10 gm. fat, 667 mg. sodium, 35 mg. cholesterol.

Spinach Rice Stew

Makes 6 servings.

Nutrient Value Per Serving: 346 calories, 9 gm. protein, 9 gm. fat, 653 mg. sodium, 21 mg. cholesterol.

    1   small onion, finely chopped (⅓ cup)
    1   carrot, diced (½ cup)
    1   celery stalk, diced (⅓ cup)
    1   leek OR: 1 bunch green onions with tops,
        chopped (¾ cups)
    1   package (10 ounces) frozen whole-leaf
        spinach
    4   tablespoons (½ stick) butter or margarine
    2   cups long-grain white rice
    4   cups beef broth*
    ⅛   teaspoon pepper
        Salt (optional)
    1   jar (8 ounces) pimiento, drained and
        chopped
    ½   cup grated Parmesan, Romano or Cheddar
        cheese (optional)
Meat (optional):
    1   package (8 ounces) brown-and-serve
        sausages, thinly sliced

1. Cook the onion, carrot, celery, leek and spinach in 3 tablespoons of the butter in a kettle or Dutch oven, stirring to break up the spinach, for 10 minutes. Add the rice; cook, stirring constantly, until the rice is opaque, for about 2 minutes.
2. Add the broth. Bring to boiling. Lower the heat; cover; simmer, stirring occasionally, for 15 minutes or until the rice is tender. Add the pepper and salt to taste, if you wish. Stir in the remaining butter and pimiento.
3. Ladle into a tureen or soup bowls. Sprinkle with the grated cheese, if you wish.

Optional Meat: Brown the sausage in a skillet. Remove with a slotted spoon. Place the slices on top of the stew; omit the last tablespoon of butter and the cheese.
Nutrient Value Per Serving: 472 calories, 13 gm. protein, 20 gm. fat, 939 mg. sodium, 47 mg. cholesterol.

*** Note:** To reduce the mg. of sodium per serving, use a reduced-sodium bouillon cube, bouillon powder or broth.

Tex-Mex Stuffing (page 180)—a blend of sweet and hot peppers, chili and corn. Other stuffings from top: Apple-Pecan (page 181), Apple-Pecan Rice (page 181), Pork and Spinach (page 182), Cranberry Cornbread (page 182).

Other Accompaniments

Flavoring Stuffings

When stuffing poultry, try flavoring them with combinations of ingredients and seasonings, such as sautéed onions, celery, mushrooms or sausage; mixed dried fruits, apples, oranges, raisins, cranberries, spinach, parsley, sage, marjoram or thyme.

Combinations that marry well with seafood include other seafoods, such as chopped shrimp, crab, lobster, scallops, oysters or clams. Fill mild-flavored fillet rolls such as sole, snapper, cod or flounder with spinach, dill, tarragon, wine, cheese and nuts. As with poultry, sautéed onions, celery and mushrooms work well.

Meat stuffings might include other forms of the meat being stuffed, such as ground pork or lamb stuffing in a crown roast of pork or lamb. Sautéed onions, celery and mushrooms accompany meat stuffings nicely. The particular type of meat will determine exactly what flavor combination you might like. Some that work well with one meat would not work with others, such as pork and sauerkraut versus lamb and sauerkraut. Individual taste and preference will determine combinations when selecting meat stuffings. A general rule of thumb to remember is to serve rich stuffings with milder meat, poultry or fish and lighter stuffings with richer meats.

Quantity Reference Chart For Stuffing

Amount of Stuffing	Size of Bird It Will Stuff	Number of Servings
2 cups	3 to 4 pounds	2 to 3
3 cups	5 to 6 pounds	4 to 5
4 cups	6 to 8 pounds	6
6 cups	8 to 10 pounds	8
8 cups	10 to 12 pounds	10
12 cups	12 to 15 pounds	12 to 14
16 cups	15 to 20 pounds	18 to 20

Tips on Preparing Stuffings

1. When preparing stuffings, chop as many ingredients as possible in advance. Store the ingredients in individual containers in the refrigerator and mix together just before ready to use.
2. Stuff the bird, roast or fish just before cooking. Prestuffing is a sure way to increase the risk of bacteria growth that could lead to food poisoning. To reduce the risk of food poisoning even more, never stuff anything that is to be frozen, before or after cooking. Never allow stuffing to remain in foods after serving. Remove stuffing and store both stuffing and stuffed food separately in covered containers in the refrigerator.
3. If using raw pork or sausage in a stuffing, sauté until no longer pink in a skillet before combining with other ingredients.
4. Spoon or drop stuffing loosely in the item to be stuffed. If packed too tightly, the stuffing will become heavy when heated, due to expansion.
5. Allow about ½ to ¾ cup of stuffing per pound of food to be stuffed. Any leftover stuffing that does not fit into the food to be stuffed should be placed in a separate lightly greased baking dish and baked along with the stuffed food during the last ¾ to 1 hour of baking.

Tex-Mex Stuffing

Use to stuff turkey or chicken breasts, or bake separately at 350° for 45 minutes.
Makes 10 cups (enough for a 12-pound turkey or 5 whole chicken breasts).

Nutrient Value Per 1 Cup: 466 calories, 10 gm. protein, 20 gm. fat, 852 mg. sodium, 128 mg. cholesterol.

- 1 *large onion, finely chopped (about 1 cup)*
- ¼ *cup (½ stick) butter or margarine*
- 1 *large sweet green pepper, halved, seeded and finely chopped (1 cup)*
- 3 *medium-size celery stalks, finely chopped (1 cup)*
  Turkey giblets, finely chopped (optional)
  Turkey liver, finely chopped (optional)
- 2 *canned hot jalapeño peppers, seeded and finely chopped*
- 1 *clove garlic, finely chopped*
- 8 *cups crumbled cornbread*
- 2 *hard-cooked eggs, coarsely chopped*
- 2 *cans (8 ounces each) corn niblets, drained*
- 1 *cup turkey or chicken broth*

2 *teaspoons chili powder*
½ *teaspoon salt*
¼ *teaspoon pepper*

1. Sauté the onion in the butter in a large skillet until softened, for about 3 minutes. Stir in the green pepper and celery; sauté for 3 minutes. Stir in the turkey giblets and liver, if using, the jalapeño peppers and garlic; sauté for 5 minutes.
2. Combine the cornbread, hard-cooked eggs and corn in a large bowl. Pour in the broth; toss to moisten. Add the sautéed vegetables, chili powder, salt and pepper.
3. Stuff the turkey and roast according to your favorite recipe. Or, spoon the dressing into a greased, shallow 3-quart baking dish. Bake, covered, in a preheated moderate oven (350°) for 45 minutes. Uncover the last 10 minutes for a crusty top.

Apple-Pecan Stuffing

Sensational as a stuffing for pork chops, ham or turkey; or bake separately at 350° for 40 minutes. Makes 14 cups (enough for a 14-pound turkey).

Nutrient Value Per Cup: 629 calories, 18 gm. protein, 29 gm. fat, 1,111 mg. sodium, 79 mg. cholesterol.

2 *cups coarsely broken pecans*
6 *tablespoons butter or margarine*
1 *large onion, chopped (1 cup)*
2 *medium-size celery stalks with leaves, diced*
6 *cups packaged plain croutons OR: 6 cups toasted bread cubes (12 slices)*
4 *large tart apples, pared, cored and cut into ½-inch cubes*
5½ *ounces cooked ham, cut into ¼-inch cubes (1 cup)*
3 *eggs, slightly beaten*
¼ *cup chopped parsley*
2 *teaspoons leaf thyme, crumbled*
½ *teaspoon pepper*

1. Sauté the pecans in 2 tablespoons of the butter in a large skillet until golden, for 3 minutes. Transfer the nuts with a slotted spoon to a large bowl.
2. Sauté the onion and celery in the remaining 4 tablespoons of butter in the same skillet until the onion softens, for 3 minutes. Do not brown. Combine with the pecans in the bowl.

3. Add the croutons, apples, ham, eggs, parsley, thyme and pepper to the pecan-vegetable mixture; toss gently to mix.
4. Stuff the turkey and roast according to your favorite recipe. Or, spoon into a greased, shallow 4½-quart baking dish. Bake, covered, in a preheated moderate oven (350°) for 40 minutes or until heated through. Uncover for the last 5 minutes of baking time for a crusty top.

MICROWAVE DIRECTIONS
650 Watt Variable Power Microwave Oven
Directions: Combine the butter or margarine, onion and celery in a 3-quart microwave-safe baking dish or casserole with a cover. Cover tightly. Microwave at full power for 8 minutes. Stir in the remaining ingredients. Cover tightly. Microwave at full power for 8 more minutes. Serve immediately or cover dish with foil and set aside for up to 20 minutes before serving.

Apricot-Pecan Rice Stuffing

Use to stuff turkey, or bake separately at 350° for 35 minutes.
Makes 12 cups (enough for a 12- to 14-pound turkey).

Nutrient Value Per Cup: 366 calories, 6 gm. protein, 20 gm. fat, 268 mg. sodium, 15 mg. cholesterol.

2 *cups coarsely broken pecans*
6 *tablespoons butter or margarine*
1 *large onion, chopped (1 cup)*
2 *large celery stalks, diced (1 cup)*
   Turkey giblets, finely chopped (optional)
   Turkey liver, finely chopped (optional)
6 *cups cooked white rice*
2 *cups coarsely chopped dried apricots*
¼ *cup chopped parsley*
2 *teaspoons leaf thyme, crumbled*
1 *teaspoon leaf sage, crumbled*
½ *teaspoon salt*
¼ *teaspoon pepper*
1 *can (13¾ ounces) chicken broth*

1. Sauté the pecans in 2 tablespoons of the butter in a large skillet until golden, for 3 minutes. Transfer the nuts with a slotted spoon to a large bowl.
2. Sauté the onion and celery in the remaining 4 tablespoons of butter in the same skillet until the onion softens, for about 3 minutes; do not let the onion brown. Add the finely chopped giblets and liver, if using, and sauté for 5 minutes longer. Combine with the pecans in the bowl. ☞

3. Add the rice, apricots, parsley, thyme, sage, salt and pepper to the pecan-vegetable mixture; toss gently to mix. Pour in the chicken broth; stir well to moisten.

4. Stuff the turkey and roast according to your favorite recipe. Or, spoon the stuffing into a greased, shallow 3-quart baking dish. Bake, covered, in a preheated moderate oven (350°) for 35 minutes or until heated through.

Pork and Spinach Stuffing

Use to stuff turkey, or bake separately at 350° for 35 minutes.
Makes 8 cups (enough for a 10- to 12-pound turkey).

Nutrient Value Per Cup: 270 calories, 15 gm. protein, 17 gm. fat, 295 mg. sodium, 153 mg. cholesterol.

1 *large onion, finely chopped (1 cup)*
2 *cloves garlic, finely chopped*
6 *tablespoons butter or margarine*
  Turkey giblets, finely chopped (optional)
1 *pound ground pork*
  Turkey liver, finely chopped (optional)
2 *packages (10 ounces each) frozen chopped spinach, thawed and drained*
3 *cups day-old white bread cubes (6 slices)*
3 *eggs, slightly beaten*
½ *cup chopped parsley*
1 *teaspoon leaf thyme, crumbled*
1 *teaspoon leaf marjoram, crumbled*
½ *teaspoon pepper*
¼ *teaspoon salt*

1. Sauté the onion and garlic in 3 tablespoons of the butter in a large skillet until the onion softens, for about 3 minutes. Transfer to a large bowl.
2. Melt the remaining 3 tablespoons of butter in the skillet. Sauté the giblets, if using, for 10 minutes until tender. Add the pork, breaking up with a wooden spoon; continue to cook until no longer pink, for about 7 minutes. Stir in the liver, if using; cook for 2 minutes. Combine the pork mixture with the onion in the bowl.
3. Combine the spinach, bread cubes, eggs, parsley, thyme, marjoram, pepper and salt with the pork mixture in the bowl.
4. Stuff the turkey and roast according to your favorite recipe. Or, spoon the dressing into a greased, shallow 2-quart baking dish.

Bake, covered, in a preheated moderate oven (350°) for 35 minutes or until heated through. Uncover for the last 5 minutes of baking time for a crusty top.

Cranberry Cornbread Stuffing

This tasty berry stuffing zips up chicken, turkey or duck.

Use as a stuffing, or bake separately at 350° for 45 minutes.
Makes 16 cups (enough for a 14- to 16-pound turkey).

Nutrient Value Per Cup; 324 calories, 8 gm. protein, 13 gm. fat, 609 mg. sodium, 50 mg. cholesterol.

2 *cups cranberries, fresh or frozen, thawed if frozen*
1 *cup water*
½ *cup sugar*
1 *pound sausage meat*
8 *cups crumbled cornbread (homemade or store-bought cornbread)*
2 *large Red Delicious apples, pared, cored and diced (about 3 cups)*
2 *medium-size celery stalks, diced (½ cup)*
1 *medium-size onion, finely chopped (½ cup)*
¼ *cup chopped parsley*
2 *teaspoons leaf thyme, crumbled*
2 *teaspoons leaf marjoram, crumbled*
½ *teaspoon salt*
¼ *teaspoon pepper*

1. Combine the cranberries, water and sugar in a medium-size saucepan. Bring to boiling. Lower the heat; simmer for 10 minutes. Drain well. Transfer to a large bowl.
2. Sauté the sausage in a medium-size skillet, breaking up into small pieces with a wooden spoon, until lightly browned and no longer pink, for about 5 minutes. Drain the excess fat. Combine with the cranberries in the bowl.
3. Add the cornbread, apples, celery, onion, parsley, thyme, marjoram, salt and pepper to the cranberry-sausage mixture; toss gently to mix.
4. Stuff the turkey and roast according to your favorite recipe. Or, spoon the stuffing into a greased, shallow 4½-quart baking dish. Bake, covered, in a preheated moderate oven (350°) for 45 minutes or until heated through. Uncover for the last 10 minutes of baking time for a crusty top.

182

Savory Thanksgiving Stuffing

Use to stuff turkey, or bake separately at 350° for 35 minutes.
Makes 14 cups (enough for a 12- to 14-pound turkey).

Nutrient Value Per Cup: 148 calories, 4 gm. protein, 6 gm. fat, 414 mg. sodium, 14 mg. cholesterol.

- 2 **large onions, diced (2 cups)**
- 2 **cups diced celery**
- 2 **cloves garlic, finely chopped**
- 6 **tablespoons butter or margarine**
- 15 **cups cubed day-old French bread (two 7-ounce loaves)**
- ⅓ **cup chopped parsley**
- 2 **teaspoons ground sage**
- 1 **teaspoon poultry seasoning**
- ½ **teaspoon pepper**
- 3 **cups chicken broth**

1. Sauté the onions, celery and garlic in 4 tablespoons of the butter in a skillet for 3 minutes or until the onions soften.
2. Combine the sautéed vegetables, bread cubes, parsley, sage, poultry seasoning and pepper in a large bowl. Mix well.
3. Melt the remaining 2 tablespoons of butter in a saucepan. Add the butter and chicken broth to the stuffing; toss to mix. Stuff the turkey and roast according to your favorite recipe. Or spoon into a 13 x 9 x 2-inch baking pan or other shallow baking dish. Bake, uncovered, in a preheated moderate oven (350°) for 35 minutes or until heated through.

Sweet Red Pepper Sauce

Makes 2 cups.

Nutrient Value Per ½ Cup: 107 calories, 2 gm. protein, 7 gm. fat, 279 mg. sodium, 0 mg. cholesterol.

- 2 **tablespoons oil, preferably olive**
- 4 **sweet red peppers (about 1½ pounds), cored, seeded and cut into chunks**
- 1 **medium-size onion, chopped (½ cup)**
- 1 **small tomato, cut into chunks**
- ½ **teaspoon salt**
- ¼ **teaspoon pepper**
  Few drops liquid red-pepper seasoning

1. Heat the oil in a large skillet over low heat. Add the peppers, onion and tomato. Cover and cook for 45 minutes, stirring occasionally, until the vegetables are very soft.
2. Place the vegetables in the container of an electric blender or food processor. Cover; whirl until puréed. Season with the salt, pepper and red-pepper seasoning.

Green and Yellow Squash Pickle Chips

Makes 6 pints.

Nutrient Value Per ¼ Cup: 44 calories, 1 gm. protein, 0 gm. fat, 726 mg. sodium, 0 mg. cholesterol.

- 6 **medium-size zucchini (about 2 pounds), cut into ¼-inch-thick slices (about 6 cups)**
- 6 **medium-size yellow squash (about 2 pounds), cut into ¼-inch-thick slices (about 6 cups)**
- 1 **very large onion, quartered lengthwise, then cut crosswise into ½-inch-thick slices (about 2 cups)**
- ⅓ **cup coarse kosher salt**
- 3½ **cups distilled white vinegar**
- 2 **cups sugar**
- 1 **tablespoon whole mustard seed**
- 1 **teaspoon celery seed**
- ½ **teaspoon turmeric**
- ½ **teaspoon dry mustard**

1. Combine the zucchini, yellow squash and onion in a very large glass or plastic bowl. Sprinkle with the salt; toss well. Cover with a layer of ice cubes. Let stand for 3 hours at room temperature.
2. When ready to can, wash 6 pint-size canning jars and lids and bands in hot soapy water. Rinse. Leave the jars in hot water until needed. Place the lids and bands in a saucepan of simmering water until ready to use.
3. Drain and rinse the vegetables under cold running water. Drain thoroughly.
4. Combine the vinegar, sugar, mustard seed, celery seed, turmeric and dry mustard in a large stainless steel or enamel saucepan. Bring to boiling. Add the drained vegetables. Return to boiling. Remove from the heat.

5. Pack the pickle chips into the clean, hot canning jars, using a wide-mouth funnel; leave a ¼-inch headspace. Make sure there is enough liquid to cover the pickles; if necessary, add additional vinegar. Run a long, thin nonmetallic spatula around the inside of the jars to release trapped air bubbles. Wipe the jar rims and threads clean with a damp cloth. Cover the jars with the hot lids; screw on the bands firmly.

6. Process the jars in a boiling water bath for 10 minutes (the water should cover the jars by 1 or 2 inches). Remove the jars from the boiling water to a wire rack. Let stand for 12 hours. Test for seals. Label, date and store in a cool, dark place.

Mediterranean Onion Relish

Serve as a relish with hamburgers or other charcoal-grilled meats and poultry, or as a tasty vegetable side dish, warm or cold.

Makes about 3 cups.

Nutrient Value Per ½ Cup: 128 calories, 3 gm. protein, 5 gm. fat, 294 mg. sodium, 0 mg. cholesterol.

> 2 **tablespoons olive or vegetable oil**
> 1½ **pounds Spanish onions, cut in slivers**
> 1 **tablespoon light brown sugar**
> 1 **can (16 ounces) whole tomatoes**
> ¼ **cup dry white wine OR: ¼ cup chicken broth**
> ¼ **cup raisins**
> 1 **tablespoon cider vinegar**
> ½ **teaspoon salt**
> ¼ **teaspoon fennel seeds, lightly crushed**
> ⅛ **teaspoon leaf thyme, crumbled**

1. Heat the oil in a large skillet. Add the onions. Cook, stirring often, until lightly browned, for about 10 minutes. Reduce the heat to low. Add the brown sugar. Cook over low heat, stirring constantly, until the sugar melts.

2. Break up the tomatoes. Pour into the skillet with the wine, raisins, vinegar, salt, fennel and thyme. Bring to boiling. Lower the heat; cover and cook for 10 minutes or until the onions are tender. If the relish is too thin, boil gently, uncovered, to reduce to a thicker consistency. Serve warm or chilled. Store in the refrigerator for up to 4 days.

> **Turmeric**
>
> The root of an East Indian plant of the ginger family.

Curried Corn and Red Pepper Relish

Makes 6 pints.

Nutrient Value Per Tablespoon: 13 calories, 0 gm. protein, 0 gm. fat, 35 mg. sodium, 0 mg. cholesterol.

> 8 **cups fresh corn kernels (about 18 ears)**
> 2 **cups chopped sweet red pepper (2 medium-size)**
> 1½ **cups chopped onions (3 medium-size)**
> 3 **cups distilled white vinegar**
> 1½ **cups sugar**
> 2 **tablespoons curry powder**
> 1 **tablespoon coarse kosher salt**
> 2 **teaspoons dry mustard**

1. Wash 6 pint-size canning jars and lids and bands in hot soapy water. Rinse. Leave the jars in hot water until needed. Place the lids and bands in a saucepan of simmering water until ready to use.

2. Combine the corn, red peppers, onions, vinegar, sugar, curry powder, salt and mustard in a large stainless steel or enamel saucepan. Bring to boiling over medium-high heat; cool for 5 minutes.

3. Pack the relish into the clean, hot canning jars, using a wide-mouth funnel; leave a ¼-inch headspace. Make sure there is enough liquid to cover the relish; if necessary, add additional vinegar. Run a long, thin nonmetallic spatula around the inside of the jar to release any air bubbles. Wipe the jar rims and threads clean with a damp cloth. Cover the jars with the hot lids; screw on the bands firmly.

4. Process the jars in a boiling water bath for 10 minutes (the water should cover the jars by 1 to 2 inches). Remove the jars from the boiling water to a wire rack. Let stand for 12 hours. Test for seals. Label, date and store jars in a cool, dark place.

Mixed Vegetable Relish

Makes 6 pints.

Nutrient Value Per Tablespoon: 18 calories, 0 gm. protein, 0 gm. fat, 150 mg. sodium, 0 mg. cholesterol.

- 5 **cups finely chopped zucchini (1¼ pounds)**
- 4 **cups finely chopped onions (1¼ pounds)**
- 4 **cups fresh corn kernels or drained, canned whole kernels**
- 2 **cups finely chopped sweet red peppers (¾ pound)**
- 2 **cups finely chopped sweet green peppers (¾ pound)**
- ¼ **cup coarse kosher salt**
- 3 **cups distilled white vinegar**
- ⅓ **cup Dijon-style mustard**
- 2 **teaspoons dry mustard**
- 1½ **teaspoons celery seed**
- ¼ **teaspoon cayenne pepper**

1. Combine the zucchini, onions, corn and sweet peppers in a very large glass or plastic bowl. Sprinkle with the salt; toss well. Cover with a clean kitchen towel; let stand for 4 hours.
2. When ready to can, wash 6 pint-size canning jars and lids and bands in hot soapy water. Rinse. Leave the jars in hot water until needed. Place the lids and bands in a saucepan of simmering water until ready to use.
3. Drain the vegetables, discarding the liquid. Squeeze out the excess liquid with your hands. Place in a large stainless steel or enamel saucepan. Add the sugar, vinegar, mustards, celery seed and cayenne; stir to combine. Bring to boiling over medium-high heat; cook for 10 minutes.
4. Pack the relish into the clean, hot canning jars, using a wide-mouth funnel; leave a ¼-inch headspace. Make sure there is enough liquid to cover the relish; if necessary, add additional vinegar. Run a long, thin nonmetallic spatula around the inside of the jars to release trapped air bubbles. Wipe the jar rims and threads clean with a damp cloth. Cover the jars with the hot lids; screw on the bands firmly.
5. Process the jars in a boiling water bath for 10 minutes (the water should cover the jars by 1 or 2 inches). Remove the jars from the boiling water to a wire rack. Let stand for 12 hours. Test for seals. Label, date and store in a cool, dark place.

Cranberry-Orange Relish

Makes 3 cups.

Nutrient Value Per Tablespoon: 25 calories, 0 gm. protein, 0 gm. fat, 0 mg. sodium, 0 mg. cholesterol.

- 2 **cups fresh whole cranberries**
- 1 **orange, unpeeled, quartered and seeded**
- ½ **lemon, unpeeled, quartered and seeded**
- 1 **cup sugar**
- ¼ to ½ **cup Cointreau or orange-flavored liqueur**
- **Orange slices for garnish**

1. Combine the cranberries, orange and lemon in the work bowl of a food processor. Cover; whirl until finely chopped. Transfer to a medium-size bowl.
2. Stir in the sugar and Cointreau. Let stand, covered, for 12 hours at room temperature. Then refrigerate until ready to serve. Garnish with the orange slices.

Chocolate-Filled Mimosa-Lemon Roll (page 201)

Luscious, melt-in-your-mouth cakes
and crunchy or chewy cookies—perfect
for discriminating dessert lovers.

Chocolate-Filled Mimosa-Lemon Roll (page 201), Orange-Ambrosia Cake (page 195), Lemon Curd Charlotte with Blueberry Topping (page 270)—the names themselves bring forth visions of dessert ecstasy. What better way to end a meal or to show someone how special you consider him or her to be than with a "made from scratch" cake!

There are extra-festive cakes like the ones mentioned above, cakes to be decorated for special occasions, cakes for bakers on-the-run, as well as layer cakes, cake rolls, sheet cakes, tube cakes, filled and frosted cakes—whatever your taste, you're sure to find something here that appeals to your sweet tooth!

And don't forget cookies. What would Christmas be without the smell of holiday cookies baking? Or Easter? Or Valentine's Day? What would coming home from school be like without milk and cookies? (Our Monster Chip, page 209, is perfect for this occasion!) There's even something for the calorie-conscious: Portuguese Walnut Squares (page 211), at a mere 43 calories per serving, will let you have a snack without feeling guilty.

We offer bar cookies, drop cookies, filled and frosted cookies, rolled and cut cookies and fruit and nut cookies. If cakes and cookies are your pleasure, you're in for a real treat!

(Note: While all of our delicious cakes and cookies would be enjoyed by guests, we've placed an 🍸 [entertaining] symbol above only those desserts that are especially decorative or appealing.)

Cakes

Poppy Seed Cake

Cake Baking Tips

- If you want your cake to have the best volume, shape and texture possible, use the ingredients, measurements and pan size called for in the recipe. Follow the directions carefully.
- Remember to preheat the oven to the proper temperature for 10 minutes before baking.
- Cake is done:
—When the cake shrinks slightly from the sides of the pan.
—When a fingertip is lightly pressed on the top of the cake and the top springs back to shape.
—When a cake tester or wooden pick inserted near the center of the cake comes out clean, with no batter or moist particles clinging to it.
- Cake may turn out heavy and soggy if the oven temperature is too low.
- Cake may fall if the oven door is opened too soon, if the oven is too hot or if there is not enough flour in the batter.

Poppy Seed Cake

Bake at 325° for 55 minutes.
Makes 14 servings.

Nutrient Value Per Serving: 346 calories, 6 gm. protein, 17 gm. fat, 221 mg. sodium, 134 mg. cholesterol.

2⅔ cups sifted *all-purpose flour*
1¼ teaspoons *baking powder*
 1 teaspoon *baking soda*
 1 teaspoon *salt*
 1 cup (2 sticks) *unsalted butter*
1¾ cups *sugar*
 5 eggs, separated
 1 cup *buttermilk*
⅓ cup *poppy seeds*
 1 tablespoon *grated lemon rind*
   10X (confectioners') sugar (optional)

1. Preheat the oven to slow (325°). Grease and flour a 12-cup (10-inch) Bundt® pan.
2. Sift together the flour, baking powder, soda and salt.
3. Beat together the butter and 1½ cups of the sugar in a large bowl until light and fluffy. Beat in the yolks one at a time.
4. Add the sifted dry ingredients alternately with the buttermilk to the egg yolk mixture,

starting and ending with the dry ingredients and beating well after each addition; beat until smooth. Beat in the poppy seeds and lemon rind. Set aside.
5. Beat the egg whites until foamy. Gradually beat in the remaining ¼ cup of sugar until the meringue forms soft peaks. Fold into the batter until no white remains. Pour into the prepared pan.
6. Bake in the preheated slow oven (325°) for 55 minutes or until the top springs back when lightly touched with a fingertip. Let stand for 5 minutes. Loosen the cake around the tube and sides with a spatula. Invert onto a wire rack. Cool completely. Just before serving, sprinkle with the 10X sugar, if you wish.

Fudge Cake

Bake at 350° for 25 to 30 minutes.
Makes 24 servings.

Nutrient Value Per Serving: 174 calories, 3 gm. protein, 9 gm. fat, 74 mg. sodium, 55 mg. cholesterol.

2¼ cups sifted *all-purpose flour*
 1 cup *unsweetened cocoa powder*
 2 teaspoons *baking soda*
½ teaspoon *salt*
 1 cup (2 sticks) *unsalted butter, softened*
1½ cups *sugar*
 3 eggs
 2 teaspoons *vanilla*
1¾ cups *water*
   Choice of Frosting (recipes follow)

1. Preheat the oven to moderate (350°). Generously grease a 15 x 10 x 1-inch jelly-roll pan.
2. Sift together the flour, cocoa, baking soda and salt onto a piece of wax paper.
3. Beat the butter, sugar, eggs and vanilla in a bowl with an electric mixer at high speed until light and fluffy, for about 3 minutes.
4. Add the flour mixture and water. Beat at medium speed, scraping down the sides frequently, until the mixture is smooth. Spread the batter evenly in the prepared pan.
5. Bake in the preheated moderate oven (350°) for 25 to 30 minutes or until the center springs back when lightly pressed with a fingertip. Cool completely on a wire rack.
6. Top with the Mocha Frosting, Whipped Cream and Chocolate Cutouts, Boston Cream Topping (all on this page) or your choice of frosting or topping. Cut into 24 pieces (4 cuts lengthwise, 6 crosswise).

1. Melt the chocolate in the top of a double boiler over hot, not boiling, water. Cover the cookie sheet with aluminum foil. Pour the chocolate onto the foil. Spread evenly with a metal spatula to a ⅛-inch thickness. Place in the refrigerator until firm.
2. Beat together the heavy cream, 10X sugar and vanilla in a small bowl until stiff peaks form. Spoon into a pastry bag fitted with a large tip.
3. Score the top of the cake into 24 pieces (4 lines lengthwise and 6 lines crosswise) with a sharp knife. Pipe the whipped cream onto the top of each serving.
4. Remove the chocolate from the refrigerator. Cut into small designs with an aspic cutter. Or cut into 1-inch squares; cut the squares in half diagonally. Place one cutout upright in each whipped cream garnish.

Mocha Frosting

Makes 24 servings.

Nutrient Value Per Serving: 108 calories, 0 gm. protein, 4 gm. fat, 2 mg. sodium, 11 mg. cholesterol.

1 tablespoon instant coffee
¼ cup warm milk
½ cup (1 stick) unsalted butter, softened
1 box (1 pound) 10X (confectioners') sugar

Dissolve the instant coffee in the milk in a small saucepan. Beat the butter in a medium-size bowl with an electric mixer until fluffy. Beat in the 10X sugar alternately with the coffee mixture until smooth and spreadable; add a little more milk, if necessary. Spread evenly over the top of the cake.

Whipped Cream and Chocolate Cutouts

Makes 24 servings.

Nutrient Value Per Serving: 49 calories, 0 gm. protein, 5 gm. fat, 4 mg. sodium, 14 mg. cholesterol.

2 squares (1 ounce each) semisweet chocolate
1 cup heavy cream
2 tablespoons 10X (confectioners') sugar
½ teaspoon vanilla

Boston Cream Topping

Makes 24 servings.

Nutrient Value Per Serving: 47 calories, 1 gm. protein, 2 gm. fat, 16 mg. sodium, 26 mg. cholesterol.

⅓ cup sugar
¼ cup cornstarch
2 cups milk
2 eggs
1 teaspoon vanilla
2 squares (1 ounce each) semisweet chocolate

1. Combine the sugar and cornstarch in a saucepan. Gradually stir in the milk. Bring to boiling over medium heat, stirring constantly. Simmer for 1 minute.
2. Beat the eggs in a bowl until light and fluffy. Gradually stir in some of the hot cornstarch mixture. Return the egg mixture to the saucepan, stirring. Return to boiling, stirring constantly. Stir in the vanilla. Spread the topping evenly over the cake.
3. Melt the semisweet chocolate in the top of a double boiler over hot, not boiling, water. Drizzle the chocolate over the pudding topping.

Apple-Date-Nut Cake

Bake at 350° for 55 to 60 minutes.
Makes 12 servings.

Nutrient Value Per Serving: 447 calories, 5 gm. protein, 19 gm. fat, 203 mg. sodium, 77 mg. cholesterol.

1¾ cups unsifted all-purpose flour
  2 teaspoons unsweetened cocoa powder
  1 teaspoon baking soda
  1 teaspoon ground cinnamon
  ½ teaspoon ground cloves
  ½ cup (1 stick) butter or margarine, softened
  1 cup sugar
  2 eggs
  4 cups chopped, pared tart apples
       (2 to 3 large apples)
  1 cup chopped walnuts or pecans
  ½ cup chopped pitted dates
  ½ cup cold coffee
       Old-Fashioned Caramel Frosting (recipe
       follows)
       Chopped apple (optional)

1. Preheat the oven to moderate (350°). Grease a 6½-cup tube pan. Dust with the flour; tap out the excess.
2. Combine 1½ cups of the flour, cocoa powder, baking soda, cinnamon and cloves in a small bowl; set aside.
3. Beat together the butter and sugar in a large bowl until smooth and creamy. Beat in the eggs, one at a time, until well blended.
4. Combine the apples, nuts and dates in a medium-size bowl. Add the remaining ¼ cup of flour; toss together until all the nut and fruit pieces are well coated with the flour.
5. Add the flour mixture alternately with the coffee to the creamed butter mixture, beginning and ending with the flour, until the batter is smooth. Stir in the apple mixture. Spoon into the prepared pan.
6. Bake in the preheated moderate oven (350°) for 55 to 60 minutes or until the top springs back when lightly touched with a fingertip. Cool the cake in the pan on a wire rack for 15 minutes. Gently loosen the cake around the edge with a small metal spatula. Carefully turn out the cake onto a rack to cool completely.
7. Frost with the Old-Fashioned Caramel Frosting and garnish with the chopped apple, if you wish.

Old-Fashioned Caramel Frosting: Melt ¼ cup (½ stick) of butter in a small saucepan over low heat. Add ½ cup of firmly packed light brown sugar; stir for 2 minutes. Stir in 2 tablespoons of milk. Bring to boiling, stirring constantly. Remove from the heat. Gradually beat in 1½ cups of 10X (confectioners') sugar until smooth and creamy. Add 1 teaspoon of vanilla. If necessary, add more milk, a tablespoon at a time, to make the frosting thin enough to spread.

Matzo Honey Cake

This cake has the texture of a sponge cake but the flavor of a dense honey cake.

Bake at 350° for 45 minutes.
Makes 16 servings.

Nutrient Value Per Serving: 111 calories, 3 gm. protein, 2 gm. fat, 62 mg. sodium, 103 mg. cholesterol.

  6 eggs, separated
  ⅔ cup sugar
  ¼ cup honey
  ¼ cup orange juice
  1 tablespoon grated lemon rind
  1 tablespoon lemon juice
  ½ cup matzo cake flour*
  ½ cup potato flour (starch)
  ¼ teaspoon salt
       Honey (optional)

1. Preheat the oven to moderate (350°). Line the bottom of a 9 x 9 x 2-inch-square baking pan with wax paper.
2. Beat the egg yolks in a large bowl until thick and lemon-colored. Add the sugar, 2 tablespoons at a time, beating well after each addition. Beat in the honey, orange juice, lemon rind and juice. Fold in the matzo cake flour, then the potato flour.
3. Beat the egg whites and salt in a large, clean bowl until stiff, but not dry, peaks form. Gently fold the whites into the batter. Pour into the prepared pan.
4. Bake in the preheated moderate oven (350°) for 45 minutes or until a cake tester comes out clean. Cool on a wire rack. (The center of the cake will sink slightly.) When cooled, turn the cake out of the pan; remove the wax paper from the bottom. Place the cake, top-side up, on a serving plate. Drizzle with the honey, if you wish.

* Note: If matzo cake flour is not available, process matzo meal in a blender on high speed until the texture of flour is attained.

Piña Colada Down-Up Cake

Bake at 350° for 50 minutes.
Makes 12 servings.

*Nutrient Value Per Serving: 523 calories, 6 gm. protein,
20 gm. fat, 285 mg. sodium, 86 mg. cholesterol.*

- ⅓ **cup butter or margarine**
- ½ **cup firmly packed light brown sugar**
- 1 **can (20 ounces) sliced pineapple in juice,
  well drained**
- 4 **maraschino cherries, halved**
- 3½ **ounces flaked coconut (half of 7-ounce
  package)**
- 3 **cups sifted all-purpose flour**
- 1¾ **cups granulated sugar**
- 1 **tablespoon baking powder**
- ½ **teaspoon salt**
- 3 **eggs**
- 1¼ **cups milk**
- ¾ **cup golden Jamaican rum**
- ½ **cup vegetable oil**
- 1 **teaspoon vanilla**

1. Place the butter in a 13 x 9 x 2-inch metal
   baking pan. Place the pan over low heat
   until the butter melts, stirring occasionally.
   Remove from the heat. Sprinkle the brown
   sugar evenly over the bottom. Arrange the
   pineapple slices in an attractive pattern over
   the butter-sugar mixture; cut 1 or 2 slices
   into quarters or halves for a neat fit, if
   necessary. Place the cherry halves in the
   center of the pineapple rings. Sprinkle with
   the coconut. Set aside.
2. Preheat the oven to moderate (350°).
3. Sift together the flour, sugar, baking
   powder and salt into a large mixer bowl.
4. Beat the eggs slightly in a medium-size
   bowl. Mix in the milk, rum, oil and vanilla.
   Pour into the dry ingredients. Beat at low
   speed until blended. Increase speed to
   medium; beat for 2 minutes. Carefully pour
   over the mixture in the pan.
5. Bake in the preheated moderate oven (350°)
   for 50 minutes or until the center of the
   cake springs back when lightly touched
   with a fingertip. Remove to a wire rack. Let
   stand for 5 minutes. Loosen the sides; invert the cake carefully onto a large serving
   platter. Cool to room temperature.

Raspberry Sherbet Cake

*Wow your guests with this elegant, refreshing dessert.
They'll think you spent hours in the kitchen.*

Makes 12 servings.

*Nutrient Value Per Serving: 179 calories, 2 gm. protein,
4 gm. fat, 81 mg. sodium, 28 mg. cholesterol.*

- 1 **box (11¾ ounces) frozen layered Boston
  cream cake**
- 1 **quart lemon sherbet**
- ½ **pint raspberries
  Mint for garnish (optional)**

1. Cut the frozen cake crosswise into 10 equal
   slices, each about ½ inch thick. Halve each
   slice vertically. Press the 14 slices, with the
   sides touching, around the side of an 8-inch
   springform pan; arrange the slices so the
   frosting is on top and a frosted edge is
   between two slices. Arrange the remaining
   cake slices in the bottom of the pan.
2. Soften the sherbet in a large, chilled metal
   bowl. Carefully spoon the sherbet into the
   lined pan and spread evenly with a metal
   spatula. Tightly cover the surface of the
   sherbet with plastic wrap. Freeze.
3. To serve, garnish the top with clusters of
   raspberries, and sprigs of mint, if you wish.

Golden Fruitcakes

Golden Fruitcakes

Dried pears and apricots add a lighter touch to this fruitcake, mixed with whole, blanched hazelnuts.

Bake at 300° for 1 hour, 45 minutes for smaller cake; 2 hours, 45 minutes for 9-inch cake. Makes a 3-cup mold and a 9-inch round (36 servings).

Nutrient Value Per Serving: 372 calories, 5 gm. protein, 18 gm. fat, 119 mg. sodium, 66 mg. cholesterol.

  1 *pound dried pears, chopped*
  1 *pound dried apricots, chopped*
  ½ *cup Triple Sec or orange liqueur*
  4 *cups all-purpose unsifted flour*
  2 *teaspoons baking powder*
  1½ *cups (3 sticks) butter or margarine,*
       at room temperature
  2 *cups sugar*
  6 *eggs*
  1 *teaspoon ground cinnamon*
  1 *teaspoon ground mace or nutmeg*
       Grated rind of 1 orange
  1 *pound whole hazelnuts, blanched**
  ½ *pound whole dried pears*
  ¼ *pound whole dried apricots*
       Whole blanched hazelnuts
       Crystal Glaze (recipe follows)

1. Toss the chopped dried pears and apricots with the Triple Sec in a large bowl; cover with foil. Let stand for at least 2 hours, preferably overnight, tossing occasionally.
2. Grease very well and flour a 3-cup mold, tapping out the flour. Grease very well a 9-inch (loose-bottom) baking pan; line the bottom with wax paper; grease.
3. Sift together 3 cups of the flour and the baking powder onto wax paper.
4. Preheat the oven to slow (300°).
5. Beat the butter or margarine and sugar until light and fluffy in a large bowl with an electric mixer at high speed. Add the eggs, one at a time, beating well after each addition. Beat in the cinnamon, mace or nutmeg and grated orange rind. Drain the chopped fruits; add the drained liqueur to the butter-sugar mixture. Add the sifted flour mixture, beating only until blended.
6. Toss the remaining 1 cup of flour with the chopped fruits and nuts; fold into the batter. Spoon the 2 cups of the mixture into the 3-cup mold; spoon the remainder into a 9-inch pan. Smooth the tops with a spoon. Decorate the top of the 9-inch pan with the whole dried pears, apricots and hazelnuts, pressing in lightly.
7. Bake in the preheated slow oven (300°) for 1 hour, 45 minutes for the small mold and for 2 hours, 45 minutes for the large pan or until a skewer inserted in the center comes out clean. Loosely cover the top of the large pan with aluminum foil after 30 minutes, so the fruit does not burn.
8. Cool in the pans on wire racks for 15 minutes. Loosen around the sides; invert onto the racks. Cool completely. Wrap tightly with aluminum foil and store in an airtight metal tin.
9. At serving time, brush the Crystal Glaze on top. Decorate with additional dried fruit and nuts, if you wish.

* Note: To blanch the hazelnuts, place the nuts in a single layer in an ungreased pan; bake in a preheated moderate oven (350°) for 10 minutes, stirring once or twice, or until the skins begin to crack and peel away from the nutmeat. Briskly rub the nuts, a handful at a time, in a clean tea towel to remove as much of the skin as possible.

Crystal Glaze: Makes ½ cup. Heat ⅓ cup of light corn syrup with 2 tablespoons of brandy or orange juice in a small saucepan until bubbly, stirring often.

Flouring Nuts and Fruits

Nuts and fruits will not sink to the bottom of a cake if they are lightly coated with flour before they are added to the batter.

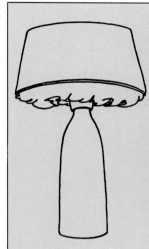

HANGING FOAM CAKES

Remove angel food, chiffon or sponge cakes from the oven. Cool by inverting and placing the pan over the top of a filled 1-quart or 1-liter *glass* bottle for 1 hour or until cold. (The cake will not fall out.) The air can circulate around the whole cake and will cool it faster.

Hot-Milk Sponge Cake

Grandma always thought of this cake as fresh berries appeared in the garden.

Bake at 325° for 50 minutes.
Makes 10 servings (one 9-inch tube cake).

Nutrient Value Per Serving: 151 calories, 3 gm. protein, 2 gm. fat, 120 mg. sodium, 83 mg. cholesterol.

  1 cup **u**nsifted all-purpose flour
  1 teaspoon baking powder
  ¼ teaspoon salt
  3 eggs
  1 cup sugar
  ¼ cup hot milk
  1 teaspoon vanilla

1. Preheat the oven to slow (325°).
2. Sift the flour, baking powder and salt onto wax paper.
3. Beat the eggs in a large bowl with an electric mixer at high speed, until thick and fluffy; slowly beat in the sugar until the mixture is almost doubled in volume and very thick. Turn the speed to low; beat in the hot milk and vanilla.
4. Fold in the flour mixture, one-third at a time, with a wire whisk, just until blended.

time, with a wire whisk, just until blended. Pour into an ungreased 9-inch angel-cake tube pan.

5. Bake in the preheated slow oven (325°) for 50 minutes or until the center springs back when lightly pressed with a fingertip.
6. Invert the pan, placing the tube over a quart- or liter-size glass bottle; let hang for 1 hour or until cooled. Loosen the cake around the tube and down the side with a narrow-bladed knife. Remove from the pan. Serve with fresh fruit or well-drained canned fruit, if you wish.

Angel, Chiffon and Sponge Cakes

● Always bake in ungreased pans so these light, airy cakes can cling to the sides of the pan and rise to their full height.

Orange Chiffon Cake

Truly an all-American variety, the chiffon cake is one of the best of the sponge-type cakes to come along in this century. It was created in the 1930's following the development of the angel food cake.

Bake at 325° for 1 hour, 10 minutes.
Makes 12 servings (one 10-inch cake).

Nutrient Value Per Serving: 318 calories, 4 gm. protein, 11 gm. fat, 187 mg. sodium, 113 mg. cholesterol.

2½ cups **sifted** cake flour
1⅓ cups sugar
  1 tablespoon baking powder
  ¼ teaspoon salt
  ½ cup vegetable oil
  5 egg yolks
  ½ cup water
  2 tablespoons grated orange rind
  ¼ cup orange juice
  7 to 8 egg whites (1 cup)
  ½ teaspoon cream of tartar
     Orange Glaze (recipe follows)

1. Sift the flour, 1 cup of the sugar, the baking powder and salt into a medium-size bowl. Make a well in the center and add in order: oil, egg yolks, water, orange rind and orange juice; beat with a spoon until smooth. Preheat the oven to slow (325°).
2. Beat the egg whites and cream of tartar in a large bowl with an electric mixer on high ☞

speed until foamy white and doubled in volume. Gradually beat in the remaining sugar until the meringue stands in firm peaks.

3. Pour the egg yolk mixture over the beaten egg white mixture; fold the mixture gently until no streaks of white remain. Pour the batter into an ungreased 10-inch tube pan.

4. Bake in the preheated slow oven (325°) for 1 hour and 10 minutes or until the top springs back when lightly pressed with a fingertip.

5. Invert the pan on a funnel or soda bottle to keep the top of the cake off the countertop; let the cake cool completely upside down. When cool, loosen the cake around the tube and down the side with a spatula. Remove from the pan. Drizzle with the Orange Glaze or sprinkle with 10X (confectioners') sugar and serve with fresh fruits, if you wish.

Orange Glaze: Combine 1 cup of 10X (confectioners') sugar with 2 tablespoons of orange juice in a small bowl until smooth.

Leftover Egg Whites

Store leftover egg whites in an airtight container in the refrigerator for up to 4 days. Use in soufflés and meringues.

Chocolate-Peanut Butter Torte

Who could resist this sinfully rich dessert? It's layered with chocolate and peanut butter fillings and slathered with chocolate-flavored cream cheese frosting and whipped cream. And, it requires no baking!

Chocolate-Peanut Butter Torte

Makes 12 servings.

Nutrient Value Per Serving: 639 calories, 12 gm. protein, 37 gm. fat, 349 mg. sodium, 232 mg. cholesterol.

24 ladyfingers (two 3-ounce packages), split in half lengthwise
¾ cup (1½ sticks) butter, softened
4 cups sifted 10X (confectioners') sugar
1 tablespoon vanilla
1 tablespoon amaretto liqueur
4 eggs
½ cup extra-chunky peanut butter
2 squares (1 ounce each) unsweetened chocolate, melted and cooled
Chocolate-Peanut Butter Frosting (recipe follows)

1. Line a 9x5x3-inch metal loaf pan with 2 sheets of aluminum foil, 1 laid crosswise and 1 laid lengthwise; allow the foil to extend several inches beyond the rim.

2. Arrange 7 ladyfinger halves, flat-side up, in the bottom of the pan, parallel to the short end of the pan. Line each long side with 7 ladyfinger halves, standing upright and flat-side in. Line each short end with 3 ladyfinger halves.

3. Beat together the butter, 10X sugar, vanilla and amaretto in a large bowl until well blended. Add the eggs, one at a time, beating well after each addition, until smooth and fluffy.

4. Transfer 2 cups of the butter mixture to a small bowl. Add the extra-chunky peanut butter; mix well. Spoon evenly over the bottom of the ladyfinger-lined pan. Tap the pan on the counter to settle the filling. Smooth evenly with a spatula. Arrange 7 ladyfinger halves, parallel to the short end of the pan, over the peanut butter mixture. Wedge 3 ladyfinger halves lengthwise, down one long side of the pan.

5. Stir the melted chocolate into the remaining butter mixture in the large bowl. Spoon over the ladyfingers; spread evenly. Arrange 10 ladyfinger halves as in Step 4. Crumble the remaining ladyfinger half over the top, filling the spaces between the ladyfingers.

6. Fold the overhanging foil over the top; wrap securely. Freeze for at least 6 hours or overnight.

7. Fold back the foil. Invert the torte onto the serving platter. Remove the pan; carefully remove the foil. Frost the sides and top with Chocolate-Peanut Butter Frosting.*

Freeze, uncovered, for 1 hour until the frosting is firm.

8. To serve, cut into thin slices with a thin-bladed sharp knife. Garnish with whipped cream, if you wish.

Chocolate-Peanut Butter Frosting: Beat together 4 packages (3 ounces each) of softened cream cheese, 2 cups of *sifted* 10X (confectioners') sugar and 1 tablespoon of milk in a medium-size bowl until fluffy. Beat in ⅓ cup of smooth peanut butter and ⅓ cup of unsweetened cocoa powder until well mixed.

* *Note:* If the ladyfingers begin to crumble when applying the frosting, carefully cover the cake with a very thin layer of frosting. Place in the freezer until firm. Spread evenly with the remaining frosting.

Room-Temperature Eggs?

Eggs perform best at room temperature (they beat faster and yield greater volume). Take them out of the refrigerator about 1 hour before using. Refrigerator-cold eggs, however, are easier to separate.

Orange-Ambrosia Cake

Bake at 325° for 35 to 40 minutes.
Makes 12 servings.

Nutrient Value Per Serving: 849 calories, 9 gm. protein, 40 gm. fat, 342 mg. sodium, 243 mg. cholesterol.

1½ **cups (3 sticks) butter, at room temperature**
1 **package (8 ounces) cream cheese, at room temperature**
3 **cups sugar**
5 **eggs**
2 **eggs, separated**
3 **cups sifted all-purpose flour**
1 **teaspoon orange extract**
1 **teaspoon pineapple extract**
Filling:
½ **cup sugar**
2 **tablespoons cornstarch**
1 **cup orange juice**
1 **can (11 ounces) mandarin oranges, well drained**
1 **can (20 ounces) crushed pineapple, well drained**
2 **cans (3½ ounces each) flaked coconut**

1 **cup coarsely ground pecans (4 ounces)**
Frosting (recipe follows)

1. Preheat the oven to slow (325°). Grease and flour four 9-inch-round layer-cake pans.*
2. Beat together the butter and cream cheese in a medium-size bowl with an electric mixer until light and fluffy, for about 3 minutes. Gradually add the sugar and continue beating for 5 minutes. Add the eggs and yolks, one at a time, beating well after each addition. (Reserve the 2 egg whites for the Frosting.)
3. Fold in the flour and the orange and pineapple extracts. Divide the batter evenly among the 4 pans. (If using 2 pans, reserve half the batter.)
4. Bake in the preheated slow oven (325°) for 35 to 40 minutes or until a cake tester inserted in the centers comes out clean. Cool the cakes in the pans for 10 minutes. Turn the cakes out onto wire racks to cool completely.
5. Prepare the Filling: Combine the sugar and cornstarch in a medium-size saucepan. Gradually stir in the orange juice until well combined. Cook over medium heat, stirring, until the mixture thickens, for 4 to 5 minutes. Chill for 1 hour before using.
6. Fold the oranges, pineapple, 1 can of the coconut and the pecans into the chilled Filling.
7. Place 1 cake layer on a plate. Spread evenly with a third of the Filling. Repeat with the remaining layers, leaving the top plain. Cover the sides and top with the Frosting. Press the remaining coconut against the top and sides.

Frosting: Combine ½ cup of sugar, ¼ cup of light corn syrup and 2 tablespoons of water in a small saucepan. Cover and bring to boiling. Uncover; cook over medium heat until a small amount of mixture dropped into cold water forms a soft ball or until a candy thermometer registers 234°. While the sugar is boiling, beat 2 reserved egg whites in a medium-size bowl until stiff peaks form. Pour the hot syrup over the whites in a thin stream, beating constantly with an electric mixer on medium speed. Beat in ⅛ teaspoon of pineapple extract, ⅛ teaspoon of orange extract, 1 teaspoon of vanilla. For coloring, add 2 drops of yellow food coloring, if you wish. Beat until stiff, about 5 minutes.

* *Note:* If you only have 2 cake pans, bake the layers in two batches. The original recipe calls for 5 layers, but we found 4 layers easier to work with.

FROSTING CAKE LAYERS

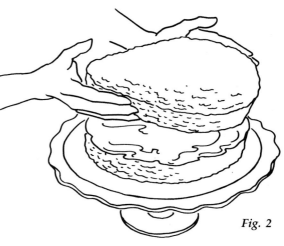

Fig. 2

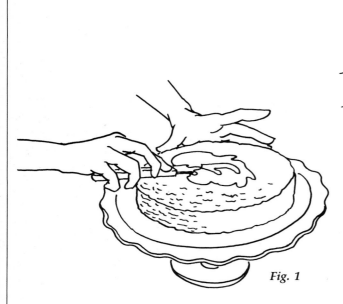

Fig. 1

Rub your hand around the edge of the cake layer to loosen and rub off any cake crumbs. (*Note:* This gives a smooth surface for the frosting.)

Place the cake layer, rounded-side down, on a cake plate; spread, with a generous layer of frosting, to the edge, leaving a thicker layer of frosting around the edge of the layer (FIG. 1). Place the second layer, rounded-side up, over the filled layer (FIG. 2). Top a spatula with a generous amount of frosting and spread it in a swirling motion up the side to the top of the cake to cover and make a decorative edge to the cake (FIG. 3).

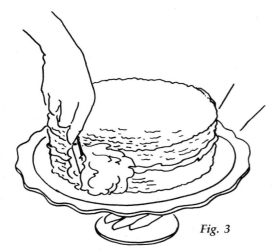

Fig. 3

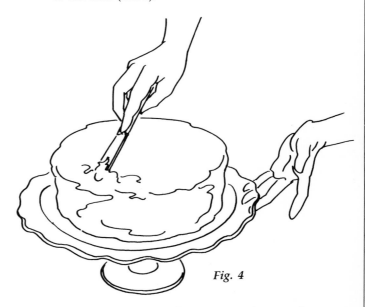

Fig. 4

Baker's Tip: If there is a tear in the side of the cake, mix ½ cup of prepared frosting with 3 tablespoons of water to make a very thin mixture. Spread it over the broken surface to coat evenly; allow it to dry before frosting the cake.

Spread the remaining frosting over the top of the cake, making swirling motions with the spatula for a decorative finish (FIG. 4).

Chocolate Supreme

Chocolate Supreme

Bake at 350° for 25 minutes.
Makes 12 servings.

Nutrient Value Per Serving: 690 calories, 10 gm. protein, 38 gm. fat, 459 mg. sodium, 189 mg. cholesterol.

¾ *cup boiling water*
¾ *cup unsweetened cocoa powder*
 1 *cup buttermilk*
2½ *cups unsifted all-purpose flour*
1½ *teaspoons baking soda*
 ½ *teaspoon baking powder*
 ½ *teaspoon salt*
¾ *cup (1½ sticks) butter, softened*
 2 *cups sugar*
 4 *eggs*
1½ *teaspoons vanilla*
    Frosting (recipe follows)
    Chocolate Curls (recipe follows)

1. Preheat the oven to moderate (350°). Grease and flour three 9-inch-round layer-cake pans.
2. Pour the boiling water over the cocoa powder in a medium-size bowl; stir to dissolve the cocoa. Stir in the buttermilk; the mixture should be cool. Set aside.
3. Sift together the flour, baking soda, baking powder and salt onto wax paper.
4. Beat together the butter and sugar in a large bowl with an electric mixer at medium speed until light and fluffy. Add the eggs, one at a time, beating well after each addition. Stir in the vanilla.
5. Beat the dry ingredients into the butter mixture, alternating with the cocoa mixture, beginning and ending with the dry ingredients. Pour into the prepared pans, dividing the batter equally.
6. Bake in the preheated moderate oven (350°) for 25 minutes or until the centers spring ☞

back when lightly pressed with a fingertip. Cool the cakes in the pans on wire racks for 10 minutes. Turn the cakes out of the pans onto the racks to cool completely.

7. Place one cake layer on a serving plate. Spread the top with one-third of the Frosting. Stack the second layer on top and spread with another third of the Frosting. Repeat with the remaining layer and Frosting. Top with the Chocolate Curls. Refrigerate until ready to serve.

Frosting: Beat 2 cups of heavy cream with ¼ cup of *sifted* 10X (confectioners') sugar and 1 teaspoon of vanilla in a large bowl with an electric mixer at high speed until stiff.

Chocolate Curls: Draw a swivel-bladed vegetable peeler across the flat side of an 8-ounce chocolate candy bar (at room temperature), letting the chocolate curl. Lift the curls with a wooden pick and place on the cake.

Christmas Cassata

A multilayered fruit, chocolate and ricotta cake.

Bake at 325° for 20 minutes.
Makes 10 servings.

Nutrient Value Per Serving: 424 calories, 7 gm. protein, 30 gm. fat, 74 mg. sodium, 180 mg. cholesterol.

Cake:
½ teaspoon grated orange rind
½ cup sugar
3 eggs, separated
1½ teaspoons Grand Marnier, or orange-flavored liqueur
½ cup **sifted** all-purpose flour

Fillings:
2½ squares (1 ounce each) semisweet chocolate
1 scant cup ricotta cheese
2 tablespoons finely chopped red glacé cherries and green glacé pineapple
¾ cup heavy cream
¼ cup 10X (confectioners') sugar
1½ teaspoons Crème de Cacao OR: ¼ teaspoon almond extract
1½ teaspoons Grand Marnier OR: ½ teaspoon orange extract
Whipped Cream Frosting (recipe follows)

Christmas Cassata

1. Preheat the oven to slow (325°). Line a 9 x 9 x 2-inch baking pan with wax paper; oil the paper. Set aside.

2. Prepare the Cake: Mix together the grated orange rind and sugar in a small bowl. Beat the egg yolks in a medium-size bowl until thick. Gradually beat in the sugar mixture until light and fluffy. Stir in the Grand Marnier. Fold in the flour until well blended.

3. Beat the egg whites in a small bowl until stiff peaks form. Stir one-quarter of the whites into the yolk mixture to lighten. Fold in the remaining whites. Pour into the prepared pan, spreading evenly to the edges.

4. Bake in the preheated slow oven (325°) for 20 minutes or until the cake is light and golden and the top springs back when lightly touched with a fingertip. Cool the cake in the pan on a wire rack.

5. Prepare the Fillings: Melt 1 square of the chocolate in the top of a double boiler or in a small bowl over hot water. Cool. Chop the remaining chocolate into pea-size pieces. Set aside.

6. Divide the ricotta in half between 2 bowls. Beat the melted chocolate into one bowl. Stir the chopped chocolate and glacé fruits into the other bowl. Whip the cream in a small bowl until soft peaks form. Fold half of the whipped cream along with the Crème de Cacao into the melted chocolate-ricotta mixture. Fold the remaining whipped cream along with the Grand Marnier into the chopped chocolate-ricotta mixture.

7. Line a 8½ x 4½ x 2⅝-inch loaf pan with plastic wrap, letting about 2 inches overhang the long sides.

8. Turn out the cooled cake onto a work surface; remove the wax paper. Cut the cake in half horizontally with a serrated knife. Then cut the cake in half to make 4 layers, 9 x 4½ inches. Place one layer in the bottom of the prepared loaf pan. Spread with half of the melted chocolate-ricotta filling. Place the second layer of the cake in the pan. Spread with half of the chopped chocolate-ricotta filling. Top with a third and fourth layer, alternating with the remaining fillings. Cover the top of the cassata with overhanging plastic wrap. Place in the freezer for at least 4 hours or until firm. The cassata can be frozen for up to several days at this point.

9. Three hours before serving, remove the cake from the freezer. Loosen from the sides of the pan with a knife. Pulling the ends of the plastic wrap, carefully lift the cake out onto a serving platter; remove the plastic wrap. Spoon the Whipped Cream Frosting into a pastry bag fitted with a decorative tip. Pipe the frosting over the sides and top of the cassata. Decorate with additional glacé cherries and glacé pineapple, if you wish. Refrigerate until ready to serve.

Whipped Cream Frosting: Beat 2 cups of heavy cream in a medium-size bowl until soft peaks form. Gradually beat in ⅓ cup of 10X (confectioners') sugar until stiff. Stir in 1½ teaspoons of vanilla and 2 tablespoons of Grand Marnier.

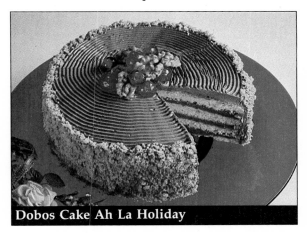
Dobos Cake Ah La Holiday

Dobos Cake Ah La Holiday

Bake at 350° for 20 minutes.
Makes 12 servings.

Nutrient Value Per Serving: 764 calories, 10 gm. protein, 58 gm. fat, 492 mg. sodium, 428 mg. cholesterol.

  6 eggs separated
1¼ cups sugar
  2 tablespoons lemon juice
  1 cup sifted all-purpose flour
  ¼ cup cornstarch
  ½ teaspoon salt
     Chocolate Frosting (recipe follows)
  1 cup ground walnuts
     Walnuts and glacé fruit for garnish
     (optional)

1. Preheat the oven to moderate (350°). Grease two 9-inch-round layer-cake pans. Line ☞

the bottoms with wax paper; grease the paper with vegetable shortening.

2. Beat the egg yolks in a medium-size bowl until thick and pale yellow. Gradually beat in the sugar until the yolks are thick and fluffy. Beat in the lemon juice.

3. Sift together the flour, cornstarch and salt over the yolk mixture all at once; fold into the yolk mixture with a rubber spatula.

4. Beat the egg whites in a medium-size bowl until stiff peaks form. Stir in one-quarter of the beaten whites into the yolk mixture to lighten. Fold in the remaining whites until no streaks remain. Spread the batter into the prepared pans, dividing equally.

5. Bake in the preheated moderate oven (350°) for 20 minutes or until the tops spring back when lightly touched with a fingertip. Cool the cakes in the pans on wire racks for 10 minutes. Turn the cakes out onto the racks; remove the wax paper and let cool. Cut each layer in half horizontally with a serrated knife.

6. Fill and stack the layers with the Chocolate Frosting. Frost the top layer. Make a design with a decorating comb, if you wish. Cover the sides with the ground walnuts. Garnish the top with the walnuts and the glacé fruit, if you wish.

Chocolate Frosting: Melt 4½ squares (1 ounce each) of semisweet chocolate in the top of a double boiler or in a small bowl over hot water. Beat 6 egg yolks and ½ cup of sugar in a medium-size bowl until pale yellow. Stir in ¾ cup of heavy cream and ⅛ teaspoon of salt. Stir into the melted chocolate. Cook over hot water, stirring occasionally, until thick. Remove from the heat. Beat in 1½ cups (3 sticks) of softened butter, 1 tablespoon at a time. If the frosting cools too rapidly to incorporate the butter, place over hot water for a minute or two. Cool the frosting in the refrigerator or over ice water until it reaches a good spreading consistency.

ROLLING A CAKE ROLL

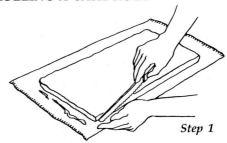

Step 1 Invert the cake onto a clean towel which has been sprinkled with confectioners' sugar; cut off the crisp edges with a long, thin serrated knife.

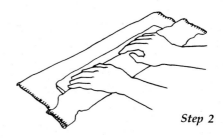

Step 2 Gently roll the warm cake and towel along the length of the cake. Place the cake and towel on a wire rack to cool.

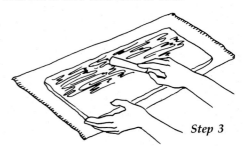

Step 3 Gently unroll the cake and spread with the filling.

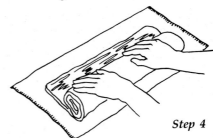

Step 4 Reroll the cake and filling without the towel.

Chocolate-Filled Mimosa-Lemon Roll

Looking for a special summer dessert? This easy and delicious lemon roll is it.

Bake at 375° for 12 minutes.
Makes 8 servings.

Nutrient Value Per Serving: 414 calories, 5 gm. protein, 13 gm. fat, 316 mg. sodium, 133 mg. cholesterol.

 1 **cup** sifted *cake flour*
 1 **teaspoon** baking powder
 ¼ **teaspoon** salt
 3 **eggs**
 ¾ **cup** granulated sugar
 ⅓ **cup** water
 2 **teaspoons** grated lemon rind
   10X (confectioners') sugar
   Rich Chocolate Filling (recipe follows)
   Mimosa-Lemon Frosting (recipe follows)
   Green and yellow food coloring

1. Preheat the oven to moderate (375°). Grease a 15 x 10 x 1-inch jelly-roll pan. Line the bottom with wax paper; grease the paper; sprinkle lightly with flour.
2. Sift together the cake flour, baking powder and salt onto a second piece of wax paper.
3. Beat the eggs in a medium-size bowl with an electric mixer until fluffy. Gradually add the granulated sugar, beating constantly, until the mixture is very thick and forms ribbons when the beaters are raised. Gently stir in the water and lemon rind until well mixed.
4. Fold in the flour mixture. Spread the batter evenly in the prepared pan.
5. Bake in the preheated moderate oven (375°) for 12 minutes or until the cake is golden and the center springs back when lightly touched with a fingertip.
6. Loosen the cake around the edges with a small spatula. Invert the pan carefully onto a clean towel dusted with 10X sugar. Peel off the wax paper. Trim ¼ inch from the sides of the cake. Roll up the cake and towel together, starting at a short end. Place, seam-side down, on a wire rack to cool completely.
7. Prepare the Rich Chocolate Filling.
8. Unroll the cooled cake and towel. Spread the cake evenly with the Rich Chocolate Filling. Reroll from the short end, using the towel as a guide. Refrigerate while making the Mimosa-Lemon Frosting.
9. Place 2 tablespoons of the Mimosa-Lemon Frosting in a small cup and 3 tablespoons in a second cup. Tint the 2 tablespoons of frosting light green, and the 3 tablespoons bright yellow. Spoon the tinted frostings into 2 small wax paper cones with the ends snipped off.
10. Spread the remaining Mimosa-Lemon Frosting over the cake roll. Pipe the green mimosa stems with yellow flowers over the cake. Refrigerate until ready to serve.

Rich Chocolate Filling: Combine 1 package (3½ ounces) of chocolate-flavored pudding mix, 1⅔ cups of milk and 2 tablespoons of butter in a small saucepan. Cook over medium heat, stirring constantly, until the mixture comes to a full rolling boil. Cool completely.

Mimosa-Lemon Frosting: Beat ¼ cup (½ stick) of butter or margarine in a small bowl until creamed. Beat in 1 cup of 10X (confectioners') sugar and 1 tablespoon of lemon juice until well blended. Beat in another 1 cup of 10X (confectioners') sugar and enough water or milk, about 1 tablespoon, until the frosting is smooth and spreadable.

Unique Cakes

Chocolate Heart Cake

Bake according to the package directions.
Makes 12 servings.

Nutrient Value Per Serving: 482 calories, 5 gm. protein, 32 gm. fat, 269 mg. sodium, 123 mg. cholesterol.

 1 **package** any flavor cake mix for 2-layer cake
 2 **cups** heavy cream
 ½ **teaspoon** vanilla
 ¼ **cup** 10X (confectioners') sugar
 3 **tablespoons** unsweetened cocoa powder
 1 **bag** (6 ounces) semisweet chocolate pieces
   Gold ribbon bow (optional)

1. Grease and flour two 8-inch heart-shaped cake pans. Prepare, bake and cool the cake, following the package directions for two 8-inch layers.
2. Combine the cream, vanilla, 10X sugar and cocoa in the bowl. Refrigerate.
3. Melt the chocolate pieces in a double boiler over hot, not boiling, water. *(continues on page 203)*

Chocolate Heart Cake (page 201)

Line the bottom of one heart-shaped pan with foil. Spread the chocolate evenly over the bottom. Place in the freezer until firm.

4. When the cakes are completely cool, beat the refrigerated cream mixture just until stiff. Spoon 1½ cups into a pastry bag fitted with a large star tip. Spoon ½ cup into a pastry bag fitted with an adapter and small star tip.
5. Fill and frost the cake layers on a serving plate with the remaining cocoa cream, swirling cream on the top and sides.
6. Using the pastry bag with the large star tip, pipe a shell border around the base of the cake. Pipe a line down the center of the cake.
7. Remove the chocolate heart from the cake pan. Carefully heat the blade of a sharp knife. Cut the heart in half. Return to the freezer for 1 minute to reset the chocolate. When the chocolate is firm again, peel off the aluminum foil and separate the halves. Using the pastry bag with the small star tip, pipe a border of small stars around the outer edge on the smooth side of each half of the chocolate heart.
8. Set half of a chocolate heart into a row of cream in the center of the cake top. Using the large star tip, pipe a puff of cream under the heart to prop it at an angle, so the outer edge is about 1 inch above the edge of the cake. Repeat with the other half.
9. Change the small star tip on the adapter to a medium rose tip.
10. Press the gold bow into the cream at the bottom point of the heart, if you wish.
11. Pipe a row of rosebuds down the seam of the heart. Extend the bud over the edge to cover the center of the bow, if using. Refrigerate until ready to serve.

Happy Birthday Teddy Bear Cake

Bake according to the package directions.
Makes 12 servings.

Nutrient Value Per Serving: 703 calories, 3 gm. protein, 29 gm. fat, 255 mg. sodium, 69 mg. cholesterol.

1 *package any flavor cake mix for 2-layer cake*
2 *recipes Decorator Frosting (recipe follows)*
4 *teaspoons instant coffee powder*
1 *teaspoon warm water*

Miniature marshmallows
Wooden picks
Green and yellow food coloring
¼ *teaspoon unsweetened cocoa powder*
Birthday candles

1. Prepare, bake and cool the cake mix, following the label directions for a 13 x 9 x 2-inch baking pan.
2. Prepare 2 recipes of the Decorator Frosting. Spoon 1½ cups into a pastry bag fitted with a medium star tip. Measure 1 cup into a small bowl, ¼ cup into a custard cup, 2 tablespoons into a second custard cup and 1 tablespoon into a third custard cup.
3. Place the cake, upside down, on a 14 x 10-inch or larger serving tray or board. Frost with the remaining unmeasured white frosting. Using a bag with a medium star tip, pipe a reverse shell border around the top edge of the cake. Pipe a shell border around the bottom edge of the cake.
4. Stir the instant coffee into the 1 teaspoon of warm water. Beat into the 1 cup of frosting in a small bowl until evenly colored. Spoon into a pastry bag fitted with a small star tip.
5. To make the sitting teddy bears on top of the cake: Push 2 miniature marshmallows onto a wooden pick, allowing ¼ inch of the pick to extend beyond the marshmallows at one end and about 1 inch on the other. Pipe small stars to completely cover the sides of the marshmallows. Holding the top ¼ inch of the wooden pick, push the long end of the pick into the cake until the teddy bear body is sitting on the cake. Insert straight into the cake for the sitting teddy bears and at an angle for the resting teddy bears. Press a quarter of a marshmallow on the end of the pick for the head; cover completely with piped stars. Pipe on the ears, arms and legs as pictured on page 204. Pipe small white stars on the faces for the eyes.
6. To make the teddy bears on the sides of the cake: Pipe a ¾-inch puff of frosting onto the side of the cake for the body. Pipe the large star above it for the head; cover both completely with small stars. Pipe on the ears, arms and legs. Pipe small white stars on the faces for the eyes.
7. To make the teddy bears standing on their heads: Push 2 wooden picks through a stack of 2 marshmallows to form an X with the center inside the marshmallows. Insert one wooden pick end into the star tip on the ☞

Happy Birthday Teddy Bear Cake

Decorator Frosting

Makes about 2¼ cups.

Nutrient Value Per Tablespoon: 74 calories, 0 gm. protein, 3 gm. fat, .12 mg. sodium, 0 mg. cholesterol.

- ½ cup vegetable shortening
- 1 box (1 pound) 10X (confectioners') sugar
- ¼ teaspoon almond extract
- 3 to 4 tablespoons warm water

Combine the shortening, sugar, almond extract and the 3 tablespoons of water in a large bowl. Beat until smooth and easy to spread. If necessary, add more water.

Big Burger Cake

Family Circle's Big Burger Cake

Bake at 350° for 25 to 30 minutes.
Makes 12 servings.

Nutrient Value Per Serving: 823 calories, 7 gm. protein, 37 gm. fat, 257 mg. sodium, 69 mg. cholesterol.

- 1 package any yellow cake mix for 2-layer cake
- 2 recipes Decorator Frosting (recipe above)
  Orange and red paste food coloring
  Red, yellow and green liquid food coloring
- ¼ cup finely chopped walnuts or pecans
- ⅔ cup plus 2 tablespoons unsweetened cocoa powder
- 3 tablespoons warm water
- 2 tablespoons instant coffee powder
- 1 can (8 ounces) almond paste
- 1 tablespoon sunflower kernels, toasted

pastry bag filled with the coffee frosting so that the tip touches the marshmallow. Gently pull back the tip, piping a coating of frosting on the pick, extending ½ inch from the marshmallow. Repeat on the other wooden pick on the small end of the marshmallows. Pipe small stars to cover the marshmallows. Push the frosted wooden picks into the cake until the teddy bear is stable. Pipe the paws at the end of the arms. Pipe the head on the body just above the arms.

8. Using the piping technique, described in Step 7, coat the top 2 wooden picks with the frosting. Pipe the paws at the end of the legs.
9. Pipe a message on the cake with the remaining light brown frosting, if you wish.
10. Color the ¼ cup of frosting green. Spoon into a small patry bag fitted with a leaf tip. Pipe leaves around the bears.
11. Color the 2 tablespoons of frosting yellow. Spoon into a small pastry bag fitted with a small star tip. Pipe small stars for flowers on the leaves.
12. Stir the cocoa into the 1 tablespoon of frosting. Spoon into a small parchment bag with a small hole cut in the end. Pipe, or apply with a wooden pick, noses and centers of eyes on the bears. Pipe clusters of dots on the leaves for flowers. Insert birthday candles into the leaves and into the bears' arms just before serving.

1. Preheat the oven to moderate (350°). Grease and flour three 8-inch-round layer-cake pans.
2. Prepare the cake mix according to the package directions. Divide evenly between the 3 pans. Bake according to the package directions, but only for 25 to 30 minutes or until the tops spring back when lightly pressed with a fingertip. Cool according to the package directions. Set all 3 layers, right-side up, on cooling racks.
3. Prepare 2 recipes of the Decorator Frosting. Spoon ½ cup into each of 3 small bowls. Color one light orange, to resemble cheese. Color another with red and yellow liquid coloring, to resemble Russian dressing. Fold in the chopped nuts. Color the third with the red paste food coloring, to resemble tomato.
4. Spoon 1½ cups of the white frosting into a medium-size bowl. Set aside the 2 tablespoons of cocoa. Stir the remaining cocoa and 2 tablespoons of the warm water into the 1½ cups of frosting until smooth and evenly colored to make cocoa frosting for the hamburgers. Add the reserved 2 tablespoons of the cocoa and the instant coffee, stirred into 1 tablespoon of the warm water, to the remaining frosting to make mocha frosting for the buns.
5. Knead several drops of the green and 1 drop of yellow food coloring into the almond paste. Divide into 12 pieces. Roll out the pieces between wax paper to form uneven shapes resembling lettuce leaves.
6. Frost halfway up the side of the first cake layer with the mocha frosting. Place the layer, unfrosted-side up, on a cake plate. Thickly frost the top half of the side of the layer with a little less than half the cocoa frosting. Round the edges and rough with a fork to resemble a hamburger. Frost the top of the layer with the cocoa frosting.
7. Spoon all of the orange frosting on top of the layer. Spread with a spatula to cover the top and extend over the sides at places to resemble melted cheese. Top with 6 almond paste lettuce leaves.
8. Turn the second cake layer over on a cooling rack. Frost the bottom and halfway down the side with the mocha frosting. Turn, right-side up, on top of the almond paste leaves on the first layer. To make the tomato, spread a thin layer of the red frosting with a spatula around the unfrosted half of the side of the cake and over the top of the cake.
9. Spoon all of the frosting which resembles Russian dressing on top of the red frosting. Spread with a spatula to cover the top of the cake and extend partway down the sides in some places to resemble the dressing. Top with the remaining 6 almond paste lettuce leaves.
10. Turn the remaining cake layer over on a cooling rack. Thickly frost halfway down the side of the layer with the cocoa frosting. Round the edges and rough with a fork to resemble a hamburger. Frost the bottom of the cake with the remaining cocoa frosting.
11. Turn the cake layer, right-side up, onto the almond paste leaves on the cake. Frost the unfrosted top half of the side and top of the cake with the remaining mocha frosting, rounding the top to look like the hamburger bun. Sprinkle with the sunflower kernels.

From top to bottom:

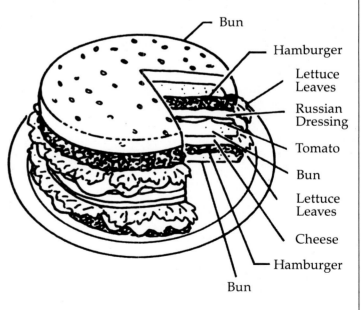

Bun
Hamburger
Lettuce Leaves
Russian Dressing
Tomato
Bun
Lettuce Leaves
Cheese
Hamburger
Bun

Sidewalk Sundae Cake

Sidewalk Sundae Cake

Bake according to the package directions.
Makes 12 servings.

*Nutrient Value Per Serving: 611 calories, 4 gm. protein,
26 gm. fat, 255 mg. sodium, 69 mg. cholesterol.*

- 1 **package any flavor cake mix for 2-layer cake**
- 6 **cups unsifted 10X (confectioners') sugar**
- 12 **tablespoons (¾ cup) vegetable shortening**
- ¼ **teaspoon almond extract**
- 4 **tablespoons warm water**
- 1 **tablespoon unsweetened cocoa powder**
- 1 **tablespoon instant coffee powder**
- 4 **to 6 medium-size fresh strawberries, washed, hulled and sliced**
- 1 **tablespoon chopped walnuts**
- 1 **large strawberry, washed, with stem left on**

1. Grease and flour one 9-inch-round layer-cake pan and one 8-inch heart-shaped cake pan. Prepare, bake and cool the cake, following the package directions.
2. Prepare the white frosting: Combine 2 cups of the 10X (confectioners') sugar, 4 tablespoons of the shortening, the almond extract and 2 tablespoons of the warm water in a medium-size bowl. Beat until smooth.
3. Prepare the mocha frosting: Combine 2 cups of the 10X (confectioners') sugar, 4 tablespoons of the shortening, the cocoa and the instant coffee stirred into the remaining 2 tablespoons of warm water, in a medium-size bowl. Beat until smooth.
4. Prepare the strawberry frosting: Combine the remaining 2 cups of 10X (confectioners') sugar, 4 tablespoons of vegetable shortening and 4 sliced strawberries in a medium-size

bowl. Beat until smooth. If the frosting is too stiff, beat in more strawberries until the consistency matches the other frostings.
5. Place a round cake layer at one end of a 19 x 11-inch, or larger, tray or board. Fit the heart-shaped cake tightly against the round layer.* Trim the heart cake so the sides are in a straight line with the sides of the round layer; these will be the sides of the cone. Trim any scraps to fit into the hollows on either side of the areas where the cakes meet.
6. Frost the trimmed heart cake, the trimmings fitted into the hollows on either side of the cake and the lower one-quarter of the round layer with the mocha frosting to make the cone. Be very careful to frost gently and in one direction over the cut edges. Score as pictured at left, to resemble a cone.
7. Frost the remaining part of the round cake with the strawberry frosting to resemble the ice cream. Swirl half of the white frosting over the top center of the strawberry frosting. Sprinkle with the nuts. Place the remaining white frosting in a pastry bag fitted with a medium star tip. Tuck doilies, cut in half, under the edges of the cake, if you wish. Pipe a shell border around the base of the cake, starting at the bottom point of the cone, and working up one side to the top, and then up the other side. Place the large strawberry at the top of the cake; fasten with a wooden pick to hold in place, if necessary.

**Note:* Instead of using a platter on which to serve the cake, cut a piece of cardboard ½ inch larger than the cake, using the unfrosted cakes fitted together as a guide. Cover the cardboard with aluminum foil and doilies.

Dad's Golden Car Cake

Dad's Golden Car Cake

Bake according to the package directions.
Makes 10 servings.

*Nutrient Value Per Serving (not including cake decorations):
782 calories, 4 gm. protein, 31 gm. fat, 209 mg. sodium,
.54 mg. cholesterol.*

1 **package pound cake mix**
 Firm cardboard
 Aluminum foil
 Wooden picks
2 **recipes Decorator Frosting (recipe, page 204)**
 Green and yellow food coloring
¼ **cup unsweetened cocoa powder**
1 **tablespoon warm water**
 Chocolate sprinkles
6 **chocolate cookies (1½ inches)**
 Silver dragees
4 **square cherry-flavored hard candies**
4 **small white gumdrops**
2 **small red gumdrops**
8 **small red cinnamon candies**

1. Prepare, bake and cool the cake mix, following the label directions for a 9 x 5 x 3-inch loaf pan.
2. Cut an 11 x 5-inch rectangle from firm cardboard. Round off the corners. Cover with foil.
3. To make the back of the car: Cut across the cake's width (A) on top, starting 1 inch from the top left edge and slanting to a point ¾ inch from the left end and 1 inch below the top of the cake. Cut in from the left side to remove a piece of the cake.
4. To make the front of the car: Cut across the cake's width (B) on top, starting 4 inches from the top right edge and slanting to a point 3½ inches from the right end and 1 inch below the top of the cake. Cut in from the right side to remove a piece of the cake.
5. Set the large remaining cake on the cardboard so the back end is even with one end of the cardboard. From the larger of 2 removed pieces, cut a 1-inch-wide piece (C) across the width from the outside baked end; this piece should match the piece removed from the back. These will be the 2 axles (A and C) for underneath the car. Trim the remainder of the large removed piece (B) so it fits snugly in front of the car and covers the

remaining cardboard base. Fasten to the front of the cake with 2 wooden picks.
6. Prepare the 2 recipes of the Decorator Frosting. Spoon ½ cup of the white frosting into a pastry bag fitted with an adapter and writing tip. Spoon ¾ cup of the white frosting into a small bowl and reserve. Measure 1 tablespoon of the white frosting into a small cup. Spoon ½ cup of the frosting into a small bowl and color green. Place the green frosting in a small pastry bag fitted with a leaf tip. Spoon 1 cup of the white frosting into a small bowl; stir in the cocoa and the 1 tablespoon of warm water until smooth and easy to spread. Measure 1 tablespoon of the cocoa frosting and add to the 1 tablespoon of white frosting to make a light cocoa frosting. Color the remaining unmeasured white frosting yellow.
7. Using the green frosting, outline a 12 x 6-inch oval on a serving platter, tray or board to make a grass border. Fill in the oval with the chocolate sprinkles to make a driveway.
8. Frost the 2 pieces of cake reserved for the axles with the cocoa frosting. Place on the chocolate driveway so they are 3 inches apart.
9. With a small spatula, frost window areas on the car cake with the ¾ cup of white frosting, reserving some for the wheels and bumpers; press gently and in only one direction over the cut areas. Frost the rest of the car yellow, reserving some of the yellow frosting.
10. Carefully set the car on the axles so the rear axle is 1½ inches from the rear of the car.
11. Frost a ½-inch circle of white onto 5 of the chocolate cookies. Press 7 silver dragees into the frosting on each wheel to make the hubcaps. Fill any areas where the cake axles do not extend to the edge of the cardboard base with the cocoa frosting. Press the cookie wheel at the end of each axle.
12. Using the white frosting and the writing tip, pipe the grill onto the front of the car. Pipe a double row of dots around the silver dragees on the remaining frosted cookie. Pipe some of the white frosting on the back of the unfrosted cookie; press the back of the frosted cookie onto it. Press the double cookie into place on the back of the car for the spare tire.
13. Spoon the remaining yellow frosting into a pastry bag fitted with a small star tip. ☞

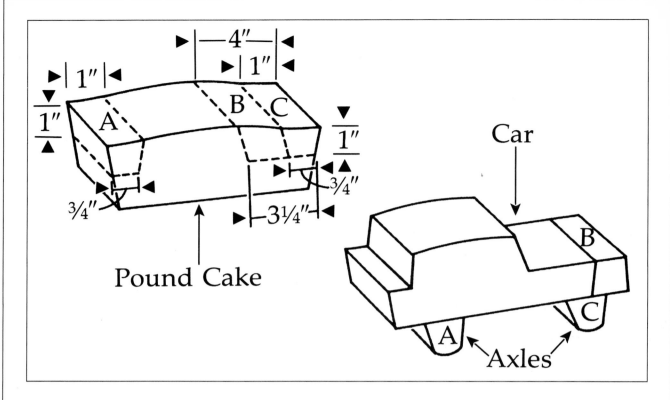

4"

1"

1"

B C

A

1"

3/4"

3/4"

3 1/4"

Pound Cake

Car

B

A

C

Axles

Pipe a star border along all the edges of the car, outlining and dividing the windows. Pipe a series of stars outlining the fenders and covering the tops of the cookie wheels. Pipe stars to fill in and build up the fender areas. Fill in the area between the front fender and the grill with flat stars.

14. Frost a ½-inch band of white along the front and back of the car for bumpers. Press 2 square red candies in the center of each for the license plates. Press 2 white gumdrops on either side of the front grill for headlights, and 1 red gumdrop on either side in the back for the taillights.

15. Change from the writing tip to a small star tip on the pastry bag of white frosting. Outline the headlights with small white stars. Press 2 small red candies into the frosting at either side for the running lights on the front and back of the car.

16. If you wish, press silver dragees in rows on any white bumper areas still visible, and on the front of the hood for ornaments.

17. Mix together 1 tablespoon of the remaining cocoa frosting and 1 tablespoon of the remaining white frosting in a small cup. Clean the writing tip. Fill the tip with the light cocoa frosting and place in the

adapter on the bag of the white frosting. Pipe the windshield wipers onto the front of the car. If the frosting begins to flow white, clean the tip and refill with the light cocoa frosting.

Cake Storage

● Cakes with a butter cream frosting can be left at room temperature. Cover the cut surface of the cake with plastic wrap and place it in a cake keeper, or invert a large bowl over the cake plate. The cake will keep for 2 or 3 days this way. (In hot weather, it is still best to refrigerate the cake.)
● Cakes with a cream frosting or filling should be refrigerated, with plastic wrap over the cut part.
● Unfrosted cakes freeze best—for up to 4 months. Wrap in aluminum foil, plastic wrap or large plastic bags; thaw at room temperature for 1 hour.
● Frosted cakes should be frozen on a piece of cardboard or a cookie sheet until firm, then wrapped in aluminum foil, plastic wrap or very large plastic bags; freeze cakes for up to 3 months and thaw at room temperature for 2 hours.

Cookies

> ### Cookie Tips
>
> • Use a cold cookie sheet to prevent the cookies from losing their shape.
> • Cookies should be of a uniform thickness and size so they will bake in the same amount of time.
> • Bake one sheet at a time and be sure that the cookie sheet has at least 1 inch of space around its edges.
> • Watch the cookies closely. Because oven temperatures vary, they may bake a little faster or slower than the regular baking time.
> • Unless the recipe indicates otherwise, always remove the cookies from the cookie sheet to a wire rack immediately. The cookies will continue to bake if left on the sheet.

The Monster Chip

Strings of gooey melted chocolate pull apart to reveal even more chocolate and pecans inside. The cookies are slightly crisp around the edges and moist and chewy within. One cookie is large enough to share with a friend. Or, you just may want to eat the whole cookie yourself.

Bake at 325° for 15 to 17 minutes.
Makes 12 very large cookies.

Nutrient Value Per Cookie: 409 calories, 6 gm. protein, 27 gm. fat, 155 mg. sodium, 44 mg. cholesterol.

- 3 bars (3 ounces each) semisweet chocolate
- 1¼ cups pecan halves
- 1 cup plus 2 tablespoons unsifted all-purpose flour
- ½ teaspoon baking soda
- ½ cup (1 stick) butter or margarine, at room temperature
- ⅓ cup smooth peanut butter
- ½ cup granulated sugar
- ½ cup firmly packed light brown sugar
- 1 egg
- 1 teaspoon vanilla

1. Preheat the oven to slow (325°). Lightly grease 2 large cookie sheets.
2. Break the chocolate bars into squares; then cut each square diagonally in half. Set aside ½ cup of the pecan halves; coarsely chop the remainder. Stir together the flour and baking soda on wax paper to mix well.
3. Beat together the butter, peanut butter, granulated sugar and brown sugar in a medium-size bowl until light and fluffy. Beat in the egg and vanilla until mixed. Stir in the flour mixture until blended; stir in the chopped pecans.
4. Using a ¼-cup measure, shape the dough into 12 mounds. Space the mounds evenly on the prepared cookie sheets. Push the chocolate pieces and reserved pecan halves into the mounds.
5. Bake in the preheated slow oven (325°) for 15 to 17 minutes or until golden brown around the edges and only lightly colored on top. If baking the 2 sheets of cookies in the same oven, switch the position of the sheets halfway through the baking. Let the cookies cool on the cookie sheets for about 3 minutes to firm up slightly. Carefully lift the cookies with a pancake turner onto brown paper; let stand for 5 minutes. Transfer to wire racks to cool completely.

Granola-Fruit Squares

Bake at 375° for 25 minutes.
Makes 16 squares.

Nutrient Value Per Square: 264 calories, 4 gm. protein, 14 gm. fat, 186 mg. sodium, 23 mg. cholesterol.

- 1 cup chopped dried apricots (6 ounces)
- 1 cup chopped dates (6 ounces)
- ¾ cup water
- 2 teaspoons grated lemon rind
- 2 teaspoons lemon juice (optional)
- 1 cup chopped walnuts
- 1¼ cups unsifted all-purpose flour
- ½ teaspoon baking soda
- ½ teaspoon salt
- 1½ cups quick-cooking oats (not instant)
- ¾ cup firmly packed dark brown sugar
- ¾ cup (1½ sticks) butter or margarine, melted

1. Preheat the oven to moderate (375°). Lightly grease a 9 x 9 x 2-inch-square baking pan.
2. Combine the apricots, dates and water in a small saucepan. Bring to boiling. Lower the heat; simmer, stirring occasionally, until the water is absorbed, for about 5 minutes. Let cool.
3. Stir the lemon rind and juice and walnuts into the apricot mixture.
4. Combine the flour, baking soda, salt, oats and brown sugar in a large bowl. Stir in the melted butter; the mixture will be crumbly. ☞

5. Reserve 1 cup of the crumb mixture. Pat the remainder evenly over the bottom of the prepared pan. Spoon the apricot mixture evenly over the crumb base. Sprinkle with the reserved crumb mixture.

6. Bake in the preheated moderate oven (375°) for 25 minutes. Remove to a wire rack to cool. Cut into 16 squares. Wrap in foil packets, about 4 to a packet. If taking on a picnic, refrigerate for several hours or overnight to make the squares very firm for travel.

7. To pack, place squares where they will not be crushed by other food.

MICROWAVE DIRECTIONS
650 Watt Variable Power Microwave Oven
Ingredient Changes: Do not melt the ¾ cup of butter.
Directions: Combine the apricots, dates and water in a microwave-safe 1½-quart bowl. Microwave, uncovered, at full power for 4 to 5 minutes or until the water is absorbed and the mixture is fairly smooth, stirring every minute. Stir in the lemon rind and juice and walnuts. Combine the flour, baking soda, salt, oats and sugar on wax paper; set aside. Cut the butter into 6 pieces; place in a 9-inch microwave-safe dish. Microwave, uncovered, at full power for 1 minute or until the butter is melted. Pour the flour mixture over the butter. Mix thoroughly with a fork. Remove 1 cup for topping. Press the remaining flour mixture into an even layer over the bottom of the dish. Spread the apricot mixture evenly over the crust. Sprinkle the reserved crust mixture over the top. Place the baking dish on an inverted saucer in the microwave oven. Microwave, uncovered, at full power for 6 minutes or until puffed and set, rotating a quarter turn every 2 minutes. Place the dish directly on a countertop to cool.

Chopping Dried Fruits

To make cutting apricots, dates and other dried fruits a little easier, cut with kitchen scissors, occasionally dipping in water.

Oatmeal-Prune Cookies

A chewy, jumbo-size cookie filled with tender prunes and crunchy walnuts.

Bake at 375° for 12 minutes.
Makes 3½ dozen cookies.

Nutrient Value Per Cookie: 141 calories, 2 gm. protein, 8 gm. fat, 67 mg. sodium, 8 mg. cholesterol.

1½ cups **sifted** *all-purpose flour*
1 *teaspoon salt*
½ *teaspoon baking soda*
1 *cup vegetable shortening*
¾ *cup firmly packed brown sugar*
½ *cup granulated sugar*
1 *egg*
1 *teaspoon vanilla*
½ *cup dairy sour cream*
1¾ *cups quick-cooking rolled oats*
1 *package (12 ounces) pitted prunes, cut into small pieces (1¾ cups)*
1 *cup coarsely chopped walnuts*

1. Preheat the oven to moderate (375°).
2. Sift together the flour, salt and baking soda onto wax paper.
3. Beat the shortening, brown sugar, sugar, egg, vanilla and sour cream in a large bowl with an electric mixer until light and fluffy. Add the flour mixture, blending thoroughly. Fold in the oats, prunes and walnuts.
4. Drop by heaping teaspoonfuls, 3 inches apart, on 2 large, greased cookie sheets (9 to a sheet). Carefully spread each into a 2½-inch round.
5. Bake in the preheated moderate oven (375°) for 12 minutes or until golden brown. Remove the cookie sheets from the oven and let stand for 1 minute. Remove to wire racks to cool.

Apricot-Oatmeal-Pecan Bars

Bake at 375° for 30 minutes.
Makes 12 bar cookies.

Nutrient Value Per Cookie: 301 calories, 3 gm. protein, 14 gm. fat, 89 mg. sodium, 26 mg. cholesterol.

1½ *cups* unsifted *all-purpose flour*
1 *cup old-fashioned oats, uncooked*
⅔ *cup firmly packed light brown sugar*
1 *teaspoon baking powder*
¾ *teaspoon ground cinnamon*
¼ *teaspoon salt*
½ *cup plus 2 tablespoons (1¼ sticks) chilled unsalted butter or margarine, cut into pieces*
¾ *cup apricot preserves or jam*
1½ *teaspoons vanilla*
½ *cup chopped pecans*

1. Preheat the oven to moderate (375°). Line a 9 x 9 x 2-inch-square baking pan with heavy-duty aluminum foil (or use a double thickness of regular weight), allowing a little overhang.
2. Combine the flour, oats, sugar, baking powder, cinnamon and salt in a large bowl. Cut in the butter with a fork until the butter is the size of small peas.

3. Press two-thirds of the mixture, about 2¼ cups, evenly into the bottom of the pan.
4. Combine the preserves and vanilla in a small bowl. Spread evenly over the oat mixture.
5. Stir the pecans into the remaining oat mixture. Sprinkle evenly over the preserves, gently pressing to compact.
6. Bake in the preheated moderate oven (375°) for 30 minutes or until lightly browned along the edges.
7. Cool completely in the pan on a wire rack. Carefully lift from the pan, using the foil overhang to help you. Refrigerate or freeze until very firm. Cut into 12 bars with a serrated knife. To freeze, wrap the bars individually in plastic wrap or aluminum foil before freezing.

Portuguese Walnut Squares

Made special with port or Madeira wine.

Bake at 350° for 15 to 20 minutes.
Makes about 64 squares.

Nutrient Value Per Square: 43 calories, 0 gm. protein, 3 gm. fat, 20 mg. sodium, 8 mg. cholesterol.

 6 *tablespoons all-purpose flour*
 ½ *teaspoon baking powder*
 ½ *cup (1 stick) butter, softened*
 ¾ *cup firmly packed light brown sugar*
 1 *egg, slightly beaten*
 2 *tablespoons milk*
 4 *tablespoons red port or Madeira wine*
 ½ *teaspoon vanilla*
 1 *cup walnuts, very finely chopped or ground*
    Sugar Glaze (recipe follows)

1. Combine the flour and baking powder on a piece of wax paper. Grease and flour a 9 x 9 x 2-inch-square baking pan.
2. Preheat the oven to moderate (350°).
3. Beat the butter and sugar in a large bowl with an electric mixer until light and fluffy, for about 3 minutes. Beat in the egg. Add the milk, 2 tablespoons of the wine and the vanilla. Stir in the flour mixture and nuts just until blended. Spoon into the pan.
4. Bake in the preheated moderate oven (350°) for 15 to 20 minutes or until a wooden pick inserted in the center comes out clean. Brush the top of the warm cake with the remaining 2 tablespoons of wine. Cool completely. Cut into about sixty-four 1-inch squares. Store in tin between layers of wax

paper. To serve, drizzle each square with the glaze.

Sugar Glaze: Mix ½ cup of 10X (confectioners') sugar and 2 teaspoons of milk until drizzling consistency.

Portuguese Walnut Squares

Rum-Butter Frosted Brownies

Bake at 350° for 30 minutes.
Makes 40 bars (about 2½ x 1 inches).

Nutrient Value Per Cookie: 227 calories, 2 gm. protein, 14 gm. fat, 94 mg. sodium, 46 mg. cholesterol.

 4 *squares (1 ounce each) unsweetened chocolate*
 1 *cup (2 sticks) butter or margarine*
 1 *cup sifted all-purpose flour*
 ¼ *teaspoon salt*
 4 *eggs*
 2 *cups sugar*
 2 *teaspoons vanilla*
 1½ *cups chopped walnuts*
    Rum-Butter Cream (recipe follows)
 8 *squares (1 ounce each) semisweet chocolate*
 1 *white chocolate candy bar (3 ounces)*

1. Preheat the oven to moderate (350°). Grease a 13 x 9 x 2-inch baking pan.
2. Melt the unsweetened chocolate and butter in a saucepan over low heat. Let cool.
3. Sift together the flour and salt onto wax paper.
4. Beat the eggs in a medium-size bowl until fluffy. Gradually beat in the sugar until the mixture is thick. Stir in the chocolate mixture and vanilla. Fold into the flour mixture ☞

211

until well blended. Stir in the walnuts. Spread evenly in the prepared baking pan.

5. Bake in the preheated moderate oven (350°) for 30 minutes or until shiny and firm on top. Cool in the pan on a wire rack.

6. Spread the brownies with the Rum-Butter Cream.

7. Melt the semisweet chocolate in the top of a double boiler over hot water. Let cool. Spread evenly over the Rum-Butter Cream.

8. Meanwhile, melt the white chocolate bar in a 1-cup glass measure set in hot water in a saucepan. Pour the white chocolate into a pastry bag fitted with a small writing tip, holding over wax paper to catch drips.

9. Immediately pipe the white chocolate in parallel straight lines across the width of the cake at ½-inch intervals. Lightly draw a wooden pick alternately up and down the cake through the white chocolate, at ½-inch intervals. Let stand until firm. Cut into 40 bars (7 cuts lengthwise, 4 cuts crosswise).

Rum-Butter Cream: Blend ½ cup (1 stick) of softened butter with half a 1-pound box of 10X (confectioners') sugar in a medium-size bowl. Beat in the remaining half box of 10X sugar alternately with 3 to 4 tablespoons of golden rum until the frosting is of good spreading consistency.

Whole-Wheat Apple Cookies

Tuck these nutritious cookies into back-to-school lunches!

Bake at 375° for 10 minutes.
Makes about 8½ dozen cookies.

Nutrient Value Per Cookie: 46 calories, 1 gm. protein, 2 gm. fat, 31 mg. sodium, 5 mg. cholesterol.

1   cup whole-wheat flour
1   cup unsifted all-purpose flour
1   teaspoon baking soda
1   teaspoon ground cinnamon
½   teaspoon ground cloves
½   teaspoon salt
½   cup (1 stick) butter or margarine, softened
1⅓ cups firmly packed light brown sugar
1   egg
1   large tart apple, pared, cored and finely chopped (about 1 cup)
1   cup raisins
1   cup chopped walnuts
    Lemon Glaze (recipe follows)
    Toasted sunflower seeds

1. Preheat the oven to moderate (375°). Grease 2 large cookie sheets.

2. Combine the whole-wheat flour, all-purpose flour, baking soda, cinnamon, cloves and salt in a small bowl. Set aside.

3. Beat together the butter and brown sugar in a large bowl until smooth and creamy; beat in the egg.

4. Blend the flour mixture into the butter mixture until the dry ingredients are completely mixed in; the mixture will be a little crumbly. Stir in the apples, raisins and walnuts until combined.

5. Drop the mixture by rounded teaspoonfuls, 2 inches apart, on the prepared cookie sheets.

6. Bake in the preheated moderate oven (375°) for 10 minutes or until lightly browned. Remove the cookies with a spatula from the cookies sheets to a wire rack. While still warm, top each with ⅛ to ¼ teaspoon of the Lemon Glaze. Sprinkle each with about ⅛ to ¼ teaspoon of the sunflower seeds. Cool completely.

Lemon Glaze: Combine 1 cup of 10X (confectioners') sugar, 2 tablespoons of lemon juice, 1 tablespoon of butter or margarine, softened, and 1 tablespoon of hot water in a small bowl. Beat together until well blended and smooth. Makes about ½ cup.

MICROWAVE DIRECTIONS
650 Watt Variable Power Microwave Oven
Directions: Prepare the cookie dough as directed above. Using a rounded teaspoonful, shape the dough into mounds. Evenly space 8 cookie mounds on a 13 x 9-inch microwave-safe baking tray. Microwave, uncovered, at full power for 2 minutes. Cool the cookies on a baking tray for 5 minutes. Transfer to a wire rack to cool. The dough can be stored, tightly covered, in the refrigerator for up to 5 days and fresh cookies baked as desired.

⚡🎯 Almond Butter Fingers

Bake at 350° for 15 minutes.
Makes about 4 dozen.

Nutrient Value Per Cookie: 57 calories, 1 gm. protein, 4 gm. fat, 31 mg. sodium, 8 mg. cholesterol.

½ **cup chopped blanched almonds**
1½ **tablespoons granulated sugar**
¾ **cup (1½ sticks) butter or margarine, softened**
⅓ **cup granulated sugar**
1 **teaspoon almond extract**
1¾ **cups sifted all-purpose flour**
1 **egg white, slightly beaten**
    10X (confectioners') sugar (optional)

1. Preheat the oven to moderate (350°).
2. Combine the almonds with the 1½ tablespoons of sugar in a small bowl. Reserve.
3. Beat together the butter, ⅓ cup of sugar and the almond extract in a medium-size bowl until smooth. Stir in the flour. Gather the dough into a ball and flatten slightly. Divide in half.
4. Roll out each half on a floured surface to a rectangle, ¼ inch thick and about 3 inches wide and 12 inches long. Even the edges with a ruler to measure 2½ inches wide. Cut crosswise into bars, ¾ inch wide. Brush the tops with the egg white. Sprinkle evenly with the almond-sugar mixture. Lift the bars with a spatula to an ungreased cookie sheet, spacing 1 inch apart.
5. Bake in the preheated moderate oven (350°) for 15 minutes or until golden brown. Transfer the cookies with a metal spatula to wire racks to cool. Store in a tightly covered container for up to 2 weeks. Dust with the 10X sugar, if you wish.

⚡🎯 Lemon-Walnut Rounds

Fresh lemon cookies with a sugary nut topping that can be made as quick-drop or refrigerator cookies.

Bake at 375° for 12 minutes.
Makes 4½ dozen cookies.

Nutrient Value Per Cookie: 78 calories, 1 gm. protein, 4 gm. fat, 66 mg. sodium, 19 mg. cholesterol.

3 **cups sifted all-purpose flour**
1 **teaspoon baking powder**
½ **teaspoon salt**
1 **cup (2 sticks) butter or margarine, softened**
1 **cup sugar**
2 **eggs**
1 **tablespoon grated lemon rind**
6 **tablespoons finely chopped walnuts**
2 **tablespoons sugar**

1. Sift together the flour, baking powder and salt onto wax paper.
2. Beat the butter or margarine with the cup of sugar, the eggs and lemon rind in a large bowl with an electric mixer until light and fluffy. Stir in the flour mixture. Chill for 3 hours or until firm enough to handle.
3. Preheat the oven to moderate (375°).
4. Roll the dough between the palms of the hands, a level tablespoon at a time, into balls.* Place 2 inches apart on 2 large ungreased cookie sheets. Flatten slightly with the bottom of a greased and sugared glass.
5. Combine the walnuts and the remaining 2 tablespoons of sugar. Sprinkle each cookie with the nut topping, pressing into the top of the cookie.
6. Bake in the preheated moderate oven (375°) for 12 minutes or until the edges of the cookies begin to brown. Cool on wire racks.

*** Note:** Quick shaping trick—Chill the dough for 3 hours; shape into two equal rolls, 7 inches long and 2 inches in diameter. Refrigerate overnight in wax paper. Cut into ¼-inch rounds; place on an ungreased cookie sheet; brush the tops with milk and sprinkle with the nut topping. Bake at 375° for 12 minutes.

Snickerdoodles

The Pennsylvania Dutch claim as their own this fragrant cinnamon-nutmeg cookie, sometimes called "schneckenoodles."

Bake at 400° for 10 minutes.
Makes 4 dozen cookies.

Nutrient Value Per Cookie: 88 calories, 1 gm. protein, 5 gm. fat, 43 mg. sodium, 11 mg. cholesterol.

2¾ **cups sifted** *all-purpose flour*
  2 *teaspoons cream of tartar*
  1 *teaspoon baking soda*
 ½ *teaspoon salt*
  1 *cup vegetable shortening*
1¼ *cups sugar*
  2 *eggs*
  1 *teaspoon vanilla*
  2 *tablespoons sugar*
  1 *tablespoon ground cinnamon*
  1 *teaspoon ground nutmeg*

1. Preheat the oven to hot (400°).
2. Sift together the flour, cream of tartar, baking soda and salt onto wax paper.
3. Beat together the shortening and the 1¼ cups of sugar in a large bowl with an electric mixer until light and fluffy. Beat in the eggs and vanilla. Stir in the flour mixture.

4. Combine the 2 tablespoons of sugar, the cinnamon and nutmeg.
5. Roll the dough between the palms of the hands, 1 level tablespoon at a time, into balls. Roll each in the sugar mixture. Place 2 inches apart on 2 large ungreased cookie sheets.
6. Bake in the preheated hot oven (400°) for 10 minutes or until lightly browned. Remove with a metal spatula to wire racks to cool.

Valentine Cookies

Valentine Cookies

Bake at 325° for 18 to 20 minutes.
Makes six 6-inch heart-shaped cookies.

Nutrient Value Per Cookie: 756 calories, 8 gm. protein, 24 gm. fat, 273 mg. sodium, 108 mg. cholesterol.

¾ *cup (1½ sticks) butter or margarine, softened*
½ *cup sugar*
1 *egg*
2½ *cups sifted all-purpose flour*
   Valentine Cookie Glaze (recipe follows)

1. To make pattern: Enlarge the heart (see FIG. 1) on folded brown paper. Open, for the full pattern. Or use a 6-inch cookie cutter if you have one.
2. Beat together the butter, sugar and egg in a large bowl until smooth. Gradually beat in the flour to make a firm dough. Shape into a ball. Wrap in wax paper. Refrigerate for 20 minutes.
3. Preheat the oven to slow (325°).
4. Divide the dough in half. Cover half with plastic wrap. Roll out the other half on a lightly floured surface to a ¼-inch thickness. Cut into three 6-inch hearts around the pattern, or use the cookie cutter. Transfer the cookies with a spatula to an ungreased cookie sheet, spacing 1 inch apart. Repeat with the other half of the dough.
5. Bake in the preheated slow oven (325°) for 18 to 20 minutes or just until the edges begin to turn golden; do not let brown. Remove the cookies to a wire rack to cool completely. Frost with the Valentine Cookie Glaze.

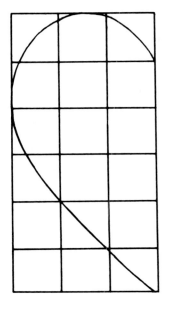

Heart Pattern
FIG. 1

1 sq. = 1"

Valentine Cookie Glaze

Makes enough frosting for six 6-inch cookies.

Nutrient Value Per Serving: 301 calories, 2 gm. protein, 0 gm. fat, 26 mg. sodium, 0 mg. cholesterol.

1 box (1 pound) 10X (confectioners') sugar
¼ teaspoon cream of tartar
3 egg whites
½ teaspoon almond extract
  Red paste food coloring

1. Combine the 10X sugar, cream of tartar, egg whites and almond extract in a small bowl. Beat with an electric mixer just until smooth and completely combined; the glaze will be very spreadable, rather than stiff.
2. Divide the frosting into 2 bowls. Color one red. Frost the top surfaces of the cookies with red or white glaze. Set aside at room temperature, loosely covered, to dry overnight. Cover the bowls of frosting tightly; refrigerate.
3. The next day, spoon the glazes into pastry bags fitted with small writing tips. Decorate as illustrated (page 214).

Easter Cookies

Bake at 350° for 7 to 8 minutes.
Makes 36 cookies.

Nutrient Value Per Cookie: 107 calories, 1 gm. protein, 3 gm. fat, 75 mg. sodium, 15 mg. cholesterol.

2½ cups sifted all-purpose flour
1 teaspoon baking powder
½ teaspoon salt
½ cup (1 stick) butter, softened
⅔ cup sugar
1 egg
1 to 2 teaspoons grated orange rind
1 tablespoon orange juice
  Decorating Frosting (recipe follows)

1. Sift together the flour, baking powder and salt onto wax paper.
2. Beat together the butter and sugar in a large bowl until smooth. Beat in the egg, orange rind and juice.
3. Add the flour mixture, a third at a time, stirring well.
4. Shape the dough into a ball; flatten slightly. Wrap in plastic wrap. Refrigerate for several hours or overnight. ☞

Easter Cookies

5. To bake the cookies, preheat the oven to moderate (350°).
6. Roll out half the dough on a lightly floured surface to a ⅛-inch thickness. Cut into bunny, chick or flower shapes with 3- to 3½-inch cutters. Place on 2 large, lightly greased cookie sheets. Repeat with the other half of the dough.
7. Bake in the preheated moderate oven (350°) for 7 to 8 minutes or until light golden around the edges; the cookies should not brown. Remove to wire racks with a metal spatula. Cool completely. Frost and decorate with the Decorating Frosting.

Decorating Frosting

Makes enough to decorate 36 cookies.

Nutrient Value Per Cookie: 39 calories, .27 gm. protein, 0 gm. fat, 4 mg. sodium, 0 mg. cholesterol.

 3 *egg whites*
 ½ *teaspoon cream of tartar*
 3½ *cups* sifted *10X (confectioners') sugar*
 1 *tablespoon water*
     Food coloring (optional)

1. Beat the egg whites and cream of tartar in a medium-size bowl until foamy. Slowly beat in the 10X (confectioners') sugar; continue beating until thick and creamy. Measure out 1¼ cups of the frosting; cover with damp paper toweling; set aside.

2. Thin the remaining frosting with the 1 tablespoon of water. Tint with the food coloring, if you wish. Spread evenly over the cookies.
3. Place the reserved frosting in a pastry tube fitted with a writing tip. Decorate the cookies as pictured above.

Almond Cornets à la Crème

Bake at 375° for 6 to 8 minutes.
Makes about 24 cornets.

Nutrient Value Per Cornet: 55 calories, 0 gm. protein, 5 gm. fat, 24 mg. sodium, 7 mg. cholesterol.

 ½ *cup coarsely ground almonds*
 ½ *cup 10X (confectioners') sugar*
 ¼ *cup (½ stick) butter, very soft*
 1 *tablespoon* unsifted *all-purpose flour*
 2 *teaspoons heavy cream*
 3 *to 4 sugar ice-cream cones, tightly wrapped in aluminum foil, or other cone-shape form*
     Grenadine Crème (recipe follows)

1. Grease and flour 2 large cookie sheets.
2. Preheat the oven to moderate (350°).
3. Blend together the almonds, sugar, butter and flour in a small bowl with a wooden spoon until smooth. Stir in the heavy cream.
4. Drop 3 level teaspoons of the almond mixture onto the prepared cookie sheets,

4 inches apart. Spread each into a 2-inch round. (Bake and roll only 3 cookies at a time.)

5. Bake in the preheated moderate oven (375°) for 6 to 8 minutes or until the cookies are light brown and bubbly in the centers. Let stand on the cookie sheet on a wire rack for 1 minute. Loosen the cookies with a spatula, one at a time; quickly shape around the tip of the wrapped sugar cone to form the cornet or horn. Remove the almond cone from the form. Place on the wire rack to cool completely. If the cookies become too stiff to shape, return to the oven for a minute or two. Repeat with the almond mixture.

6. To serve, pipe or spoon the Grenadine Crème into each cornet and serve at once. Or, arrange the cornets on a serving plate with the Grenadine Crème and let guests fill their own. Garnish with strawberries, if you wish.

To Make Ahead: Make unfilled cornets 1 or 2 days ahead. Store in a tightly covered container at room temperature.

Grenadine Crème: Beat 1 cup of heavy cream, 3 tablespoons of grenadine syrup and 1 teaspoon of lemon juice until stiff. Refrigerate until ready to serve, for up to 2 hours. Makes 2 cups.

Butter Fancies

Refrigerate this soft dough for several hours or overnight before rolling. If the dough becomes too soft to handle when rerolling, refrigerate until firm.

Bake at 375° for 6 minutes.
Makes forty 3-inch cookies (10 sandwich cookies and 20 frosted cookies).

Nutrient Value Per Sandwich Cookie: 154 calories, 1 gm. protein, 5 gm. fat, 96 mg. sodium, 26 mg. cholesterol.

Nutrient Value Per Frosted Cookie: 119 calories, 1 gm. protein, 6 gm. fat, 70 mg. sodium, 19 mg. cholesterol.

1½ cups **unsifted** all-purpose flour
1 teaspoon baking powder
½ teaspoon baking soda
½ cup (1 stick) butter or margarine, softened
1 egg
½ cup sugar
1½ tablespoons milk

1 teaspoon vanilla
⅔ cup currant or other flavor jelly
Butter-Cream Frosting (recipe follows)
¼ cup chopped pistachio nuts

1. Sift together the flour, baking powder and baking soda onto wax paper.
2. Beat together the butter, egg and sugar in a large bowl with an electric mixer until fluffy, for about 3 minutes. Stir in the milk and vanilla. Stir in the flour mixture until blended and smooth. Wrap the dough and chill for several hours or overnight.
3. Preheat the oven to moderate (375°).
4. Divide the dough into fourths. Roll out one-fourth of the dough, keeping the remainder of dough refrigerated, on a lightly floured surface to a ⅛-inch thickness. Cut out the cookies from the dough with a 3-inch-round cookie cutter. Reroll the scraps of dough and cut out as many rounds as you can (you should have a total of about 10). Arrange on an ungreased cookie sheet, 1 inch apart.
5. Repeat with the remaining dough, cutting the centers out of the last fourth of dough with a 1½-inch star-shape or round cookie cutter. Carefully remove the cut out stars and place on a separate cookie sheet, 1 inch apart.
6. Bake the rounds in the preheated moderate oven (375°) for 6 minutes or until the cookies are set and lightly browned. Bake the stars for 4 minutes or until set and lightly browned. Transfer the cookies and stars to wire racks to cool.
7. For sandwich cookies, spread about 1 tablespoon of the jelly on the bottom side of 10 of the cookies. Place a cookie with the cut-out center on each, to make 10 sandwich cookies. Spread the remaining cookies with the Butter-Cream Frosting and top half of them with the cookie star. Sprinkle the remaining cookies with the chopped pistachios.

Butter-Cream Frosting: Beat together ¼ cup (½ stick) of softened butter, 1 tablespoon of milk, ½ teaspoon of vanilla and 1 cup of *sifted* 10X (confectioners') sugar in a medium-size bowl until smooth. Slowly beat in 1 additional cup of *sifted* 10X sugar until the frosting is of good spreading consistency. Beat in several drops of food coloring to tint, if you wish. Makes about ¾ cup.

Cookies from Grandma's Kitchen

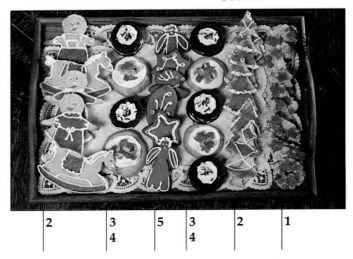

2   3   5   3   2   1
     4   4

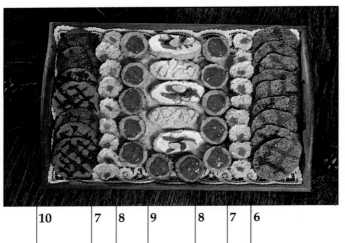

10   7   8   9   8   7   6

1. Danish Spritz Cookies (page 219)
2. Orangy Sugar Cookies (page 219)
3. Frozen Chocolate Cookie Cakes (page 219)
4. Fruit and Nut Cookies (page 220)
5. Brown Molasses Cookies (page 221)
6. Small Sand Cookies (page 221)
7. Coconut Flake Cookies (page 221)
8. Almond Tartlets (page 222)
9. Almond Macaroons (page 222)
10. Pecan Wafers (page 223)

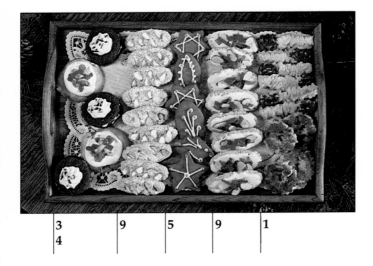

3   9   5   9   1
4

⬛ Danish Spritz Cookies

Bake at 350° for 8 to 10 minutes.
Makes 4 dozen cookies.

Nutrient Value Per Cookie: 70 calories, 1 gm. protein, 4 gm. fat, 39 mg. sodium, 27 mg. cholesterol.

1 **cup (2 sticks) butter, softened**
⅔ **cup sugar**
3 **egg yolks**
½ **teaspoon almond extract**
2½ **cups sifted all-purpose flour**
1 **egg white, slightly beaten (optional)**
  Chocolate shot and colored decorating
   sugar for garnish (optional)

1. Preheat the oven to moderate (350°).
2. Beat together the butter, sugar, egg yolks and almond extract in a large bowl with an electric mixer until fluffy. Stir in the flour blending well.
3. Spoon the dough into a pastry bag fitted with a star tip or into a cookie press with a star plate. Press out the dough into 3-inch lengths, 1 inch apart, on ungreased cookie sheets. Gently push into wreaths, "S" shapes, candy canes or leave straight.
4. Bake in the preheated moderate oven (350°) for 8 to 10 minutes or until the edges are lightly browned.
5. If you wish, brush the warm cookies with egg white and sprinkle with the chocolate shot or colored sugar. Cool on wire racks.

⬛ Orangy Sugar Cookies

Bake at 375° for 8 minutes.
Makes 3 dozen large cookies.

Nutrient Value Per Cookie: 84 calories, 1 gm. protein, 3 gm. fat, 54 mg. sodium, 7 mg. cholesterol.

2¼ **cups sifted all-purpose flour**
1 **tablespoon baking powder**
¼ **teaspoon salt**
½ **cup (1 stick) butter, softened**
2 **tablespoons grated orange rind**
1 **cup sugar**
¼ **cup orange juice**
2 **tablespoons lemon juice**
  Corn syrup for garnish (optional)
  Colored decorating sugar and silver
   dragees for garnish (optional)
  Decorating Frosting (recipe follows)

1. Sift together the flour, baking powder and salt onto wax paper.
2. Beat together the butter, orange rind and sugar with an electric mixer until fluffy. Stir in the orange and lemon juices. Sift in the dry ingredients until blended. Chill for several hours or overnight until firm.
3. Preheat the oven to moderate (375°).
4. Roll out the dough, one-third at a time, on a floured surface to a ⅙-inch thickness. Cut out with floured cookie cutters. Arrange, 1 inch apart, on 2 large ungreased cookie sheets.
5. Bake in the preheated moderate oven (375°) for 8 minutes or until set and lightly golden. Cool on wire racks.
6. If you wish, brush the tops of the cookies with the corn syrup and sprinkle with the colored sugar and silver dragees. Decorate with white or colored Decorating Frosting.

Decorating Frosting: Combine 1 egg white, ½ teaspoon of cream of tartar and 1 cup of 10X (confectioners') sugar in a small bowl. Beat with an electric mixer until stiff but a good spreading consistency. Cover with a damp towel until ready to use. If you wish, stir food coloring into small amounts of the frosting before using. Pipe or spread onto the cookies.

⬛ Frozen Chocolate Cookie Cakes

Bake at 350° for 10 minutes.
Makes 2 dozen cookies.

Nutrient Value Per Cookie: 149 calories, 1 gm. protein, 10 gm. fat, 64 mg. sodium, 35 mg. cholesterol.

1 **cup sifted all-purpose flour**
½ **teaspoon baking soda**
⅛ **teaspoon salt**
½ **cup (1 stick) butter**
6 **squares (1 ounce each) semisweet chocolate**
¼ **cup light corn syrup**
⅓ **cup sugar**
1 **teaspoon vanilla**
1 **egg**
1 **cup heavy cream**
2 **tablespoons 10X (confectioners') sugar**
2 **tablespoons orange-flavored liqueur**
  Candy decorations for garnish (optional) ☞

1. Preheat the oven to moderate (350°). Cover 2 large cookie sheets with aluminum foil; grease with vegetable shortening.
2. Sift together the flour, baking soda and salt onto wax paper.
3. Heat the butter, chocolate, corn syrup and sugar in a medium-size saucepan over low heat until the butter and chocolate are melted. Stir until smooth; cool for 5 minutes.
4. Stir the vanilla, egg and flour mixture into the chocolate mixture. Beat until smooth.
5. Drop the mixture by level teaspoons, 2 inches apart, onto the prepared cookie sheets. Spread with a small spatula into an even circle, 1½ inches in diameter.
6. Bake in the preheated moderate oven (350°) for 10 minutes or until the cookies have flattened and become firm. Cool completely on foil on a wire rack.
7. Remove the cookies from the foil and match into stacks of three cookies each.
8. Beat the cream with the 10X sugar and liqueur in a small bowl until stiff. Spoon into a pastry bag fitted with a large star tip. Pipe a star onto each cookie in each of the stacks. Reassemble the stacks, pushing the cookies together until they are about ¼ inch apart. Sprinkle the top star with the candy decorations, if you wish.
9. Place the cookies in a deep dish or pan. Cover tightly; freeze until ready to serve.

Fruit and Nut Cookies

Bake at 350° for 15 minutes.
Makes 4½ dozen cookies.

Nutrient Value Per Serving: 95 calories, 1 gm. protein, 4 gm. fat, 51 mg. sodium, 17 mg. cholesterol.

½ *cup dried apricots, diced*
1 *cup boiling water*
2 *cups* **sifted** *all-purpose flour*
1 *teaspoon baking powder*
½ *teaspoon baking soda*
⅔ *cup butter, softened*
1 *cup sugar*
1 *teaspoon grated orange rind*
1 *teaspoon grated lemon rind*
2 *eggs*
1 *tablespoon lemon juice*
½ *cup dairy sour cream*
¼ *cup diced candied orange peel*
¾ *cup diced candied pineapple*
⅔ *cup chopped walnuts*
   Frosting (recipe follows)
   Apricots, candied pineapple and walnuts for garnish (optional)

1. Combine the apricots and the 1 cup of boiling water in a small bowl. Set aside for 10 minutes. Drain well. Reserve.
2. Preheat the oven to moderate (350°). Lightly grease 2 large cookie sheets with vegetable shortening.
3. Sift together the flour, baking powder and baking soda onto wax paper.
4. Beat together the butter, sugar, orange and lemon rinds, eggs and lemon juice in a large bowl with an electric mixer until fluffy.
5. Stir in the flour mixture and sour cream until blended. Fold in the apricots, candied orange and pineapple, and walnuts. Drop by tablespoonfuls, 1½ inches apart, onto the prepared cookie sheets.
6. Bake in the preheated moderate oven (350°) for 15 minutes or until the edges are golden and the centers feel firm to the touch. Remove to racks to cool completely.
7. Spread the cookies with the Frosting and garnish with more apricots, pineapple and walnuts, if you wish.

Frosting: Blend in a small bowl 1¼ cups of 10X (confectioners') sugar, 1 tablespoon of light corn syrup, ¼ teaspoon of vanilla and 1½ tablespoons of hot water until blended and a good spreading consistency.

Small Sand Cookies

Bake at 375° for 8 to 10 minutes.
Makes 4 dozen cookies.

Nutrient Value Per Cookie: 85 calories, 1 gm. protein, 5 gm. fat, 41 mg. sodium, 22 mg. cholesterol.

1⅓ cups firmly packed dark brown sugar
 1 cup (2 sticks) butter, softened
 2 egg yolks
 2 cups sifted all-purpose flour
 3 squares (1 ounce each) semisweet chocolate, melted
 Candy decorations for garnish (optional)

1. Beat together the brown sugar, butter and egg yolks in a large bowl with an electric mixer until fluffy. Gradually beat in the flour until smooth. Chill for several hours or overnight until firm.
2. Preheat the oven to moderate (375°). Grease 2 large cookie sheets with vegetable shortening.
3. Roll out the dough on a floured surface to a ⅛-inch thickness. Cut out with a floured 2-inch-round cookie cutter. Arrange, 1½ inches apart, on the prepared cookie sheets.
4. Bake in the preheated moderate oven (375°) for 8 to 10 minutes. Transfer from the cookie sheets to wire racks to cool.
5. When completely cool, drizzle the cookies with the melted chocolate. Sprinkle with the candy decorations, if you wish.

Brown Molasses Cookies

Bake at 375° for 10 to 12 minutes.
Makes 6 dozen cookies.

Nutrient Value Per Cookie: 78 calories, 1 gm. protein, 1 gm. fat, 34 mg. sodium, 6 mg. cholesterol.

4 cups sifted all-purpose flour
 1 teaspoon baking soda
 1 teaspoon baking powder
 ⅓ cup butter, softened
 2 tablespoons grated orange rind
 1 cup granulated sugar
 1 egg
 1 cup light molasses
 Vanilla Decorating Icing (recipe follows)
 Silver dragees for garnish

1. Sift together the flour, baking soda and baking powder onto wax paper.

2. Beat together the butter and orange rind in a large bowl with an electric mixer until creamy. Add the sugar and egg. Beat until light and fluffy. Beat in the molasses. Add the flour mixture and beat on low speed just until well blended.
3. Divide the dough in half, wrap in wax paper and refrigerate overnight.
4. When ready to make the cookies, preheat the oven to moderate (375°). Lightly grease 2 large cookie sheets with vegetable shortening.
5. Roll out the dough on a lightly floured board to a ⅛-inch thickness. Cut out the cookies with floured cookie cutters. Arrange, 1½ inches apart, on the prepared cookie sheets.
6. Bake in the preheated moderate oven (375°) for 10 to 12 minutes or until firm. Remove the cookies from the cookie sheets to wire racks; cool completely.
7. Spoon the Vanilla Decorating Icing into a pastry bag fitted with a writing tip. Pipe the decorations onto the cooled cookies. Decorate with the silver dragees.

Vanilla Decorating Icing: Blend in a bowl 1 box (1 pound) of 10X (confectioners') sugar with ½ teaspoon of salt, 1 teaspoon of vanilla and 3 to 4 tablespoons of milk to make a smooth, firm frosting.

Coconut Flake Cookies

Bake at 325° for 15 minutes.
Makes 5 dozen cookies.

Nutrient Value Per Cookie: 44 calories, 0 gm. protein, 3 gm. fat, 23 mg. sodium, 9 mg. cholesterol.

1 cup sifted all-purpose flour
 ⅛ teaspoon salt
 ⅛ teaspoon ground cinnamon
 ⅛ teaspoon ground nutmeg
 ½ cup (1 stick) butter, softened
 ¼ cup firmly packed dark brown sugar
 1 egg yolk
 ½ teaspoon vanilla
 ¼ teaspoon almond extract
 2 teaspoons grated orange rind
 2 teaspoons grated lemon rind
 2 egg whites, slightly beaten
 2 cans (3½ ounces each) flaked coconut
 Red and green candied pineapple, cut into ¼-inch cubes, for garnish

1. Preheat the oven to slow (325°). Grease 2 large cookie sheets with vegetable shortening.
2. Sift together the flour, salt, cinnamon and nutmeg onto wax paper.
3. Beat together the butter, brown sugar, egg yolk, vanilla, almond extract, orange and lemon rinds in a medium-size bowl with an electric mixer until fluffy. Add the flour mixture; beat at low speed until smooth.
4. Drop the dough by half teaspoonfuls into the beaten whites; toss in the coconut to coat evenly. Place, 1 inch apart, on the prepared cookie sheets. Press 1 candied pineapple cube into the center of each cookie.
5. Bake in the preheated slow oven (325°) for 15 minutes or until the coconut is golden. Transfer to wire racks to cool.

Almond Tartlets

Bake at 325° for 20 to 25 minutes.
Makes 7 dozen cookies.

Nutrient Value Per Cookie: 57 calories, 1 gm. protein, 3 gm. fat, 23 mg. sodium, 12 mg. cholesterol.

 1 **cup blanched almonds**
 1 **cup (2 sticks) butter, softened**
 ½ **teaspoon almond extract**
 ½ **teaspoon lemon extract**
 ⅔ **cup sugar**
 2 **egg yolks**
 2 **cups sifted all-purpose flour**
 1 **jar (12 ounces) currant jelly or apricot preserves**

1. Grind the almonds in a food processor or blender to a fine powder.
2. Beat together the butter, almond extract, lemon extract, sugar and egg yolks in a large bowl with an electric mixer until light and fluffy. Add the ground almonds and flour. Beat at low speed until a firm dough forms.
3. Preheat the oven to slow (325°).
4. Place small cupcake papers in 1-inch muffin pans (gem pans). Divide the dough into ¾-inch balls. Press one ball into each cupcake paper to cover the sides and bottom, hollowing out the center to form a tartlet.
5. Bake in the preheated slow oven (325°) for 20 to 25 minutes or until the edges are golden. Remove from the pans and cool

completely on wire racks.
6. Spoon about ½ teaspoon of the jelly or preserves into each tart. If the tartlets are to be stored for several days, do not fill them until ready to serve.

MICROWAVE DIRECTIONS
650 Watt Variable Power Microwave Oven
Directions: Prepare the tartlets as directed above, placing the papers in a 1-inch muffin pan to form the tartlets. Remove from the pan and arrange, just in papers, 12 at a time, in a circle with 3 in the center, on a microwave-safe baking sheet. Microwave, uncovered, at full power for 1 minute and 40 seconds. Remove to a cooling rack. Cool and fill as directed above. If you wish, the unbaked, formed tartlets may be frozen. Microwave, unthawed, as directed above when ready to use. Do not increase the time.

Almond Macaroons

Bake at 300° for 15 minutes.
Makes 2½ dozen cookies.

Nutrient Value Per Cookie: 81 calories, 2 gm. protein, 3 gm. fat, 5 mg. sodium, 0 mg. cholesterol.

 1½ **cups blanched almonds, toasted**
 1 **cup sugar**
 2 **large egg whites**
 ½ **teaspoon almond extract**
    Icing (recipe follows)
    Red and green candied pineapple, sliced unblanched almonds for garnish (optional)

1. Preheat the oven to slow (300°).
2. Grind the nuts to a fine powder in a food processor. Add the sugar; process just to combine.
3. Beat the whites until stiff, not dry. Fold in the almond mixture and the extract until the mixture forms a smooth paste.
4. Cut 30 rectangles, 3½ x 1½ inches, from brown paper. Divide the dough into 30 pieces. Shape each into a 2-inch-long roll. Flatten onto the paper to make a 2½ x 1-inch oval. Place the papers on a cookie sheet.
5. Bake in the preheated slow oven (300°) for 15 minutes or until firm and dry on the surface. Cool completely on racks.
6. Frost the cookies with the Icing. Return to the cool oven just until the surface of the frosting is firm. Decorate with the optional garnishes.

Icing: Beat 1 egg white in a bowl until stiff. Add 1 cup of 10X (confectioners') sugar and 1 teaspoon of lemon juice. Beat to a good spreading consistency.

Poinsettia Cookies

Poinsettia Cookies

Bake at 350° for 8 to 10 minutes.
Makes 5 dozen.

Nutrient Value Per Cookie: 53 calories, 1 gm. protein, 3 gm. fat, 68 mg. sodium, 13 mg. cholesterol.

2½ **cups sifted all-purpose flour**
1 **teaspoon salt**
1 **cup (2 sticks) butter**
1 **cup sifted 10X (confectioners') sugar**
1 **egg**
1½ **teaspoons almond extract**
1 **teaspoon vanilla**
   Red decorating sugar
   Edible silver decorating shot

1. Sift together the flour and salt onto wax paper.
2. Beat the butter in a medium-size bowl until light. Beat in the 10X sugar until light and fluffy. Beat in the almond extract and vanilla. Blend in the flour mixture. Shape the dough into 2 equal balls. Wrap each in wax paper. Chill for 2 hours or overnight, or until firm.
3. When ready to make the cookies, preheat the oven to moderate (350°). Grease 2 large cookie sheets with vegetable shortening.
4. Roll out the dough, one half at a time, into a 12 x 10-inch rectangle, ⅛ inch thick. (Work in a cool room since the dough is very rich and soft.) Cut into 2-inch squares. Cut each corner of each square diagonally toward the center about ¾ inch. Turn down the alternate corners, placing the tips in the center to achieve a pinwheel effect. Sprinkle the center of each cookie with red sugar and press a silver ball in the center. Place,

1 inch apart, on the prepared cookie sheets.
5. Bake in the preheated moderate oven (350°) for 8 to 10 minutes; watch carefully so the edges of the cookies do not overbrown. Remove the cookies from the sheets to wire racks to cool.

Pecan Wafers

Bake at 350° for 12 to 15 minutes.
Makes 5 dozen cookies.

Nutrient Value Per Cookie: 38 calories, 0 gm. protein, 2 gm. fat, 14 mg. sodium, 2 mg. cholesterol.

3 **egg whites**
⅛ **teaspoon salt**
1¼ **cups firmly packed light brown sugar**
3 **tablespoons melted butter**
1 **teaspoon vanilla**
2 **tablespoons unsifted all-purpose flour**
1 **cup finely chopped pecans**
   Corn syrup, red and green sugar for garnish (optional)

1. Cover 2 large cookie sheets with aluminum foil; grease with vegetable shortening. Preheat the oven to moderate (350°).
2. Beat the egg whites with salt in a medium-size bowl with an electric mixer until stiff.
3. Combine the sugar, butter, vanilla and flour in a medium-size bowl. Fold the mixture into the egg whites just until uniformly combined. Fold in the nuts.
4. Drop by slightly rounded teaspoonfuls, 3 inches apart, on the prepared cookie sheets.
5. Bake in the preheated moderate oven (350°) for 12 to 15 minutes or until the centers and edges are evenly colored. Cool on foil. If not crisp when cooled, return to the oven for 2 to 3 minutes. Store in an airtight container.
6. If you wish, brush two parallel lines of the syrup in each direction on the cookies while warm. Sprinkle red sugar over one line in each direction, and green over the others.

Leftover Yolks

Store leftover uncooked egg yolks, covered with water, in an airtight container for 2 to 3 days in the refrigerator. Drain the water from the yolks before using them in custards or sauces.

 GLORIOUS
ENDINGS

Almond-Stuffed Apples With Two Sauces
(page 233), Apple-Plum Clafouti (page 235).

224

I f cakes and cookies aren't quite what you crave today, if it's pie that sets your mouth watering, or if you're an ice cream-aholic, or if you simply love fresh fruit, you won't have any trouble finding your palate's desire in this chapter!

And while dessert may be the pièce de résistance for many lovers of fine food, it need not always be rich in order to satisfy that insatiable craving for a little something sweet to end a meal. In fact, it can even serve to balance out the day's nutritional requirements from the Basic 4! For example, our Apple-Plum Clafouti (page 235) is loaded with fresh fruit. Coconut Custard Pie (page 226) uses three cups of fresh milk.

Dessert can be as simple as a bowl of bright red Strawberry Kissel (page 295) or as elegant as Apricot Ice-Cream and Chablis-Ice Bombe (page 240). It can be a new twist on an old theme, like the Maple-Pumpkin Pie (page 231), or an age-old standby, like Lemon Meringue Pie (page 228).

Nor does this thin-is-in society in which we live have to stifle your sweet tooth, as you'll see when you whip up our imaginative and delicious reduced-calorie creations—for instance, Summer-Light Cheesecake (page 243) at 94 calories per serving.

When planning dessert to round out and finish a particular meal, give special consideration to what will go before it. If the main course is to be on the heavier side, select a simpler dessert. On the other hand, a gloriously rich confection might be just the thing to top off a lighter meal.

Dessert Pies

Pie-Making Pointers

Baker's Tips: Here are a few pointers to help make pastry flaky, light and picture-perfect.
● Handle pastry dough *as little as possible*; unlike bread dough, pastry dough that's overhandled will become tough. As soon as the dough holds together, form a ball; divide it in half; shape it into a round about 1" high on a lightly floured pastry cloth. Roll the dough out to a specific size. Repeat with other half.
● Always roll dough from the center to the edge. The crust will be even in size and thickness. As you roll out the dough, turn it gently to prevent sticking.
● Use your pie plate as a size guide. Turn it upside down on the rolled dough and check the size for additional rolling needed. As a general rule, it's best to roll out the dough 2 inches larger than the pie plate.
● Fold the rolled pastry in half over the rolling pin; lay one half over the pie plate to help center it and flip the other half over the rest of the pie plate.
● Be sure to fit the dough *loosely* in the pie plate. If dough is stretched taut, it will shrink during baking and break.
● For lattice pies as well as pastry shells, turn the edges of the dough under and pinch to form a stand-up edge. There is no need to seal in juices as there is with most double-crust pies.
● Trimmings from pastry can be rerolled. When cut and sprinkled with sugar and cinnamon, they make extra treats.
● To catch any runovers during baking, slide a piece of aluminum foil on the oven rack below the pie.

Coconut Custard Pie

Old-fashioned favorites become no-fail when you start with a refrigerated piecrust and egg-rich filling.

Bake shell at 425° for 3 minutes, then bake pie at 325° for 40 minutes.
Makes 6 servings (one 9-inch pie).

Nutrient Value Per Serving: 414 calories, 10 gm. protein, 24 gm. fat, 430 mg. sodium, 204 mg. cholesterol.

1 **package (15 ounces) refrigerated all-ready piecrust OR: ½ of an 11-ounce package piecrust mix**
3 **cups milk**

4 **eggs**
⅓ **cup sugar**
¼ **teaspoon salt**
1 **can (3½ ounces) flaked coconut**
1 **teaspoon vanilla**
 Ground nutmeg

1. Preheat the oven to hot (425°).
2. Unfold the piecrust, following the label directions; pat into a 9-inch pie plate; make a stand-up edge. If using a piecrust mix, prepare the mix, following the label directions for a 9-inch pastry shell with a high fluted edge.
3. Bake in the hot oven (425°) for 3 minutes. Remove the shell; cool on a wire rack. Lower the oven temperature to 325°.
4. Heat the milk in a medium-size saucepan until bubbles appear around the edge.
5. Beat the eggs slightly in a large bowl with a wire whisk; stir in the sugar and salt; slowly stir in the milk. Stir in the coconut and vanilla. Pour into the partly baked pastry shell. Sprinkle with the nutmeg.
6. Bake in the preheated slow oven (325°) for 40 minutes or until the center is almost set, but still soft. (Do not overbake; the custard will set as it cools.) Cool on a wire rack. Serve warm or chilled.

Frozen Orange 'n' Cream Pie

Frozen Orange 'n' Cream Pie

Ice cream and a store-bought chocolate piecrust are the beginnings for this frosty pie.

Makes 8 servings.

Nutrient Value Per Serving: 257 calories, 4 gm. protein, 13 gm. fat, 183 mg. sodium, 30 mg. cholesterol.

- **1** quart vanilla ice cream
- **1** package (6 ounces) chocolate-flavored ready-to-use piecrust
- **4** orange sections
- **1** square (1 ounce) semisweet chocolate, melted
  Pressurized whipped cream

1. Soften the ice cream in a chilled large bowl. Carefully spoon it into the pie shell, spreading evenly with a metal spatula. Cover the ice cream with plastic wrap; freeze the pie until solid.*
2. Dip one end of each orange section into the melted chocolate. Arrange on a cookie sheet. Refrigerate for 30 minutes or until the chocolate is set.
3. To serve, carefully run a sharp knife under the dipped orange sections to loosen them from the cookie sheet. Garnish the pie with whipped cream and orange sections.

Note: To remove the piecrust to a serving dish, as we did for the photograph, remove the plastic cover from the pie and set aside. Freeze the crust in its aluminum foil pan for several hours. Carefully turn back the sides of the foil pan; lift the crust from the pan and set in the plastic cover. Refreeze for several hours or until very firm. Fill as directed in the above recipe.

> ### Lemons, Limes and Oranges
>
> Should be grated before squeezing when a recipe calls for both grated rind and juice.

Citrus Chiffon Pie

Lemon, orange and grapefruit are the citrus flavors in this smooth, creamy chiffon pie from southern California.

Bake crust at 375° for 8 minutes.
Makes 8 servings (one 9-inch pie).

Nutrient Value Per Serving: 398 calories, 6 gm. protein, 21 gm. fat, 284 mg. sodium, 193 mg. cholesterol.

Citrus Chiffon Pie

- **1⅓** cups graham cracker crumbs
- **1¼** cups sugar
- **¼** cup (½ stick) butter, softened
- **2** medium-size lemons
- **1** medium-size orange
- **½** medium-size grapefruit
- **4** eggs, separated
- **1** envelope unflavored gelatin
- **¼** teaspoon salt
- **1** cup heavy cream, whipped
  Lemon slices (optional)
  Orange slices (optional)

1. Preheat the oven to moderate (375°).
2. Mix together the graham cracker crumbs, ¼ cup of the sugar and the butter in a small bowl until well blended. Press firmly into an even layer over the bottom and side of a 9-inch pie plate.
3. Bake the crust in the preheated moderate oven (375°) for 8 minutes. Cool on a wire rack.
4. Grate the rind of 1 lemon, the orange and ½ grapefruit.
5. Squeeze the juice from the lemons, orange and grapefruit. Strain.
6. Beat the egg yolks in a small, heavy saucepan or in the top of a double boiler until well mixed. Stir in the fruit juices, gelatin, salt and ½ cup of the sugar. Cook over low heat or hot water, stirring constantly, until thickened. Remove from the heat; stir in the grated rinds. Turn into a large bowl. Chill, stirring occasionally, until thickened to ☞

the consistency of uncooked egg whites.

7. Beat the egg whites in a medium-size bowl until soft peaks form. Gradually beat in the remaining ½ cup of sugar until stiff peaks form. Fold into the gelatin mixture until no streaks of white remain. Spoon into the prepared crust. Chill for at least 4 hours.

8. Just before serving, top with the whipped cream. Garnish with the lemon and orange slices, if you wish.

Even Crust

To obtain a more even bottom and side crust, gently press the side and bottom of a standard metal measuring cup (any measure) along the side and bottom of the pie plate.

Lemon Meringue Pie

One of America's all-time favorite pies. To keep meringue from "weeping," keep away from drafts after baking.

Bake shell at 425° for 5 minutes, then bake pie at 425° for 5 minutes.
Makes 6 servings (one 9-inch pie).

Nutrient Value Per Serving: 530 calories, 6 gm. protein, 19 gm. fat, 371 mg. sodium, 198 mg. cholesterol.

    ½ of an 11-ounce package piecrust mix
    1⅓ cups sugar (for filling)
    ½ cup cornstarch
    ¼ teaspoon salt
    2¼ cups water
    4 eggs, separated
    2 tablespoons butter or margarine
    1 tablespoon grated lemon rind
    ½ cup lemon juice
    ¼ teaspoon cream of tartar
    ½ cup sugar (for meringue)

1. Preheat the oven to hot (425°). Prepare the piecrust mix, following the label directions for a 9-inch pastry shell with a high fluted edge.

2. Bake the shell in the preheated hot oven (425°) for 5 minutes or until golden. Remove the shell; cool on a wire rack.

3. Combine the 1⅓ cups of sugar, cornstarch and salt in a medium-size saucepan with a wooden spoon; gradually stir in the water until smooth.

4. Cook over medium heat, stirring constantly, until the mixture thickens and bubbles.

Cook for 1 minute. Remove the saucepan from the heat.

5. Beat the egg yolks lightly in a small bowl; slowly blend in about ½ cup of the hot cornstarch mixture in the saucepan. Cook over low heat for 2 minutes, stirring constantly; remove from the heat. (Do not overcook.)

6. Stir in the butter or margarine, grated lemon rind and juice; pour into the cooled pastry shell. Press a piece of plastic wrap directly on the filling to prevent the formation of a skin. (Remove before topping the pie.) Cool to room temperature.

7. Beat the egg whites with the cream of tartar in a medium-size bowl with an electric mixer at high speed, until foamy white. Slowly add the ½ cup of sugar, 1 tablespoon at a time, beating until the meringue stands in firm peaks.

8. Press the meringue into large puffs on the cooled pie, using a pastry bag with a large notched tip, or spread the meringue over the cooled filling with a spatula, being sure to seal the edge of the pie with the meringue and making peaks at the top of the meringue.

9. Bake in the preheated hot oven (425°) for 5 minutes or just until the peaks turn golden. Cool the pie on a wire rack, away from drafts. Serve at room temperature.

Country Blueberry Pie

⬛◣ ◀◀ Country Blueberry Pie

Memories of country kitchens and warm summer days belong with slices of this super pie.

Bake at 425° for 15 minutes, then at 350° for 35 minutes.
Makes 6 servings (one 9-inch pie).

Nutrient Value Per Serving: 552 calories, 4 gm. protein, 24 gm. fat, 500 mg. sodium, 14 mg. cholesterol.

- 4 cups (2 pints) fresh blueberries OR:
  2 packages (1 pound each) dry-pack frozen blueberries
- 1 cup sugar
- ¼ cup unsifted all-purpose flour
- ¼ teaspoon salt
- ½ teaspoon ground nutmeg
- 1 package (11 ounces) piecrust mix
- 1 tablespoon butter or margarine
  Milk or cream
  Sugar

1. Preheat the oven to hot (425°).
2. Wash the berries gently; drain well; place in a large bowl. Sprinkle with the sugar, flour, salt and nutmeg; toss to mix with a rubber scraper.
3. Prepare the piecrust mix, following the label directions for a 9-inch double-crust pie. Line a 9-inch pie plate with the crust. Reserve the other crust for the top. Spoon the berry mixture into the bottom crust; dot with the butter or margarine.
4. Roll out the remaining pastry to an 11-inch round and cut a 4-inch cross, with a pastry wheel or knife, in the center of the pastry. Lift the pastry with the rolling pin and center on the pie. Turn back the pastry sections to show the blueberries. Trim the overhang to ½ inch.
5. Pinch the crust edges together; turn up and in. Pinch again to form a stand-up edge; flute. Brush the pastry with the milk or cream, using a pastry brush; sprinkle with the sugar.
6. Bake in the preheated hot oven (425°) for 15 minutes; then lower the oven temperature to moderate (350°) and continue to bake for 35 minutes longer or until the pastry is golden and the juices bubble up. Cool for 1 hour on a wire rack before serving.

◀◀ ⬛ Currant-Walnut-Apple Pie

Toast nuts at 350° for 10 to 15 minutes; bake pie at 400° for 50 to 55 minutes.
Makes 6 servings (one 9-inch pie).

Nutrient Value Per Serving: 876 calories, 7 gm. protein, 50 gm. fat, 585 mg. sodium, 50 mg. cholesterol.

- 1 package (11 ounces) piecrust mix
- 1 cup coarsely chopped walnuts
- ½ cup sugar
- 2 tablespoons unsifted all-purpose flour
- ½ teaspoon ground cinnamon
- ¼ teaspoon ground nutmeg
- ⅛ teaspoon salt
- 1 tablespoon brandy
- 2 pounds (6 medium-size) McIntosh apples, pared, quartered, cored and thinly sliced (about 6½ cups)
- 2 tablespoons currants
- 1 tablespoon sugar
- 1 tablespoon hot water
  Brandied Hard Sauce (recipe follows)

1. Preheat the oven to moderate (350°).
2. Prepare the piecrust, following the label directions for a 9-inch double-crust pie. Line a 9-inch pie plate with the crust. Reserve the other crust for the top.
3. Spread ½ cup of the nuts in a shallow baking pan. Toast in the preheated moderate oven (350°), stirring often, for 10 to 15 minutes or until browned. Cool. Reserve for garnish. Increase the oven temperature to hot (400°).
4. Combine the ½ cup of sugar, the flour, cinnamon, nutmeg, salt and brandy in a large bowl; add the apple slices, the remaining ½ cup of walnuts and the currants; toss gently to mix well.
5. Spoon the apple mixture into the pastry-lined pie plate. Cut the reserved top crust into 1-inch strips. Weave the strips over the filling in a lattice design. Trim the overhang to 1 inch; fold under, flush with the rim. Pinch to make a stand-up edge; flute.
6. Bake the pie in the preheated hot oven (400°) for 40 minutes.
7. Meanwhile, prepare the garnish: Stir together the sugar and the water in a small bowl. Add the reserved ½ cup of toasted walnuts. When the pie has baked for 40 minutes, sprinkle the outer edge of the pie with the nut mixture. *(Continues on page 231.)*

Top: Maple-Pumpkin Pie (page 231), Indian Pudding (page 247), Currant-Walnut-Apple Pie (page 229).

8. Bake the pie for 10 to 15 minutes longer or until the apples are easily pierced with a knife and the pastry is golden brown. Cool on a wire rack. Serve warm with the Brandied Hard Sauce.

Brandied Hard Sauce: Beat ½ cup (1 stick) of softened butter in a medium-size bowl with an electric mixer until fluffy. Beat in 1½ cups of *sifted* 10X (confectioners') sugar with 2 tablespoons of heated brandy until smooth. Makes 1 cup.

Maple-Pumpkin Pie

Bake at 425° for 15 minutes, then at 350° for 55 minutes.
Makes 6 servings (one 9-inch pie).

Nutrient Value Per Serving: 401 calories, 6 gm. protein, 21 gm. fat, 601 mg. sodium, 120 mg. cholesterol.

- ½ **of an 11-ounce package piecrust mix**
- 2 **eggs**
- 1 **can (1 pound) pumpkin**
- ½ **cup sugar**
- ¼ **cup maple syrup**
- 1 **teaspoon ground cinnamon**
- ½ **teaspoon salt**
- ½ **teaspoon ground ginger**
- ¼ **teaspoon ground cloves**
- 1⅔ **cups half and half (½ cream, ½ milk) or light cream**
  Whipped cream (optional)
  Maple-flavored candies (optional)
  Kumquats and mint leaves (optional)

1. Preheat the oven to hot (425°). Prepare the piecrust mix, following the label directions for a 9-inch pastry shell with a high fluted edge.
2. Beat the eggs slightly in a large bowl. Beat in the pumpkin, sugar, maple syrup, cinnamon, salt, ginger and cloves until well combined. Stir in the half and half. Pour the pumpkin filling into the pie shell.
3. Bake in the preheated hot oven (425°) for 15 minutes. Lower the oven temperature to moderate (350°). Cover the crust with aluminum foil if browning too fast. Bake for another 55 minutes or until the custard is almost set, but still soft in the center; do not overbake. Cool the pie on a wire rack. Garnish with the whipped cream, maple-flavored candies or kumquats and mint leaves, if you wish.

MICROWAVE DIRECTIONS
650 Watt Variable Power Microwave Oven
Directions: Prepare the pastry shell as above in a 9-inch microwave-safe pie dish. Microwave at full power for 4 minutes. Remove from the oven and brush the edges with browning liquid, if desired. Set aside. Combine the pumpkin, sugar, maple syrup, cinnamon, salt, ginger, cloves and half and half in a 2-quart microwave-safe mixing bowl; stir to mix well. Microwave at full power for 8 minutes. Meanwhile, mix the eggs in a small bowl; brush a little over the bottom of the pastry shell. Mix the remaining eggs into the pumpkin mixture. Pour into the pastry shell. Microwave at half power for 20 minutes or until the top of the filling looks quite dry. Remove; cool to room temperature. Chill.

Freezing Pie Shells

Make 2 pie shells; use 1 and freeze the other for future use.
- Wrap unbaked pie shells in aluminum foil and freeze. To use, thaw the unbaked shell at room temperature for about 30 minutes and use in the recipe as directed.
- Cool a baked pie shell before wrapping and freezing. Warm the frozen shell in a preheated moderate oven (375°) for 10 minutes, if you wish.

Fruit Desserts

Watermelon Basket

Makes 18 servings.

Nutrient Value Per Serving: 89 calories, 2 gm. protein, 1 gm. fat, 8 mg. sodium, 0 mg. cholesterol.

- 1 **watermelon (8 to 10 pounds)**
- 2 **cantaloupes**
- 1 **ripe pineapple**
- 1 **quart strawberries, rinsed and hulled**
- 1 **bunch seedless grapes**

1. Remove the top third of the watermelon, cutting horizontally across the top of the melon with a long, thin knife.
2. Hollow out the bottom and top sections with a melon baller. Place the watermelon balls in a large bowl.
3. Cut the edge of the watermelon basket into a zigzag pattern with a sharp knife.
4. Halve and seed the cantaloupes. Scoop ☞

out the balls with a melon baller. Add to the watermelon balls.

5. Halve and core the pineapple. Cut the fruit into cubes. Add to the bowl along with the strawberries and grapes. Toss gently to mix. Spoon into the watermelon basket.

6. Cover the basket with plastic wrap, making sure all the fruit and cut surfaces are covered. Refrigerate for up to 2 hours.

Red Fruits

Strawberries, raspberries and whipped cream—what could be better, and easier?

Makes 6 servings.

Nutrient Value Per Serving: 147 calories, 1 gm. protein, 8 gm. fat, 9 mg. sodium, 27 mg. cholesterol. The above calculation does not include sugar for whipped cream.

 2 **pints strawberries, hulled and halved, if large**
 1 **package (10 ounces) frozen raspberries, thawed**
 ½ **cup heavy cream**
    Sugar

1. Place the strawberries in a glass serving dish or individual sherbet glasses.
2. Place the raspberries in the container of an electric blender or food processor. Cover; whirl until puréed. Spoon the purée over the strawberries. Chill thoroughly.
3. To serve: Beat the heavy cream with the sugar to taste, in a small bowl until stiff. Top the strawberries with the whipped cream.

Cherry-Nut Tarts

These easy-to-make cherry tarts, made with ready-to-use graham cracker tart shells, may be prepared a day ahead and refrigerated. Save the protective plastic tart-shell inserts to use as covers.

Makes 2 servings.

Nutrient Value Per Serving: 229 calories, 1 gm. protein, 10 gm. fat, 155 mg. sodium, 5 mg. cholesterol.

 2 **ready-to-use graham cracker tart shells (from a 4-ounce package; freeze remaining shells in package for another use; or to make 6 tarts,***
 1 **teaspoon melted butter**
 2 **teaspoons dark brown sugar**

 1 **tablespoon finely chopped pecans**
 ½ **cup prepared cherry pie filling (use remainder of 1-pound can as sauce for ice cream, or for 6 tarts,***
 ¼ **teaspoon grated lemon rind**

1. Remove the plastic inserts from the 2 tart shells; leave the shells in the foil. Wash the inserts and reserve.
2. Combine the melted butter, brown sugar and pecans in a small bowl.
3. Combine the pie filling with the lemon rind in a bowl. Spoon into the tart shells. Sprinkle half the nut mixture over each.
4. Invert the reserved plastic tart inserts and use to cover the filled tarts. Secure to the foil tart pan with several pieces of tape. Place the tarts in a covered plastic container, if you wish. Refrigerate for several hours or overnight.
5. If preparing for a picnic, pack with a frozen ice pack.

* Note: To prepare 6 tarts, stir ¾ teaspoon of grated lemon rind into 1 can (1 pound) of prepared cherry pie filling. Spoon evenly into 6 tart shells (one 4-ounce package). Combine 1 tablespoon of melted butter, 2 tablespoons of dark brown sugar and 3 tablespoons of finely chopped pecans in a bowl. Sprinkle over the tops of the tarts, dividing equally.

Danish Apple Dessert

This classic Scandinavian dessert, layered in a straight-sided glass bowl, makes an attractive buffet dessert centerpiece.

Makes 8 servings.

Nutrient Value Per Serving: 423 calories, 4 gm. protein, 24 gm. fat, 109 mg. sodium, 63 mg. cholesterol.

 8 **medium-size Golden Delicious apples**
 1 **tablespoon lemon juice**
 1 **tablespoon butter or margarine**
 1 **tablespoon granulated sugar**
 ¼ **cup (½ stick) butter or margarine**
 1 **cup zwieback crumbs (16 toasts)**
 ½ **cup firmly packed light brown sugar**
 ½ **cup chopped blanched almonds**
 1 **teaspoon ground cinnamon**
 1 **cup heavy cream**
 2 **tablespoons 10X (confectioners') sugar**
 1 **teaspoon vanilla**
    Red and green apple slices for garnish (optional)

1. Pare, core and slice each apple into 12 wedges.

Toss the wedges with the lemon juice in a large bowl until completely coated.

2. Melt the 1 tablespoon of butter in a large (12-inch) skillet over medium heat. Add the apples and sprinkle with the granulated sugar. Cook, covered, stirring occasionally, for 15 minutes or until the apples are tender, but not brown.

3. Meanwhile, melt the ¼ cup of butter in another skillet. Stir in the zwieback crumbs, brown sugar, almonds and cinnamon until well blended. Toast over low heat, stirring occasionally, for 15 minutes or until golden.

4. Sprinkle half of the crumb mixture evenly over the bottom of a 2-quart serving bowl. Layer the apples over the top of the crumb mixture. Sprinkle the remaining crumb mixture over the top. Chill for several hours or serve at room temperature.

5. At serving time, beat together the cream, 10X sugar and vanilla in a small bowl until stiff. Garnish the top with the whipped cream and the apple slices, if you wish.

Pear-Walnut Torte

The buttery, cake-like base for this torte is filled with pears and sprinkled with a ground walnut-brown sugar topping. Serve with vanilla ice cream or a custard sauce.

Bake at 375° for 35 minutes.
Makes 8 servings.

Nutrient Value Per Serving: 540 calories, 7 gm. protein, 28 gm. fat, 207 mg. sodium, 145 mg. cholesterol.

- 1 *cup unsifted all-purpose flour*
- ¼ *teaspoon baking powder*
- ½ *cup (1 stick) butter or margarine, softened*
- ½ *cup granulated sugar*
- 3 *eggs*
- 1 *teaspoon vanilla*
- 1 *cup finely chopped walnuts*
- ¼ *cup firmly packed light brown sugar*
- 3 *tablespoons all-purpose flour*
- 3 *tablespoons butter or margarine, softened*
- 3 *to 4 large ripe pears, such as Bartlett or Bosc (about 2 pounds)*
- 2 *tablespoons lemon juice*
- 2 *tablespoons granulated sugar*
- ½ *cup currant jelly*

1. Preheat the oven to moderate (375°). Grease and flour an 11-inch-round tart pan with a removable bottom.

2. Combine the 1 cup of flour and the baking powder in a small bowl; set aside.

3. Beat together the butter and granulated sugar in a large bowl until smooth and creamy. Beat in the eggs until light and fluffy. Gradually beat in the flour mixture until the batter is smooth. Beat in the vanilla.

4. Sprinkle ½ cup of the walnuts in the bottom of the prepared pan. Spoon the cake batter over the walnuts.

5. Combine the remaining walnuts, brown sugar, the 3 tablespoons of flour and 3 tablespoons of butter in a small bowl; mix until well blended.

6. Pare the pears. Halve lengthwise and core. Slice each half into thirds and toss with the lemon juice in a bowl to completely coat. Press the pears into the batter to form an attractive design. Sprinkle with the granulated sugar and walnut-sugar mixture.

7. Place the tart pan on a baking sheet and bake in the preheated moderate oven (375°) for 35 minutes or until the cake top springs back when lightly touched with a fingertip. Cool in the pan on a wire rack for 45 minutes. Gently loosen the cake around the edge and remove the sides of the pan. Serve warm or cooled.

8. Melt the currant jelly in a small saucepan over low heat. Carefully brush over the top of the cooled torte.

Almond-Stuffed Apples with Two Sauces

A glorious end to a special dinner—poached stuffed apple in a pool of custard feathered with a strawberry sauce. The stuffed apple and strawberry sauce can be made a day ahead.

Makes 4 servings.

Nutrient Value Per Serving: 425 calories, 7 gm. protein, 14 gm. fat, 40 mg. sodium, 145 mg. cholesterol.

- 4 *small apples, such as McIntosh, Cortland or Rome Beauty (about 1 pound)*
- ½ *cup toasted blanched almonds, finely chopped*
- 5 *tablespoons sugar*
- ⅛ *teaspoon almond extract*
- ¾ *cup dry red wine*
- 3 *tablespoons orange-flavored liqueur*
   Orange rind strips from ½ orange
   Lemon rind strips from ½ lemon ☞

Vanilla Custard Sauce:
 1 *cup milk*
 1 *tablespoon cornstarch*
 2 *tablespoons sugar*
 2 *teaspoons orange-flavored liqueur*
 ½ *teaspoon vanilla*
 2 *egg yolks*
 1 *package (10 ounces) strawberries in syrup, thawed and drained*

1. Cut a ½-inch slice off the top of each apple, leaving the stem on. Scoop out the core with the melon ball cutter, being sure not to go through the bottom of the apples.
2. Combine the almonds, 2 tablespoons of the sugar and the almond extract in a small bowl. Stuff the apples. Replace the apple tops.
3. Combine the wine, orange-flavored liqueur, the remaining 3 tablespoons of sugar, and the orange and lemon rinds in a medium-size saucepan. Bring to boiling, stirring to dissolve the sugar. Add the apples to the pan. Lower the heat; cover; cook until the apples are tender, for about 10 minutes, basting the apples frequently. Remove the apples from the pan with a slotted spoon to a plate to cool.*
4. Prepare the Vanilla Custard Sauce: Pour ¾ cup of the milk into a small saucepan. Heat gently until small bubbles appear around the edge. Meanwhile, combine the remaining ¼ cup of milk and the cornstarch in a small bowl; stir until smooth. Add the cornstarch mixture, sugar, orange-flavored liqueur and vanilla to the milk. Bring to boiling, stirring constantly. Remove from the heat. Gradually pour ¼ cup of the hot liquid into the egg yolks in a small bowl, beating constantly. Gradually pour the mixture back into the saucepan, stirring constantly. Place the saucepan in a large bowl of ice and water to cool the custard; whisk occasionally to prevent a skin from forming.
5. Meanwhile, place the strawberries in the container of an electric blender or food processor. Cover; whirl until puréed. Set aside.
6. To serve, pour the Vanilla Custard Sauce onto each of four dessert plates to form a pool. Make small wax paper cones with very small open tips; fasten with tape. Fill a cone with the strawberry purée. Pipe two thin circles over the custard on each plate, equally placed between the center and

edge. Fill more cones with the purée as needed. To "feather," gently pull the blunt edge of a thin knife or a wooden pick over the custard and strawberry sauce from the center of each plate to the edge in a spoke-like pattern. Place the cooked apple in the center of each plate.

* Note: The poaching liquid can be stored in the refrigerator and used later as a sauce for ice cream or cut-up fresh fruit.

Poached Pears with Hot Caramel Sauce

An elegant but simple dessert! For the best effect, make sure the pears are well chilled, and the sauce hot.

Makes 6 servings.

Nutrient Value Per Serving: 367 calories, 1 gm. protein, 15 gm. fat, 16 mg. sodium, 54 mg. cholesterol.

 6 *firm-ripe pears such as Bartlett, Bosc or Comice*
 2 *tablespoons lemon juice*
 4 *to 5 cups water*
Caramel Sauce:
 1 *cup heavy cream*
 1 *cup sugar*
 1 *teaspoon vanilla*
    Toasted sliced almonds

1. Core the pears from the bottom. Pare the pears without removing the stems. Brush well with the lemon juice to prevent discoloration.
2. Bring the water to boiling in a large skillet. Place the pears in the skillet. Lower the heat and simmer, turning and basting the pears occasionally, until firm-tender, for 8 to 10 minutes. Transfer the pears and liquid to a deep bowl; make sure the pears are completely submerged. Refrigerate until well chilled.
3. Prepare the Caramel Sauce: Heat the cream in a small saucepan just until bubbles form around the edge; do not let boil.
4. Heat the sugar in a large, heavy skillet over medium-high heat, stirring constantly. When the sugar begins to melt, reduce the heat to low and continue to stir constantly, until the sugar is dissolved and the mixture is light brown.
5. Slowly add the warm cream, stirring

constantly until the sauce is smooth. (If some of the sugar crystallizes, cook, stirring constantly, until the crystals dissolve.) Remove from the heat. Stir in the vanilla.

6. To serve, drain the pears thoroughly. Place on individual serving plates. Spoon the hot sauce over the pears. Garnish with the almonds.

Note: For advance preparation, make the Caramel Sauce ahead. Reheat very slowly over low heat, stirring constantly, until hot.

Apple-Plum Clafouti

An easy-to-prepare dessert—just pour the batter over the sliced fruit and bake. Be sure to serve it while still puffy and warm.

Bake at 375° for 30 minutes.
Makes 6 servings.

Nutrient Value Per Serving: 195 calories, 6 gm. protein, 4 gm. fat, 77 mg. sodium, 143 mg. cholesterol.

> 1 **Golden Delicious apple, peeled, cored and thinly sliced**
> 2 **purple plums, pitted and cut into ¼-inch-thick wedges**
> ¼ **cup plus 1 tablespoon sugar**
> 1 **cup milk**
> 3 **eggs**
> ½ **cup unsifted all-purpose flour**
> 2 **tablespoons apple brandy**
> 1 **teaspoon vanilla**
> ¼ **teaspoon almond extract**
> **Pinch salt**
> **10X (confectioners') sugar**
> **Lightly whipped heavy cream (optional)**

1. Preheat the oven to moderate (375°). Grease a shallow 1½- to 2-quart baking dish.

2. Toss the apple and plum wedges with the 1 tablespoon of sugar.

3. Place the remaining ¼ cup of sugar, the milk, eggs, flour, apple brandy, vanilla, almond extract and salt in the container of an electric blender or food processor. Cover; whirl until the batter is smooth.

4. Place the fruit in the prepared baking dish. Pour the batter evenly over the fruit.

5. Bake in the preheated moderate oven (375°) for 30 minutes or until puffed and golden and springy to the touch. Sprinkle with the 10X sugar. Serve immediately. Pass with the whipped cream, if you wish.

Fresh Apple Brûlées

Individual apple custards with a caramelized sugar topping.

Bake at 350° for 30 minutes, then broil for 2 to 3 minutes.
Makes 8 servings.

Nutrient Value Per Serving: 425 calories, 5 gm. protein, 31 gm. fat, 36 mg. sodium, 286 mg. cholesterol.

> 2 **to 3 large Golden Delicious apples, pared, cored and finely chopped (about 2⅔ cups)**
> 1 **tablespoon lemon juice**
> 6 **egg yolks**
> 2 **cups heavy cream**
> ¼ **cup sugar**
> 1 **tablespoon vanilla**
> ½ **cup slivered blanched almonds, toasted**
> ¾ **cup firmly packed brown sugar**

1. Preheat the oven to moderate (350°).

2. Toss together the apples and lemon juice in a small bowl until completely coated. Spoon about ⅓ cup of the apples into each of eight 6-ounce baking dishes.

3. Beat the yolks slightly in a large bowl. Stir in the cream, sugar and vanilla. Pour about ½ cup of the cream mixture into each baking dish. Place the baking dishes in a large, shallow baking pan and place on the oven rack. Pour in boiling water to a depth of about ½ inch.

4. Bake in the preheated moderate oven (350°) for 30 minutes or until the custards are almost set. Remove from the pan of water to a wire rack to cool. Refrigerate for several hours or until chilled.

5. To serve, sprinkle about 1 tablespoon of the almonds over each custard. Sieve the brown sugar over each, dividing equally.

6. Broil about 6 inches from the heat until the sugar caramelizes, for about 2 to 3 minutes; watch carefully to prevent burning. Serve immediately.

Peach Melba Shortcake for a Crowd

A package of yellow cake mix makes short work of this large shortcake, which can be divided into large or small portions to feed any size crowd.

Bake at 350°, following package directions for a 13 x 9-inch cake.
Makes 12 large servings or 24 small servings.

Nutrient Value Per Large Serving: 405 calories, 3 gm. protein, 20 gm. fat, 253 mg. sodium, 54 mg. cholesterol.
Nutrient Value Per Small Serving: 203 calories, 2 gm. protein, 10 gm. fat, 127 mg. sodium, 27 mg. cholesterol.

    1 package (18.25 ounces) yellow cake mix
    ⅓ cup peach preserves
    4 medium-size peaches (about 1¼ pounds)
    1½ cups raspberries, fresh or individually
         frozen
    2 cups heavy cream
    ¼ cup 10X (confectioners') sugar
    ½ teaspoon vanilla
    1 tablespoon lemon juice
Raspberry Sauce:
    1 package (10 ounces) frozen raspberries,
         thawed

1. Preheat the oven to moderate (350°). Grease and flour a 13 x 9 x 2-inch baking pan, shaking out the excess flour.
2. Prepare, bake and cool the cake mix, following the package directions for a 13 x 9-inch cake.
3. Place the cake, top-side down, on a serving tray. Carefully split the cake in half horizontally, using a long serrated knife.* Remove and reserve the top layer (actually the bottom of the cake). Spread the peach preserves over the cut surface of the layer on a tray.
4. Peel, pit and dice 2 of the peaches. Sprinkle over the preserves along with 1 cup of the raspberries.
5. Combine the cream, sugar and vanilla in a medium-size bowl; beat until stiff. Spread about one-third of the cream over the fruit. Carefully cover with the reserved cake layer, cut-side down.
6. Spread the top with a thin layer of whipped cream. Spoon the remaining cream into a pastry bag fitted with a star tip. Pipe a decorative border around the edge of the cake. Then pipe lines across the top, forming 12 equal rectangles.
7. Peel, pit and slice the remaining 2 peaches;

brush with the lemon juice. Arrange on the cake with the remaining ½ cup of raspberries. Refrigerate until serving time.
8. Meanwhile, prepare the Raspberry Sauce: Purée the undrained thawed raspberries in an electric blender or food processor. Pour into a serving pitcher or bowl. Cover and refrigerate.
9. To serve, cut the cake into 12 large servings or 24 small servings. Pass the Raspberry Sauce.

* Note: For easy splitting of the cake, insert toothpicks at the half-height point all around the cake use the toothpicks as a guide for the knife.

Warm Blueberry Scone Shortcakes

Pecan scones are topped with a warm, spicy blueberry sauce and cinnamon-flavored whipped cream.

Bake at 400° for 12 minutes.
Makes 4 servings.

Nutrient Value Per Serving: 460 calories, 6 gm. protein, 22 gm. fat, 482 mg. sodium, 117 mg. cholesterol.

    1 cup buttermilk baking mix
    2 tablespoons chopped pecans
    2 tablespoons sugar
    1 egg, slightly beaten
    1 teaspoon butter or margarine, melted
Blueberry Sauce:
    2 cups fresh blueberries
    ¼ cup sugar
    1 tablespoon cornstarch
    1 tablespoon lemon juice
    ⅛ teaspoon ground cinnamon
    ⅛ teaspoon ground allspice
         Cinnamon Cream (recipe follows)

1. Preheat the oven to hot (400°).
2. Combine the baking mix, pecans and the 2 tablespoons of sugar in a medium-size bowl; stir to mix well. Stir in the egg to make a soft dough.
3. Turn out on a lightly floured surface and shape into a ball. Knead gently 5 times. Pat out with floured hands to make a 4½-inch square. Cut diagonally to make 4 equal triangles. Place on an ungreased cookie sheet. Brush with the melted butter.
4. Bake in the preheated hot oven (400°) for about 12 minutes or until golden brown.

236

5. Meanwhile, prepare the Blueberry Sauce: Rinse and pick over the berries. Stir together the ¼ cup of sugar, cornstarch, lemon juice, cinnamon and allspice in a small saucepan until smooth and well blended. Add the blueberries. Cook over medium heat, stirring constantly, until the mixture thickens and bubbles. Remove from the heat. Cool slightly.

6. To serve, place the scones on individual dessert plates. Spoon the Blueberry Sauce over. Top with the Cinnamon Cream.

To Make Ahead: Prepare the scones and Blueberry Sauce the day before; cool the scones completely; wrap securely in aluminum foil and refrigerate. Transfer the sauce to a medium-size bowl, cover with plastic wrap and refrigerate. To serve, heat the scones in a preheated moderate oven (350°) for 15 minutes or until warm as desired. Place the sauce in a small saucepan and heat over low heat until bubbly. Proceed as the recipe directs.

Cinnamon Cream: Combine ½ cup of heavy cream, 1 tablespoon of 10X sugar and ¼ teaspoon of cinnamon in a small bowl; beat until stiff.

MICROWAVE DIRECTIONS (For Blueberry Sauce)
650 Watt Variable Power Microwave Oven
Directions: Combine the 2 cups of fresh blueberries, ¼ cup of sugar, 1 tablespoon of cornstarch, 1 tablespoon of lemon juice, ⅛ teaspoon of cinnamon and ⅛ teaspoon of allspice in a 1-quart microwave-safe casserole. Microwave, uncoverd, at full power for 2 minutes. Stir well. Microwave for 2 minutes longer or until the mixture is thickened and bubbly. Cool slightly and continue with Step 6, above.

Classic Strawberry Shortcake

Bake at 425° for 20 minutes.
Makes 6 servings.

Nutrient Value Per Serving: 639 calories, 7 gm. protein, 39 gm. fat, 499 mg. sodium, 127 mg. cholesterol.

  2 cups **sifted** *all-purpose flour*
 10 *tablepoons sugar*
  1 *tablespoon baking powder*
  ¼ *teaspoon salt*
  ½ *cup (1 stick) butter or margarine*
  ¾ *cup milk*
  1 *quart ripe strawberries*
  ¼ *cup kirsch or light rum*
 1½ *cups heavy cream*
  ½ *teaspoon vanilla*
     Fresh mint sprig for garnish (optional)

1. Preheat the oven to hot (425°). Grease an 8-inch-round layer-cake pan.

2. Combine the flour, 4 tablespoons of the sugar, the baking powder and salt in a medium-size bowl; stir to mix. Cut in the butter with a pastry blender or 2 knives until the mixture resembles coarse meal. Make a hole in the center; pour in the milk all at once. Stir gently just until the mixture makes a soft dough. Spread evenly in the prepared pan.

3. Bake in the preheated hot oven (425°) for 20 minutes or until lightly browned. Cool in the pan on a wire rack for 5 minutes. Remove the shortcake from the pan; cool on the wire rack.

4. Meanwhile, reserve 3 strawberries for garnish. Slice the remaining strawberries into a large bowl. Sprinkle with 4 tablespoons of the sugar and the kirsch; let stand for 30 minutes, stirring occasionally.

5. Beat the cream, the remaining 2 tablespoons of sugar and vanilla in a medium-size bowl until stiff.

6. To serve, split the shortcake in half horizontally. Set the bottom half on a serving plate. Spoon half of the strawberries and all of the juice over the biscuit bottom. Spread half of the cream over the strawberries. Cover with the top half of the biscuit. Sprinkle with the remaining strawberries. Spoon on the remaining cream. Garnish with the reserved whole strawberries and mint sprig, if you wish.

To Make Ahead: The shortcake may be baked in advance, wrapped well and frozen. When ready to serve the shortcake, remove from the freezer several hours before and allow to come to room temperature before completing the dessert.

Chocolate Tortoni

Ice-Cream Desserts

Chocolate Tortoni

Makes 12 servings.

Nutrient Value Per Serving: 447 calories, 8 gm. protein, 39 gm. fat, 81 mg. sodium, 60 mg. cholesterol.

- 1 **cup almond-macaroon cookie crumbs**
- 2 **tablespoons butter or margarine, melted**
- 2 **squares (1 ounce each) unsweetened chocolate**
- 1 **package (6 ounces) semisweet chocolate bits**
- 4 **egg whites**
- ⅛ **teaspoon cream of tartar**
- ⅛ **teaspoon salt**
- ¼ **cup sugar**
- 2 **cups heavy cream**
- 2 **teaspoons sugar**
- 1 **teaspoon vanilla**
- ½ **cup toasted chopped almonds**

Garnish:
- **Whipped cream**
- **Whole toasted almonds, dipped in semisweet chocolate**
- **Strawberries**
- **Chocolate leaves (optional)**

1. Combine the cookie crumbs and melted butter in a small bowl; blend well. Firmly press the mixture in an even layer over the bottom of an 8-inch springform pan. Chill while preparing the tortoni mixture.
2. Melt the unsweetened chocolate in the top of a double boiler over hot, not boiling, water. In a separate double boiler, melt the semisweet chocolate bits over hot, not boiling, water. Remove from the heat; cool both chocolates to room temperature.
3. Beat the egg whites with the cream of tartar and salt in a small bowl until foamy. Gradually beat in the ¼ cup of sugar, 1 tablespoon at a time, until soft peaks form.
4. Beat the 2 cups of heavy cream in a large bowl until stiff. Beat in the 2 teaspoons of sugar, the vanilla and melted unsweetened chocolate; blend well.
5. Fold the beaten egg whites, toasted almonds and melted semisweet chocolate into the whipped cream mixture until no streaks of white remain; there may be some small chunks of chocolate.
6. Turn into the prepared pan. Smooth the top with a rubber spatula. Cover the pan with aluminum foil. Freeze until firm or for up to 3 days.
7. To serve, remove the side of the pan. Garnish with the whipped cream, almonds, strawberries and chocolate leaves, if you wish.

Note: To make the chocolate leaves, wash and thoroughly dry fresh green leaves with well-marked veins. Melt semisweet chocolate in the top of a double boiler over hot, not boiling, water. Carefully brush the melted chocolate on the underside of the leaves, using a small, narrow spatula or pastry brush. Place the leaves, chocolate-side up, on a plate or cookie sheet. Freeze or refrigerate just until the chocolate is completely firm. Carefully peel away the green leaves, starting at the stem end. Store the chocolate leaves, covered, in the freezer.

For Homemade Whipped Cream

Place the beaters and bowl in the refrigerator, along with the heavy cream, to chill for 1 hour. Beat the heavy cream in the chilled bowl until stiff. For sweetened whipped cream, fold 2 tablespoons of 10X (confectioners') sugar for each cup of heavy cream used into the whipped cream.

Strawberry Ice-Cream Brownie Bombe

A brownie mix makes this spectacular dessert even easier.

Bake at 350° for 30 minutes.
Makes 12 servings.

Nutrient Value Per Serving: 550 calories, 6 gm. protein, 31 gm. fat, 241 mg. sodium, 74 mg. cholesterol.

- 1 **package (23 ounces) double-fudge brownie mix**
- ½ **cup walnuts, chopped**
- ½ **cup strawberry preserves**
- 1 **quart strawberry ice cream, softened**
- 2 **cups (1 pint) heavy cream**
  Few drops red food coloring
- ¼ **cup 10X (confectioners') sugar**
  Chocolate-covered strawberries for garnish (optional) ☞

Strawberry Ice-Cream Brownie Bombe

1. Preheat the oven to moderate (350°). Grease two 8-inch-round layer-cake pans. Line the bottoms with wax paper; grease the paper. Place a 1½-quart bowl in the refrigerator to chill.
2. Prepare the brownie mix, following the package directions for cake-like brownies. Stir the walnuts into the batter. Pour into the prepared pans, dividing equally.
3. Bake in the preheated moderate oven (350°) for 30 minutes or just until the cakes begin to pull away from the sides of the pans. Cool the cakes in the pans on a wire rack to room temperature. Remove the cakes from the pans.
4. Line the chilled bowl with aluminum foil. Cut and fit one brownie layer to evenly line the inside of the bowl. Spread the strawberry preserves over the brownie layer. Place in the freezer until cold. Wrap the second layer in plastic wrap; refrigerate.
5. Spoon the ice cream into the lined bowl, packing down firmly. Smooth the top. Cover with plastic wrap; freeze until firm.
6. To assemble: Unwrap the refrigerated brownie layer; place on a serving plate. Remove the plastic wrap from the ice-cream bombe top and unmold the ice-cream bombe onto the brownie layer. Remove the foil. Return to the freezer while preparing the cream, or for up to 3 days. Beat the cream with a few drops of the red food

coloring in a medium-size bowl until slightly thickened. Beat in the 10X sugar until stiff. Spoon about 1½ cups of the whipped cream into a pastry bag fitted with a star tip. Refrigerate. Frost the bombe with the remaining cream. Pipe the cream in lines decoratively up the sides and around the base of the bombe. Return to the freezer until the cream is hard.
7. Garnish the bombe with the chocolate-dipped strawberries, if you wish.

Apricot Ice-Cream and Chablis-Ice Bombe

A delicately flavored white wine ice is the hidden treat in this cooling dessert.

Makes 12 servings.

Nutrient Value Per Serving: 148 calories, 2 gm. protein, 5 gm. fat, 44 mg. sodium, 20 mg. cholesterol.

- 1 can (17 ounces) unpeeled apricot halves, chilled and drained
- 1 quart vanilla ice cream, softened
- 1½ cups water
- ½ cup sugar
  Outer yellow peel from 1 lemon, cut in single strip
- 1½ teaspoons gelatin
- 1 cup Chablis wine
- 2 tablespoons lemon juice
  Whipped cream, chopped pistachio nuts, apricot halves and fresh mint leaves for garnish (optional)

1. Chill an 8-cup bombe mold.
2. Purée the drained apricots in a blender or food processor. Stir the puréed apricots into the softened ice cream in a medium-size bowl. Place in the freezer to stiffen to a spreading consistency.
3. Line the mold with the apricot ice cream to within ¼ inch of the top edge, leaving a hollow center. Cover with plastic wrap and freeze until firm.
4. Combine the water, sugar and lemon peel in a medium-size saucepan. Bring to boiling, stirring to dissolve the sugar. Lower the heat; simmer for 15 minutes without stirring.
5. Sprinkle the gelatin over ¼ cup of the wine in a small bowl. Let stand to soften for about 5 minutes. Stir into the hot sugar syrup until dissolved. Stir in the remaining

Apricot Ice-Cream and Chablis-Ice Bombe

¾ cup of wine and the lemon juice. Remove the lemon peel. Cool to room temperature. Chill.
6. Pour the chilled wine mixture into the ice-cream-lined mold. Cover with plastic wrap and freeze overnight or for up to 3 days.
7. To serve, unmold onto a chilled serving plate. Garnish with the whipped cream, chopped pistachio nuts, apricot halves and mint, if you wish. Serve immediately.

Removing an Ice-Cream Mold

To serve, place a towel, wrung out in hot water, over the bottom of the mold and turn out onto a chilled serving platter.

Frozen Irish Coffee

Makes 6 servings.

Nutrient Value Per Serving: 228 calories, 1 gm. protein, 9 gm. fat, 10 mg. sodium, 27 mg. cholesterol.

- **4 cups freshly brewed hot espresso or very strong regular coffee**
- **½ cup granulated sugar**
- **¾ cup Irish whiskey**
- **½ cup heavy cream**
- **2 teaspoons 10X (confectioners') sugar**
- **¼ teaspoon vanilla**
- **1 square (1 ounce) semisweet chocolate, coarsely grated**

1. Combine the coffee, granulated sugar and whiskey in a 6-quart pitcher. Cool.
2. Pour the coffee into ice cube trays or a 13 x 9 x 2-inch pan. Freeze until firm.
3. Unmold the coffee cubes. If using a baking pan, cut into 2-inch chunks. Place one-quarter of the chunks in a food processor fitted with a metal blade. Process until smooth.
4. With the motor running, add another quarter of the cubes; process until smooth. Spoon into the freezer container. Repeat with the remaining cubes. Freeze until firm.
5. Several hours before serving, return the frozen coffee to the food processor. Process just until smooth. Scoop into serving dishes. Freeze until ready to serve.
6. Beat the cream, 10X sugar and vanilla until stiff. Refrigerate until ready to serve.
7. To serve, top with the whipped cream and sprinkle with the grated chocolate.

To Make Ahead: Frozen coffee can be made several days ahead through Step 4. Scoop into dishes several hours before serving.

Calorie-Lite Desserts

Ambrosia Summer Rice Pudding

Makes 10 servings.

Nutrient Value Per Serving: 111 calories, 1 gm. protein, 1 gm. fat, 3 mg. sodium, 0 mg. cholesterol.

1 **can (20 ounces) pineapple chunks in juice**
1 **can enriched precooked rice**
2 **teaspoons grated orange rind**
2 **navel oranges, peeled, sectioned**
1 **banana, thinly sliced**
½ **cup fresh blueberries, pitted cherries or sliced strawberries**
7 **tablespoons flaked coconut**

1. Drain the pineapple juice into a medium-size saucepan; reserve the chunks. Bring the pineapple juice to boiling. Stir in the rice. Remove from the heat; cover. Let cool.
2. Combine the pineapple chunks, orange rind and sections, banana, berries, coconut and rice in a large bowl. Refrigerate for several hours or until well chilled.

Glazed Strawberry Tartlets

Makes 10 individual tartlets.

Nutrient Value Per Serving with Flavored Gelatin: 142 calories, 2 gm. protein, 5 gm. fat, 162 mg. sodium, 0 mg. cholesterol. Nutrient Value Per Serving with Sugar-Free Flavored Gelatin: 113 calories, 2 gm. protein, 5 gm. fat, 157 mg. sodium, 0 mg. cholesterol.

1 **package (3 ounces) strawberry-flavored gelatin OR: 1 package (.3 ounces to make 4 servings) sugar-free strawberry-flavored gelatin**
¾ **cup boiling water**
4 **ice cubes**
3½ **cups fresh strawberries**
10 **ready-to-use individual graham cracker tart shells**

1. Stir the gelatin into the boiling water in a saucepan until the gelatin is completely dissolved. Remove from the heat. Stir in the ice cubes until melted. Pour into a medium-size bowl. Refrigerate until the mixture is slightly syrupy and partially set, for about 20 minutes.

2. Reserve 10 attractive large or 20 small berries for the top of the tartlets. Wash, dry and hull all the berries. Set aside the reserved whole berries; thinly slice the remaining berries. Combine the sliced berries with half of the gelatin mix; mix lightly to coat. Spoon the gelatin-coated slices into the tart shells.
3. If the reserved whole berries are large, quarter lengthwise and arrange 4 quarters on top of each tart. If the berries are small, halve lengthwise and arrange the halves on top of each tart. Spoon the remaining gelatin glaze over the berries. Refrigerate until set, for about 1 hour.

Nutty Baked Apples

Instead of a high-calorie cake or pie for dessert, serve these delectable baked apples. Warm or chilled, they're just the kind of light dessert that spells better nutrition.

Bake at 350° for 20 to 25 minutes.
Makes 8 servings.

Nutrient Value Per Serving: 176 calories, 1 gm. protein, 5 gm. fat, 1 mg. sodium, 0 mg. cholesterol.

8 **large baking apples**
4 **teaspoons lemon juice**
½ **cup broken walnuts**
8 **teaspoons honey**
 Ground cinnamon
½ **cup coffee- or vanilla-flavored yogurt (optional)**
 Ground nutmeg

1. Preheat the oven to moderate (350°).
2. Wash the apples. Remove the core of each from the stem end, leaving the other end closed. Pare 1 inch of the apple skin away from the stem end. Drizzle the lemon juice over the pared areas and in the cavities. Fill the cavities with the broken walnuts.

Add 1 teaspoon of the honey to each cavity. Sprinkle the tops lightly with the cinnamon. Place the apples in a 13 x 9 x 2-inch baking pan.

3. Bake in the preheated moderate oven (350°) for 20 to 25 minutes or until fork-tender but firm. Remove from the oven. Chill until ready to serve. Warm the apples before serving, if you wish. Top each apple with a dollop of the yogurt, if you wish, and a light sprinkling of the nutmeg.

Summer-Light Cheesecake

Makes 12 servings.

Nutrient Value Per Serving: 94 calories, 11 gm. protein, 3 gm. fat, 97 mg. sodium, 53 mg. cholesterol.

1 **tablespoon diet margarine, at room temperature**
⅓ **cup graham cracker crumbs**
2 **envelopes unflavored gelatin**
⅓ **cup cold water**
2 **eggs, separated**
1 **cup skim milk**
1 **pound lowfat pot-style uncreamed cottage cheese**
   Artificial sweetener equivalent to 24 teaspoons sugar
1 **tablespoon grated orange rind**
⅛ **teaspoon salt**
1 **cup pressurized low-calorie or regular whipped cream**
Garnish (optional):
   Navel orange slices
   Fresh mint leaves
   Sugared grapes

1. Grease the bottom and sides of an 8-inch springform pan with the diet margarine. Reserve 2 tablespoons of the crumbs for the top of the cheesecake; sprinkle inside the pan with the remaining crumbs. Refrigerate for 1 hour or freeze for 20 minutes.

2. Sprinkle the gelatin over the cold water in a small bowl; set aside to soften, for 5 minutes.

3. Beat the yolks in the top of a double boiler until well combined. Stir in the milk. Cook over hot, not boiling, water, stirring constantly, until the mixture thickens and lightly coats the back of a spoon, for 8 to 10 minutes. Remove from the heat and stir in the gelatin mixture until the gelatin is completely dissolved.

4. Combine the cottage cheese, artificial sweetener and orange rind in the container of an electric blender or a food processor; whirl until the mixture forms a smooth purée.

5. Combine the egg yolks and cheese mixtures in a large bowl. Refrigerate until slightly thickened, for about 20 minutes.

6. Beat together the egg whites and salt in a medium-size bowl until stiff and glossy peaks form. Gently fold the whites into the chilled cheese mixture.

7. Fill a 1-cup measure with the pressurized whipped cream; fold into the cheese mixture. Spoon into the prepared pan. Refrigerate for 4 hours or until set.

8. To serve, remove the sides of the springform pan. Using the fingers, press the reserved 2 tablespoons of graham cracker crumbs around the outer edge of the cheesecake. If you wish, garnish the top with the orange slices, fresh mint leaves and grapes.

Brandied Raspberry Sauce

Other Desserts

▧ ◀◀ ▤
Brandied Raspberry Sauce

Delicious served over lemon sherbet or fresh peach ice cream.

Makes about 1⅔ cups.

Nutrient Value Per ⅓ Cup: 172 calories, 0 gm. protein, 0 gm. fat, 0 mg. sodium, 0 mg. cholesterol.

- 1 **package (12 ounces) frozen dry-pack whole raspberries OR: 3 cups fresh raspberries**
- ¾ **cup sugar**
- 2 **tablespoons cornstarch**
- ¼ **cup brandy, Grand Marnier or other orange-flavored liqueur**

1. Combine the raspberries and sugar in a medium-size saucepan.
2. Dissolve the cornstarch in the liqueur in a small bowl. Stir into the raspberries until well combined.
3. Cook over medium heat, stirring frequently, until the sauce thickens and bubbles, for about 5 minutes. Do not overcook.
4. Cool to room temperature. Store in a tightly covered container in the refrigerator.

▧ ◀◀ ▢
Gingered Pear and Lemon Sauce

Spruce up vanilla or chocolate ice cream with this thick, fruity sauce.

Makes about 2 cups.

Nutrient Value Per ¼ Cup: 87 calories, 0 gm. protein, 0 gm. fat, 1 mg. sodium, 0 mg. cholesterol.

- 3 **firm pears**
- 1 **cup water**
- ½ **cup sugar**
- ⅛ **teaspoon ground ginger**
- 2 **teaspoons grated lemon rind**
- 3 **tablespoons lemon juice**
- 1 **tablespoon cornstarch**

1. Peel, core and coarsely chop the pears. Combine the pears, water, sugar, ginger, lemon rind and 2 tablespoons of the lemon juice in a medium-size saucepan.

2. Cook over medium heat just until the pears are fork-tender, for 15 to 20 minutes. Let cool.
3. Purée the pear mixture through a food mill or in a food processor. Return to the saucepan.
4. Dissolve the cornstarch in the remaining tablespoon of lemon juice in a small bowl. Stir into the puréed pear mixture to blend.
5. Cook over medium heat, stirring frequently, just until the mixture thickens and bubbles, for about 5 minutes. Do not overcook.
6. Cool to room temperature. Store in a tightly covered container in the refrigerator.

▧ ◀◀
Spicy Blueberry Topping

This topping combines deliciously with lemon sherbet.

Makes about 2 cups.

Nutrient Value Per ¼ Cup: 75 calories, 0 gm. protein, 0 gm. fat, 2 mg. sodium, 0 mg. cholesterol.

- 1 **pint fresh blueberries**
- ½ **cup sugar**
- 1 **teaspoon ground cinnamon**
- ½ **teaspoon ground nutmeg**
- 1 **tablespoon cornstarch**
- ⅓ **cup orange juice**

1. Wash and stem the blueberries. Combine the blueberries, sugar, cinnamon and nutmeg in a medium-size saucepan.
2. Dissolve the cornstarch in the orange juice in a small bowl. Stir into the blueberry mixture until well combined.
3. Cook over medium heat, stirring, just until the mixture thickens and bubbles, for about 5 minutes. Do not overcook.
4. Cool to room temperature. Store in a tightly covered container in the refrigerator.

▧ ◀◀ ▤ ▢
Harlequin Pumpkin Mousse

Makes 10 servings.

Nutrient Value Per Serving: 354 calories, 4 gm. protein, 24 gm. fat, 148 mg. sodium, 74 mg. cholesterol.

- 2 **envelopes (2 tablespoons) unflavored gelatin**
- ½ **cup cold water**
- 1 **teaspoon grated orange rind**

☞

Harlequin Pumpkin Mousse

¾ cup orange juice
1 tablespoon lemon juice
1 teaspoon ground cinnamon
1 teaspoon ground ginger
¼ teaspoon ground nutmeg
1 tablespoon brandy
½ cup sugar
1 cup heavy cream
2 tablespoons 10X (confectioners') sugar
2 cups canned pumpkin purée
1 cup dairy sour cream
¾ cup glacé cherries and pineapple, cut into small pieces
2 squares (1 ounce each) semisweet chocolate
1 cup heavy cream, whipped, for garnish
  Candied orange rind for garnish (optional)

1. Lightly oil a 6-cup soufflé dish or other straight-sided round mold. Set aside.
2. Sprinkle the gelatin over the cold water in a small saucepan. Let stand to soften for about 5 minutes. Place over low heat and stir to dissolve the gelatin. Add the orange rind and juice, lemon juice, cinnamon, ginger and nutmeg; stir until blended. Remove from the heat; stir in the brandy and sugar. Chill for 8 to 10 minutes, stirring occasionally, until slightly syrupy.
3. Meanwhile, beat the heavy cream with the 10X sugar in a small bowl until stiff.
4. Combine the pumpkin purée and sour cream in a small bowl. Fold in the whipped cream and glacé fruits. Fold in the gelatin mixture until well blended. Pour into the prepared mold. Chill for several hours or until set, or overnight.
5. Line the bottom of a removable 7-inch tart pan or other 7-inch circle with wax paper.
6. Melt the chocolate in the top of a double boiler or in a small bowl over simmering water. Beat until shiny. Spread evenly over the lined circle. Refrigerate just until the chocolate begins to harden but is still pliable, for about 10 minutes. Cut the chocolate into 8 equal wedge-shaped triangles. Return to the refrigerator to set, for about 1 hour.
7. Run a thin-bladed knife around the side of the mousse. Dip the mold briefly in hot water. Invert onto a serving plate.
8. To garnish: Peel the wax paper from the triangles. Place a small dot of whipped cream in the center of each triangle. Gently press the triangles against the mousse along the outside, pointed-ends up and wide bases almost touching each other. Garnish the top with the candied orange rind, if you wish. Pipe whipped cream rosettes around the base and top edge.

Gelling Gelatin

An envelope of unflavored gelatin (1 tablespoon) will gel 2 cups of liquid.

> **When Beating Egg Whites...**
>
> For the best volume, egg whites should always be at room temperature when you beat them. Be sure not to let any yolk get into the whites; fat in the yolks will decrease the volume.

Lemon Mousse

Prepare this mousse a day or two ahead.

Makes 10 servings.

Nutrient Value Per Serving: 196 calories, 2 gm. protein, 10 gm. fat, 30 mg. sodium, 115 mg. cholesterol.

> **Grated rind of 2 large lemons (2 tablespoons)**
> **Juice of 2 large lemons (about 6 tablespoons)**
> 2 **eggs, separated**
> 1 **egg**
> 1 **cup plus 2 tablespoons sugar**
> 1 **cup heavy cream**
> **Garnish:**
> **Chocolate curls**
> **Strips of lemon zest**

1. Combine the lemon rind and juice, egg yolks, the 1 egg and ½ cup of the sugar in the top of a double boiler.
2. Cook over hot, not boiling, water, stirring constantly until thickened, for 8 to 10 minutes. Remove from the heat and transfer to a medium-size bowl. Cover and refrigerate for about 20 minutes or until cooled. (Or, to cool quickly, place in a large bowl of ice and water, stirring the lemon mixture frequently.)
3. Beat the egg whites in a small bowl until foamy-white. Beat in ½ cup of the sugar, a tablespoon at a time, until the meringue forms soft peaks.
4. Beat together the cream and the remaining 2 tablespoons of sugar in a small bowl until soft peaks form.
5. Gradually fold the whipped cream, then the meringue, into the cooled lemon mixture until no streaks of white remain. Pour into 10 individual dessert dishes or a 4- to 5-cup serving bowl. Freeze until firm, for about 4 hours or one or two days ahead.
6. Remove the mousse from the freezer to the refrigerator for about 15 to 30 minutes before serving, to allow the mousse to soften. To serve, garnish with the chocolate curls and lemon zest.

Indian Pudding

Bake individual ramekins at 325° for 45 minutes, or a baking dish for 1½ hours. Makes 10 servings.

Nutrient Value Per Serving: 226 calories, 5 gm. protein, 9 gm. fat, 213 mg. sodium, 54 mg. cholesterol.

> 4 **cups milk**
> ¼ **cup (½ stick) butter or margarine**
> ½ **cup yellow cornmeal**
> ½ **cup molasses**
> ¼ **cup sugar**
> 1 **medium-size apple, pared, cored and chopped (1 cup)**
> ½ **cup raisins**
> 4½ **teaspoons ground cinnamon**
> 1½ **teaspoons ground ginger**
> ½ **teaspoon salt**
> 1 **egg, slightly beaten**
> **Whipped cream (optional)**
> **Ground cinnamon (optional)**
> **Thin apple slices (optional)**

1. Preheat the oven to slow (325°). Grease 10 ramekins (3¼"-diameter with a ⅔-cup capacity) or a shallow 1½-quart baking dish.
2. Combine 2½ cups of the milk and the butter in a medium-size saucepan. Heat until the butter melts. Stir together ½ cup of the remaining milk and the cornmeal in a small bowl. Add to the saucepan. Bring to boiling. Lower the heat; simmer for 20 minutes or until the mixture thickens, stirring frequently so the mixture does not burn.
3. Stir the molasses, sugar, apple, raisins, cinnamon, ginger and salt into the saucepan. Stir a little of the hot milk mixture into the egg in a small bowl; return to the saucepan, stirring. Continue to cook, stirring frequently, for 5 minutes longer.
4. Spoon the pudding into the prepared ramekins or baking dish. Pour the remaining 1 cup of milk over the individual ramekins or baking dish; do not stir.
5. Bake in the preheated slow oven (325°) for 45 minutes for the ramekins or 1½ hours for the baking dish, or until the pudding is set. Serve warm. Garnish with the whipped cream, ground cinnamon and apple slices, if you wish.

Top: Frozen Coffee 'n' Cream (page 251), Tropical Refresher (page 253), Grapefruit Campari (page 251).

*Hot and cold drinks, cocktails,
punches—something for everyone
and every occasion.*

Whether it's a glass of milk to accompany a family dinner or an elegant cup of Cassis Punch Royale (page 250) served at a gala celebration, the right choice of beverage can make an occasion more enjoyable.

Who can resist a tall, frosty glass of Tropical Refresher (page 253) after a competitive game of tennis? Ice-cold and garnished with a slice of lemon and a sprig of mint, this fresh fruit thirst-quencher is bound to make your win more enjoyable (or your loss easier to take).

On a cold, wintry day, nothing can be more soothing than a steaming hot Claret Cup (page 254)! Served in earthenware mugs, this may be just what's needed to revive a group of après-skiers.

Selecting the right container can go a long way toward making a drink more special. The variety is endless—you can use footed, fluted and stemmed glasses; cups, mugs and steins; heat-resistant clear glass and wafer-thin bone china— the list goes on. Steaming, hot, frothy drinks team up perfectly with mugs or steins. Cold drinks served in glasses that have a frosty coating, or in glasses that are frosty from prechilling, certainly look all the more appetizing, and when drinks *look* this good, they even seem to *taste* better.

When you plan your next celebration, don't forget to give extra attention to beverages!

Punches

Simple Drink Garnishes

- Maraschino cherry
- Lemon/lime slice
- Halved orange slice
- Lemon/lime rind twist
- Orange rind twist
- Lemon/lime wedge
- Fresh mint sprig
- Fresh strawberry
- Peach slice
- Powdered 10X sugar
- Shaved chocolate
- Orange wedge
- Fresh stemmed cherry
- Seedless grape
- Fresh raspberry
- Melon chunk
- Banana chunk
- Toasted almond slices
- Cinnamon sugar
- Mandarin orange section
- Pineapple spear
- Coffee bean

Strawberry-Limon Punch

Makes thirty-six ½-cup servings.

Nutrient Value Per Serving: 72 calories, 0 gm. protein, 0 gm. fat, 1 mg. sodium, 0 mg. cholesterol.

- 2 **packages (10 ounces each) frozen strawberries, thawed**
- 1 **can (12 ounces) frozen lemonade concentrate, thawed**
- 1 **can (12 ounces) frozen limeade concentrate, thawed**
- 2 **tablespoons grenadine**
- 2 **bottles (1 liter each) ginger ale, chilled**
- 1 **bottle (1 liter) seltzer, chilled**
  Ice cubes
  Lemon and lime slices for garnish

1. Purée the strawberries in a blender or food processor until smooth. Pour into a large pitcher. Stir in the juice concentrates and grenadine. Refrigerate.
2. Just before serving, pour the strawberry mixture into a large punch bowl. Pour in the ginger ale and seltzer. Add the ice cubes. Garnish with the lemon and lime slices.

Golden Punch

This slightly sweet fruit punch will quickly quench your thirst. Double the recipe if you want extra drinks.

Makes six 8-ounce servings.

Nutrient Value Per Serving: 125 calories, 1 gm. protein, 0 gm. fat, 3 mg. sodium, 0 mg. cholesterol.

- 1 **quart orange juice**
- 2 **cans (6 ounces each) pineapple juice**
- 1 **can (6 ounces) apricot nectar**
- 2 **tablespoons honey (optional)**
- 3 **sprigs fresh mint, crushed**

1. A day ahead, combine the orange juice, pineapple juice and apricot nectar in a 2-quart container. Pour some of this mixture into an ice cube tray and freeze. Add the honey, if you wish, and the crushed mint to the remaining juice mixture. Stir to dissolve the honey. Refrigerate overnight.
2. To pack for a picnic, remove the mint and pour the juice into a 2-quart insulated picnic jug. Add the frozen punch cubes; stir.

Cassis Punch Royale

Makes about 24 servings.

Nutrient Value Per Serving: 91 calories, 0 gm. protein, 0 gm. fat, 5 mg. sodium, 0 mg. cholesterol.

- **Red and green grapes for ice block**
- ½ **cup Crème de Cassis (black currant liqueur)**
- 1 **bottle (750 ml.) white wine, chilled**
- 2 **bottles Champagne, chilled**
  Whole fresh or frozen strawberries (optional)

1. Prepare the ice block: Fill a fancy mold that will fit inside a punch bowl with ice cubes. Add cold water to almost fill. Arrange clusters of the grapes in the mold, half in the ice and water and half out. Place in the freezer until firm enough to unmold. Unmold, dipping in warm water to loosen, if necessary; be careful not to break the grapes. Return to the freezer until ready to use.
2. Just before serving, pour the Cassis and wine into the punch bowl. Add the ice block with the grapes on top. Slowly pour in the Champagne. Add a strawberry to each glass, if you wish.

To Make Ahead: Make the ice block several days ahead.

Cocktails

Frozen Coffee 'n' Cream

Makes 2 servings.

Nutrient Value Per Serving: 434 calories, 5 gm. protein, 14 gm. fat, 126 mg. sodium, 60 mg. cholesterol.

 1 **pint coffee ice cream**
 ½ **cup coffee-flavored liqueur**
    Club soda
    Chocolate curls (optional)

1. Prechill the container of an electric blender and 2 large glasses.
2. Make 2 small scoops of the ice cream; place on a cookie sheet in the freezer. Soften the remainder of the ice cream in the refrigerator for 15 minutes.
3. Combine the softened ice cream and liqueur in a blender. Cover; whirl until smooth. Pour into the chilled glasses. Add a splash of the club soda. Place a scoop of the ice cream in each glass and garnish with the chocolate curls, if you wish.

Grapefruit Campari

Makes 1 serving.

Nutrient Value Per Serving: 291 calories, 0 gm. protein, 0 gm. fat, 22 mg. sodium, 0 mg. cholesterol.

 1 **orange slice**
    Granulated sugar
    Ice cubes
 3 **ounces (6 tablespoons) Campari**
 3 **ounces (6 tablespoons) grapefruit juice**
    Club soda
    Half orange slice (optional)

1. Rub the rim of one tall 14-ounce glass with 1 orange slice. Dip the rim into the granulated sugar and place in the freezer for 1 hour.
2. Place several ice cubes in a chilled glass. Add the Campari and grapefruit juice. Fill the glass with the club soda; stir thoroughly. Garnish with the orange slice, if you wish.

Sunshine Delight

Makes 1 serving.

Nutrient Value Per Serving: 174 calories, 4 gm. protein, 1 gm. fat, 87 mg. sodium, 3 mg. cholesterol.

    Ice cubes
 ⅔ **cup orange juice**
 ⅓ **cup buttermilk**
 1 **ounce (2 tablespoons) vodka***
    Dash grenadine
 1 **orange slice (optional)**

1. Prechill one 14-ounce glass.
2. Place the ice cubes in a chilled glass. Combine the juice, buttermilk, vodka and grenadine; pour over the cubes in the glass. Garnish with the orange slice, if you wish.

To Make Ahead: Combine the juice, buttermilk, vodka and grenadine in a small bowl. Cover with plastic wrap and refrigerate. To serve, proceed as the recipe directs.

*** Note:** Omit the vodka, if you wish.

Kiwi Zest

Makes 1 serving (1 cup).

Nutrient Value Per Serving: 265 calories, 1 gm. protein, 0 gm. fat, 32 mg. sodium, 0 mg. cholesterol.

 1 **kiwi, peeled and chopped**
 1½ **ounces (3 tablespoons) gin**
 2 **tablespoons light corn syrup**
 1 **drop green food coloring (optional)**
 ¾ **cup crushed ice**
 ½ **teaspoon slivered orange peel**
    Kiwi slice (optional)

1. Prechill the container of an electric blender and one 8-ounce glass.
2. Combine the chopped kiwi, gin, corn syrup, food coloring, if using, and the crushed ice in the chilled container of the electric blender. Cover; whirl until smooth. Pour into the chilled glass. Garnish with the orange peel and kiwi slice, if you wish.

Cold Drinks

Lemonade Syrup

An easy-to-make flavor base for lemonade, an iced tea punch and a wine cooler.

Makes 3 cups syrup.

- 2 cups sugar
- 1 cup water
  Grated rind of 2 large lemons
    (2 tablespoons)
- 1 cup lemon juice (about 6 large lemons)

1. Combine the sugar and water in a small saucepan. Bring to boiling over moderate heat, stirring until the sugar is dissolved and the mixture is clear. Cover and boil for 2 minutes. Cool the syrup to room temperature.
2. Stir the grated rind and lemon juice into the cooled syrup. Pour into a 3-cup jar with a tight-fitting lid. Refrigerate and use as a flavoring base for the following drinks.

Lemonade: Combine ⅔ cup of club soda or cold water and 2 tablespoons of the syrup in a tall glass; stir to blend. Add ice cubes and garnish with fresh mint and lemon slices, if you wish. Makes 1 serving.
Nutrient Value Per Serving: 67 calories, 0 gm. protein, 0 gm. fat, 29 mg. sodium, 0 mg. cholesterol.

Wine Cooler: Combine ⅓ cup of dry white wine, ⅓ cup of club soda or tonic water and 2 tablespoons of the lemonade syrup in a tall glass; stir to blend. Add ice cubes. Makes 1 serving.
Nutrient Value Per Serving: 132 calories, 0 gm. protein, 0 gm. fat, 18 mg. sodium, 0 mg. cholesterol.

Tea and Lemon Punch: Prepare the punch following the directions for the Wine Cooler, but substituting cold tea for the wine. Makes 1 serving.
Nutrient Value Per Serving: 68 calories, 0 gm. protein, 0 gm. fat, 14 mg. sodium, 0 mg. cholesterol.

Banana-Cinnamon Shake

Makes 2 servings.

Nutrient Value Per Serving: 146 calories, 6 gm. protein, 2 gm. fat, 71 mg. sodium, 6 mg. cholesterol.

- ½ cup 1%-fat milk
- ½ cup lowfat plain yogurt
- 1 medium-size ripe banana, cut into chunks
- 4 ice cubes
- 1 tablespoon sugar
- 1 tablespoon vanilla
- ¼ teaspoon ground cinnamon

Combine the milk, yogurt, banana, ice cubes, sugar, vanilla and cinnamon in the container of an electric blender. Cover; whirl until thick and smooth. Divide between 2 glasses.

Blue, Blue Russian

Makes 4 servings.

Nutrient Value Per Serving: 142 calories, 1 gm. protein, 2 gm. fat, 8 mg. sodium, 4 mg. cholesterol.

- 1½ cups blueberries, fresh or frozen dry-pack
- ½ cup sugar
- 1 cup water
- ½ lemon, seeded
- 5 small cinnamon sticks
- 8 teaspoons dairy sour cream

1. Combine the blueberries, sugar, water, lemon and 1 cinnamon stick in a medium-size saucepan; stir to mix. Bring to boiling over medium-high heat. Lower the heat; simmer for 15 minutes. Remove from the heat and cool completely.
2. Remove the cinnamon stick. Pour the blueberry mixture into the container of an electric blender. Cover; whirl until smooth. Refrigerate until completely chilled. Also chill four 6-ounce glasses.
3. To serve, pour the chilled mixture into each of the 4 chilled glasses.* Swirl 2 teaspoons of the sour cream into each glass with a cinnamon stick.

Note: We especially like this drink with a splash of seltzer.

Tropical Refresher

Makes 2 servings.

Nutrient Value Per Serving: 65 calories, 1 gm. protein, 0 gm. fat, 3 mg. sodium, 0 mg. cholesterol.

- ½ **cup chopped fresh pineapple**
- ¼ **cup orange juice**
- ¼ **cup pineapple juice**
- ¼ **to ½ cup crushed ice**
- 1 **tablespoon lemon juice**
  Lemon-lime soda
- 2 **lemon slices for garnish**
  Fresh mint (optional)

1. Prechill the container of an electric blender and 2 glasses.
2. Combine the chopped pineapple, orange juice, pineapple juice, crushed ice and lemon juice in the chilled blender container. Cover; whirl until smooth.
3. Pour half of the juice mixture into each glass. Fill with the lemon-lime soda. Garnish each glass with a lemon slice and mint, if you wish.

Iced Tampa Tea

Makes 4 servings.

Nutrient Value Per Serving: 72 calories, 0 gm. protein, 0 gm. fat, 3 mg. sodium, 0 mg. cholesterol.

- 2 **cups chilled brewed tea**
- 1 **can (12 ounces) ginger ale**
- ½ **cup orange juice**
- ½ **cup cranberry juice**
- 4 **teaspoons lemon juice**
- 2 **teaspoons sugar**
  Ice cubes
- 4 **strawberries**

1. Prechill a 1½-quart pitcher and 4 glasses.
2. Combine the tea, ginger ale, orange juice, cranberry juice, lemon juice and sugar in the pitcher; stir thoroughly. Place several ice cubes in the chilled glasses. Pour equal amounts of tea into each. Garnish each glass with a strawberry.

Hot Drinks

Glögg

Makes 12 four-ounce servings.

Nutrient Value Per Serving: 264 calories, .26 gm. protein, .03 gm. fat, 4 mg. sodium, 0 mg. cholesterol.

- 1 **bottle (⅘ quart) dry red wine**
- ½ **cup seedless raisins**
  Rind of ½ orange, cut in strips
- 8 **whole cloves**
- 1 **half-piece stick cinnamon**
- 10 **cardamom seeds, coarsely broken**
- 1 **bottle (⅘ quart) aquavit**
- 10 **sugar cubes**
  Whole blanched almonds

1. Combine the wine and raisins in a large saucepan. Tie the orange rind, cloves, cinnamon and cardamom seeds in a double thickness of cheesecloth. Add to the saucepan; cover. Bring very slowly just to simmering; simmer for 15 minutes, but do not boil. Remove the spice bag.
2. Heat the aquavit slowly in a medium-size saucepan.
3. Place the sugar cubes in a large metal punch bowl. Pour about ½ cup of the hot aquavit over the top. Ignite with a long match; let stand until the sugar dissolves. Stir in the hot wine mixture, remaining aquavit and almonds. Serve in a heatproof punch glass.

Hot Herbed Tomato Juice

Makes 6 servings.

Nutrient Value Per Serving: 42 calories, 2 gm. protein, 0 gm. fat, 390 mg. sodium, 0 mg. cholesterol.

- 6 **small green onions**
- 2 **cans (18 ounces each) tomato juice**
- 2 **tablespoons lemon juice**
- 1 **tablespoon Worcestershire sauce**
- ½ **teaspoon dried dillweed, crumbled**
- ½ **teaspoon leaf chervil, crumbled**

1. Slice a 1- to 2-inch piece from the bulb end of the green onions. Chop the pieces; reserve. To curl the onion, make thin, ☞

lengthwise cuts through the top of the green ends, leaving enough stalk uncut so the onion doesn't separate.

2. Combine the tomato juice, lemon juice, Worcestershire, dillweed, chervil and chopped white portion of the onion in a medium-size saucepan. Bring to boiling.

3. Pour the tomato mixture into a blender or food processor fitted with a metal blade. Blend until smooth. Pour into heatproof glasses or mugs. Garnish with the onion curls.

Claret Cup

Warmed Burgundy wine is teamed with lemonade for a conversation starter.

Makes 6 servings.

Nutrient Value Per Serving: 154 calories, .16 gm. protein, .02 gm. fat, 6 mg. sodium, 0 mg. cholesterol.

    3 cups water
    1 tablespoon mixed pickling spices
    1 can (6 ounces) frozen concentrate for
         lemonade, thawed
    3 cups red Burgundy, heated (do not boil)
         Lemon slices
         Whole cloves

Combine the water and spices in a small saucepan; bring to boiling; lower the heat; simmer for 5 minutes; strain into a heatproof pitcher; stir in the lemonade and wine. Pour into mugs; float a lemon slice studded with cloves.

WINEGLASS SHAPES

The classic tulip-shaped wine glasses (above left) might be considered all-purpose; the smaller version (center) is traditionally for white wine. The little glass is for sherry. The fluted or tulip-shaped champagne glass (right) keeps the bubbly effervescent.

The Party Bar

How to Buy

Liquor and wine have gone metric. Here's a rundown on what's what.

Metric measure replaces:	U.S. measure
500 milliliter or ½ liter (16.9 oz.)	the pint
750 milliliter (25.4 oz.)	the fifth
one liter (33.8 oz.)	the quart
two liters (67.6 oz.)	the ½ gallon
four liters (135.2 oz.)	the gallon

How Much to Buy

Below is a chart indicating how many drinks you should get from bottles of liquor or wine. If serving wine with dinner, however, figure on fewer glasses to a bottle: 5 to 6 to a liter (quart); 3 to 4 to 750 milliliter (fifth).

	Number of drinks per bottle	
	one liter	750 milliliter
whiskey, gin, vodka (mixed drinks, highballs–1½-oz. servings)	22	17
table wines (red, white, rosé –4- to 5-oz. servings)	6-8	5-6
sherry (3-oz. servings)	11	8
cordials (1-oz. servings)	33	25
Champagne, sparkling wine (4- to 5-oz. servings)	6-8	5-6

Note: Keep in mind that people are drinking lighter these days. However, as a general rule, figure two drinks per person for the first two hours, one drink per person after that.

Good Inexpensive Wines: How to Choose and Serve

No doubt about it—there *are* some food and wine combinations that seem to bring out the best in both. That's why you'll find our match-up chart so handy. It lists suggestions for wines to accompany everything from appetizers to desserts. And the great thing about serving "good" wines is that "good" doesn't have to be expensive.

From Buying to Serving Wines

1. Always consume less expensive wines shortly after purchase.

2. When buying inexpensive wines, choose whites not more than two years old; three to four years is the cutoff for red wines.

3. Be sure corked bottles are stored on their sides to keep the cork moist.

4. If you can't decide *which* wine to buy, choose a bottle from a producer whose wines you have liked before.

5. Never buy more than one bottle of a wine that you're unfamiliar with. Try that bottle; buy more if you like it.

6. Refrigerate white and rosé wines only until chilled—for a few hours.

7. Chill light reds only slightly. Serve full-bodied reds at normal room temperature.

8. For a low-calorie before-dinner drink, try the new "light" wines. Or splash some soda into a glass of white, rosé or red wine for a refreshing, low-calorie spritzer.

9. Don't serve wine with very spicy foods like curry or chili—beer is better. If you're serving a vinegary salad with dinner, leave wine off your menu as well.

10. Cork any leftover wine tightly and refrigerate. Use up as soon as possible.

Food and Wine Go-togethers

Foods	Wine Description
Appetizers; hors d'oeuvres; egg dishes; delicate fish; plain chicken; mild cheese dishes; main-dish salads; Chinese food	Light to medium-bodied, fruity whites and rosé
Shellfish; oily fish; chicken in sauce; pasta; turkey; creamed dishes; main-dish salads; sandwiches	Full-bodied whites, rosés and light-bodied reds
Pork; ham; sausages; turkey; lamb; pasta	Medium-bodied dry reds
Hearty soups; pasta; roast beef; steaks; pot roast; venison; cheese	Full-bodied dry reds
Hamburgers; hot dogs; pizza; baked beans; casseroles	Anything you like or whatever wine is already open
Fruit salads; desserts; cakes	Semisweet or sweet whites and rosés

Fruit and Cream Brûlée (page 263), Mixed Vegetable Salad (page 70), Turkey in Chili-Mole Sauce (page 261).

*Favorite foods from around
the world—plus theme menus,
tips and more.*

T aco stands, sushi bars, Chinese take-out restaurants—judging by the multi-ethnic nature of the foods we're eating today, America is truly living up to its image as the world's melting pot. No longer limited to major cities, where there have always been large concentrations of people from different cultures, appreciation for the foods of other nations has been spreading rapidly throughout the country in recent years.

The skyrocketing interest in international cooking and eating has led many grocery stores and supermarkets to devote entire aisles to international products. And why not? When a meal becomes a journey to another world, it can often be as healthy as it is fun. Our ever-increasing awareness of good nutrition has prompted us to learn a great deal about healthier eating habits and preparation techniques practiced in many other countries. Studies of what people eat in countries where there are lower incidences of heart disease and cancer of the colon, for example, have led us to revise our own dietary guidelines. We now know it's better to eat a variety of foods, avoid too much saturated fat and cholesterol as well as sugar and salt, and to eat foods high in starch and fiber.

International cooking translates into fun entertaining. Imagine planning an evening around a specific country, with the entire menu devoted to its native dishes and with table appointments and decorations designed to carry out the theme!

Organizing and executing an international "gala," like planning any party, will require thought and consideration, so we've prepared a checklist of points to consider as you begin. (Look through the chapter for more party tips.)

1. Type of party—do you want a casual barbecue, a formal sit-down dinner, or something in between?

2. Number of guests—the larger the group, the more make-ahead recipes you'll want in your menu.

3. Seating arrangements and traffic—is your "eating area" large enough to accomodate the number of guests? Consider how traffic will flow.

4. Inventory check—do you have an adequate supply of utensils, plates, chairs, hangers, ice, etc.?

5. Party helpers—can you count on family or close friends to assist you at the bar or in the kitchen?

6. Repair check—have you fixed those loose chair legs, snags in the carpet and leaky faucets to prevent embarassing accidents at the party?

Remember to plan ahead to leave as few last-minute details as possible just before the party. That way, you'll be free to enjoy more time with your guests!

Chili-Cheese Rolls with Avocado Dip

MEXICAN PIÑATA SUMMER BUFFET
FOR 10 TO 12

Chili-Cheese Rolls with Avocado Dip, page 259
Corn Chips with Salsa, page 259
Mexican Corn Soup with Lemon, page 260
Honey, Avocado and Daikon Salad with Lemon Dressing, page 260
Turkey in Chili-Mole Sauce, page 261
Pork and Chick-Peas Mexicana, page 262
Rosy-Future Punch, page 262   Assorted Beers
Fruit and Cream Brûlée, page 263
Coffee   Tea

To add some merriment to your buffet, purchase several paper-mâché piñatas and suspend in safe areas. Provide sticks for your guests to break open and reap the rewards inside.

Note: When preparing the above menu for your Mexican Buffet, make the following adjustments:

1. Double the Salsa recipe.
2. Make the soup two times rather than doubling at one time.
3. Double the salad, the Pork and Chick-Peas Mexicana, and the Fruit and Cream Brûlée.

Avocado Turning Dark?

To prevent an avocado from turning dark after cutting, brush with lemon juice as soon as it's peeled or, if using a recipe including lemon juice, mash with the lemon juice before adding the remaining ingredients.

Chili-Cheese Rolls with Avocado Dip

Try the Avocado Dip with fresh vegetables or tortilla chips as dippers.

Makes 50 rolls.

Nutrient Value Per Serving: 70 calories, 3 gm. protein, 3 gm. fat, 28 mg. sodium, 13 mg. cholesterol.

- 50 **wonton skins (1-pound package)***
- 2 **egg whites, beaten with 1 tablespoon water**
- 8 **ounces Monterey Jack cheese, cut into ½ x ½ x ¼-inch cubes**
- ¾ **cup finely chopped, drained green chilies Vegetable oil for frying Avocado Dip (recipe follows)**

1. Place the wonton skins on a work surface with a point facing you. (Keep the remaining skins covered with plastic wrap while you work.) Brush lightly with the beaten egg white.
2. Place a cheese cube in the center of the wrapper; top with ¼ teaspoon of the chilies. Bring one corner up and over the filling; repeat with the adjacent corners, one at a time, pressing down the points firmly together over the filling. Roll into a neat package. Place on a cookie sheet; cover with plastic wrap to prevent drying. Repeat with

the remaining wonton wrappers, cheese cubes and chopped chilies.

3. Pour the oil into an electric skillet or deep saucepan to a depth of 3 inches. Heat to 375°. Deep-fry 8 rolls at a time for 30 seconds or until golden brown; keep the rolls submerged with a slotted spoon. Drain on paper toweling. Serve immediately with the Avocado Dip.

To Make Ahead: Prepare the recipe through Step 2. When ready to serve, proceed as the recipe directs. The Avocado Dip may also be prepared in advance. If preparing in advance, cover the surface with plastic wrap and refrigerate until ready to serve.

Avocado Dip: Combine 1 cup of mashed avocado, 1 finely chopped clove of garlic, 2 tablespoons of dairy sour cream, 2 tablespoons of yogurt, 1 teaspoon of lemon juice and ¼ teaspoon of pepper.

* Note: You can find wonton skins in the freezer or produce sections of your supermarket.

Salsa

Makes about 2 cups.

Nutrient Value Per Serving: 32 calories, .72 gm. protein, 2 gm. fat, 93 mg. sodium, 0 mg. cholesterol.

- 1 **can (1 pound) tomatoes, drained**
- 1 **medium-size onion, chopped (½ cup)**
- 2 **canned green chilies, seeded and chopped**
- 2 **tablespoons chopped parsley**
- 1 **tablespoon olive or vegetable oil**
- 1 **tablespoon white vinegar**

Break up the tomatoes with a spoon in a small bowl. Add the onion, green chilies, parsley, oil and vinegar; mix well. Chill for at least 1 hour.

Mexican Corn Soup with Lemon

A zesty blend of fresh corn, jalapeño peppers and chili powder in an egg-lemon broth that is sensational served hot or cold.

Makes 6 servings.

Nutrient Value Per Serving: 167 calories, 8 gm. protein, 9 gm. fat, 475 mg. sodium, 107 mg. cholesterol.

- 1   medium-size onion, chopped (½ cup)
- 1   clove garlic, finely chopped
- 2   tablespoons butter or margarine
- 2   cups fresh corn kernels OR: 1 package (10 ounces) frozen corn kernels, thawed and drained
- ½   to 1 teaspoon hot chili powder
- 3   cups chicken broth
- ½   to 1 teaspoon finely chopped canned or pickled jalapeño peppers
- 1   cup milk
- 2   eggs
- ¼   cup lemon juice (2 large lemons)
      Sour cream (optional)
      Chopped jalapeño peppers (optional)
      Strips of lemon zest

1. Sauté the onion and garlic in the butter in a medium-size saucepan until softened, for about 3 minutes; do not let brown. Stir in the corn and chili powder. Add the chicken broth. Bring to boiling. Lower the heat and simmer for 20 minutes.
2. Strain the soup into a large bowl. Place the solids along with the finely chopped jalapeño peppers in the container of an electric blender or food processor. Return the liquid to the saucepan. Whirl the blender until the mixture is coarsely smooth, for about 30 seconds. Return the puréed vegetables to the liquid in the saucepan. Stir in the milk until thoroughly combined. Bring to boiling; lower the heat.
3. Slightly beat together the eggs and lemon juice in a small bowl. Slowly stir in ½ cup of the hot soup. Stir back into the soup in the saucepan. Heat gently, stirring constantly, for 1 minute; do not let boil.
4. Ladle into warm soup bowls. Garnish with a dollop of the sour cream, the chopped jalapeño peppers, if you wish, and lemon zest.

MICROWAVE DIRECTIONS
650 Watt Variable Power Microwave Oven
Directions: Combine the onion, garlic and butter in a microwave-safe 2-quart casserole. Microwave, uncovered, at full power for 3 minutes. Add the corn, chili powder and 1 cup of the chicken broth. Cover. Microwave at full power for 10 minutes. Transfer the mixture to an electric blender. Add 1 cup of the remaining chicken broth. Whirl until puréed. Mix together the milk and eggs in the same casserole; stir in the puréed mixture, the remaining 1 cup of broth, jalapeño peppers and lemon juice. Cover. Microwave at full power for 10 minutes, stirring after 5 minutes. Serve as in the above recipe.

Jalapeño Pepper Hotline

Avoid touching face, eyes, nose, mouth or other sensitive areas when handling jalapeño peppers. The juice from these peppers will burn and sting, even several hours later.

Honeydew, Avocado and Daikon Salad with Lemon Dressing

Try as an appetizer or as part of a cold buffet. The dressing goes well with other fruit salads.

Makes 6 servings.

Nutrient Value Per Serving: 160 calories, 4 gm. protein, 10 gm. fat, 243 mg. sodium, 99 mg. cholesterol.

Lemon Dressing:
      Grated rind of 1 large lemon (1 tablespoon)
      Juice of 1 large lemon (about 3 tablespoons)
- 2   egg yolks
- 1   teaspoon sugar
- ½   teaspoon salt

⅛ teaspoon cayenne pepper
½ cup dairy sour cream
1 teaspoon Dijon-style mustard
3 cups honeydew melon strips (2 x ¼-inch)
   (about ½ medium-size)
2 cups daikon*, jicama*, cucumber, zucchini
   or summer squash strips (2 x ½-inch)
1 large or 2 small ripe avocados, pared and
   cut into 2 x ½-inch strips
12 cups shredded lettuces, including
   watercress or radish sprouts for extra bite
¼ cup total of chopped cilantro*, parsley and
   green onion

1. Prepare the Lemon Dressing: Combine the
   lemon rind and juice, egg yolks, sugar, salt
   and cayenne pepper in the top of a double
   boiler; mix until well blended. Cook over
   hot, not boiling, water, stirring constantly,
   until thickened, for about 2 to 3 minutes.
   Remove from the heat and transfer the
   mixture to a small bowl. Cover and
   refrigerate until cool, for 15 to 20 minutes.
   (Or, to cool quickly, place the bowl in a
   large bowl of ice and water, stirring the
   lemon mixture occasionally.) Fold in the
   sour cream and mustard. Refrigerate the
   dressing until ready to prepare the salad.
2. Combine the melon, daikon and avocado
   strips in a large bowl. Add half of the
   dressing; toss gently until well combined.
3. To serve, line a shallow serving bowl with
   the greens and mound the fruit-vegetable
   mixture in the center. Pour on the
   remaining dressing and sprinkle with the
   chopped parsley mixture.

* *Note:* Daikon is a long, mild-flavored white Japanese
radish. Jicama is a root vegetable with a crisp texture
resembling water chestnuts. Cilantro, or Chinese parsley,
is a pungent herb used in American Southwestern,
Mexican and Middle Eastern cooking. All can be found
in the produce section of your supermarket.

More Lemon Juice

For a larger juice yield from a lemon, roll the
lemon at room temperature on the counter
several times, using slight pressure from the
hand while rolling.

Turkey in Chili-Mole Sauce

*This variation of the popular Mexican mole (pronounced
mo-lay) sauce is flavored with chili powder, ground nuts
and semisweet chocolate. Prepare the dish 1 or 2 days
ahead, and the flavor will improve.*

Bake at 325° for 1 hour and 30 minutes.
Reheat at 350° for 45 to 60 minutes.
Makes 10 servings.

*Nutrient Value Per Serving: 574 calories, 70 gm. protein,
27 gm. fat, 585 mg. sodium, 175 mg. cholesterol.*

1 fresh or thawed frozen turkey (about
   10 pounds), cut up into 8 pieces
4 to 6 tablespoons vegetable oil
½ cup chopped onion (1 medium-size)
½ cup chopped carrot
½ cup chopped celery
2 teaspoons salt
4 cups water
2 to 3 tablespoons chili powder
2 medium-size onions, cut up
2 to 3 cloves garlic, coarsely chopped
1 can (1 pound) whole tomatoes, undrained
8 tortilla chips
½ teaspoon ground cinnamon
½ teaspoon ground coriander
¼ teaspoon anise seeds, crushed
½ cup finely ground toasted almonds
½ cup finely ground toasted walnuts
1½ squares (1 ounce each) semisweet chocolate
Garnish (optional):
   Red and green chili peppers
   Parsley

1. Preheat the oven to slow (325°).
2. Working in batches, brown the turkey pieces,
   on all sides in the oil in a large skillet.
   Transfer to a large, deep roasting pan.
3. Sauté the onion, carrot and celery in the same
   skillet until soft. Stir in the salt and water.
   Bring to boiling, scraping up the browned
   bits from the bottom and side of the skillet
   with a wooden spoon; pour over the turkey.
   Cover the roasting pan tightly with foil.
4. Bake the turkey in the preheated slow oven
   (325°) for 1 hour and 15 to 30 minutes or
   until tender.
5. Remove the turkey pieces to a platter; keep
   warm. Strain the broth through a large
   sieve into a large bowl; there should be at
   least 4 cups of broth. Discard the vegetables
   in the sieve.
6. Combine 1 cup of the hot broth with the
   chili powder in a small bowl. Reserve the ☞

3 other cups of broth.

7. Place the cut-up onions, garlic, tomatoes with their liquid, tortilla chips, cinnamon, coriander and anise seeds in the container of an electric blender or food processor. Cover; whirl until smooth.

8. Prepare the Mole Sauce: Skim 4 tablespoons of fat from the top of the turkey broth and place in a large saucepan or Dutch oven. Heat; stir in the chili powder mixture. Bring slowly to boiling, stirring constantly; cook for 2 minutes. Stir in the tomato sauce from the blender and the ground almonds and walnuts. Return to boiling. Lower the heat; cook, stirring often, for 5 minutes. Stir in the chocolate; cook, stirring, until the chocolate is melted and mixed into the sauce, for about 10 minutes. Add 2 cups of the remaining broth; cook for another 45 minutes, stirring often. Add additional broth if the sauce becomes too thick. Add salt to taste.

9. Meanwhile, remove and discard the large bones from the turkey. Cut the meat into small pieces. Arrange in a single layer in 1 or 2 shallow baking dishes. Spoon the mole sauce over. Let cool slightly. Cover; refrigerate for 1 to 2 days.

10. To reheat and serve: Reheat, loosely covered, in a preheated moderate oven (350°) for 45 to 60 minutes or until heated through. Garnish with the red and green chili peppers and parsley, if you wish.

Pork and Chick-Peas Mexicana

Begin your Mexican fiesta with guacamole and corn chips, and end with a platter of orange slices dusted with cinnamon sugar.

Makes 8 servings.

Nutrient Value Per Serving: 379 calories, 32 gm. protein, 16 gm. fat, 590 mg. sodium, 72 mg. cholesterol.

2   pounds boneless lean pork, cut into 1-inch cubes
¼   cup all-purpose flour for coating, or as needed
¼   cup olive or vegetable oil, or as needed
6   green onions, sliced
2   cloves garlic, finely chopped
1   can (16 ounces) whole tomatoes
1   can (15 ounces) tomato sauce
1   can (4 ounces) chopped green chilies
½   pound carrots (3 medium-size), sliced
2   teaspoons chili powder
½   teaspoon salt
½   teaspoon ground cumin
½   teaspoon leaf oregano, crumbled
¼   teaspoon ground coriander
¼   teaspoon pepper
1   pound zucchini, trimmed and sliced
1   can (20 ounces) chick-peas, drained

1. Pat the pork dry with paper toweling. Coat the pork with the flour, shaking off the excess.

2. Heat about 2 tablespoons of the oil in a large flameproof casserole. Brown the meat in batches, adding more oil as necessary. As the meat browns, remove to a plate.

3. Sauté the green onions and garlic in the fat remaining in the casserole until tender but not browned, for about 3 minutes.

4. Add the tomatoes, breaking up with a wooden spoon, the tomato sauce, chilies, carrots, chili powder, salt, cumin, oregano, coriander, pepper and reserved pork; scrape up any browned bits from the bottom of the casserole with a wooden spoon. Bring to boiling. Lower the heat; cover; simmer for 1 hour.

5. Add the zucchini and chick-peas. Cover; simmer for 15 minutes or until the meat is tender and the mixture is heated through.

Rosy-Future Punch

A few sips of this punch, and the day will be instantly sunny.

Makes 20 servings.

Nutrient Value Per Serving: 224 calories, 0 gm. protein, 0 gm. fat, 14 mg. sodium, 0 mg. cholesterol.

½   cup 10X (confectioners') sugar
1½ cups tequila
¾   cup orange-flavored liqueur
¼   cup lemon juice
1   pint strawberries OR: 1 package (12 ounces) frozen dry-pack strawberries, crushed
1   quart frozen lemon ice or lemon sherbet
3   bottles (750 ml. each) dry white wine, chilled
1   bottle (28 ounces) club soda, chilled
    Fresh mint (optional)
    Strawberries (optional)

1. Combine the 10X (confectioners') sugar, tequila, liqueur and lemon juice in a bowl; stir until the sugar is dissolved. Add the strawberries. Refrigerate for 3 hours to allow the flavors to blend.
2. To serve, pour the strawberry mixture into a 7½- to 8-quart punch bowl; mix well. Add the lemon ice. Pour in the wine and club soda. Garnish with the mint and strawberries, if you wish.

Ripening Pineapples

Pinapples do not ripen after they are picked, so don't buy them if they are underripe and expect them to ripen when you get them home.

◁◁ ⍻ ◻

Fruit and Cream Brûlée

A festive fruit dessert topped with sour cream and caramelized sugar.

Makes 8 servings.

Nutrient Value Per Serving: 319 calories, 2 gm. protein, 11 gm. fat, 38 mg. sodium, 21 mg. cholesterol.

1 **small pineapple, peeled, quartered, cored and sliced**
1 **pound red and green seedless grapes**
¼ **cup rum**
1¼ **cups firmly packed brown sugar
    Butter or margarine for greasing cookie sheet**
1 **container (16 ounces) dairy sour cream
    Red and green grapes (optional)**

1. Place the pineapple slices and grapes in a large bowl. Sprinkle with the rum and ¼ cup of the brown sugar; toss the fruit gently to coat. Cover; chill for several hours.
2. Butter a cookie sheet. Force 1 cup of the brown sugar through a sieve onto the cookie sheet in a layer ¼ inch thick.
3. Broil the sugar 4 inches from the heat until it is almost melted and forms a lacy pattern, for 1 to 2 minutes. Watch carefully to prevent overbrowning. Cool on a wire rack.
4. To serve: Turn the fruit into a serving bowl. Spoon the sour cream evenly over the top. Just before serving, carefully break the sugar topping into large pieces; place on the sour cream. Garnish with the grapes, if you wish.

Glossary of Mexican Terms

Burrito: A rolled flour tortilla filled with meat and cheese.
Ceviche: Raw marinated fish (usually scallops) served with lime juice and coriander (cilantro).
Chiles rellenos: Cheese-stuffed chili peppers.
Chimichanga: A deep-fried large flour tortilla "package" stuffed with various fillings.
Enchiladas: Corn tortillas filled with a variety of ingredients, baked and served with a sauce of tomatoes, cheese, guacamole and other seasonings.
Flan: Caramel custard.
Flautas: Little tubes of tortillas filled, rolled and fried.
Frijoles: Beans.
Huevos Rancheros: "Ranch-style eggs" of tortillas and eggs, usually served with tomatoes and chili sauce.
Margarita: A combination of tequila, orange-flavored liqueur and lime juice in a glass whose rim has been salted.
Mole: A creamy sauce usually made with deep, dark unsweetened chocolate, frequently served with chicken.
Quesadillas: Crescent-shaped totillas topped with cheese and baked.
Taco: A corn tortilla folded almost in half and fried crisp; stuffed with meat, cheese and shredded lettuce on top.
Tamales: Another form of corn flour, or masa, that's mixed with water and lard or shortening to form a light and fluffy dough. The dough is spread on softened corn husks, topped with filling and more dough, to cover the filling, and they are steamed until the tamale pulls away from the corn husk. These can be wrapped in aluminum foil and refrigerated.
Tequila: A strong alcohol made from the agave root which is the basis for the margarita.
Tortillas: The basic thin pancake-like bread made from cornmeal or flour.
Corn Tortillas: Made with masa, or instant corn flour, that is mixed with warm water to make a soft dough. The dough is shaped into balls, then flattened with a tortilla press. The flattened tortilla is placed on a hot griddle and cooked until bubbles appear on top, then turned and cooked on the second side.
Flour Tortillas: Made with wheat flour, shortening and water, mixed with the fingers to form a soft dough, then rolled out with a rolling pin and cooked on a griddle.

CHINESE NEW YEAR CELEBRATION
FOR 4

Twice-Cooked Sweet and Sour Spareribs, page 264 (halve the recipe)

Egg Drop Soup, page 264

Chinese Duckling, page 265

Steamed Rice   Stir-Fried Broccoli with Oyster Sauce*

Mandarin Salad, page 266

Orange Sherbet   Fortune Cookies

Green Tea

Provide each of your guests with an inexpensive set of chopsticks and encourage each person to attempt to use them even if they've never tried them before.

*Oyster sauce may be found in oriental markets or the gourmet section of your grocery store. If unable to find oyster sauce, omit and serve stir-fried broccoli.

Egg Drop Soup

Twice-Cooked Sweet and Sour Spareribs

Makes 4 servings.

Nutrient Value Per Serving: 794 calories, 30 gm. protein, 63 gm. fat, 902 mg. sodium, 120 mg. cholesterol.

- **1 rack spareribs (about 3 pounds)**
- **¼ cup white vinegar**
- **¼ cup catsup**
- **¼ cup sugar**
- **2 tablespoons soy sauce**
- **2 tablespoons water**
- **2 teaspoons cornstarch**
- **3 tablespoons peanut or vegetable oil**
- **2 medium-size onions, thinly sliced**
- **2 medium-size sweet green peppers, halved, seeded and cut into thin strips**
- **1 clove garlic, finely chopped**

1. Ask your butcher to cut a rack of spareribs into individual ribs and saw crosswise into 1½-inch pieces.
2. Drop the ribs into 4 quarts of boiling water. Lower the heat; simmer for 30 minutes. Drain. Dry with paper toweling.
3. Combine the vinegar, catsup, sugar, soy sauce, water and cornstarch in a bowl. Reserve.
4. Heat the oil in a wok or large skillet. Add the onions and green peppers; stir-fry for 2 minutes. Add the spareribs and garlic; stir-fry for 1 minute. Add the catsup sauce; cook for 2 minutes longer or until bubbly.

Egg Drop Soup

Try this famous Chinese soup as the first course for your next dinner party.

Makes 6 servings.

Nutrient Value Per Serving: 51 calories, 4 gm. protein, 2 gm. fat, 739 mg. sodium, 91 mg. cholesterol.

4 cups chicken broth
4 green onions, sliced
1 bay leaf
2 eggs
1 tablespoon water
Green Onion Fans (recipe follows)

1. Bring the chicken broth, sliced green onions and bay leaf to boiling in a large saucepan. Lower the heat and simmer for 10 minutes.
2. Beat the eggs and water in a cup until well blended with a fork.
3. Bring the broth mixture to boiling; stir in the beaten egg, just until set. Remove from the heat.
4. Ladle into soup bowls and garnish with the Green Onion Fans.

Green Onion Fans: Makes 6 servings. Trim 6 green onions and cut to a 6-inch length from the bottom. Cut lengthwise down the green leaves to separate into many pieces. Let stand in ice water until the green leaves curl.

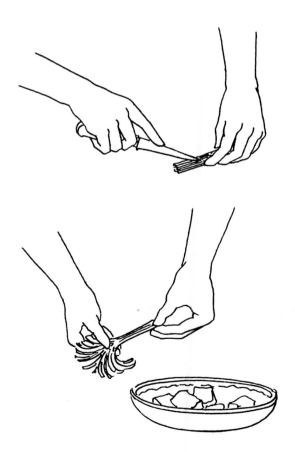

Chinese Duckling

Duckling is considered very special and is served mainly as a banquet dish in the northern province of Soochow, China. Prepared correctly, the duckling is so tender that no carving is necessary, only forks or chopsticks.

Roast at 350° for 1 hour.
Simmer for 2 hours longer.
Makes 4 servings.

Nutrient Value Per Serving: 678 calories, 35 gm. protein, 49 gm. fat, 723 mg. sodium, 145 mg. cholesterol.

1 frozen duckling, thawed (about 4 pounds)
2 eating oranges
4½ cups water
2 leeks, cut into 2-inch pieces
¼ cup mild soy sauce
½ cup dry sherry
2 tablespoons dark corn syrup

1. Preheat the oven to moderate (350°).
2. Remove the giblets from the duckling and use for making broth.
3. Remove the peel from the oranges with a sharp knife in one continuous spiral, cutting through and removing the white part and membrane around the orange meat; reserve. Cut the oranges in half; slice into ¼-inch slices.
4. Place the duckling on a rack in a roasting pan. (Add 2 cups of the water to the pan to catch the drippings and prevent the oven from smoking.)
5. Roast the duckling in the preheated moderate oven (350°) for 1 hour. Before removing from the oven, pierce the skin with the tines of a fork to let the fat run out.
6. Combine the leeks, soy sauce and sherry in a Dutch oven or large kettle. Place the duckling on top, breast-side up. Bring to boiling. Add the remaining 2½ cups of water; bring to boiling again. Lower the heat; cover; simmer for 1 hour, basting occasionally.
7. Roll up the orange spiral; stuff into the cavity. Pour the corn syrup over the duck. Continue cooking for 1 hour more, basting once with the pan juices.
8. Remove the cover; simmer for 10 minutes.
9. Place the duck on a platter. Arrange the orange slices around and over it. Keep warm. Simmer the juices remaining in the Dutch oven until thickened. Pour over the duck before serving.

Cutting a Duck for Serving

You also can use this method to cut Cornish hens or even small chickens.

1. Let the roasted duckling stand for at least 15 minutes. Cut with poultry scissors, starting at the opening and ending at the neck.

2. Turn the bird over and start cutting with the scissors on either side of the back bone to separate into halves.

3. Follow the natural line between the breast and thigh and cut into even quarters.

Duckling

Ducklings were first brought from China over 100 years ago by Long Island sea captains, and for many years, were grown commercially only on Long Island. However, today most come from the Midwest, and weigh between 4 and 6 pounds and are most often found frozen, but sometimes fresh. Since they are very fatty, do not stuff, except with onion, apple or orange wedges which should be discarded. Prick the skin well before roasting and continue pricking during the cooking. Allow about one-quarter to one-half duckling per person. To serve, cut into quarters with poultry or kitchen scissors.

Mandarin Salad

Chow mein (noodles) adds crunch to an Oriental-style salad.

Makes 6 servings.

Nutrient Value Per Serving: 199 calories, 3 gm. protein, 14 gm. fat, 272 mg. sodium, .9 mg. cholesterol.

1 head leaf lettuce, washed and chilled
  Curly endive, washed and chilled
1 can (11 ounces) mandarin orange segments
  Sliced water chestnuts
  Chow mein (noodles)
⅓ cup peanut or vegetable oil
1 teaspoon ground ginger
½ teaspoon salt

1. Break the lettuce into bite-size pieces and arrange in a salad bowl. Drain the mandarin oranges, reserving the syrup.
2. Add the mandarin orange segments and sliced water chestnuts to the salad bowl; arrange the noodles in the center of the salad greens.
3. Combine the oil, 3 tablespoons of the reserved mandarin orange syrup, the ginger and salt in a jar with a screw top; cover and shake well.
4. Drizzle the dressing over the salad and toss well, just before serving.

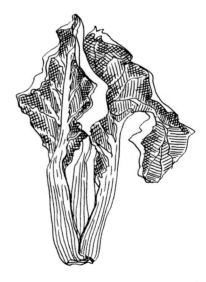

At a Sit-Down Dinner

- It's nice to serve the appetizer in the living room with cocktails.
- If you don't have someone to help you serve the meal, put the soup on the table just before the guests are seated, to make serving less complicated.
- Have a rolling cart or a tray nearby to make the removal of dishes easier.

Prepare in Advance

When you entertain, have the food prepared ahead whenever possible.

- Appetizers should be made and refrigerated, then reheated, if necessary.
- Most soups can be made and refrigerated, then reheated just before serving.
- Breads may be wrapped in aluminum foil, ready for warming.
- Make green salads (without the dressing) 1 or 2 hours ahead and refrigerate in a plastic bag or a glass bowl, covered with plastic wrap. Add the dressing just before serving.
- Prepare as much of the entrée ahead as possible. Have the ingredients and implements ready to use for any last-minute sauces or other cooking.
- The dessert should be made ahead, ready to be served.

Glossary of Chinese Terms

Bird's Nest Soup: Made from a bird's nest and coated with a gelatinous substance after cleaning and soaking. It's edible cooked in a soup, with stuffing for fowl or cooked with sugar in a dessert.

Chop Suey: American concept of Chinese food, usually prepared with water chestnuts, bamboo shoots, bean sprouts, soy sauce and rice.

Chow Mein: Similar concept as Chop Suey. A combination of ingredients available to the Chinese cooks in the American Old West who made do with what was available.

Egg Foo Yung: A non-Chinese scrambled egg and vegetable combination.

Hot and Sour Soup (Suan La Lang): A rich, slightly thickened soup of mushrooms, pork, bean curd, vinegar and hot pepper.

Pupu Platter: Precooked appetizer tidbits that need to be reheated over a flame.

Shark's Fin Soup: A lightly thickened soup made from shredded shark's fin.

Shrimp Balls: A minced shrimp and egg-white dish.

Tree or Cloud Ear: A small, ear-shaped, dried fungus possessing a delicate taste and crunchy texture.

Tofu: Bean curd (produced by cooking and puréeing soybeans until smooth). The bland custardlike mixture is formed into small cakes for frying or boiling. Eaten as a vegetable or used in soups and meat dishes.

Wonton: A noodle dough filled with a mixture of finely chopped meat, fish or vegetables and folded into triangles. May be served fried, steamed or boiled in a soup.

QUEEN'S BIRTHDAY PARTY
FOR 6

Fresh Vegetable Tray with Dip, page 268
Lightly Curried Deviled Eggs, page 269
British Oyster Bake, page 271
Mixed Green Salad with Vinaigrette Dressing
Whipped Potatoes with Parsley, page 271
Oven-Baked Carrots, page 271
Herbed Baked Puffs, page 272   *Butter*
Lemon Curd Charlotte with Blueberry Topping, page 272
Coffee   Tea

Just for fun, place at each setting small, individual drawstring bags made from elegant deep purple fabric, such as satin or velveteen, and containing inexpensive costume jewelry.

For More Colorful and Tender Fresh Vegetables for Dipping

To bring out the color and slightly tenderize the dipping vegetables, separately immerse the broccoli, cauliflower and carrots in boiling water for 2 to 3 minutes. Repeat with the zucchini and yellow squash for about 1 to 2 minutes. Plunge immediately into ice water. When cooled, drain thoroughly, store separately in plastic bags and refrigerate until ready to serve.

Fresh Vegetable Tray with Dip

This fresh vegetable appetizer is always a party favorite. Prepare the vegetables and dip ahead.

Makes 12 appetizer servings.

Nutrient Value Per Serving: 239 calories, 7 gm. protein, 16 gm. fat, 528 mg. sodium, 33 mg. cholesterol.

1 *medium-size head broccoli, divided into flowerets (stalks reserved for another use)*
1 *medium-size head cauliflower, divided into flowerets (stalks reserved for another use)*
6 *medium-size carrots, pared and cut into 2 x 1-inch sticks*
2 *large zucchini, diagonally cut into ¼-inch-thick slices*
2 *large yellow squash, diagonally cut into ¼-inch-thick slices*
1 *large sweet green pepper, halved, seeded and cut into ¼-inch-wide strips*
1 *pint cherry tomatoes*
2 *containers (16 ounces each) dairy sour cream*
2 *packages (1 ounce each) buttermilk salad dressing mix*

Arrange the vegetables attractively on a large platter. Combine the sour cream and salad dressing mix in a serving bowl. Use the vegetables as dippers.

Dramatic Presentation

The vivid colors of freshly prepared vegetables make an attractive presentation. Mason jars, unusual cut-glass bowls and antique crocks all make interesting containers for fresh crudité or marinated vegetables. Offer fresh raw vegetables in a clay flowerpot or in a basket lined with fresh lettuce leaves. Use raw vegetables also for a dip container— hollow out cabbages, tomatoes, peppers, fill with dip and surround with fresh vegetables.

> **To Hard-Cook Eggs**
>
> Place the eggs in a saucepan and add cold water to cover the eggs by about 1 inch. Bring rapidly to boiling, cover, remove from the heat and let stand for 15 minutes. Drain and rinse under cold running water until the eggs are cold. Crack the shells on the countertop for easy peeling.

Lightly Curried Deviled Eggs

Prepare the filling ahead and refrigerate the filling and hard-cooked whites separately in covered containers. Fill the whites just before serving to prevent drying out.

Makes 24 halves.

Nutrient Value Per Half: 68 calories, 3 gm. protein, 6 gm. fat, 153 mg. sodium, 139 mg. cholesterol.

12 *hard-cooked eggs, well chilled*
 1 *tablespoon drained sweet pickle relish*
 1 *teaspoon dry mustard*
 1 *tablespoon salt (or to taste)*
 ¼ *teaspoon pepper*
 ¼ *teaspoon curry powder*
 ⅓ *to ½ cup mayonnaise or salad dressing*
     Chopped pimiento and parsley sprigs for garnish (optional)

1. Peel the hard-cooked eggs. Cut the eggs in half lengthwise. Carefully remove the yolks from the whites, without breaking the whites. Refrigerate the whites in a tightly covered container.
2. Mash the yolks in a small bowl. Stir in the pickle relish, dry mustard, salt, pepper, curry and mayonnaise until well blended. Cover and refrigerate.
3. To serve, spoon the filling into the hollows in the egg whites. Garnish with the pimiento and tiny sprigs of parsley, if you wish.

Party Garnishes

Finishing touches for salads:
- Green onion fans
- Sliced stuffed green olives
- Halved pitted ripe olives
- Tinted pineapple slices
- Crescent-shaped celery
- Fresh dill sprigs
- Peach slices
- Orange sections
  (More ideas for garnishes below and on next page.)

GORGEOUS GARNISHES

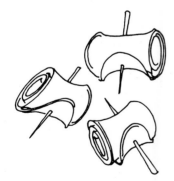

Carrot Curls: Pare carrots; curl long thin, shavings with a vegetable parer or knife; roll them up and fasten with wooden toothpicks.
- This technique can also be used with limp cooked bacon, rolled and fastened with picks. Try it on chocolate by making long strokes with a parer; decorate cake and pies.

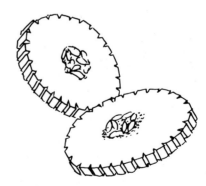

Cucumber Cartwheels: Wash cucumbers and slice thin (do not pare). Serrate the edges of the slice all around with a paring knife.
- This technique can also be used on lemons, limes, oranges, zucchini, squash and carrots.
- Use in a poultry plate, seafood, salads and beverages.

MORE GORGEOUS GARNISHES

Fluted or Turned Mushrooms: Use medium-size mushrooms and cut off stems close to the caps. With a knife, mark the center of each cap. Starting there, make a carved cut about ⅛ inch deep to the edge. Repeat around the cap to make 8 evenly spaced cuts. Make a second carved cut just behind each line, slanting the knife slightly so you can lift out a narrow strip, as shown. Brown the caps in butter.
- Use in steak platters, poultry and seafood.

Radish Roses: Make four evenly spaced cuts from the tip almost to the stem on the radishes. Place the radishes in ice water. The petals will spread.
- Use in salads and meat platters.
- Try also a radish fan by following the directions for Strawberry Fans, leaving a little greenery on and placing in cold water.

Strawberry Fans: Make four lengthwise cuts from the top of a berry to about ¼ inch from the bottom. Spread the slices to form a fan. Leaving the green on the berry gives it a special effect.
- Use in salads, desserts and gelatins.
- This technique can also be used on plum tomatoes, pickles, zucchini chunks and yellow squash.

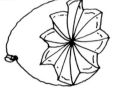 

Lemon Twists: Slice lemons with a knife. Mark the center of each slice and make a cut to the end. Twist with the fingers.
- This technique can also be used on limes, tomatoes and oranges.
- Use for fish and seafood plates and beverages.

Vandyked Lemons: Make deep right-angled cuts at the center of a lemon with a small, sharp paring knife. Continue until the entire lemon is cut. Pull apart.
- Use as garnish on large meat or fish platters.
- This technique can also be used on limes or oranges.

Pepper Cups: Wash red, yellow or green peppers, core and seed. Leave the edges plain or serrate for a different effect. Fill with favorite dips, toppings or salad dressings.
- This technique can also be used on tomatoes, melons, hard-cooked egg whites and oranges.

Garnishing Tips
- Appearance is a first when it comes to serving your meals. Serve molds, slaws, cheese mixes or stuffed fruits and vegetables on a bed of curly dark greens.
- Sprinkle the servings with paprika, grated cheese, chopped nuts or parsley; or green sprigs such as chives, parsley, mint, dill weed and watercress tied with a pimiento strip or a colorful thin ribbon.

British Oyster Bake

Bake at 350° for 30 minutes.
Makes 6 servings.

*Nutrient Value Per Serving: 384 calories, 19 gm. protein,
22 gm. fat, 701 mg. sodium, 127 mg. cholesterol.*

- 4 **cans (8 ounces each) oysters OR: 2 pints fresh oysters**
- 1 **cup light cream or half and half (half cream, half milk)**
- ¼ **cup (½ stick) butter or margarine**
- 1 **small onion, chopped (¼ cup)**
- 1 **package (5 ounces) oyster crackers, crushed**
- ¼ **cup chopped parsley**
- ½ **teaspoon salt**
- 1 **teaspoon Worcestershire sauce Dash liquid red-pepper seasoning**
- 1 **package (10 ounces) frozen peas, cooked and drained Paprika**

1. Drain the liquid from the oysters; measure ½ cup. Combine with the light cream in a 2-cup measure.
2. Preheat the oven to moderate (350°).
3. Melt the butter or margarine in a medium saucepan; sauté the onion until transparent. Stir in the crushed oyster crackers, parsley and salt; mix.
4. Spread half the buttered crackers in a 6-cup shallow casserole; spoon the drained oysters over; cover with the remaining buttered crackers.
5. Stir the Worcestershire sauce and red-pepper seasoning into the cream mixture; pour over the crackers.
6. Bake in the preheated moderate oven (350°) for 30 minutes or until the top is golden; spoon the peas around the edge; sprinkle with the paprika before serving.

Whipped Potatoes with Parsley

Yogurt, skim milk and margarine replace the usual cream or milk and butter.

Makes 12 servings.

*Nutrient Value Per Serving: 101 calories, 3 gm. protein,
1 gm. fat, 14 mg. sodium, 1 mg. cholesterol.*

- 4 **pounds all-purpose potatoes, pared and halved if large**
- ½ **cup plain yogurt**
- ⅓ **cup skim milk, heated**
- ¼ **cup (½ stick) margarine, softened (optional)**
- ¼ **cup chopped parsley Chopped parsley (optional)**

1. Place the potatoes in a large saucepan. Add the water to a depth of 1 inch. Bring to boiling. Lower the heat; cover and simmer for 20 minutes or until the potatoes are fork-tender.
2. Drain the potatoes. Place in a large bowl. Add the yogurt, hot skim milk and softened margarine, if using, and chopped parsley. Beat until light and fluffy, adding more skim milk for a fluffier consistency, if you wish. Garnish with the additional chopped parsley, if you wish.

Oven-Baked Carrots

You'll keep all the vitamins when you cook vegetables this way.

Bake at 350° for 40 minutes.
Makes 6 servings.

*Nutrient Value Per Serving: 69 calories, .92 gm. protein,
4 gm. fat, 432 mg. sodium, 10 mg. cholesterol.*

- 1 **bag (1 pound) carrots, sliced**
- ½ **cup water**
- 1 **small onion, thinly sliced**
- 1 **clove garlic, finely chopped**
- 1 **teaspoon salt**
- 2 **tablespoons butter or margarine**

1. Preheat the oven to moderate (350°).
2. Combine the carrots, water, onion, garlic and salt in a 4-cup casserole; dot with the butter or margarine; cover.
3. Bake in the preheated moderate oven (350°) for 40 minutes or until crisp-tender.

Herbed Baked Puffs

Bake at 400° for 50 minutes.
Makes 8 large puffs.

Nutrient Value Per Serving: 201 calories, 5 gm. protein, 15 gm. fat, 188 mg. sodium, 168 mg. cholesterol.

- **1 cup water**
- **½ cup (1 stick) butter or margarine**
- **1 teaspoon dry mustard**
- **1 cup unsifted all-purpose flour**
- **4 eggs**
- **⅓ cup chopped parsley**
- **¼ cup chopped green onion**
- **⅛ teaspoon salt**
- **⅛ teaspoon pepper**

1. Preheat the oven to hot (400°).
2. Combine the water, butter and mustard in a large saucepan. Bring to a rolling boil.
3. Add the flour all at once. Stir vigorously with a wooden spoon until the mixture forms a thick ball that leaves the sides of the pan clean. Remove from the heat. Let stand for 5 minutes.
4. Add the eggs, one at a time, beating well after each addition, until the paste is smooth and shiny. Beat in the parsley, green onion, salt and pepper.
5. Using about ⅓ cup of the paste for each puff, place eight puffs, 2 inches apart, on an ungreased baking sheet. Smooth out any points with a finger dipped in cold water.
6. Bake the puffs in the preheated hot oven (400°) for 40 minutes or until puffed and golden. Without removing the puffs from the oven, carefully make a 1-inch slit inside each puff with a small knife. Continue baking for 10 minutes until deep golden and very firm. Remove with a metal spatula to a wire rack to cool completely.
7. Slice off the tops of the puffs. Remove any soft dough from the inside and discard. Place the puffs in an airtight container and freeze.
8. To serve, place on a baking sheet and heat the frozen puffs in a preheated moderate oven (375°) for about 6 minutes or until thawed, dry and firm.

Lemon Curd Charlotte with Blueberry Topping

Bake at 375° for 12 minutes.
Makes 8 servings.

Nutrient Value Per Serving: 712 calories, 12 gm. protein, 41 gm. fat, 366 mg. sodium, 426 mg. cholesterol.

- **1 cup sifted cake flour**
- **1 teaspoon baking powder**
- **¼ teaspoon salt**
- **9 eggs**
- **1¾ cups sugar**
- **⅓ cup water**
- **1 teaspoon vanilla**
- **10X (confectioners') sugar**
- **½ cup (1 stick) butter, cut in small pieces**
- **2 teaspoons grated lemon rind**
- **⅓ cup plus ¼ cup lemon juice**
- **2 envelopes unflavored gelatin**
- **1½ cups plain yogurt**
- **2 cups heavy cream**
- **Blueberry Topping (recipe follows)**

1. Preheat the oven to moderate (350°).
2. Grease a 15 x 10 x 1-inch jelly-roll pan; line with wax paper; grease the paper.
3. Sift the flour, baking powder and salt onto the wax paper.
4. Beat 3 of the eggs in a bowl until very thick and creamy. Gradually add ¾ cup of the sugar, beating constantly until very thick. Stir in the water and vanilla. Gently fold in the dry ingredients until blended. Spread the batter evenly into the prepared pan.
5. Bake in the preheated moderate oven (375°) for 12 minutes or until the cake springs back when lightly touched with a fingertip. Remove from the oven. Dust a clean kitchen towel with the 10X sugar. Loosen the cake around the edges with a small spatula. Invert onto the towel. Peel off the paper. Roll up the cake with the towel from the short side. Place, seam-side down, on a wire rack to cool thoroughly.
6. Beat together the remaining 6 eggs, 1 cup of sugar, butter, lemon rind and the ⅓ cup of lemon juice in the top of a double boiler. Cook over hot, not boiling, water, stirring constantly, until the mixture thickens, for 15 minutes. Remove the lemon curd from the heat. Cool. Measure out 1 cup; set aside.

(Continues on page 274.)

Lemon Curd Charlotte with Blueberry Topping

7. Sprinkle the gelatin over the remaining ¼ cup of lemon juice in a small saucepan. Let soften for 3 minutes. Place over low heat; stir to dissolve the gelatin. Stir into the remaining curd, along with the yogurt; blend well.

8. Beat 1 cup of the heavy cream in a small bowl until stiff. Gently fold into the lemon curd-yogurt mixture. Refrigerate.

9. Unroll the cake. Spread evenly with the reserved 1 cup of curd. Reroll from the short side. Cut into 8 equal slices. Line the side of an 8-inch springform pan with the slices. Turn the curd mixture into the cake-lined pan. Smooth the top. Cover; refrigerate for 5 to 6 hours.

10. To serve, place the charlotte on a serving plate. Carefully remove the sides of the pan. Spoon some of the Blueberry Topping over the lemon curd filling. Pass the remainder. Beat the remaining 1 cup of cream until stiff. Pipe around the outer top edge and base. Garnish with mint and strips of lemon rind, if you wish.

To Make Ahead: Make the charlotte and topping the day before. Garnish with whipped cream before serving.

Blueberry Topping: Combine ⅓ cup of sugar, 1 tablespoon of cornstarch and ¼ cup of orange juice in a medium-size saucepan. Cook over medium heat, stirring constantly, for 2 to 3 minutes. Add 1 pint of fresh or frozen blueberries. Cook until the mixture thickens and clears, for about 5 minutes. Refrigerate until chilled.

Strawberry Topping Variation (as pictured on the cover of this book): Prepare the recipe as directed through Step 7. Cover and refrigerate the reserved lemon curd. Unroll the cake. Spread with one jar (12 ounces) strawberry preserves. Reroll from the short side. Cut the roll into 8 equal slices, wiping the knife with damp paper toweling after each cut. Line the side of an 8-inch springform pan with the slices. Turn the lemon mixture into the cake-lined pan. Smooth the top. Cover and refrigerate for 5 to 6 hours. To serve, place the charlotte on a serving plate. Carefully remove the sides of the pan. Beat the remaining 1 cup of cream until stiff. Spread a very thin layer of whipped cream over the top. Pipe the remaining cream around the outer edge and base. Fill the center and garnish the base with

hulled strawberries (about 1 pint). Garnish with mint and strips of lemon rind, if you wish. Serve with the reserved lemon curd as a sauce.

Nutrient Value Per Serving: 520 calories, 8 gm. protein, 28 gm. fat, 246 mg. sodium, 284 mg. cholesterol.

Glossary of British and Irish Terms

Bubble and Squeak: Fried cabbage and potatoes sometimes served over cold roast beef.
Colcannon: An Irish dish of cabbage and mashed potatoes.
Flummery: A molded dessert of egg yolks, lemon juice, brandy and wine.
Fool: Cooked puréed fruits in cream.
Kedgeree: An English fish dish made with curry and rice.
Kippers: Smoked, split herrings.
Plum Pudding: Raisins, other dried fruits, nuts, bread crumbs, beef suet, spices and eggs steamed in a pudding mold for 12 hours.
Shepherd's Pie: Ground meat and vegetables in gravy topped with mashed potatoes and browned in the oven.
Deep-Dish Steak-and-Kidney Pie: Just as it reads, with a crust pastry.
Toad-in-the-Hole: Fried sausages baked in Yorkshire pudding.
Trifle: Sponge cake, custard, cream and, often, sherry.
Welsh Rabbit (or Rarebit): Melted cheese, mustard, beer and/or milk mixed together and served on white toast.

BASTILLE DAY HOLIDAY
FOR 6

Potato and Leek Pâté, page 275

Endive and Caper Salad with Buttermilk Dressing, page 277

Chicken Provençale with Hot Cooked Rice, page 277

Ratatouille, page 280 (make the recipe twice)

Crusty French Bread   Butter

White Wine

Open Fresh Fruit Pie with Finnish Vanilla Sauce, page 280

Demitasse   Tea

Potato and Leek Pâté

Potato and Leek Pâté

Makes 8 servings.

Nutrient Value Per Serving (without dressing): 154 calories, 3 gm. protein, 8 gm. fat, 222 mg. sodium, 22 mg. cholesterol.

1½ **pounds russet baking potatoes**
½   **teaspoon salt**
2   **large leeks, washed and trimmed**
1   **envelope unflavored gelatin**
¼   **cup dry white wine**
⅓   **cup butter or margarine, melted**
⅓   **cup plain yogurt**
2   **green onions, sliced**
2   **tablespoons chopped chives**
¼   **teaspoon salt**
⅛   **teaspoon pepper**
     Curly lettuce (optional)
     Chives (optional)
     Pimiento Vinaigrette (recipe follows)

Creamy Celery Seed Dressing (recipe follows)

1. Scrub the potatoes and cook in boiling salted water to cover in a large saucepan just until easily pierced with a fork. Drain. Let cool. Peel. Press through a potato ricer or food mill. Set aside.
2. Trim the green stems from the leeks. Cut the white parts into ½-inch slices. Reserve. Cook the stems in a small amount of boiling water until soft and pliable, for 10 minutes. Drain. Cool.
3. Cut the green stems lengthwise on one side; open the stems flat in one piece. Line a greased 7⅜ x 3⅝ x 2¼-inch loaf pan with the stems; reserve some to cover the top.
4. Cook the reserved slices of the white part of the leeks in a small amount of boiling water in a saucepan until tender, for about 20 minutes. Drain. Chop finely. Stir into the potato.
5. Sprinkle the gelatin over the wine in a small saucepan. Let soften for 5 minutes; stir over low heat to dissolve the gelatin.
6. Add the gelatin, butter, yogurt, green onions, chives, salt and pepper to the potato; mix well. Turn into the prepared pan, smoothing the top. Cover with the reserved leek greens. Cover with plastic wrap. Chill for 5 to 6 hours or until firm.
7. To serve, remove the plastic wrap. Invert onto a cutting board. Cut the pâté into 8 equal slices. Place on individual plates. Garnish with the curly lettuce and chives, if you wish. Spoon the Pimiento Vinaigrette and Creamy Celery Seed Dressing on the plate on either side of the pâté.

Chicken Provençale

To Make Ahead: The pâté can be made up to 2 days ahead, the dressings a day ahead, and refrigerate tightly covered.

Pimiento Vinaigrette: Combine ½ cup of olive or vegetable oil, 1 tablespoon of lemon juice, 1 tablespoon of red wine vinegar, ½ teaspoon of dry mustard, 1 clove garlic, finely chopped, ½ teaspoon of leaf basil, crumbled, 1 jar (4 ounces) of chopped, drained pimiento, ¼ teaspoon of salt and ⅛ teaspoon of pepper in a jar with a lid. Cover; shake well. Makes 1 cup.
Nutrient Value Per 2 Tablespoons: 125 calories, 0 gm. protein, 14 gm. fat, 72 mg. sodium, 0 mg. cholesterol.

Creamy Celery Seed Dressing: Combine ⅓ cup of olive or vegetable oil, ⅓ cup of tarragon vinegar, 2 tablespoons of sugar, 1 tablespoon of whole celery seeds, ½ teaspoon of salt, ¼ teaspoon of pepper, 1 cup of plain yogurt and 1 cup of dairy sour cream in a bowl. Mix. Cover; refrigerate until ready to use. Makes 2⅔ cups.
Nutrient Value Per 2 Tablespoons: 65 calories, 1 gm. protein, 6 mg. fat, 63 mg. sodium, 6 mg. cholesterol.

Endive and Caper Salad with Buttermilk Dressing

Choose endive that are tightly closed and crisp; avoid those with brownish cut ends, as they can have a bitter taste. Buttermilk makes the dressing lowfat but flavorful.

Makes 8 servings.

Nutrient Value Per Serving: 22 calories, 2 gm. protein, 0 gm. fat, 97 mg. sodium, 1 mg. cholesterol.

4 Belgian endive
4 celery stalks, finely sliced
1 sweet red pepper, cored, seeded and coarsely diced
1 cup buttermilk
1 tablespoon snipped fresh dill
4 teaspoons drained capers

1. Wash and trim the endive; separate the outer leaves. Arrange a bed of outer leaves on a large serving plate or bowl.
2. Slice the remaining hearts of endive into ½-inch-thick pieces. Combine the endive, celery and diced pepper in a medium-size bowl. Spoon onto the endive leaves.
3. Combine the buttermilk and dill in a small bowl; spoon over the salad. Sprinkle with the drained capers.

To Make Ahead: The buttermilk dressing may be prepared the day before or several hours before and refrigerated for the flavor to develop.

Chicken Provençale

Makes 8 servings.

Nutrient Value Per Serving: 740 calories, 54 gm. protein, 41 gm. fat, 654 mg. sodium, 203 mg. cholesterol.

2 broiler-fryers (3½ pounds each), cut up
⅓ cup all-purpose flour for coating, or as needed
¼ cup olive or vegetable oil, or as needed
1 teaspoon salt
¼ teaspoon pepper
1 large onion, chopped (1 cup)
3 cups thickly sliced celery
2 cloves garlic, finely chopped
1 can (28 ounces) Italian-style plum tomatoes, coarsely chopped
1 cup dry white wine
2 teaspoons leaf thyme, crumbled
1 teaspoon fennel seeds, slightly crushed
2 bay leaves
   Pinch saffron (optional)
1 large navel orange
3 cups hot cooked rice

1. Wash the chicken. Pat dry with paper toweling. Coat lightly with the flour, shaking off the excess.
2. Heat 2 tablespoons of the oil in a large flameproof casserole. Brown the chicken in batches, adding more oil as necessary. As the chicken browns, transfer to a plate. Season with the salt and pepper.
3. Pour off all but 2 tablespoons of the fat from the casserole. Sauté the onion and celery in the casserole for 3 minutes. Add the garlic; sauté for 30 seconds.
4. Add the tomatoes, wine, thyme, fennel, bay leaves and saffron, if using; scrape up any browned bits from the bottom of the casserole with a wooden spoon. Return the chicken to the casserole.
5. Remove the outer rind (without the white pith) of the orange with a vegetable peeler. Add the rind to the casserole; reserve the peeled orange. Bring to boiling. Lower the heat; cover; simmer for 20 minutres or until the chicken is tender.
6. To serve, section the reserved peeled orange and arrange on top. Serve with the rice.

From top right: Fresh Apple Brûlées (page 235), Open Fresh Fruit Pie (page 280),
Poached Pears with Hot Caramel Sauce (page 234), Danish Apple Dessert (page 232).

Ratatouille

Makes 4 servings.

Nutrient Value Per Serving: 193 calories, 5 gm. protein, 11 gm. fat, 576 mg. sodium, 0 mg. cholesterol.

- 3 tablespoons vegetable oil
- 1 large onion, sliced
- 1 clove garlic, finely chopped
- 1 small zucchini, trimmed and cut into sticks
- 1 small yellow squash, trimmed and cut into sticks
- 1 small eggplant, cut into 1-inch pieces
- 1 large sweet green pepper, halved, seeded and cut into squares
- 1 large sweet red pepper, halved, seeded and cut into squares
- ½ pound mushrooms, sliced
- 1 can (1 pound) low-sodium tomatoes, drained and cut into quarters
- 1 teaspoon salt (or to taste)
- 1 teaspoon mixed Italian herbs, crumbled
- ¼ teaspoon pepper

1. Heat the oil in a large skillet or wok over high heat. Add the onion and garlic and stir-fry for 2 minutes. Add the zucchini, yellow squash, eggplant, peppers and mushrooms; stir-fry for 3 minutes or until the vegetables are shiny and bright.
2. Add the tomatoes, salt, Italian herbs and pepper; stir-fry, just to blend; cover the skillet or wok; reduce the heat to low.
3. Steam for 5 minutes or just until the vegetables are crisp-tender.

Open Fresh Fruit Pie

This dessert, which looks like a fresh fruit pizza, is a chance for the artistic cook to show off. To serve, cut in wedges and pass the Finnish Vanilla Sauce instead of whipped or heavy cream.

Bake crust at 450° for 7 minutes.
Makes 12 servings.

Nutrient Value Per Serving: 264 calories, 3 gm. protein, 11 gm. fat, 164 mg. sodium, 77 mg. cholesterol.

- 1½ cups packaged piecrust mix
- 1 egg yolk
- 1 tablespoon water
- ¾ cup apricot preserves
- 1 to 2 large pears, halved, cored and thinly sliced (2 cups)
- 4 large plums, halved, pitted and thinly sliced (2 cups)
- 1 tablespoon lemon juice
- ½ cup seeded red grapes
  Finnish Vanilla Sauce (recipe follows)

1. Preheat the oven to very hot (450°). Lightly grease a 12-inch pizza pan.
2. Prepare the piecrust, following the directions for a single-crust pie. Roll out the dough on a lightly floured surface into a circle 13 to 13½ inches in diameter. Gently fold the dough over into quarters to form a triangle. Transfer to the prepared pan. Unfold and gently press the dough into the pan so it fits evenly. Trim the edges, leaving a ½-inch overhang. Turn the overhang under to make a stand-up edge; flute. Prick holes all over the crust with a fork.
3. Beat together the egg yolk and water in a small bowl. Gently brush the egg wash over the fluted edge.
4. Bake the tart crust in the preheated very hot oven (450°) for 7 minutes or until lightly browned. Remove to a wire rack to cool.
5. Melt the preserves in a small saucepan over low heat. Force through a sieve with the back of a spoon into a small bowl. Brush the pastry with ¼ cup of the strained preserves.
6. Toss the pears and plums with the lemon juice in a large bowl until completely coated. Arrange the pear and plum slices, overlapping, in a circle around the outside edge of the tart. Arrange the grapes in the center.
7. Brush the fruits carefully with the remaining strained preserves. Refrigerate until chilled. Serve with the Finnish Vanilla Sauce.

Finnish Vanilla Sauce: Combine 2 cups of milk, 3 tablespoons of sugar, 2 egg yolks and 1 tablespoon of cornstarch in a medium-size heavy saucepan. Cook, stirring constantly, over medium-high heat until the mixture is thick and bubbly. Remove from the heat; continue to stir for about 1 minute. Stir in 1 teaspoon of vanilla. Cover the surface with plastic wrap and cool completely.

> ### Prevent Fruit Darkening
>
> To prevent cut fruits from darkening, pour a little lemon juice in a bowl or use a powdered fruit protector prepared according to the package directions; toss with the fruits.

Glossary of French Terms

Amandine: Made with almonds.

Béarnaise: A sauce of white wine, tarragon, vinegar and shallots cooked with egg yolk and butter.

Béchamel: A sauce consisting of butter, flour and milk, which is frequently the basis for other sauces.

Beurre Blanc: A light butter sauce flavored with shallots and vinegar.

Bisque: A shellfish soup seasoned with paprika and red pepper.

Blanquette de Veau: Boiled veal with mushrooms, white onions and a white sauce.

Boeuf à la Bourguignonne: Beef cooked with red wine and herbs and garnished with vegetables.

Bordelaise: A sauce of red wine, brown stock, shallots, tomato sauce and herbs.

Bouillabaisse: A stew made of various fish, tomatoes, saffron and other seasonings.

Brioche: A rich egg-yeast pastry shaped like a muffin with a top knob.

Canard: Duck, served with a varitety of sauces, usually orange, cassis or peppercorns.

Champignon: Mushroom.

Chateaubriand: The French version of porterhouse steak, containing the T-bone and part of the tenderloin.

Consommé: Clear broth made of meat or poultry, to which may be added julienne vegetables, truffles or bits of meat.

Coquilles Saint-Jacques: Scallops, usually served in a creamy sauce with mushrooms.

Coulibiac de Saumon: Salmon with flavored rice enrobed in brioche dough.

Crème: Cream.

Crème Fraiche: A thick, rich, slightly sour cream.

Dijonnaise: A mustard sauce.

Escargots: Snails, usually served with garlic butter and parsley.

Foie Gras: The liver of a fattened goose or duck.

Glacé: Frozen or iced.

Grillade: Grilled meat.

Madrilene: Consommé with tomatoes.

Marrons: Chestnuts.

Meunière: Sole or other fish which is floured, sautéed in butter, and served with the sautéed butter sauce and lemon wedge.

Mornay: A béchamel sauce thickened with Parmesan cheese.

Mousseline: Hollandaise sauce containing whipped cream.

Pêches Melba: Peaches with vanilla ice cream and raspberry sauce, named after opera singer Nellie Melba by Escoffier.

Poires Belle Hélène: Poached pears in syrup, served with vanilla ice cream and chocolate sauce.

Pois: Peas.

Pommes: Apples.

Pommes de Terre: Potatoes.

Ratatouille: A mixture of eggplant, sweet green peppers, tomatoes, zucchini, onions and garlic served hot or cold.

Sabayon: French style of zabaglione containing whipped egg yolks, wine and sugar.

Steak au Poivre: Steak cooked with a black, green, white or red peppercorn crust.

Steak Tartare: A combination of raw, ground beef, capers and onions.

Vacherin: Dessert of meringue shell filled with fruit in whipped cream.

Veloute: A basic white sauce of flour cooked with butter and bouillon.

Vichyssoise: A cold leek and potato soup named after the chef's hometown.

Vinaigrette: A simple salad dressing of oil, vinegar and, frequently, mustard.

ITALIAN HERITAGE DAY FEAST
FOR 12
Tortellini Pick-Ups, page 282
Cubed Vegetable Salad with Lemon Dressing, page 282 (double the recipe)
Cherry Tomatoes with Pesto, page 283 (double the recipe)
Italian Bake Roma, page 283
Hard Rolls   *Butter*
White Wine
Kiwi Tart, page 284
Espresso   *Tea*

Note: When preparing the above menu for your Italian Feast, make the following adjustments: Double the Cubed Vegetable Salad with Lemon Dressing and the Cherry Tomatoes with Pesto recipes.

Tortellini Pick-Ups

Makes 20 servings.

Nutrient Value Per Serving: 28 calories, 1 gm. protein, 2 gm. fat, 28 mg. sodium, 3 mg. cholesterol.

- 1 small zucchini, about 1¼ inches in diameter
- 20 cheese-filled tortellini
    Milk or heavy cream, as needed
- ¼ cup Pesto Mayonnaise (see Cherry Tomatoes with Pesto, page 283)
    Toasted pine nuts or slivered almonds

1. Cut the zucchini into ¼-inch-thick slices. Cook in boiling salted water for 1 minute. Drain. Plunge into ice water; drain.
2. Cook the tortellini, following the label directions. Drain. Rinse under cold water.
3. Add enough milk to the Pesto Mayonnaise in a medium-size bowl to make the mayonnaise the consistency of thick, heavy cream. Add the tortellini; toss to coat well.
4. To serve, arrange the slices of the zucchini on a serving plate. Top each with a tortellini. Garnish with the nuts.

To Make Ahead: Make the zucchini and tortellini a day ahead; refrigerate. Make the mayonnaise several days ahead; refrigerate.

Cubed Vegetable Salad with Lemon Dressing

This salad can be made a day or two ahead.

Makes 6 servings (4 cups).

Nutrient Value Per Serving: 137 calories, 2 gm. protein, 12 gm. fat, 149 mg. sodium, 0 mg. cholesterol.

- 1 large zucchini (about ½ pound), cut into ½-inch cubes
- 1 large yellow squash (about ½ pound), cut into ½-inch cubes
- 3 small tomatoes (¾ pound), seeded and cut into ½-inch cubes
- 1 stalk celery, cut into ½-inch cubes
- 1 green onion, thinly sliced

Lemon Dressing:
- ⅓ cup olive or vegetable oil
    Finely grated rind of ½ lemon (1 teaspoon)
    Juice of 1 lemon (2 tablespoons)
- 2 teaspoons Dijon-style mustard
- 1 clove garlic, finely chopped
- ½ teaspoon leaf oregano, crumbled
- ¼ teaspoon leaf basil, crumbled
- ¼ teaspoon salt
- ¼ teaspoon pepper

1. Combine the zucchini, yellow squash, tomatoes, celery and green onion in a large serving bowl.
2. Prepare the Lemon Dressing: Whisk together the oil, lemon rind and juice, mustard, garlic, oregano, basil, salt and pepper in a small bowl. Pour over the vegetables; toss to coat. Cover with plastic wrap. Marinate for 2 hours, or up to 2 days, refrigerated. Toss before serving.

Ripening Cherry Tomatoes

To hasten the ripening of cherry tomatoes or regular tomatoes, place them in a brown paper bag and leave at room temperature until as ripe as desired. Never refrigerate tomatoes.

Cherry Tomatoes with Pesto

Makes 16 servings.

Nutrient Value Per Serving: 30 calories, 0 gm. protein, 3 gm. fat, 23 mg. sodium, 2 mg. cholesterol.

- **1 pint ripe cherry tomatoes**
- **⅓ cup Pesto Mayonnaise (recipe follows)**
  Toasted pine nuts or slivered almonds (optional)

1. Cut a small slice from the top of each tomato. Hollow out each slightly, about half, with a small spoon. Turn the tomatoes upside down on paper toweling to drain.
2. About 1 hour before serving, fill each tomato with a scant teaspoon of the Pesto Mayonnaise. Garnish with the toasted pine nuts, if you wish.

To Make Ahead: The mayonnaise can be prepared a day ahead; the tomatoes scooped out serveral hours before serving.

Pesto Mayonnaise: Combine ½ cup of mayonnaise or salad dressing, ½ cup of loosely packed parsley leaves, ½ teaspoon of leaf basil, crumbled, 1 tablespoon of grated Parmesan cheese and ¼ teaspoon of finely chopped garlic in the container of an electric blender. Cover. Whirl until smooth. Blend in 2 tablespoons of finely chopped walnuts or pecans. Refrigerate until ready to use. (Leftover mayonnaise can be added to salad dressings or used as a sandwich spread.)

Italian Bake Roma

A delicious chicken and pasta dish. Bake it in two casseroles.

Bake at 350° for 30 minutes.
Makes 12 servings.

Nutrient Value Per Serving: 779 calories, 43 gm. protein, 36 gm. fat, 748 mg. sodium, 151 mg. cholesterol.

- **2 broiler-fryers, cut up (about 3 pounds each)**
- **1 medium-size onion, peeled and sliced**
- **2 teaspoons salt**
- **½ teaspoon peppercorns**
- **4 cups water**
- **1 pound mushrooms, trimmed and sliced**
- **1 small sweet green pepper, slivered**
- **¾ cup (1½ sticks) butter or margarine**
- **2 cups soft white bread crumbs (4 slices)**
- **⅓ cup all-purpose flour**
- **¼ teaspoon pepper**
- **¼ teaspoon ground nutmeg**
- **2 cups light cream or half and half (half cream, half milk)**
- **½ cup dry sherry**
- **1 package (2 pounds) thin spaghetti, broken in 2-inch lengths**
- **1 cup grated Parmesan cheese**
- **½ cup chopped parsley**
  Watercress
  Sliced mushrooms
  Pimiento

1. Combine the chicken, onion, 1 teaspoon of the salt, the peppercorns and water in a kettle. Bring to boiling; lower the heat; cover. Cook for 30 minutes or until the chicken is tender. Remove from the broth and cool until easy to handle. Strain the broth into a 4-cup measure and set aside.
2. Pull the skin from the chicken and take the meat from the bones; cube the meat; place in a large bowl.
3. Sauté the mushrooms and pepper in ¼ cup of the butter or margarine in a skillet until soft; combine with the chicken.
4. Melt the remaining butter or margarine in a large saucepan. Measure out 2 tablespoons and toss with the bread crumbs in a bowl; set aside.
5. Stir the flour, the remaining 1 teaspoon of salt, the pepper and nutmeg into the remaining butter or margarine in the saucepan; cook, stirring constantly, until bubbly. Stir in 3½ cups of the chicken broth ☞

and the cream. Continue cooking and stirring until the sauce thickens and bubbles, for 3 minutes; remove from the heat. Stir in the sherry.

6. Preheat the oven to moderate (350°).
7. While the sauce cooks, cook the spaghetti, following the label directions; drain well. Spoon into two 12-cup casseroles. Spoon the chicken mixture over the spaghetti; spoon the sauce over all.
8. Add the Parmesan cheese and parsley to the bread-crumb mixture and toss lightly to mix. Sprinkle over the mixture in the casseroles.
9. Bake in the preheated moderate oven (350°) for 30 minutes or until bubbly and the crumb topping is toasted. Garnish with bouquets of watercress, sliced mushrooms and pimiento, if you wish.

Planning Ahead

Cook's Tip: To freeze a prepared second casserole, see the instructions for How to Freeze Casseroles below.

How to Freeze Casseroles

For family and party servings:
● Line freezer-to-oven casseroles with heavy-duty aluminum foil, allowing enough overlap to cover food and make a tight seal. Spoon in the cooked food; cool; cover with the overlap. Label, date and freeze. When frozen, remove the dish; return the food to the freezer. When ready to serve, remove the foil from the frozen casserole and return to the original dish; cover. Bake, following the individual recipes.
For individual servings:
● Line individual toaster-oven-size casseroles with aluminum foil, following the directions above. At serving time, peel the foil from the food and return to the original dish; cover lightly with aluminum foil. Heat in the toaster-oven set at moderate (350°) for 30 minutes or until bubbly hot.
● Spoon the casserole mixture into boilable bags; seal, following the manufacturer's directions. Label, date and freeze. At serving time, bring a large saucepan of water to boiling; add the cooking bag and cook for 15 minutes or until the contents appear hot.

Even Graham Cracker Crust

To insure a more even bottom and side crust, press the sides and bottom of a standard metal measuring cup (any measure) along the sides and bottom of the pie plate.

Kiwi Tart

Makes 12 servings (one 9-inch tart).

Nutrient Value Per Serving: 102 calories, 3 gm. protein, 3 gm. fat, 240 mg. sodium, 6 mg. cholesterol.

1 envelope unflavored gelatin
2 tablespoons cold water
¾ cup skim milk, scalded
1 tablespoon grated orange rind
   Ice cubes and cold water to equal 1 cup
¾ cup lowfat cottage cheese
1 package (3½ ounces) vanilla-flavored instant pudding and pie filling
   9-inch graham cracker crust, purchased or homemade (recipe follows)
2 to 3 kiwi fruit, peeled and sliced
1 large strawberry

1. Sprinkle the gelatin over the 2 tablespoons of cold water in a blender. Set aside to soften, for 5 minutes. Add the hot scalded milk and orange rind. Blend until the gelatin is completely dissolved, for about 20 seconds. Add the ice water; blend until the ice is melted. Add the cottage cheese; blend until smooth. Add the pudding and pie filling; blend until thick and creamy. Pour into the prepared crust. Refrigerate until set, for about 4 hours.
2. Just before serving, arrange the kiwi slices on top of the tart. Garnish with the strawberry.

Homemade Graham Cracker Crust for Kiwi Tart: Preheat the oven to moderate (350°). Toss ¾ cup of plain graham cracker crumbs with 2 tablespoons of melted butter or margarine in a medium-size bowl. Spray a 9-inch pie plate with a vegetable cooking spray. Press the crumb mixture evenly over the bottom and sides of the plate. Bake in the preheated moderate oven (350°) for 6 to 8 minutes or until golden; be careful not to overbake. Cool completely before filling.

Glossary of Italian Terms

Aioli Sauce: Sauce of egg yolks, vinegar or lemon juice, olive oil and lots of garlic.
Amaretti: Macaroon cookies.
Bolognese: When referring to a sauce, it is a combination of chopped meat, vegetables and tomatoes.
Braciola: A flat piece of meat, rolled around a filling of meat, vegetables, herbs and seasonings.
Calamari: Squid.
Calzone: A pizza dough stuffed with cheese and ham.
Cannelloni: Large tubes of pasta stuffed with various ingredients.
Cannoli: A crisp pastry tube filled with ricotta, sugar and candied fruit.
Capellini: A very thin spaghetti.
Caponata: A dish made of eggplant, celery and anchovies in a sauce of onions, tomatoes and vinegar.
Cappelletti: Meat-stuffed small pasta similar to tortellini.
Cappuccino: A coffee blended with steaming, frothy milk.
Carbonara: For no apparent reason the name refers to a secret 19th-century society in Italy. It is made with pasta onto which bits of bacon and raw egg are dropped, then mixed together so that the egg is cooked by the heat of the pasta. Often cream is added to the recipe in America.
Cassata: A sponge cake sprinkled with Marsala wine and formed with layers of ice cream and candied fruit.
Crema: Custard.
Espresso: A very dark strong cup of coffee through which steam has been forced.

Fettuccine Alfredo: Long strands of pasta, mixed with butter, Parmesan cheese and, usually, cream.
Frittata: Omelet.
Gelato: A very rich and creamy ice cream consisting of eggs, sugar and flavoring.
Gnocchi: Pasta made with potato dough or with semolina flour.
Linguine: Flattened spaghetti strands.
Marinara: A sauce of tomatoes, onion and garlic, often with seafood usually added at the last minute.
Mortadella: A type of pork sausage.
Ossobucco: Veal shanks in a brown tomato sauce.
Pasta e Fagioli: Pasta and beans, usually in a thick tomato and garlic soup.
Pecorino: A sharp grating cheese.
Pesto: A sauce made of fresh basil, pignoli nuts, olive oil, garlic and cheese.
Piccata: A thin scallop of veal, usually prepared with lemon.
Polenta: A cooked cornmeal served as a side dish or used as a base for sauces.
Pollo: Chicken.
Primavera: A sauce made with fresh vegetables.
Prosciutto: Cured ham, which should be served in paper-thin slices.
Radicchio: A red-leafed, bitter lettuce.
Saltimbocca: Thin slices of veal and ham cooked in butter frequently with Marsala wine and served on spinach or kale.
Tortellini: Small filled pasta hats.
Vermicelli: Very thin pasta.
Zabaglione: A sweetened egg yolk and Marsala wine dessert custard.
Ziti: Hollow, tubular pasta.

SPANISH FLAMENCO PARTY
FOR 6

Cheese Rolls, page 286

Cold Parsnip Cream Soup, page 286

Mixed Green Salad

Paella Valenciana, page 286

Sangria

No-Cook Summer Fruit Flan, page 287

Coffee   Tea

Cheese Rolls

For a large crowd, make the recipe two or three times. These easy-to-make rolls can be prepared a day or two ahead. Save any leftovers for a delicious sandwich filling.

Makes 2 cheese rolls, 12 servings each.

Nutrient Value Per Serving: 140 calories, 4 gm. protein, 13 gm. fat, 349 mg. sodium, 25 mg. cholesterol.

- **2 packages (8 ounces each) cream cheese, softened**
- **2 tablespoons prepared horseradish**
- **2 tablespoons Dijon-style mustard**
- **2 tablespoons finely chopped onion**
- **2 jars (2.5 ounces each) sliced dried beef, finely chopped**
- **¾ cup finely chopped pecans**
- **¾ cup finely chopped chives or parsley**

1. Beat together the cream cheese, horseradish, mustard and onion in a small bowl with a wooden spoon until well blended. Stir in the beef.
2. Chill for about 1 hour or until the mixture is firm enough to be shaped into 2 equal-size rolls, each about 1½ inches in diameter.
3. Roll one log in the chopped pecans and the other in the chopped chives. Serve with crackers or party rounds.

Cold Parsnip Cream Soup

Makes 6 servings.

Nutrient Value Per Serving: 155 calories, 3 gm. protein, 7 gm. fat, 363 mg. sodium, 16 mg. cholesterol.

- **2 tablespoons butter or margarine**
- **1 large onion, chopped (1 cup)**
- **1 small leek, white part only, well rinsed and thinly sliced**

- **1 small, hot green chili pepper OR: canned jalapeño pepper, seeded and chopped**
- **½ teaspoon sugar**
- **½ teaspoon minced fresh gingerroot**
- **¼ teaspoon turmeric**
- **⅛ teaspoon ground nutmeg**
- **1 pound parsnips, pared and chopped**
- **1 medium-size potato, pared and chopped**
- **5 cups water**
- **1 can (13¾ ounces) chicken broth**
- **½ teaspoon white pepper**
- **⅓ cup dairy sour cream**
  Chopped parsley

1. Melt the butter in a large saucepan or Dutch oven over medium-low heat. Add the onion, leek, chili pepper, sugar, gingerroot, turmeric and nutmeg. Cook, stirring occasionally, for 5 minutes.
2. Add the parsnips and potato; cook for 5 minutes longer. Pour in the water and chicken broth. Bring to boiling. Lower the heat; simmer, uncovered, for 20 minutes or until the vegetables are tender. Season with the pepper. Cool slightly.
3. Working in batches, place the soup in the container of an electric blender or food processor. Cover; whirl until puréed. Transfer to a large bowl; cover with plastic wrap; refrigerate. To serve, stir in the sour cream. Garnish with the chopped parsley.

Paella Valenciana

Golden rice, seafood and chicken baked in a chicken-rich broth is one of Spain's best-known contributions to cuisine.

Bake at 375° for 1 hour.
Makes 6 servings.

Paella Valenciana

Nutrient Value Per Serving: 536 calories, 45 gm. protein, 20 gm. fat, 888 mg. sodium, 170 mg. cholesterol.

1 **broiler-fryer, cut up (about 3 pounds)**
1 **clove garlic, finely chopped**
¼ **cup olive or vegetable oil**
1 **large onion, chopped (1 cup)**
1 **chorizo (Spanish sausage), sliced ½ inch thick, OR: ½ cup diced cooked ham**
1½ **cups uncooked long-grain rice**
6 **strands saffron, crushed**
2 **cans (10 ounces each) condensed chicken broth**
1 **cup water**
1 **teaspoon salt**
1 **bag (1 pound) frozen, shelled and deveined shrimp, thawed**
1 **can (4 ounces) pimiento, drained and cut into chunks**
1 **bag (1 pound) frozen peas**
1 **dozen small clams, scrubbed**
1 **dozen mussels, scrubbed (optional)**

1. Brown the chicken and garlic in the oil in a large skillet; remove and reserve.
2. Preheat the oven to moderate (375°).
3. Sauté the onion in the pan drippings until soft, then add the chorizo or ham and sauté for 3 minutes; push to one side; sprinkle the rice in the pan and cook, stirring constantly, until the grains are golden; add the saffron, chicken broth, water and salt; bring to boiling; pour into a 12-cup paella dish or shallow casserole; add the browned chicken and cover the casserole.
4. Bake in the preheated moderate oven (375°) for 45 minutes; add the shrimp, pimiento and peas; top with the clams and mussels, if using; cover. Bake for 15 minutes longer or until the shrimp and rice are cooked and the cooking liquid is absorbed.

No-Cook Summer Fruit Flan

Makes 6 servings.

Nutrient Value Per Serving with Sugar: 99 calories, 8 gm. protein, 1 gm. fat, 34 mg. sodium, 47 mg. cholesterol. Nutrient Value Per Serving with Artificial Sweetener: 89 calories, 8 gm. protein, 1 gm. fat, 34 mg. sodium, 46 mg. cholesterol.

1 **egg**
1 **envelope unflavored gelatin**
¾ **cup boiling water**
1 **cup cold skim milk**
4 **envelopes (.75 ounces each) vanilla-flavored reduced-calorie dairy drink mix**
2 **teaspoons grated orange or lemon rind (optional)**
Raspberry Purée Topping (recipe follows)

1. Combine the egg and gelatin in a medium-size bowl, electric blender or food processor. Let stand to soften, for 5 minutes. Add the boiling water. Beat or blend until the gelatin is dissolved, for about 1 minute.
2. Add the skim milk, drink mix and rind, if using, to the egg mixture. Beat or blend until thoroughly combined. Pour into 6 small (6-ounce) custard cups. Refrigerate until set, for 3 to 4 hours.
3. To serve, unmold the custard cups onto individual plates. Drizzle each with a few tablespoons of the Raspberry Purée Topping.

Raspberry Purée Topping: Purée 1 cup of fresh or thawed, dry-pack frozen raspberries in a blender or food processor. Sweeten to taste with 4 teaspoons of sugar, or artificial sweetener equivalent to 4 teaspoons of sugar.

Glossary of Spanish and Portuguese Terms

Arroz con Pollo: Chicken with yellow rice and peas.
Flan: Caramel custard.
Gazpacho: A cold tomato and garlic soup.
Paella: A rice-based dish flavored with saffron, to which a variety of ingredients such as shrimp, lobster, clams, mussels, chicken, sausage, ham, peas, artichokes, tomatoes, onions and garlic may be added.
Sangria: A wine and fruit drink to which brandy is added.
Sopa de Ajo: Garlic soup.
Tapas: Hors d'oeuvres or canapés, commonly served in bars in Spain.

Greek Spinach Pie (page 290)

GREEK COSTUME PARTY
FOR 8

Belgian Endive with Herbed Cheese, page 289

Salata Diana, page 289

Greek Spinach Pie, page 290

Rice Dressing, page 291

Assorted Beers

Poached Honeyed Pears with Mint Jelly, page 291

Coffee   Tea

To make your party a little more entertaining, ask everyone to dress in a Grecian-type costume.

Note: When preparing the above menu for your Grecian party, make the following adjustments: Make the Salata Diana and the Rice Dressing twice each.

What Is Belgian Endive?

Belgian endive is the crown of creamy white young leaves of chicory.

Belgian Endive with Herbed Cheese

Makes 24 servings.

Nutrient Value Per Serving: 25 calories, 0 gm. protein, 2 gm. fat, 21 mg. sodium, 8 mg. cholesterol.

2 Belgian endive, preferably short ones
2 packages (3 ounces each) cream cheese with chives, softened
2 teaspoons chopped parsley
⅛ teaspoon garlic powder
   Alfalfa sprouts, rinsed and well drained

1. Trim the bottom from the endive. Separate each into leaves.
2. Blend together the cream cheese, parsley and garlic powder in a small bowl. Spread about 1 teaspoon on the bottom of each leaf. Garnish the tops of the leaves with the sprouts. Cover with damp paper toweling and plastic wrap.

To Make Ahead: The cream cheese filling can be prepared a day ahead. The assembled leaves can be refrigerated for up to several hours.

Salata Diana

Makes 8 servings.

Nutrient Value Per Serving: 504 calories, 18 gm. protein, 39 gm. fat, 1,222 mg. sodium, 73 mg. cholesterol.

1 large or 2 small heads romaine lettuce
1 pint small cherry tomatoes
5 green onions, both white and tender green parts, thinly sliced
4 tablespoons chopped fresh dill
4 large radishes, thinly sliced
1 medium-size cucumber, pared and cut into ¼-inch-thick rounds
1 sweet red or green pepper, halved, seeded and cut into ½-inch squares
1 jar (6 ounces) marinated artichoke hearts, drained
1 tablespoon capers
¾ cup bottled Italian dressing
½ pound feta cheese, crumbled (1½ cups)
¾ pound ready-to-eat Greek sausage or Polish kielbasa sausage, cut into ¼-inch-thick rounds
6 ounces Greek olives or other black olives (optional)
⅛ teaspoon pepper

1. Discard the tough outer leaves from the romaine lettuce. Wash and cut the head

crosswise into 1-inch-wide slices. Dry well. Wrap in paper toweling and place in plastic bags. Store in the refrigerator until ready to use.

2. Combine the cherry tomatoes, green onions, dill, radishes, cucumber, red or green pepper, artichoke hearts and capers in a large serving bowl. Add the dressing; stir to coat. Cover; refrigerate until serving time.

3. To serve, add the romaine, cheese and sausage and olives, if using, to the vegetables. Toss well to coat. Season with the pepper; toss again and serve.

For Your Information

Cucumbers and tomatoes are classified as fruits, not vegetables.

Greek Spinach Pie

This dish is authentic Spanakopita only if you use olive oil, fresh dill, feta cheese and, of course, spinach.

Bake at 325° for 25 minutes; then at 350° for 15 minutes.
Makes 8 servings.

Nutrient Value Per Serving: 629 calories, 17 gm. protein, 46 gm. fat, 897 mg. sodium, 126 mg. cholesterol.

 2 *packages (10 ounces each) frozen chopped spinach, thawed and drained*
 ½ *cup olive or vegetable oil*
 1 *medium-size onion, chopped (½ cup)*
 2 *bunches green onions, trimmed and chopped*
 ¼ *cup chopped dill*
 ¼ *cup chopped parsley*
 2 *eggs*
 ½ *pound feta cheese, chopped*
 1 *container (8 ounces) lowfat cottage cheese*
 1 *teaspoon salt*
 ¼ *teaspoon pepper*
 ½ *cup (1 stick) butter or margarine*
 ½ *cup olive or vegetable oil*
 16 *sheets phyllo leaves, from a 1-pound package frozen phyllo leaves*
    Fresh dill
    Lemon slices

1. Press the spinach through a colander with the back of a cup to remove moisture.

2. Heat ½ cup of the oil in a large skillet; sauté the chopped onion and green onions until soft. Add the drained spinach, chopped dill and parsley and cook, stirring often, for 5 minutes.

3. Beat the eggs in a large bowl; add the feta, cottage cheese, salt and pepper. Stir into the spinach mixture.

4. Melt the butter or margarine with the ½ cup of olive oil in a small saucepan.

5. Thaw the phyllo leaves, following the directions for the proper thawing procedure found on the back of the package. Remove the phyllo leaves from the package. Gently unfold the sheets; count out 16. Rewrap; return the remaining phyllo leaves to the original box and refrigerate. Plan to use within one week.

6. Brush one phyllo leaf generously with the butter-oil mixture and place one edge in the center of a 9-inch pie plate, allowing part of the leaf to hang over the edge. Turn the pie plate one-quarter and repeat brushing the leaf with the butter-oil mixture and laying one edge in the center of the pie plate. Repeat the one-quarter turns and layering of the phyllo leaves until 8 leaves have been used.

7. Brush one leaf with the butter-oil mixture and fold in half. Place one long edge down the center of the pie plate; make a one-quarter turn. Repeat with 3 more phyllo leaves; top the pie plate with a total of 12 leaves.

8. Preheat the oven to slow (325°).

9. Spoon the spinach mixture into the phyllo-layered pie plate, spreading evenly. Lift the phyllo leaves from the edge of the pie plate and fold over the filling.

10. Brush a phyllo leaf generously with the butter-oil mixture; fold in half; place down the center of the pie; repeat to cover the pie with the remaining 3 phyllo leaves.

11. Score the top into 8 wedges with a sharp knife, but do not cut through.

12. Bake in the slow preheated oven (325°) for 25 minutes; increase the oven temperature to moderate (350°); bake for 15 minutes longer or until the crust is puffed and golden. Cool in the pan on a wire rack for at least 45 minutes before serving. Garnish with the fresh dill and lemon slices.

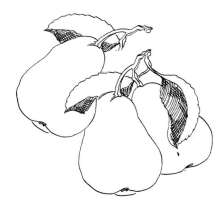

Rice Dressing

Serve as a savory side dish with grilled meats, roast chicken or a crown roast of lamb. Or, use dressing to stuff vegetables.

Makes 3 cups.

Nutrient Value Per ½ Cup: 392 calories, 12 gm. protein, 17 gm. fat, 530 mg. sodium, 27 mg. cholesterol.

- **½ pound ground lamb or beef**
- **2 tablespoons vegetable oil**
- **1 medium-size onion, finely chopped (½ cup)**
- **1 cup uncooked white rice**
- **1 can (13¾ ounces) chicken broth**
- **1 can (6 ounces) sliced mushrooms, drained**
- **⅓ cup raisins**
- **½ teaspoon salt**
- **¼ teaspoon ground cinnamon**
- **¼ teaspoon pepper**
- **1 can (17 ounces) apricot halves, drained and diced**
- **¼ cup slivered toasted almonds OR: toasted pine nuts**

1. Sauté the lamb in the oil in a large skillet until no longer pink, for about 5 minutes. Add the onion; sauté until the onion is softened, for about 10 minutes.
2. Stir the rice into the skillet. Add the chicken broth, mushrooms, raisins, salt, cinnamon and pepper to the skillet; stir to mix well. Bring to boiling. Lower the heat; cover and simmer until the rice is tender and all the liquid is absorbed, for about 20 minutes.
3. Stir in the apricots and nuts with a fork; stir for 1 for 2 minutes longer or until heated through. Serve.

Poached Honeyed Pears with Mint Jelly

A small amount of honey adds natural sweetness to these pears. Cook them a day ahead and chill until ready to serve.

Makes 8 servings.

Nutrient Value Per Serving: 62 calories, 0 gm. protein, 0 gm. fat, 2 mg. sodium, 0 mg. cholesterol.

- **8 firm pears**
- **3 cups boiling water**
- **½ cup lemon juice**
- **¼ cup honey**
- **¼ teaspoon ground nutmeg**
  Mint jelly

1. Pare, halve and core the pears. Arrange in a large skillet. Add the boiling water, lemon juice, honey and nutmeg. Bring to boiling over high heat. Lower the heat and cook, covered, for 10 minutes or until the pears are tender.
2. Place the pears in a large bowl. Pour the cooking liquid over. Chill.
3. To serve, remove the pears from the liquid with a slotted spoon. Fill the cores with the mint jelly.

Note: The cooking liquid may be cooked down to make a syrup topping for desserts.

Glossary of Greek Terms

Arni: Lamb.
Baklava: Sweet, almond-filled flaky phyllo pastry.
Dolma: Stuffed grape leaves.
Feta: A tangy sheep's or goat's milk cheese.
Kafe: Coffee.
Moussaka: Eggplant layered with ground meat, cheese and various seasonings and baked in the oven.
Ouzo: A strong, anise-flavored liqueur.
Pita: A flat bread, often containing a sandwich type of filling.
Psomi: Bread.
Spanakopita: Phyllo pastry filled with spinach and feta cheese.
Supa Avgholemono: A chicken soup with rice and lemon.

Clockwise, from lower right: Ebi No Kikka Age (page 293), Takara Mushi (page 294), Tori No Sanmi Yaki or Three-Flavored Chicken (page 294), Radish and Carrot Sunomono (page 294).

JAPANESE GARDEN FEAST
FOR 4

Ebi No Kikka Age, page 293

(Chrysanthemum-Shaped Shrimp Rolls)

Takara Mushi, page 294

(Chicken and Shrimp Custard Soup)

Radish and Carrot Sunomono, page 294

Tori No Sanmi Yaki, page 294

(Three-Flavored Chicken with Hot Cooked Rice)

Sake (Rice Wine)

Strawberry Kissel, page 295

Coffee   Tea

Add a colorful note to your Japanese Garden Feast by purchasing some outdoor Japanese lanterns to place around and light the yard or patio.

Ebi No Kikka Age
(Chrysanthemum-Shaped Shrimp Balls)

Makes 21 small shrimp balls.

Nutrient Value Per Ball: 49 calories, 4 gm. protein, 2 gm. fat, 179 mg. sodium, 25 mg. cholesterol.

½ *medium-size sweet potato, pared and cubed*
12 *ounces shrimp, peeled, deveined and chopped*
2½ *teaspoons cornstarch*
¼ *teaspoon salt*
1 *egg white, slightly beaten*
1 *teaspoon finely chopped, pared fresh gingerroot*
1 *green onion, white part only, finely chopped*
3 *canned water chestnuts, drained and finely chopped (optional)*
1½ *cups (2 ounces) white crisp Oriental noodles (Harusame*), or Chinese lo mein (noodles), broken into short lengths*
  Vegetable oil for deep frying
1½ *tablespoons sake (rice wine) OR: dry sherry*

1½ **tablespoons soy sauce**
2 **teaspoons sugar**
¼ **cup water**

1. Cook the sweet potato in boiling water to cover in a small saucepan just until barely tender, for 5 to 10 minutes. Drain.
2. Meanwhile, mash together the shrimp, 1½ teaspoons of the cornstarch and the salt, adding just enough of the egg white to make a paste, in a food processor fitted with a metal blade or with a mortar and pestle. Blend in the gingerroot and green onion. Stir in the water chestnuts, if using.
3. Toss the sweet potato cubes in the remaining 1 teaspoon of cornstarch to coat. Mold the shrimp mixture around each potato cube with moistened hands; shape to the size of a quarter. Roll each in the noodle pieces.
4. Pour the oil into a large saucepan to a depth of 3 to 4 inches. Heat the oil to 350° on a deep-fat frying thermometer. Add several balls with a slotted spoon to the oil; do not crowd the pan. Fry until golden and the noodles curl, for about 1 minute. Remove with a slotted spoon to paper toweling to drain. Repeat with the remaining balls.
5. To prepare the dipping sauce: Combine the sake, soy sauce, sugar and water in a small bowl. Serve with the shrimp balls.

* Note: *Harusame is available in Oriental grocery stores and specialty food shops.*

Takara Mushi
(Chicken and Shrimp Custard Soup)

Makes 4 servings.

Nutrient Value Per Serving: 178 calories, 27 gm. protein, 5 gm. fat, 1,124 mg. sodium, 234 mg. cholesterol.

- 1 **boneless, skinned chicken breast (8 ounces), diced (1 cup)**
- 6 **ounces shrimp, peeled, deveined and diced (¾ cup)**
- 3 **ounces canned bamboo shoots, drained and diced (¾ cup)**
- 2 **ounces fresh mushrooms, thinly sliced (1 cup)**
- ⅓ **cup frozen peas, thawed**
- 2 **eggs, slightly beaten**
- 1 **can (13¾ ounces) chicken broth**
- 2 **teaspoons soy sauce**

1. Combine the chicken, shrimp, bamboo shoots, mushrooms and peas in a medium-size heatproof bowl.
2. Combine the eggs, broth and soy sauce in a medium-size bowl. Pour over the chicken mixture. Stir to mix. Cover the bowl tightly with foil. Place the bowl on a rack in a steamer, or on a trivet in a deep saucepan, with enough boiling water to come 1 inch up the side of the bowl. Cover tightly. Steam over medium heat for 30 minutes or until the mixture is loosely set.
3. To serve, lightly spoon some of the solid ingredients from the bottom onto the surface of the soup. (The soup will have a slightly curdled appearance.)

Radish and Carrot Sunomono

Makes 12 servings (about 3 cups).

Nutrient Value Per Serving: 14 calories, 0 gm. protein, 0 gm. fat, 119 mg. sodium, 0 mg. cholesterol.

- 1 **tablespoon sweet sake (rice wine) or dry sherry**
- 2 **tablespoons rice wine vinegar**
- 1 **tablespoon sugar**
- 1 **tablespoon soy sauce**
- ½ **large daikon or white radish, cut into matchstick pieces, OR: about 9 ounces red radishes, cut into matchstick pieces (1 cup)**
- 1 **large carrot, cut into matchstick pieces (1 cup)**

Combine the sake, vinegar, sugar and soy in a large bowl. Add the radish and carrot; toss to mix. Marinate, covered, in the refrigerator for at least 1 hour.

Tori No Sanmi Yaki
(Three-Flavored Chicken)

Bake at 325° for 25 minutes; then broil for 3 to 5 minutes.
Makes 4 servings.

Nutrient Value Per Serving: 531 calories, 36 gm. protein, 21 gm. fat, 1,853 mg. sodium, 93 mg. cholesterol.

- 3 **tablespoons sesame seeds**
- 2 **cloves garlic, crushed**
- ½ **small dried red pepper, seeded**
- ¼ **teaspoon ground ginger**
- ¼ **cup sake (rice wine) OR: dry sherry**
- ⅓ **cup soy sauce**
- ¼ **cup honey**
- 2 **boneless chicken breasts, halved and with skin on**
- 1 **large sweet green pepper, cored, seeded and cut into thin strips**
- 1 **tablespoon vegetable oil**
- 6 **thin lemon slices, seeded and halved**
- 2 **cups hot cooked rice**

1. Toast the sesame seeds in a small, dry skillet over medium heat until amber in color, for about 5 minutes; shake the pan frequently.
2. Mash the seeds with the garlic, pepper and ginger with a mortar and pestle, or in a blender for food processor, until a paste forms. Add the sake, soy sauce and honey. Mash or process until well blended.
3. Place in a single layer in a nonmetal shallow dish. Pour the sesame seed mixture over; turn the chicken pieces to coat. Cover. Marinate in the refrigerator for 3 to 4 hours or overnight. Turn the pieces occasionally.
4. Preheat the oven to slow (325°). Place the chicken pieces, skin-side down, in a baking pan. Brush with the marinade.
5. Bake in the preheated slow oven (325°) for 15 minutes. Turn the chicken skin-side up. Bake for 10 more minutes, brushing occasionally with the remaining marinade.

6. Broil 7 inches from the heat for 3 to 5 minutes or until glazed on both sides.
7. Meanwhile, sauté the green pepper strips in the oil in a small skillet until slightly wilted.
8. Cut each breast diagonally into 4 equal pieces. Leave the pieces in the shape of the original breast. Arrange on a platter; tuck the lemon slices in between the chicken pieces. Garnish with the pepper strips. Serve with the rice.

Strawberry Kissel

Treat your family and friends to this delectable dessert made with one of America's favorite berries.

Makes 6 servings.

Nutrient Value Per Serving: 88 calories, .64 gm. protein, .38 gm. fat, 2 mg. sodium, 0 mg. cholesterol.

    2 pints strawberries
    ⅓ cup sugar
    2 tablespoons lemon juice
    ½ cup water
    3 tablespoons cornstarch

1. Hull and slice 1 pint of the strawberries. Set aside.
2. Hull the remaining strawberries. Place in a medium-size saucepan, mash with a fork or potato masher. Stir in the sugar and lemon juice. Bring to boiling over medium heat.
3. Combine the water and cornstarch in a small bowl. Pour into the bubbling strawberry mixture. Cook, stirring, until the mixture returns to boiling and thickens.
4. Place the saucepan in a large bowl of ice and water. Stir until cooled to room temperature. Stir in the reserved 1 pint of sliced strawberries.
5. Spoon into individual dessert dishes and refrigerate until ready to serve.

Glossary of Japanese Terms

Nori: Black seaweed.
Sake: Rice wine.
Sashimi: Raw fish exquisitely sliced and served in a variety of styles. Served with wasabi and pickled ginger.
Shiitake: A dark wild mushroom.
Sukiyaki: Thinly sliced beef and vegetables sautéed in soy sauce.
Sushi: Beautifully cut and presented vegetables, fish and eggs wrapped in vinegared rice and then in Nori (seaweed). It may be eaten with the fingers.
Tempura: A battered piece of shrimp, fish, vegetable or chicken quickly fried in oil and dipped in a soy-based sauce.
Teriyaki: Marinated meat, fish or chicken grilled over coals as a barbecue dish.
Wasabi: A pungent green horseradish served with sushi and sashimi.

Saucy Loin of Pork with Baked Apples
(page 297), Fanned Roast Potatoes (page 299),
Drunken Sauerkraut (page 298)

GERMAN BEER TASTING AND BARBECUE
FOR 8

Assorted Cheeses   Assorted Crackers

Instant Borscht, page 297

Saucy Loin of Pork with Baked Apples, page 297

Fanned Roast Potatoes, page 299

Drunken Sauerkraut, page 298

Salt Pretzels, page 299

Assorted German and Domestic Beers

Chocolate Ice-Cream Linzer Torte, page 301

Coffee   Tea

Note: When preparing the above menu for your German Barbecue, make the following adjustment: Double the Instant Borscht.

Instant Borscht

This refreshing soup is a snap to make. Keep a jar of beets and chicken broth in your refrigerator for instant assembling.

Makes 4 servings (about 3 cups).

Nutrient Value Per Serving: 77 calories, 3 gm. protein, 2 gm. fat, 502 mg. sodium, 4 mg. cholesterol.

1   *jar (16 ounces) whole beets*
1   *cup chicken broth*
1   *tablespoon sugar*
2   *tablespoons lemon juice*
1   *teaspoon distilled white or cider vinegar*
2   *teaspoons chopped fresh dill*
1   *teaspoon finely chopped green onion*
⅛   *teaspoon pepper*
2   *to 3 drops liquid red-pepper seasoning*
2   *tablespoons dairy sour cream*
2   *tablespoons plain yogurt*
    Dill sprigs for garnish (optional)

1. Drain the beets, reserving ¼ cup of the liquid. Shred the beets on the coarse side of a grater into a small bowl.
2. Stir the reserved ¼ cup of the beet liquid, the chicken broth, sugar, lemon juice, vinegar, dill, green onion, pepper and liquid red-pepper seasoning into the beets. Cover. Chill until serving time.

3. Combine the sour cream and yogurt in a small bowl.
4. Ladle the soup into cups. Top with the sour cream mixture. Garnish with the dill sprigs, if you wish.

Saucy Loin of Pork with Baked Apples

Cooking time will vary with the temperature of the fire and the weight of the meat. If using charcoal, replenish it periodically.

Makes 6 to 8 servings (with leftovers).

Nutrient Value Per Serving: 570 calories, 29 gm. protein, 34 gm. fat, 585 mg. sodium, 123 mg. cholesterol.

1   *boneless loin of pork, rolled and tied (4 to 6 pounds)*
1   *clove garlic, crushed*
½   *cup Dijon-style mustard*
¼   *cup honey*
1   *tablespoon lemon juice (½ lemon)*
½   *teaspoon chopped fresh marjoram OR: ¼ teaspoon leaf marjoram, crumbled*
¼   *cup applejack or apple brandy*
1   *tablespoon cider vinegar*
    Dash liquid red-pepper seasoning
½   *teaspoon freshly ground pepper*
6   *to 8 red baking apples*
4   *to 5 tablespoons unsalted butter or margarine, softened*
    Ground cinnamon
6   *to 8 teaspoons brown sugar*

1. Wipe the pork with damp paper toweling. Rub the pork well with the garlic.
2. Combine the mustard, honey, lemon juice, marjoram, applejack, vinegar, red-pepper seasoning and pepper in a medium-size bowl; mix well.
3. Coat the pork with ½ cup of the mustard mixture. Let stand at room temperature, lightly covered, for 3 hours. Cover and reserve the remaining basting mixture.
4. Prepare the charcoal for grilling with a drip pan in the center under the grid, or preheat a gas unit with a drip pan.
5. Place the pork on the grid or rotisserie. Cover the grill with the dome.* Cook over high heat for 20 to 22 minutes per pound, basting often with the remaining mustard mixture, until a meat thermometer inserted in the thickest part of the meat registers 170°. (If cooking over coals, replenish with new charcoal as needed.) Let the roast stand for 10 to 15 minutes before carving.
6. About 30 minutes before serving, rub each apple with 1 teaspoon of the softened butter.** Sprinkle each lightly with the cinnamon and 1 teaspoon of the brown sugar. Enclose each apple in a packet of heavy-duty aluminum foil. Place the packets around the pork on the grill. Cook, with the grill covered, until tender, for 25 to 30 minutes; the apples will give slightly when gently pressed.
7. To serve, remove the apples from the foil. Place upright on a serving dish. Make a cross with a sharp knife in the top of each apple, about ¾ inch deep. Pour any liquid in the foil packets over the apples. Top each with 1 teaspoon of the softened butter.

*Note: To construct a barbecue cone or dome, see page 124.
**Note: For the photograph on page 296, we cored the apples, leaving the bottoms intact, then rubbed them with softened butter, sprinkled with cinnamon and spooned brown sugar into the cavities.

Drunken Sauerkraut

Makes 6 to 8 servings.

Nutrient Value Per Serving: 116 calories, 3 gm, protein, 6 gm. fat, 1,124 mg. sodium, 7 mg. cholesterol.

3 strips bacon, chopped
1 cup finely chopped onion
1 package (2 pounds) sauerkraut, rinsed and drained
2 tablespoons brown sugar
½ teaspoon caraway seeds
1 can (12 ounces) beer OR: apple cider
¾ cup grated carrot
    Salt and pepper
1 tablespoon chopped parsley

1. Sauté the bacon in a medium-size heavy pot or Dutch oven until all the fat is rendered, but the bacon is not browned.
2. Add the onion; cook, stirring occasionally, for 4 minutes or until softened.
3. Stir in the sauerkraut, brown sugar, caraway seeds and beer. Bring to boiling. Lower the heat; simmer, partially covered, for 1 hour.
4. Add the carrot. Simmer, partially covered, for 30 minutes longer. If the mixture is too "wet," raise the heat slightly; cook, uncovered, a little longer. Add the salt and pepper to taste. Sprinkle with the parsley.

MICROWAVE DIRECTIONS
650 Watt Variable Power Microwave Oven
Ingredient Changes: Reduce the beer to ¾ cup. Do not chop the bacon.
Directions: Microwave the bacon on a grid in a microwave-safe dish, about 13 x 9 inches, uncovered, at full power for 3 minutes. Remove the bacon and grid; crumble the bacon. Add the onion to the dish. Microwave at full power for 3 minutes, stirring after 2 minutes. Mix in the sauerkraut, sugar, caraway, beer, carrot and bacon. Cover with wax paper. Microwave at half power for 15 minutes. Sprinkle with the salt, pepper and parsley.

Fanned Roast Potatoes

Makes 6 to 8 servings.

Nutrient Value Per Serving: 237 calories, 3 gm. protein, 15 gm. fat, 84 mg. sodium, 40 mg. cholesterol.

12 to 16 small red new potatoes
8 to 10 tablespoons unsalted butter or
   margarine, melted
   Salt and pepper
   Snipped fresh chives
   Chopped fresh tarragon OR: dried leaf
   tarragon, crumbled

1. Cut six to eight 12 x 9-inch rectangles of heavy-duty aluminum foil.
2. Cut 4 or more parallel slices into the potatoes without cutting through (place the potatoes in a large spoon before cutting and you won't cut them all the way through). Fan-open the potatoes. Place 2 on each piece of foil; pour the butter over. Sprinkle with the salt, pepper, chives and tarragon to taste. Seal the foil to form packets.
3. Place on the grill. Cover. Cook until tender, for about 45 minutes.

Note: If your grill is small, the potatoes in this recipe can be cooked before the apples in the Saucy Loin of Pork with Baked Apples recipe on page 297. Remove the potatoes and keep warm.

Salt Pretzels

Bake at 400° for 15 minutes.
Makes 12 four-inch pretzels.

Nutrient Value Per Serving: 175 calories, 5 gm. protein, 3 gm. fat, 648 mg. sodium, 46 mg. cholesterol.

1 envelope active dry yeast
1 cup very warm water
3½ to 3¾ cups sifted bread flour
¼ cup sugar
½ teaspoon salt
1 egg
2 tablespoons vegetable shortening
1 egg yolk
1 tablespoon cold water
1 tablespoon coarse kosher salt

1. Sprinkle the yeast over the very warm water in a large bowl. ("Very warm water" should feel comfortably warm when dropped on the wrist.) Stir until the yeast is dissolved.

2. Beat in 2 cups of the flour, the sugar, salt, egg and vegetable shortening until smooth; beat in enough additional flour to make a stiff dough.
3. Turn out onto a lightly floured surface. Knead until smooth and elastic, for about 10 minutes, using only as much flour as needed to keep the dough from sticking.
4. Place the dough in a lightly greased large bowl; turn to bring the greased-side up. Cover with a towel. Let rise in a warm place, away from drafts, for 1 hour or until doubled in volume.
5. Punch the dough down; turn out onto a lightly floured surface; knead for 1 minute. Invert the bowl over the dough; allow to rest for 10 minutes. Divide the dough into 12 equal pieces. Roll each with the palms of your hands into a 20-inch rope on an unfloured surface; twist into a pretzel shape. Keep the remaining pieces covered with the towel to prevent the dough from drying out. Place on lightly greased cookie sheets.
6. Beat the egg yolk in water; brush over the tops of the pretzels; sprinkle with the kosher salt. Cover with the towel; let rise again, away from drafts, for 20 minutes or until almost doubled in volume.
7. Meanwhile, preheat the oven to hot (400°).
8. Bake in the preheated hot oven (400°) for 15 minutes or until golden brown.

Chocolate Ice-Cream Linzer Torte

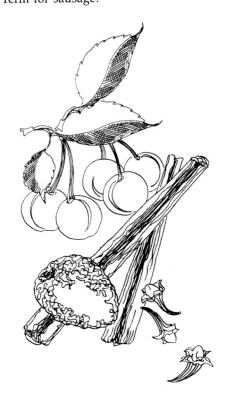

Chocolate Ice-Cream Linzer Torte

Chocolate ice cream is sandwiched between layers of chocolate meringue, then covered with whipped cream and toasted almonds.

Bake meringues at 300° for 45 minutes.
Makes 12 servings.

Nutrient Value Per Serving: 462 calories, 7 gm. protein, 27 gm. fat, 79 mg. sodium, 74 mg. cholesterol.

- ½ **cup egg whites (about 5 eggs)**
- ½ **cup granulated sugar**
- 1 **cup sifted 10X (confectioners') sugar**
- 1 **tablespoon cornstarch**
- ¼ **cup unsweetened cocoa powder**
- ½ **cup toasted ground almonds**
- 1 **jar (12 ounces) raspberry preserves**
- 1 **quart chocolate ice cream, softened**
- 2 **cups (1 pint) heavy cream**
- ⅔ **cup toasted ground almonds**
- 1 **package (12 ounces) frozen dry-pack whole raspberries OR: 3 cups fresh raspberries**

1. Preheat the oven to slow (300°). Cut three 9-inch circles from plain brown paper. Place the circles on cookie sheets.
2. Beat the egg whites in a large bowl with an electric mixer until soft peaks form. Slowly beat in the granulated sugar, 1 tablespoon at a time, until the meringue forms stiff shiny peaks.
3. Sift together the 10X sugar, cornstarch and cocoa onto wax paper. Gradually beat into the meringue, 1 tablespoon at a time, beating just until blended. Fold in the ½ cup of the toasted ground almonds.
4. Spread the meringue evenly over the brown paper circles on the cookie sheets; spread to the edge of the circles.
5. Bake in the preheated slow oven (300°) for 45 minutes. Turn off the oven; let the meringues cool completely in the oven with the oven door closed.
6. Carefully remove the cooled meringues from the brown paper, being careful not to break or crack them.*
7. To assemble: Place 1 meringue layer on a plate. Carefully spread one-third of the raspberry preserves over the meringue. Spread with half the ice cream, smoothing the sides. Repeat with the second meringue layer and the other half of the ice cream. Top with the remaining meringue layer. Press down gently to secure the layers. Freeze until firm, for about 3 hours.
8. To decorate: Beat the heavy cream in a medium-size bowl until stiff. Frost the top and sides of the torte with about two-thirds of the whipped cream. Press the ⅔ cup of the toasted ground almonds into the sides of the torte. Spoon the remaining whipped cream into a pastry bag fitted with a star tip; pipe rosettes around the outer top edge of the torte. Arrange the raspberries in the center; top them with the remaining preserves.

* Note: The meringue layers can be made several days ahead and stored in a tin with a tight-fitting cover at room temperature.

Glossary of German Terms

Blutwurst: Blood sausage.
Bratwurst: Pork sausage, usually grilled.
Hasenpfeffer: Rabbit stew with a red wine sauce.
Holstein-Schnitzel: Veal cutlet topped with a fried egg.
Lebkuchen: Honey spice cakes or cookies.
Sachertorte: A very rich, dense chocolate cake containing a layer of apricot jam.
Sauerbraten: Pot roast marinated in red wine and vinegar.
Weisswurst: White veal sausage.
Wurst: Term for sausage.

COOKING GLOSSARY

A

À la In the manner of, as in *à la maison:* in the style of the house—"the house specialty."

Al dente An Italian phrase meaning "to the tooth," used to describe spaghetti or other pasta at the perfect stage of doneness—tender, but with enough firmness to be felt between the teeth.

Antipasto Another Italian word, this one meaning "before the meal." Antipasto is a selection of hors d'oeuvres, such as salami, marinated mushrooms, tuna or anchovies.

Aspic A jelly made from the cooking liquids of beef or poultry, principally. It will jell by itself, but is often strengthened with additional gelatin and used for coating and garnishing cold foods.

Au gratin Usually a creamed mixture topped with bread crumbs and/or cheese and browned in the oven or broiler.

Au naturel A French phrase referring to foods that are cooked simply or served in their natural state.

B

Bake To cook cakes, pies, cookies, breads, other pastries and doughs, as well as casseroles, fish, ham, etc., in the oven by dry heat.

Barbecue To roast meat, poultry or fish over hot coals or other heat, basting with a highly seasoned sauce. Also, the food so cooked and the social gathering.

Baste To ladle pan fat, marinade or other liquid over food as it roasts in order to add flavor and prevent dryness.

Batter A flour-liquid mixture of fairly thin consistency, as for pancakes.

Beat To stir vigorously with a spoon, eggbeater or electric mixer.

Blanch To plunge foods, such as tomatoes and peaches, quickly into boiling water, then into cold water, to loosen skins for easy removal. Also, a preliminary step to freezing vegetables.

Blend To mix two or more ingredients until smooth.

Boil To cook in boiling liquid.

Bone To remove the bones from meat, fish or poultry. This is usually done to make eating, carving or stuffing easier.

Bouillon A clear stock made of poultry, beef or veal, vegetables and seasonings.

Bouquet garni A small herb bouquet, most often sprigs of fresh parsley and thyme plus a bay leaf, tied in cheesecloth. Dried herbs can be used in place of the fresh. The *bouquet garni* is dropped into stocks, stews, sauces and soups as a seasoner and is removed before serving—usually as soon as it has flavored the dish.

Braise To brown in fat, then to cook, covered, in a small amount of liquid.

Bread To coat with bread crumbs, usually after dipping in beaten egg or milk.

Broil To cook under a broiler or on a grill by direct dry heat.

Broth A clear meat, fish, poultry or vegetable stock made of a combination of them.

Brush To spread with melted butter or margarine, beaten egg, water or other liquid, using a small brush.

C

Calorie The measure of body heat energy produced by the burning (oxidation) of the food we eat.

Candy To cook fruit, fruit peel or ginger in a heavy syrup until transparent, which is later drained and dried. Also to cook vegetables, such as carrots or sweet potatoes, in sugar or syrup.

Caramelize To melt sugar in a skillet, over low heat, until it becomes golden brown.

Chantilly Heavy cream whipped until soft, not stiff; it may or may not be sweetened.

Chop To cut into small pieces.

Coat To cover with flour, crumbs or other dry mixture before frying.

Coat the spoon A term used to describe egg-thickened sauces when cooked to a perfect degree of doneness; when a custard coats a metal spoon, it leaves a thin, somewhat jelly-like film.

Combine To mix together two or more ingredients.

Crimp To press the edges of a piecrust together with the tines of a fork or your fingertips.

Croutons Small, fried bread cubes.

Crumb To coat food with bread or cracker crumbs. So that the crumbs will stick, the food should first be dipped in milk or beaten egg.

Crumble To break between the fingers into small, irregular pieces.

Crush To pulverize food with a rolling pin or whirl in a blender until it is granular or powdered.

Cube To cut into cubes.

Cut in To work shortening or other solid fat into a flour mixture with a pastry blender or two knives until the texture resembles coarse meal.

Cutlet A small, thin, boneless piece of meat—usually cut from the leg of veal or chicken or turkey breast.

D

Dash A very small amount—less than $\frac{1}{16}$ teaspoon.

Deep-fry To cook in hot, deep, temperature-controlled fat.

Deglaze To loosen the browned bits in a skillet or roasting pan by adding liquid while stirring and heating. A glaze is used as a flavor base for sauces and gravies.

Demitasse French for "half cup," it refers to the small cups used for after-dinner coffee and also to the strong, black coffee served in them.

Devil To season with mustard, pepper and other spicy condiments.

Dice To cut into small, uniform pieces.

Dissolve To stir a powder or solid ingredient into a liquid to make a solution.

Dot To scatter bits of butter or margarine or other seasoning over the surface of a food to be cooked.

Dough A mixture of flour, liquid and other ingredients stiff enough to knead.

Drain To pour off liquid. Also, to place fried foods on paper toweling to soak up the excess fat.

Drawn butter Melted, clarified butter or margarine; often served with boiled shellfish.

Dredge To coat with flour prior to frying.

Drizzle To pour melted butter or margarine, marinade or other liquid over food in a thin stream.

Duchesse Mashed potatoes mixed with egg, butter or margarine and cream, piped around meat, poultry or fish dishes as a decorative border, then browned in the oven or broiler just before serving.

Dust To cover lightly with flour, 10X (confectioners') sugar or other dry ingredient.

Dutch oven A large, heavy, metal cooking pot with a tight-fitting cover; used for cooking pot roasts and stews and for braising large cuts of meat and poultry.

E

Entrée A French term applying to the third course in a full French dinner. We use the term to designate the main dish of a meal.

Escalope A thin slice of meat or fish, slightly flattened and most often sautéed quickly in oil or butter.

Espresso Robust, dark Italian coffee brewed under steam pressure. It is traditionally served in small cups and, in this country (though usually not in Italy), accompanied by twists of lemon rind.

Evaporated milk Canned unsweetened milk slightly thickened by the removal of some of its water.

F

Fillet A thin, boneless piece of meat or fish.

Fillo See "Phyllo."

Fines herbes A mixture of minced fresh or dried parsley, chervil, tarragon and, sometimes, chives, used to season salads, omelets and other dishes.

Flake To break up food (salmon or tuna, for example) into smaller pieces with a fork.

Flambé, flambéed French words meaning "flaming." In the culinary sense, the verb *flamber* means to pour warm brandy over a food and to set it afire with a match.

Florentine In the style of Florence, Italy, which usually means served on a bed of spinach, topped with a delicate cheese sauce and browned in the oven. Fish and eggs are often served Florentine style.

Flour To coat with flour.

Flute To form a fluted edge with the fingers, on a piecrust edging.

Fold in To mix a light, fluffy ingredient, such as beaten egg white, into a thicker mixture, using a gentle under-and-over motion.

Fondue Switzerland's gift to good eating: a silky concoction of melted cheese, white wine and kirsch served in an earthenware crock set over a burner. To eat the fondue, chunks of bread are speared with special, long-handled fondue forks and then twirled in the semiliquid cheese mixture. *Fondue Bourguignonne* is a convivial Swiss version of a French dish: Cubes of raw steak are speared with the fondue forks, fried at the table in a pot of piping hot oil, then dipped into assorted sauces.

Frappé A mushy, frozen dessert.

Fricassee To simmer a chicken covered in water with vegetables and often wine. The chicken may be browned in butter first. A gravy is made from the broth and served with the chicken.

Fritter A crisp, golden, deep-fried batter bread, often containing corn or minced fruits or vegetables. Also, pieces of fruit or vegetable, batter-dipped and deep-fried.

G

Garnish To decorate with colorful and/or fancily cut pieces of food.

Glaze To coat food with honey, syrup or other liquid so it glistens.

Gluten The protein of wheat flour that forms the framework of cakes, breads, cookies and pastries.

Goulash A beef or pork stew, flavored with paprika.

Grate To shred into small pieces with a grater.

Grease To rub food or a container with butter, margarine or other fat.

Grill To cook on a grill, usually over charcoal.

Grind To put through a food grinder.

H

Hors d'oeuvres Bite-size appetizers served with cocktails.

Hull To remove caps and stems from berries.

I

Ice To cover with icing. Also, a frozen, water-based, fruit-flavored dessert.

Italienne, à la Served Italian style with a garnish of pasta.

J

Julienne To cut food into uniformly long, thin slivers (1½ x ¼ inches).

K

Kabobs Cubes of meat, fish or poultry and/or vegetables threaded on long skewers and grilled over coals or under the broiler.

Kasha Buckwheat groats, braised or cooked in liquid and usually served in place of rice, potatoes or another starch.

Knead To work dough with the hands until it is smooth and springy. Yeast breads must be kneaded to develop the gluten necessary to give them framework and volume.

Kosher salt A very coarse salt.

L

Lard Creamy, white, rendered pork fat.
Line To cover the bottom, and sometimes sides, of a pan with paper or thin slices of food.
Lyonnaise Seasoned in the style of Lyons, France, meaning with parsley and onions.

M

Macerate To let food, principally fruits, steep in wine or spirits (usually kirsch or rum).
Maître d'hôtel Simply cooked dishes seasoned with minced parsley, butter and lemon. *Maître d'hôtel* butter is a mixture of butter (or margarine), parsley, lemon juice and salt. It is most often used to season broiled fish, grilled steaks or chops or boiled carrots.
Marinade The liquid in which food is marinated.
Marinate To let food, principally meats, steep in a piquant sauce prior to cooking. The marinade serves to tenderize and add flavor.
Marzipan A confection made from almond paste, sugar and egg whites—often colored and shaped into tiny fruit and vegetable forms.
Mash To reduce to a pulp.
Mask To coat with sauce or aspic.
Melt To heat a solid, such as chocolate or butter, until liquid.
Meringue A stiffly beaten mixture of sugar and egg white.
Mince To cut into fine pieces.
Mix To stir together.
Mocha A flavoring for desserts, usually made from coffee or a mixture of coffee and chocolate.
Mold To shape in a mold.
Mole A sauce of Mexican origin, usually containing chilies, onion, garlic and other ingredients, especially bitter chocolate. It is usually served over poultry.
Mousse A rich, creamy, frozen dessert. Also, a velvety hot or cold savory dish, rich with cream, bound with eggs or—if cold—with gelatin.
Mull To heat a liquid, such as wine or cider, with whole spices.

N

Niçoise Prepared in the manner of Nice, France—with tomatoes, garlic, olive oil and ripe olives.
Nouvelle Cuisine A French cuisine established by classically trained younger chefs with a new and lighter twist on classic French dishes and preparation techniques. It has been adapted by many other cuisines.

O

Oil To rub a pan or mold with cooking oil.

P

Panbroil To cook in a skillet in a small amount of fat; drippings are poured off as they accumulate.
Parboil To cook in water until about half done; vegetables to be cooked *en casserole* are usually parboiled.
Pare To remove the skin of a fruit or vegetable with a swivel-blade vegetable peeler.
Pasta The all-inclusive Italian word for all kinds of macaroni, spaghetti and noodles.
Pastry A stiff dough, made from flour, water and shortening, used for piecrusts, turnovers and other dishes; it is also a rich cookie-type dough used for desserts.
Pastry bag A cone-shaped fabric, parchment or plastic bag with a hole at the tip for the insertion of various decorating tubes. Used to decorate cakes, pastries, etc.
Pâté A well-seasoned mixture of finely minced or ground meats and/or liver. *Pâté de foie gras* is made of goose livers and truffles.
Pectin Any of several, natural gelatinous substances found in the cellular structure of different fruits and vegetables. It is also manufactured in syrup form to use in helping jellies to jell.
Petits fours Tiny, fancily frosted cakes.
Phyllo Greek term for a flaky, tissue paper-thin pastry used in many Greek dishes. (Also spelled fillo.)

Pilaf Rice cooked in a savory broth, often with small bits of meat or vegetables, herbs and spices.

Pinch The amount of a dry ingredient that can be taken up between the thumb and index finger—less than ¼ teaspoon.

Pipe To press frosting, whipped cream, mashed potatoes or other soft mixtures through a pastry bag fitted with a decorative tube to make a fancy garnish or edging.

Plank A well-seasoned (oiled) hardwood plank used to serve a broiled steak or chop, usually edged with Duchesse potatoes.

Plump To soak raisins or other dried fruits in liquid until they are softened and almost returned to their natural state.

Poach To cook in barely simmering liquid, as fish fillets, for example.

Polenta A cornmeal porridge popular in Italy. Usually cooled, sliced or cubed, then baked or fried with butter and Parmesan cheese.

Pot cheese A soft uncured cheese from strained milk curds, almost identical to cottage cheese but perhaps a bit drier.

Pound To flatten by pounding.

Preheat To bring an oven or broiler to the correct temperature before cooking food.

Purée To reduce food to a smooth, velvety texture by whirling in an electric blender or pressing through a sieve or food grinder. Also, the food so reduced.

R

Ragôut A stew.

Ramekin A small, individual-size baking dish.

Reduce To boil a liquid, uncovered, until the quantity is concentrated.

Render To melt solid fat.

Rice To press food through a container with small holes. The food then resembles rice.

Risotto An Italian dish made with short-grain rice browned in fat and cooked with chicken broth until tender but firm. Mixture is creamy, not dry or runny.

Roast To cook meat or poultry in the oven by dry heat.

Roe The eggs of fish, such as sturgeon, salmon (caviar) or shad; considered delicacies.

Roll To press and shape dough or pastry with a rolling pin.

Roulade A slice of meat, most often veal or beef, rolled around any number of fillings. Also, a jelly-roll cake.

Roux A cooked, fat-flour mixture used to thicken sauces and gravies.

S

Sauté To cook food quickly in a small amount of hot fat in a skillet.

Scald To heat a liquid just until bubbles form around the edge of the pan, but the liquid does not boil.

Scallop To bake small pieces of food *en casserole,* usually in a cream sauce. Also a thin, boneless slice of meat, such as veal.

Score To make shallow, crisscross cuts over the surface of a food with a knife.

Scramble To stir eggs or an egg mixture while cooking until the mixture sets.

Scrape To remove fruit or vegetable skin by scraping with a knife.

Shirr To bake whole eggs in ramekins with cream and crumbs.

Short An adjective used to describe a bread, cake or pastry that has a high proportion of fat and is ultra-tender or crisp.

Shortening A solid fat, usually of vegetable origin, used to add tenderness to pastry, bread or cookies.

Shred To cut in small, thin slivers by rubbing food, such as Cheddar cheese, over the holes in a shredder-grater.

Sift To put flour or another dry ingredient through a sifter. (*Note:* In this book, recipes that call for *sifted* flour require that you sift the flour and then measure it, even if you use a flour that says "sifted" on the bag.)

Simmer To cook in liquid just below the boiling point.

Skewer To thread food on a long wooden or metal pin before cooking. Also, the pin itself.

Skim To remove fat or film from the surface of a liquid or sauce.

Sliver To cut in long, thin strips.

Soak To let stand in liquid.

Soufflé A light, fluffy, baked combination of egg yolk, sauce, purée and flavoring, with stiffly beaten egg whites folded in.

Spit To thread food on a long rod and roast over glowing coals or under a broiler. Also, the rod itself.

Steam To cook, covered, on a trivet over a small amount of boiling water.

Steep To let food soak in liquid until the liquid absorbs its flavor, as in steeping tea in hot water.

Stew To cook, covered, in simmering liquid.

Stir To mix with a spoon using a circular motion.

Stir-fry To cook in a small amount of oil, in a wok or skillet, over high heat, stirring or tossing constantly, for a short period of time.

Stock A liquid flavor base for soups and sauces made by long, slow cooking of meat, poultry or fish with their bones. Stock may be brown or white, depending on whether the meat and bones are browned first.

Stud To press whole cloves, slivers of garlic or other seasoning into the surface of a food to be cooked.

T

Terrine A type of container used for baking dishes such as pâtés. The prepared dish may also be referred to as a terrine.

Thicken To make a liquid thicker, usually by adding flour, cornstarch or beaten egg.

Thin To make a liquid thinner by adding liquid.

Timbale A savory meat, fish, poultry or vegetable custard, baked in a small mold. Also, pastry shells made on special iron molds—Swedish Rosettes, for example.

Torte A very rich, multilayered cake made with eggs, and, often, grated nuts. Usually it is filled, but frequently it is not frosted.

Toss To mix, as a salad, by gently turning ingredients over and over in a bowl, either with the hands or with a large fork and spoon.

Truffles A type of underground fungi considered a real delicacy. Black, dark brown or white in color and quite expensive because of their rarity and the method of obtaining them. Also, a term for an extra-rich chocolate candy.

Truss To tie into a compact shape before roasting.

Turnover A folded pastry usually made by cutting a circle or square, adding a dollop of sweet or savory filling, folding into a semicircle or triangle, then crimping the edges with the tines of a fork. Most turnovers are baked, but some are deep-fat fried.

Tutti-Frutti A mixture of minced fruits used as a dessert topping.

V

Variety meats Organ and muscular meat, such as liver, heart, kidneys and tripe.

Véronique A dish garnished with seedless green grapes.

Vinaigrette A sauce, French in origin, made from oil, vinegar, salt, pepper and herbs; usually served on cold meat, fish or vegetables.

W

Whip To beat until frothy or stiff with an eggbeater or an electric mixer.

Wok A round-bottomed, bowl-shaped Chinese cooking utensil used for stir-frying.

Z

Zest The oily, aromatic, colored part of the rind of citrus fruits.

Index